AWS EKS Essentials

A Comprehensive Guide to Setting Up, Securing, and Scaling EKS Clusters

Ebenezer Paintsil

Apress®

AWS EKS Essentials: A Comprehensive Guide to Setting Up, Securing, and Scaling EKS Clusters

Ebenezer Paintsil
eben@iconsec.net
Oslo, Norway

ISBN-13 (pbk): 979-8-8688-1330-6 ISBN-13 (electronic): 979-8-8688-1331-3
https://doi.org/10.1007/979-8-8688-1331-3

Copyright © 2025 by Ebenezer Paintsil

This work is subject to copyright. All rights are reserved by the Publisher, whether the whole or part of the material is concerned, specifically the rights of translation, reprinting, reuse of illustrations, recitation, broadcasting, reproduction on microfilms or in any other physical way, and transmission or information storage and retrieval, electronic adaptation, computer software, or by similar or dissimilar methodology now known or hereafter developed.

Trademarked names, logos, and images may appear in this book. Rather than use a trademark symbol with every occurrence of a trademarked name, logo, or image we use the names, logos, and images only in an editorial fashion and to the benefit of the trademark owner, with no intention of infringement of the trademark.

The use in this publication of trade names, trademarks, service marks, and similar terms, even if they are not identified as such, is not to be taken as an expression of opinion as to whether or not they are subject to proprietary rights.

While the advice and information in this book are believed to be true and accurate at the date of publication, neither the authors nor the editors nor the publisher can accept any legal responsibility for any errors or omissions that may be made. The publisher makes no warranty, express or implied, with respect to the material contained herein.

>   Managing Director, Apress Media LLC: Welmoed Spahr
>   Acquisitions Editor: Celestin Suresh John
>   Development Editor: James Markham
>   Coordinating Editor: Kripa Joseph

Cover designed by eStudioCalamar

Cover image designed by Unsplash.com

Distributed to the book trade worldwide by Springer Science+Business Media New York, 1 New York Plaza, New York, NY 10004. Phone 1-800-SPRINGER, fax (201) 348-4505, e-mail orders-ny@springer-sbm.com, or visit www.springeronline.com. Apress Media, LLC is a Delaware LLC and the sole member (owner) is Springer Science + Business Media Finance Inc (SSBM Finance Inc). SSBM Finance Inc is a **Delaware** corporation.

For information on translations, please e-mail booktranslations@springernature.com; for reprint, paperback, or audio rights, please e-mail bookpermissions@springernature.com.

Apress titles may be purchased in bulk for academic, corporate, or promotional use. eBook versions and licenses are also available for most titles. For more information, reference our Print and eBook Bulk Sales web page at http://www.apress.com/bulk-sales.

Any source code or other supplementary material referenced by the author in this book can be found here: https://www.apress.com/gp/services/source-code.

If disposing of this product, please recycle the paper

This book is dedicated to my wonderful family.

Table of Contents

About the Author .... **xxi**

About the Technical Reviewer .... **xxiii**

Acknowledgments .... **xxv**

Part I: 1

Chapter 1: Introduction to the Amazon Elastic Kubernetes Service.....3
    Background..4
    Kubernetes..6
    Elastic Kubernetes Service..8
    Summary...11

Chapter 2: EKS Architecture and Cluster Access Control...................13
    The EKS Architecture..14
    The Control Plane...16
        The API Server Component..17
        The ETCD Component...17
        The Controller Manager Component..17
        Scheduler Component...18
        Route 53..19
    The Data Plane..19
        Customer VPC..20
        Cluster Security Group and ENIs...20

TABLE OF CONTENTS

Cluster Network Access Control 22
Endpoint Private Access Control 23
Endpoint Hybrid Access Cluster 25
Endpoint Public Access Control 28
End-User Communication 31
Summary 32

Chapter 3: EKS Implementations 35

Endpoint Public Access Cluster 35
Control Plane Deployment 38
    Role Assignment 42
    Security Groups 44
The Data Plane VPC 45
Subnets 47
Network Infrastructure 49
Cluster Nodes 51
Node Security 53
    IAM 53
main.tf File 56
Terraform Code Deployment 56
    Account Setup 57
Code Visualization with AWS Console 58
    Cluster Endpoint 59
    Add-ons 60
    Cluster ENIs 60
    Node Security Group 61
    Command Line Interface (CLI) 62
    Testing the Cluster 63

TABLE OF CONTENTS

Cluster Security 64
    Identity and Access Management 64
    Public Endpoint Restrictions with Web Console 65
    Public Endpoint Restrictions with Code 68
    Public Endpoint Restrictions with CLI Command 68
    Network Security 69
    Security Group 71
    Additional Security Group 73
Cluster Stability 74
Cluster Deletion 76
Summary 76

Chapter 4: Endpoint Private Access Cluster 79

Cluster Creator Role Creation 79
    Role Creation 80
    Create User to Assume the Role 81
    Create EKS Describe Cluster Policy 84
    Attach EKS Describe Cluster Policy 85
    Configure Role in AWS Credential File 85
The Structure of the Code 87
Bastion Host Code 90
    Bastion Security Group 91
    Bastion Authentication 93
Network Setup 94
Worker Nodes 99
Cluster Security Group Review 101
    Cluster Security Group Code Review 104
    Additional Security Group Code Review 105

TABLE OF CONTENTS

Cluster Review 109
    Cluster Security Group 110
    Bastion Security Group Validation 110
    Cluster Security Group Validation 111
    Additional Security Group Validation 113
Connecting to the Cluster with Bastion Host 114
Impact and Benefits of Security Controls 118
Summary 118

Chapter 5: Endpoint Hybrid Access Cluster 121

Cluster Creator Role Creation 122
    Create a Role 122
    Create User to Assume the Role 123
    Create EKS Describe Cluster Policy 124
    Attach EKS Describe Cluster Policy 125
    Configure Role in AWS Credential File 126
The Structure of the Code 127
Bastion Host Code 129
    Bastion Security Group 129
Network Setup 130
    The Control Plane Module 133
Worker Nodes 134
    Cluster Security Group Code Review 135
    Additional Security Group Code Review 136
Troubleshooting the Cluster 140
Cluster Review 143
    Cluster Security Group Cleanup 143
    Additional Security Group Review 145

TABLE OF CONTENTS

Connecting to the Cluster 146
    The Endpoint Hybrid Cluster 146
    Public Cluster Access Test 147
    Private Cluster Access Test 147
Test Public Endpoint Restrictions 151
Summary 153

Chapter 6: Cluster Nodes 155

Node and Node Groups 155
Types of Nodes 157
    Managed Nodes 157
    Managed Launch Template 159
    Self-Managed 161
    Fargate 161
Managed Node Code Review 162
Managed Node Deployment 164
Managed Node Deployment Review 165
Custom Launch Templates 167
    Terraform Code Execution 171
    Custom Launch Template Instantiation 173
    User Data File 174
Self-Managed Node Deployment 175
    Creating AMI with AWS Console 175
Creating Image with Packer 181
Graceful Node Group Update 185
    Demonstration of Graceful Update Strategy 186
Cluster Upgrade Tips 189
Summary 190

TABLE OF CONTENTS

Chapter 7: EKS IP Address Management 191
Node IP Addressing 192
Cluster Deployment and Review 194
The VPC Container Network Interface 199
Pod Density 200
Pod Density Demonstration 202
Pod Density with Prefix 207
Prefix Assignment Mode Demonstration 208
    Verification 210
Summary 213

Chapter 8: EKS Addons 215
Controllers 215
Intrinsic Controllers 217
Extrinsic Controllers 218
    EKS Addon Controllers 219
    AWS Controllers for Kubernetes 221
    Operators 223
    Third-Party Addon Controllers 223
Self-Managed Addons 224
Addon Implementation 225
Code Review 227
Deployment and Validation 228
Version Upgrade 232
Controller and Deployment 235
ACK Controller Deployment 236
Summary 238

TABLE OF CONTENTS

Chapter 9: Identity and Access Management 239
IAM in EKS 240
The aws-auth ConfigMap Authentication 242
    Cluster Access Demonstration 242
Using the Kube Config File 245
The aws-auth ConfigMap Access Control Approach 247
K8s RBAC Roles 248
Role Assignment Demonstration Role 249
    Create the Test User, Alice 250
    Configure aws-auth ConfigMap 251
Manual Editing of aws-auth ConfigMap 255
Adding Cluster Editor Role 256
Using Custom Groups 258
Manual Editing of aws-auth ConfigMap with Code Editor 261
Adding Cluster Editor Role 263
Summary 265

Chapter 10: The New Cluster Access Management 267
Access Entries and Policy Association 268
Built-In Access Entry Policy 270
Access Management Authentication Modes 273
The New Cluster Access Management Implementation 274
Granting Cluster Creator Access to Alice 275
Create Cluster Admin 280
Namespace Access 282
Granting Custom Permissions with K8s RBAC 284
Assigning Permissions to IAM Roles 286

TABLE OF CONTENTS

Creating Access Entry with EKS Console 289

Disable Cluster Creator 290

Summary 291

Part II: 293

Chapter 11: Kubernetes 295

Key Benefits of Kubernetes 296

Kubernetes Architecture 297

    The API Server Component 298

    The ETCD Component 299

    Scheduler Component 300

    The Controller Manager Component 301

    The Kubelet Component 301

    The Kube-proxy Component 302

Addon 302

Pods 303

Kubernetes Component Illumination 303

Summary 309

Chapter 12: Running Apps on K8s 311

Container Packaging 311

Containerized Applications 314

Docker Desktop Installation 315

Running Containers on Cluster 316

Custom Container Image 317

Building Container Images 319

Finding the Layers 320

Image Optimization 324

TABLE OF CONTENTS

Running Custom Containers on EKS 325
Docker Hub Public Registry 326
    Run the Image on EKS 329
Private Repository 332
    Running ECR Image on EKS 334
Summary 335

Chapter 13: The Pod Object 337

Pod Specification 337
Pod Parameter Experiment 338
    Name 341
    Namespace 341
    Initial Namespace 343
    Priority 344
    Service Account 345
    Node 345
    Label 345
    Annotations 346
    Status 346
    QoS 347
    Node Selectors 347
    Tolerations 348
    Events 349
Summary 350

Chapter 14: The Service Object 351

Pod Deployment 351
Internal Access to Application 352
Port Forwarding and Proxy 353

TABLE OF CONTENTS

    Port Forwarding Example 354
    Using a Proxy 355
Using the Service Objects 357
    Node Port Service Type Example 359
    Node Port Service Type and Public Network 360
    Testing Cluster IP Service 364
Load Balancers 366
The AWS Elastic Load Balancer 367
Classic Load Balancer Implementation 370
Network Load Balancer 373
Application Load Balancer 375
    Requisites for ALB 377
    Instance Metadata 380
    ALB Controller Installation 382
    The script.sh 382
Troubleshooting Tips 385
    Create the ALB 386
    Test the Load Balancer 387
    Alternative 388
Summary 388

Chapter 15: Pod Service Accounts 391

The RBAC Method 391
    Testing Pod Access After Deployment 393
    Secret Manager Test 395
    S3 and ECR Access Test 396
IAM Roles for Service Accounts (IRSA) 398
IRSA Flow 401
    Trust Establishment 402

IRSA Authentication and Authorization Flow 403
IRSA Manual Trust Establishment 404
Changes to Terraform Code 410
Client Configuration 412
Testing the s3 Bucket 413
Testing with the Exec Command 414
Testing with the kotaicode Debug Container 415
OIDC Terraform Automation 416
Cluster Deployment 419
Testing Secret Manager with Port Forwarding 420
Testing with the Exec Command 421
Testing with the kotaicode Debug Container 421
Pod Identity 423
Terraform Code 423
Cluster Deployment 425
Testing with CLI 428
Summary 428

Chapter 16: Pod Persistence 431

Kubernetes Volumes 431
Kinds of Ephemeral Volumes 433
Ephemeral Volume Implementation 434
    Testing the Ephemeral Volume 436
The Secret Volume 436
    Testing the Secret Volume 438
Persistent Volume 438
    The Host Path Volume 439
    The Persistent Volume Subsystem 443

TABLE OF CONTENTS

    Persistent Volume Creation and Testing 444

    Out-of-Tree NFS Provisioner 450

    Persistent Volume with AWS 453

    EBS Volume 454

    EFS File Storage 461

    EFS Experiment 462

    Summary 465

Chapter 17: Pod Scaling 467

    Kubernetes Controllers 468

    Replica Sets 468

    Replica Set Manifest 469

    Replica Set Experiment 471

    Deployment 473

    Deployment Manifest 475

        Rolling Update Strategy 477

    Deployment Experiment 478

    Summary 481

Chapter 18: Pod Monitoring 483

    Kubefwd 483

    K8s Dashboard Manifest 484

        Namespace 485

        Service Account 485

        Service 486

        Secret 486

        Access Control 488

        Deployment 491

Admin User Service Account 495

Dashboard Deployment with kubefwd 496

Lens 499

K9s 500

Object Access 502

Other Common Commands 503

Summary 503

Part III: 505

Chapter 19: Cluster Autoscaling 507

The Cluster Autoscaler 507

Autoscaling Demonstration 510

Testing the CA 514

Deploy Autoscaler Controller 515

AWS Karpenter 518

Karpenter Implementation 520

Karpenter Deployment 524

    Install Karpenter Controller 525

Deploy Node Pool 526

Application Deployment 528

Karpenter vs. Cluster Autoscaler 529

Summary 530

Chapter 20: Service Mesh and VPC Lattice 531

Service Orchestration 531

AWS App Mesh 535

App Mesh Data Plane 538

App Mesh Control Plane 541

xvii

TABLE OF CONTENTS

- App Mesh Implementation 542
  - The App Mesh Cluster 543
  - App Mesh Cluster Deployment 546
- App Mesh Deployment Scenario 1 547
  - Install App Mesh Controller 548
  - Run the App Mesh 551
  - Testing the AB Services 562
  - The Three-Application Scenario 563
- App Mesh with Load Balancer Implementation 563
  - App Mesh with Load Balancer Deployment 573
  - Testing the AB Services 573
- App Mesh Traffic Management Implementation 574
  - Testing the Traffic Management App Mesh 589
- Logging with App Mesh 590
  - Software Log Sources 590
  - Operating System Log Sources 590
  - Audit Logs 591
  - Application Log Sources 591
  - Network Log Sources 591
- Changes to Terraform Configuration 593
- Logging Configuration 593
  - App Mesh Deployment 597
- Log Review 599
- VPC Lattice 602
  - The Benefits of VPC Lattice 604
- AWS Gateway API Controller 606
- Implementation Changes to Terraform Code 607

TABLE OF CONTENTS

VPC Lattice Configuration for Blue-Green Deployment 611
Testing..................616
Istio Service Mesh..................617
Istio Implementation 619
    Testing the Service Mesh 624
Istio Ingress Gateway..................624
Summary..................627

Index..................629

About the Author

Ebenezer Paintsil is a seasoned cybersecurity architect based in Norway. With over 13 years of experience, he specializes in security architecture, risk governance, DevSecOps, and cloud security. He has worked with leading organizations like Telenor and Schibsted ASA, developing robust security architectures and fostering cybersecurity cultures. He holds a PhD in Information Security from NTNU Norway and multiple certifications, including SABSA and AWS Security Specialty. His expertise covers AWS, Google Cloud, and a range of risk management frameworks.

About the Technical Reviewer

Anil Kumar Moka is a distinguished technology leader and AWS Certified Solutions Architect who has transformed data security and cloud infrastructure at some of America's largest financial institutions. As a Lead Software Engineer, he architects enterprise-scale solutions that protect sensitive data for over 100 million customers while driving substantial operational efficiencies. With more than 18 years of experience in data engineering and security, Anil has spearheaded multiple revolutionary initiatives that shaped the future of the financial industry. A respected voice in the technology community, Anil has published extensively across prestigious platforms, including Forbes.com, DZone, and Red-Gate Simple-Talk, contributing more than ten peer-reviewed articles on data security and cloud architecture.

Acknowledgments

I never wanted to begin this demanding project until it was the right time, but it has never been and perhaps it will never be. This was a rocky and truly demanding project, but you were patient and understanding – thank you my lovely family for giving me the space and time to do this. He prefers to stay anonymous but I still want to acknowledge him as a former colleague together with all my friends who inspired me to continue working on this project. To everyone who put in the effort to edit this book and worked tirelessly to coordinate the activities of this project, Kripa, John, and all the editors – I say thank you for your invaluable contributions.

PART 1

CHAPTER 1

Introduction to the Amazon Elastic Kubernetes Service

The future of your IT career could be at risk if you are not familiar with Kubernetes. With its rapid and widespread adoption, it is possible that soon, nearly all applications will be deployed within the Kubernetes ecosystem. Whether you are a security expert, developer, system administrator, data scientist, or software engineer; gaining expertise in Kubernetes is essential to staying ahead in the ever evolving technology landscape. According to the 2024 report by Edge Delta, over 60% of enterprises have adopted Kubernetes, with the Cloud Native Computing Foundation (CNCF) reporting surge in adoption rates up to 96% among the surveyed organizations. Approximately 5.6 million developers globally are using Kubernetes, representing about 31% of all backend developers. Kubernetes holds 92% share of the market for container orchestration tools. Undoubtdely, no one can underestimate the revolutionary impact of Kubernetes on today's technological landscape. This book aims to simplify and make the introduction to Kubernetes more practical, reducing the learning curve and providing you with a solid foundation to confidently explore Kubernetes on your own. The book starts with the introduction to basics of Amazon Elastic Kubernetes Service (EKS), exploring various architecture options. The focus then shifts to security and cluster implementation with Terraform covering role assignments, cluster monitoring, application load balancing, persistent storage management among others. The last part of the book covers advanced EKS concepts such as auto scaling with Karpenter, service mesh with App Mesh, Istio and application networking with VPC Lattice. No plan survives enemy contact,[1] but it is equally true that failing to plan is planning to fail.[2] So, I want to take the liberty to discuss my plan for this book. I will begin with background information and briefly conclude with the structure of the book. I hope you will follow along with my plan or at least understand where to start within the three composite parts of this book.

Background

When Google wanted to speed up large-scale orchestrations, they turned to Borg, their container orchestrator and cluster management tool. The innovation was an instant success, providing efficient resource utilization, process management, support for high-availability applications, and reduced fault-recovery time, among others. It was one of the few occasions where a complex technology simplified life for its users. With well-structured declarative job specification language, real-time job monitoring, and backend analytics, Borg had already exceeded expectation.[3]

A Borg cluster is comparable to a single data center, divided into one large cell and a few smaller, specialized cells. Each cell consists of thousands of heterogeneous servers, with varying types and numbers of processors, memory sizes, and different storage and network resource capacities.

---

[1] Sun Tzu

[2] Benjamin Franklin

[3] Verma, Abhishek, et al. "Large-scale cluster management at Google with Borg." *Proceedings of the tenth European conference on computer systems.* 2015

CHAPTER 1   INTRODUCTION TO THE AMAZON ELASTIC KUBERNETES SERVICE

As an orchestrator, Borg does most of the resource allocations behind the scenes, managing them on behalf of its users. The users (operators, developers and administrators) simply submit their tasks and watch Borg determine where in a cell to run the tasks and allocate the necessary resources for them.

A task in Borg is like a container. A container is a standard unit of software that bundles together code and all its dependencies such that the application it encapsulates can run quickly and reliably on different computing platforms.[4] A Borg job is a collection of one or more tasks that execute the same program or binary within a single Borg cell.

Borg is resource efficient. It uses a controller service to prioritize job scheduling. Jobs with higher quotas take precedence over lower ones. A job quota is made up of two components, the job's priority and the number of resources it requires over a specified period. By this, Borg can prioritize important jobs over less important ones depending on their job quotas. The higher the quotas, the higher the importance.

Borg is scalable. It can scale across thousands of computers within a cell to meet the resource demands of applications that require high availability. This capability ensures that even resource-intensive applications can run reliably at scale. Borg manages many thousands of computers simultaneously to keep resource-intensive applications available.

Borg achieves scalability with techniques like parallel processing and multithreading. Additionally, Borg is designed with the capability to free up space for new jobs by evicting less important ones. Borg also helps reduce correlated failures by distributing jobs across various failure domains, such as different machines, racks, and power domains. This ensures greater resilience and availability within the Borg cluster.

---

[4] https://www.docker.com/resources/what-container/

But not everything about Borg was innovative. And not everything made it to the world of open source. First, its name was changed to Kubernetes, meaning captain in Greek. Borg's complicated one IP address per machine was deprecated in favor of one IP address per pod.

Running all tasks on a machine on a single IP address made ports a crucial resource for task isolation and again a valuable resource for Borg to manage. Borg must schedule ports as a resource and manage their allocations, that is, which ones are in use and which ones are free. Tasks could not decide on port numbers on their own as they must pre-declare how many ports they need and wait for Borg to decide which specific ports they can use.

The optimization for power users at the expense of casual ones was discontinued. Power users have unlimited opportunity to optimize their job as compared to casual users. For example, Borg grants power users an excess of about 230 parameters to fine-tune their application at the expense of casual users.

Kubernetes rejected the job notion in favor of labels. Labels are a big part of Kubernetes when you want to differentiate resources for monitoring, efficient quarries, set network policies, security, and resource assignments.

Kubernetes

Kubernetes (K8s) is an open source orchestrator emerged from the Borg cluster and job orchestration system. In 2014, Google founded the Kubernetes open source project to develop a container orchestrator that is decoupled from their internal and proprietary Borg orchestrator.[5] Since then, K8s has become the de facto orchestrator of containerized applications and the most popular container orchestrator to date.[6]

As a container orchestrator, its major task is to run and control applications that are packaged into single or multiple containers (Pods). K8s can deploy and redeploy containers. It can monitor upscale and downscale containerized applications seamlessly.

Traditionally, application development ends once developers package an application into a web archive (war), a java archive (jar), or an executable file (exe) and ship it to the operations team for deployment. The operations (ops) team takes over, installs application dependencies, creates configuration files, and provisions the requisite platform for the application package. This approach could consume a lot of deployment time, cause undue delays in product delivery and add to operational cost.

Containers were invented to address some of these bottlenecks in product delivery. They allow developers to package applications into a self-contained and portable format (container image) that includes all requisite dependencies and configurations necessary to deploy them on any platform. This cuts off the need for dedicated operations teams thereby reducing deployment delays and operational costs.

Containers allow developers to automate application deployments and roll back quickly in case of failures. You may describe a container as a self-contained executable package of software that combines everything needed to run an application including dependencies and configurations.[7]

---

[5] Cloud Native DevOps with Kubernetes: Building, Deploying, and Scaling Modern Applications in the Cloud, Justin Domingus & John Arundel
[6] Kubernetes Deep Dive Zero To Hero In A Single Book, Nigel Poulton
[7] https://www.docker.com/resources/what-container/

Containerized applications are known as pods in K8s. A pod is used to encapsulate one or more containerized applications. They are the smallest deployable units of computing resources you can create and manage in K8s.[8]

Elastic Kubernetes Service

The Amazon Elastic Kubernetes Service (EKS) and Google's open source Kubernetes orchestrator are two independent services or orchestrators. As illustrated in Figure 1-1, EKS could be described as an orchestrator for the Google's Kubernetes (K8s) orchestrator. Similarly, K8s is an orchestrator for pods, applications, or K8s objects.

EKS orchestrates K8s, whereas K8s orchestrates pods. This hierarchy allows EKS to manage the underlying infrastructure, while K8s handles the deployment and management of containerized applications within pods.

The EKS service is responsible for provisioning and managing the lifecycle of K8s clusters. This means that EKS can create, manage, and deprovision entire K8s clusters. On the contrary, K8s is responsible for provisioning and managing the lifecycle of K8s objects, such as pods, K8s service objects, and deployments, within the clusters provisioned by EKS.

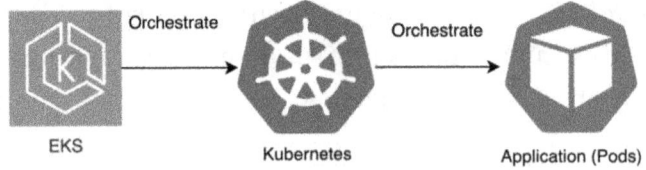

Figure 1-1. Relationship between EKS and K8s

---

[8] https://kubernetes.io/docs/concepts/workloads/pods/

CHAPTER 1   INTRODUCTION TO THE AMAZON ELASTIC KUBERNETES SERVICE

The two lifecycle management platforms, (one for **K8s clusters** by EKS and the other for **K8s objects** by Kubernetes), run independently, each by its own service. They use separate sets of commands and tools, allowing for distinct management of the cluster infrastructure and the containerized applications running within it.

For instance, you can manage K8s using the AWS web console, the **aws eks** command, and the **eksctl** tool while primarily interacting with Kubernetes objects using the **kubectl** and the **Helm** tools. The Helm tool serves as a package manager for Kubernetes, allowing you to easily download and deploy K8s objects, much like the Linux **apt** and **yum** package managers.

Kubernetes consists of two planes, the data and control planes. Setting up and facilitating communication between these two planes is always a challenge. In the cloud, the challenge is exacerbated by additional cluster management demands, operational capabilities, security, and interaction with the underlying networking, computing, and storage resources.

Amazon responded to these challenges with EKS providing a solution that frees Kubernetes cluster operators from the complexities of deployment and management of the K8s cluster in Amazon Web Services (AWS) and even in on-premises environments.

EKS simplifies cluster setup, management, and integration of K8s with AWS cloud services. It leverages the AWS services to enhance security within and outside a K8s cluster. EKS offers APIs that handle the entire lifecycle of the K8s clusters on AWS, from cluster provisioning to deprovisioning and anything in between.

With EKS, you can install and update K8s cluster worker nodes and add-ons.[9] Add-ons are software components designed to enhance the operational capabilities of cluster applications. These include tools such as observability agents that monitor the health and performance of cluster

---

[9] https://aws.amazon.com/blogs/containers/enable-private-access-to-the-amazon-eks-kubernetes-api-with-aws-privatelink/

applications, as well as K8s drivers that enable the cluster to interact with AWS's network, compute, and storage resources. Worker nodes are the computing resources that run the containerized applications.

EKS provisions K8s as a managed service eliminating the need for customers to install, patch, and maintain their own K8s control plane on AWS.[10] Amazon manages the control plane of the cluster on behalf of customers. Meanwhile, customers are responsible for worker nodes in the cluster's data plane.

Customers can opt for AWS-managed worker nodes or use their own self-managed worker nodes. You can describe the managed node option as a hybrid option where both the customer and AWS share responsibility in maintaining the nodes. For example, when worker nodes run Amazon EKS optimized Amazon Machine Image (AMI), AWS will be responsible for image update (creation of a new patched image, fixing issues with the image, etc.), and customers will be responsible for deploying the image in the cluster.[11]

This means Amazon will release patched or updated image versions every month or so, but they cannot patch or update the existing worker node of a customer with the new image since they have no access to the customer's AWS account. It will be the customer's responsibility to update the node whenever AWS releases a new update. The customer must explicitly click an update button in the AWS console or use code to update the node with the new release.

AWS offers no support for customers if they elect to use self-managed nodes. On the contrary, AWS is fully responsible for customers who opt for the Fargate nodes. Fargate nodes are serverless nodes provisioned and

---

[10] Amazon EKS – User Guide
[11] https://docs.aws.amazon.com/eks/latest/userguide/managed-node-groups.html

fully managed by AWS on the customer's behalf. AWS is fully responsible for installation, patching, troubleshooting, security, and anything that may affect the nodes.

Summary

This chapter introduced the subject matter of this book and highlighted the key differences between EKS and K8s. We discussed the brief history of K8s, its functions, and purpose. Now it should be clear that K8s is not EKS but an orchestrator for K8s, whereas K8s is an orchestrator for objects such as pods that encapsulate containerized applications.

This book is organized into three main parts. Part 1 will introduce EKS concepts, its architecture, and how to deploy them. Part 2 will revisit Kubernetes, its architecture, and how it orchestrates containerized applications. Finally, Part 3 will focus on the service and observability in application deployments on EKS clusters. We will introduce a few advanced K8s concepts such as service mesh and VPC Lattice in this part.

CHAPTER 2

EKS Architecture and Cluster Access Control

When you order a new product, you welcome it with open arms once it arrives. Next, you unbox it and ensure that the package is intact. For a well-packaged product, you can't wait to open its protective casing to dive deeper into its inner workings. Examining the individual components, understanding how to install them, and exploring how to use the product provide valuable insights into its design and functionality. In the same way, we aim to delve into Amazon EKS by uncovering its core components, analyzing how they are interconnected, and exploring the configuration options available for cluster operators. This approach will offer a clear understanding of EKS's architecture and how to tailor it to meet diverse application needs. Specifically, we will cover the EKS architecture and the three cluster network access control options available for cluster operators. This should lead us into security discussions and the implications of cluster network access control use cases.

The EKS Architecture

The Amazon Elastic Kubernetes Service (EKS) employs a unified architecture featuring three network access control choices. This architecture encompasses two distinct planes, the data plane and the control plane, depicted in Figure 2-1.

The control plane is exclusively managed by AWS, while the data plane operates within a separate AWS virtual private cloud (VPC) network that AWS customers typically oversee. In this setup, cluster operators, and developers generally manage the data plane, with AWS assuming full responsibility for the control plane.

AWS shields the control plane from direct customer access, permitting interactions solely through an application programming interface (API). We provide detailed explanations regarding the nature of these interactions and their security implications in subsequent sections.

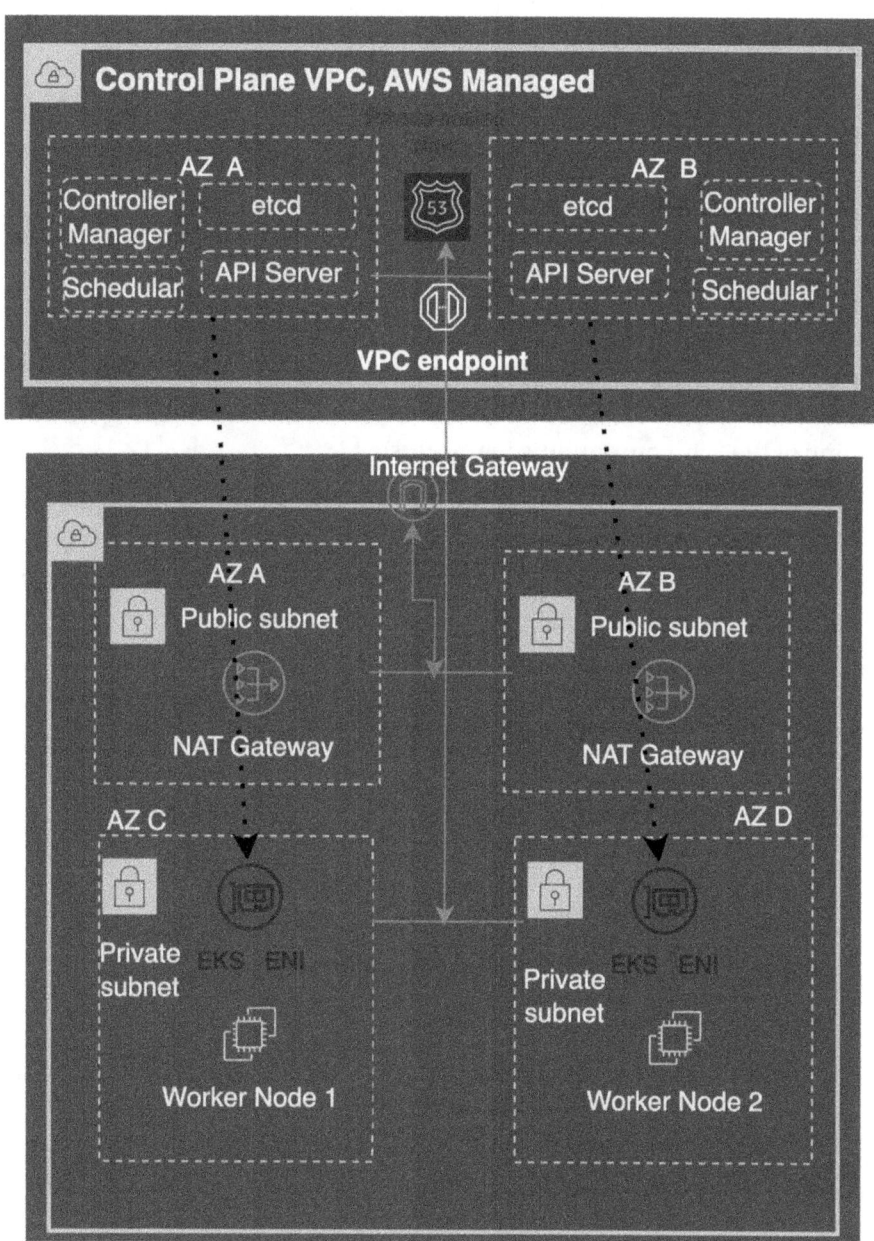

Figure 2-1. *The Amazon EKS architecture*

CHAPTER 2   EKS ARCHITECTURE AND CLUSTER ACCESS CONTROL

The Control Plane

This section explains the core components of the control plane of an EKS cluster. The control plane is the intelligent hub of the cluster where global decisions such as application scheduling and cluster management are made.[1] It is responsible for detecting and responding to cluster events such as failures, resource scheduling, and more.

The control plane is composed of AWS and Kubernetes (K8s) components. The K8s components are typically responsible for application orchestration, whereas the AWS components are for communication and hosting of the K8s components in the cluster.

The K8s components that reside in the control plane include the scheduler, the etcd database, the controller manager, and the API server as depicted in Figure 2-1. The AWS components are AWS-managed VPC, the Route 53 private hosted zone, VPC endpoint, and others.

EKS deploys the K8s components within an AWS-managed VPC, ensuring seamless communication between the data and control plane components. AWS is responsible for the control plane and its management, meaning customers or cluster operators have no direct access to it. In contrast, customers may own and manage the VPC in the data plane, depending on the type of cluster nodes they deploy. For example, customers who deploy Fargate nodes may delegate full responsibilities to AWS for both data and control planes.

---

[1] The Kubernetes Workshop: Learn how to build and run highly scalable workloads on Kubernetes, Zachary Arnold, Sahil Dua, Wei Huang, Faisal Masood, Melony Qin, and Mohammed Abu Taleb

The API Server Component

The API server acts as the communication gateway for both internal cluster components and external clients or services that seek access to the cluster. It is the sole interface through which all agents, users, or services interact with the components within the cluster. The cluster components themselves can only communicate with each other through the API server. It has exclusive access to the cluster database (etcd) which keeps the critical cluster metadata, secrets and other necessary information for cluster management.

The ETCD Component

An EKS cluster is a distributed system where several nodes or instances work together to run a workload.[2] Distributed systems are susceptible to failures due to their complex interconnections. To recover from such failures, EKS relies on the data stored in the etcd key-value database to maintain the clusters in their desired states. The etcd database holds critical metadata and essential information required to maintain the desired state of EKS clusters.

The Controller Manager Component

The controller manager component is the mother of all cluster controllers. It manages the object or cluster controllers. Cluster or object controllers maintain the desired state of their respective cluster objects. They include the node controller which monitors the health of cluster nodes and

---

[2] Božić, Velibor. (2023). Distributed computing systems. 10.13140/RG.2.2.33017.75361

manages their lifecycle, the replication controller which maintains the desired number of pod replicas in the cluster, the endpoint controller which manages the mapping of services to pods, and the service account and token controllers which manage service accounts and their associated tokens.

Typically, controllers monitor events such as create, update, and delete on resources and trigger appropriate responses to restore objects to their desired state.[3]

Controllers monitor the state of the cluster via the API server and respond to failure or undesirable events with corrective actions that may restore the cluster to its desired state. They can enforce policies on cluster objects. For instance, you can use the admission controller to allow only pods with specific labels to run on a node.

Scheduler Component

The scheduler is responsible for assigning the most appropriate node to an incoming workload or pod. It relies on decision-making algorithms and a deep understanding of the cluster environment to perform this task. The scheduler takes into account various factors, including resource requirements, hardware and software constraints, policy rules, and affinity or anti-affinity specifications to select a suitable node. Additional inputs in the decision-making process include data locality, potential inter-workload interference, and deadlines.[4]

---

[3] The Kubernetes Workshop: Learn how to build and run highly scalable workloads on Kubernetes, Zachary Arnold, Sahil Dua, Wei Huang, Faisal Masood, Melony Qin, and Mohammed Abu Taleb

[4] https://kubernetes.io/docs/concepts/overview/components/

Route 53

Route 53 is one of the AWS components found in the control plane. It is one of the domain name services or systems in EKS clusters. It is responsible for converting fully qualified domain names (FQDNs) to IP addresses. In the EKS context, Route 53 is responsible for converting the FQDN of the EKS cluster API server endpoint to an IP address to facilitate communication between cluster components.

The cluster endpoint is the URL assigned by EKS during the cluster provisioning. Its purpose is to facilitate routing of traffic between the nodes in the data plane and the API server in the control plane. Also, it allows clients or services outside the cluster to reach the API server.

Route 53 DNS requires DNS and DNS hostname support in the data plane to function. Hence, EKS cluster operators must enable these supports in the customer's VPC. Since Route 53 is hosted in the control plane, it is not directly visible within the customer's account or VPC. The core DNS is another DNS server you can find in EKS clusters. It is the default name server for K8s clusters. It is a flexible, extensible DNS server responsible for resolving the FQDNs of cluster resources to IP addresses. For instance, K8s may use the core DNS to resolve the FQDN of a service represented as **blue.namespacex.svc.cluster.local** to a local IP address. The core DNS may be implemented for cluster objects while the Route 53 may be marked for the cluster's API endpoints.

The Data Plane

The data plane is the non-intelligent part of the cluster. Its primary role is to host the nodes that run containerized applications and provide the necessary network infrastructure for the cluster. Nodes, which are EC2 instances or servers, execute tasks assigned by the scheduler in the control plane. Like the control plane, the data plane also contains K8s and EKS components. However, we will skip a detailed discussion of the K8s components for now and cover it in Part 2 of the book.

Customer VPC

The customer VPC is where EKS deploys the data plane resources. It consists of customer-managed subnets and network infrastructure, such as Elastic Network Interfaces (ENIs), Internet gateways, and network address translation (NAT) gateways. These gateways work together to enable access to the data plane from both internal and external clients or services while facilitating outbound communication from the data plane to the Internet.

Within the customer VPC, the worker nodes are responsible for running the pods in the cluster. The EKS ENIs in the VPC enable the API server to make direct inbound calls from the control plane to the data plane.

Cluster Security Group and ENIs

AWS secures network communication with security groups. Security groups are virtual firewalls that control inbound and outbound traffic associated with elastic network interfaces (ENIs).[5]

In Amazon EKS, security groups regulate traffic between the control plane and the data plane. By default, EKS sets up inbound and outbound security groups that permit unrestricted traffic flow between the two planes. However, cluster operators can modify these settings by implementing more stringent custom rules. These custom rules may allow outbound traffic on ports 53 and 443 to ensure communication from the data plane to the Route 53 DNS service and the API server, respectively.

---

[5] https://docs.aws.amazon.com/vpc/latest/userguide/vpc-security-groups.html

CHAPTER 2 EKS ARCHITECTURE AND CLUSTER ACCESS CONTROL

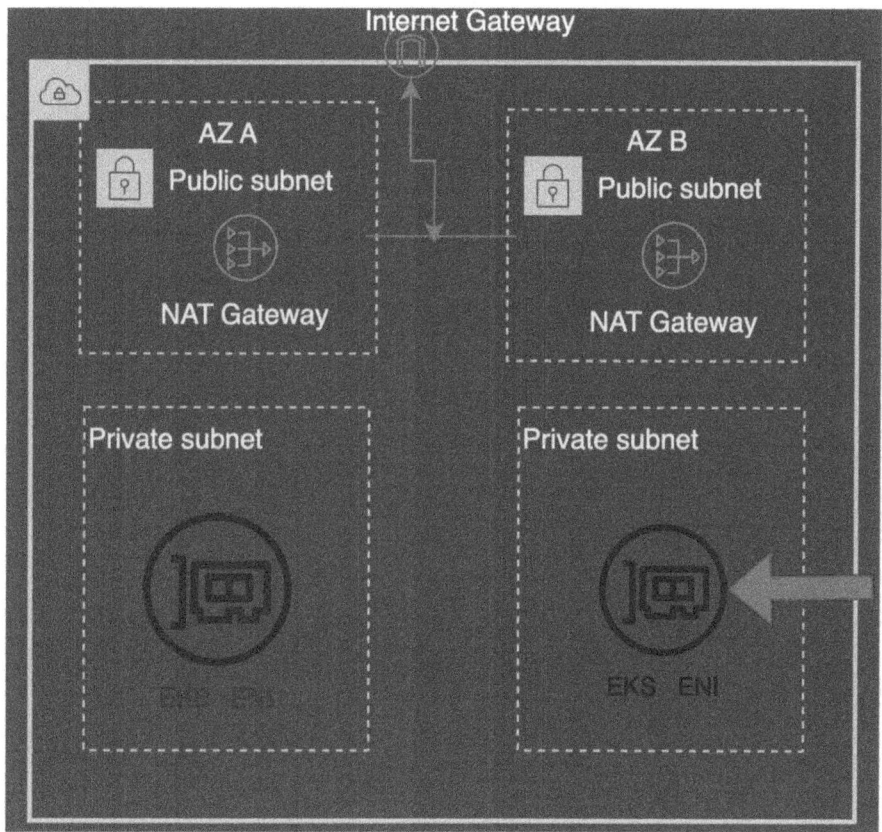

Figure 2-2. *Cluster ENIs in customer VPC*

EKS depends on two key resources to enable bidirectional communication between the control plane and the data plane, the cluster's Elastic Network Interfaces (ENIs), as shown in Figure 2-2, and the API endpoint.

The ENIs facilitate one-way inbound traffic from the control plane to the data plane, while the VPC endpoint in the control plane enables outbound traffic from the data plane to the control plane, collectively establishing two-way communication between the two planes.

The ENIs are always deployed within the customer's VPC in the data plane, even if the Kubernetes endpoint private access is not configured. This ensures continuous one-way communication from the control plane to the data plane.

ENIs enable requests like **kubectl exec deployment/catalog** and **kubectl logs**, which originate from the API server, to reach the data plane, as depicted by the black dotted lines in Figure 2-1. You can deploy two to four ENIs in any of the data plane subnets, either during the cluster creation or afterwards.

During K8s version update, EKS deletes and recreates new ENIs.[6] Unfortunately, there is no guarantee that EKS will create the ENIs in the same subnets as your preferred subnets except you limit the number of subnets for the ENIs to only two during or after cluster creation.

It is recommended to decouple the ENIs from the subnets of the worker nodes by deploying them in their separate /28 subnets. For example, in Figure 2-1 both worker nodes and ENIs share the same subnets, creating tightly coupled architecture and contributing to IPv4 address exhaustion.

Cluster Network Access Control

During cluster provisioning, EKS creates an API endpoint to allow both services and cluster operators access to the cluster. This API endpoint serves as the primary gateway and entry point for accessing the cluster once it is deployed. Controlling access to this entry point is crucial for ensuring the security of the cluster.

---

[6] https://docs.aws.amazon.com/eks/latest/userguide/network_reqs.html

Fortunately, EKS offers several ways to control access to the cluster's API endpoint at the network level. Cluster administrators or operators can choose from three access options (private, public and hybrid) based on their requirements. Each option is explained in the following sections.

Endpoint Private Access Control

The API server manages all communication to and from an EKS cluster across three distinct routes, from the external client or service to the API server, from the data plane to the API server, and from the API server to the data plane.

Communication from the API server to the data plane follows a fixed route; it always goes from the control plane to the cluster ENIs in the data plane (as shown in Figure 2-1). In contrast, the communication route for external clients, services, or data plane to the API server depends on how the cluster endpoint is configured.

If you configure a endpoint private access, then EKS will deploy a VPC endpoint in the control plane to allow only traffic originating from the customer VPC to reach the control plane via the VPC endpoint. This ensures that all communications originating from the customer's VPC of the data plane or the connected networks to the control plane remain private within the cluster.

The endpoint private access cluster is one of the three cluster network access control configurations. It is the most secure cluster network access control among the three because it restricts all traffic within the AWS private networks.[7] It enforces direct communication from the data plane to the control plane over a private VPC endpoint and from the control plane to the data plane over ENIs of the data plane.

---

[7] https://docs.aws.amazon.com/eks/latest/userguide/cluster-endpoint.html

Since the control and data planes typically reside within private AWS networks, EKS cluster administrators or services outside the customer VPC of the data plane cannot access the cluster unless they join the customer network through a VPN tunnel, Direct Connect, bastion host, or similar solutions.

For instance, the endpoint private access configuration shown in Figure 2-3 restricts cluster administrators (EKS Admins) from accessing the cluster outside the customer VPC. The EKS Admin cannot directly access the cluster's API server or API endpoint from a local client computer, as all access is confined within the cluster's VPC or network.

While restricting access to the cluster network enhances security, it can complicate tasks such as patching and node updates. Nodes and pods located in the private subnets of the data plane are unable to send outbound requests outside their local network or receive updates unless there is a route to the public Internet.

A common solution to overcome these access restrictions for pods and nodes is to introduce public subnets, equipped with NAT and Internet gateways to route traffic outside the local network, as shown in Figure 2-3. The setup allows outbound communication from the private subnets to the Internet, enabling nodes to receive the necessary updates.

The NAT and Internet gateways enable both programmatic and non-programmatic outbound communication from the worker nodes or pods to the Internet. Nonprogrammatic outbound communication refers to scenarios where a cluster operator manually login to a pod using the **kubectl exec** command and makes outbound calls within the pod.

Alternatively, pods in public subnets can use Source NAT (SNAT) to reach the Internet directly, without requiring an external NAT gateway. This setup allows Internet access for the pods while maintaining private access for the API endpoint. Administrator or operator access to the cluster remains restricted to the cluster VPC, ensuring that the API calls stay private.

CHAPTER 2 EKS ARCHITECTURE AND CLUSTER ACCESS CONTROL

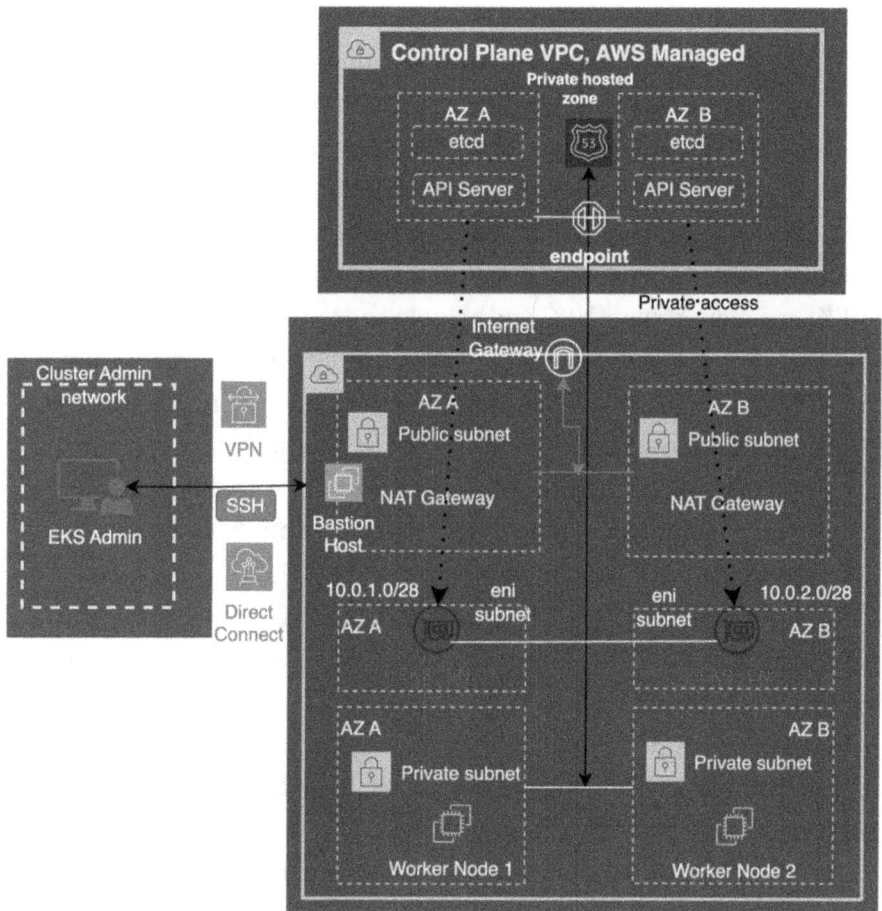

Figure 2-3. Endpoint Private with NAT and Internet gateways

Endpoint Hybrid Access Cluster

Setting up endpoint private access clusters can be complicated, especially when the cluster needs to communicate with external services, such as a Jenkins code pipeline. The Jenkins server cannot access the private endpoint of the cluster unless it is deployed within the same customer VPC or connected via VPN, Direct Connect, or similar solutions.

Where VPN tunnels or similar connectivity is not feasible, an endpoint "hybrid" access cluster that combines both public and private API endpoints in the same cluster offers a more practical solution. This setup allows external services (e.g., Jenkins code pipeline) to access the cluster through the public endpoint while maintaining private API access through the private API endpoint. This ensures secure and efficient communication for both internal and external interactions.

EKS creates a private VPC endpoint in the control plane for private access and an Internet gateway for public access. For the hybrid endpoint, administrators can choose to interact with the cluster through either the private or public endpoint, depending on their security requirements.

To enhance security, the public endpoint can be further protected using IP whitelisting, restricting access to specific public IP addresses or address ranges. Communication from the data to the control planes will continue to occur over the private endpoint within the cluster. In contrast, traffic is routed to the public Internet if the cluster administrator accesses the cluster through the public endpoint.

The public endpoint opens the cluster access for anyone with cluster access credentials if no IP whitelist is implemented. It is therefore prudent to enforce IP restrictions on the public endpoint from the EKS cluster's advanced settings in the AWS EKS console or use the **public_access_cidrs = [IP Address/32]** command in Terraform. You can also use the EKS **eksctl utils update-cluster-vpc-config --cluster=<cluster> cidrs command** to achieve the same goal.

CHAPTER 2   EKS ARCHITECTURE AND CLUSTER ACCESS CONTROL

In Figure 2-4 (black line), the private endpoint ensures that communication between the data and control planes remains private. The cluster administrators may access the cluster in both ways, either through the public or the private endpoint.

The communication between the data and control planes will remain private, routed through the ENIs and the private VPC endpoint, as illustrated in Figure 2-4.

Public access involves two Internet gateways (one in the customer VPC and the other in the VPC of the control plane) and a network load balancer (NLB) (not in shown in Figure 2-4) in the control plane that manages traffic to the control plane.[8]

---

[8] https://docs.aws.amazon.com/eks/latest/userguide/cluster-endpoint.html

CHAPTER 2   EKS ARCHITECTURE AND CLUSTER ACCESS CONTROL

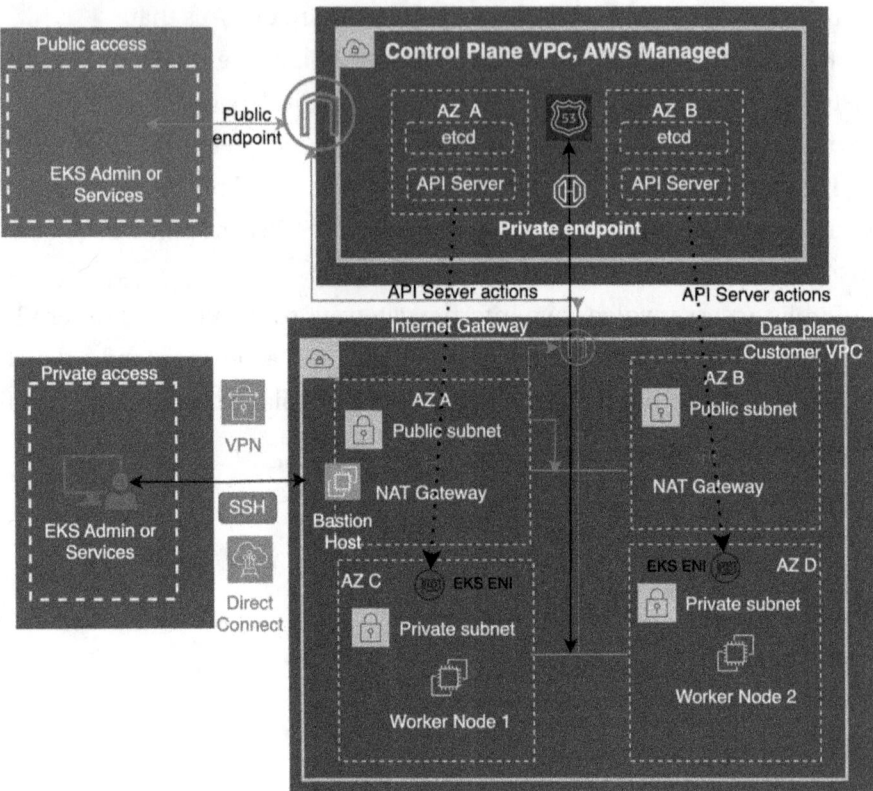

Figure 2-4. Endpoint Hybrid access setup

Endpoint Public Access Control

The endpoint public access setup is the default configuration for EKS clusters. In this setup, EKS creates a public API server endpoint, enabling cluster operators to access the cluster's API server from the Internet. The API server is secured using a combination of AWS Identity and Access Management (IAM) and K8s role-based access control (RBAC).

CHAPTER 2　EKS ARCHITECTURE AND CLUSTER ACCESS CONTROL

The default endpoint public access cluster may be implemented in less secure environments, such as test or development. In these cases, VPN or Direct Connect is not required; regular Internet access will be sufficient. To enable this setup, a new API server endpoint configuration is needed, as illustrated in Figure 2-5.

The endpoint public access clusters do not deploy private VPC endpoints to secure communication from the data plane to the control plane. As a result, it is the least secure option, as all API calls may occur over the public Internet. API calls from the worker nodes leave the customer's VPC and are routed to control plane over the internet through the Internet gateways of the cluster (see the red line in Figure 2-5).[9]

Cluster administrators will always access the API server through the public Internet. This communication path exposes the cluster API server to the public Internet access, and make it more vulnerable attacks than the endpoint private access clusters. We summarize the three configuration options Table 2-1.

---

[9] https://docs.aws.amazon.com/eks/latest/userguide/cluster-endpoint.html

CHAPTER 2   EKS ARCHITECTURE AND CLUSTER ACCESS CONTROL

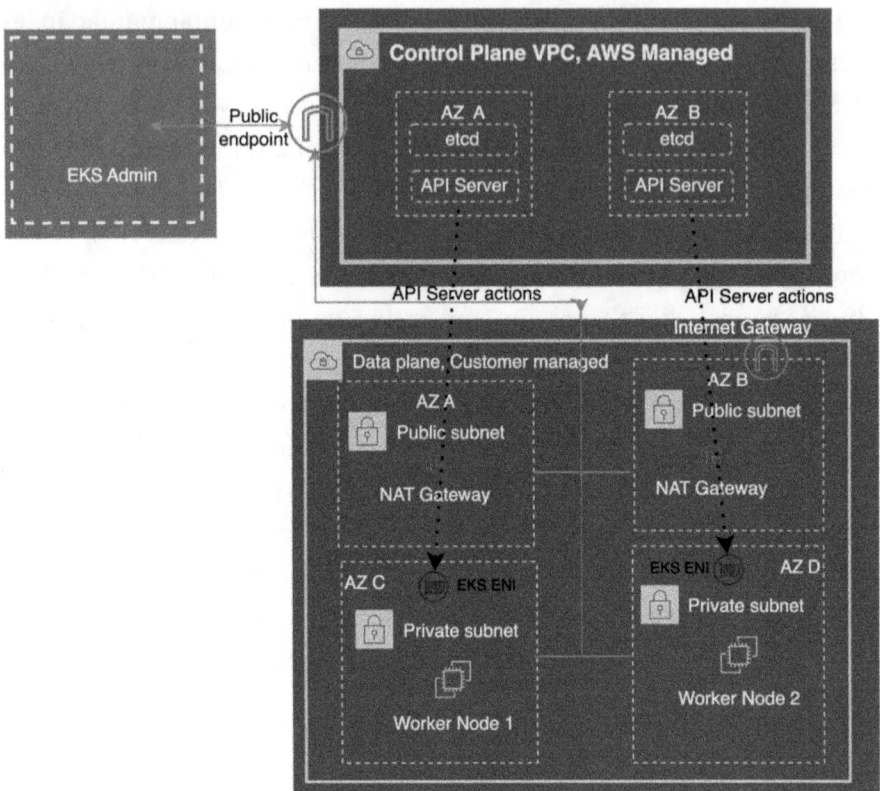

Figure 2-5. *Endpoint Public access setup*

Table 2-1. *Cluster network access control options*[10]

Endpoint Public Access	Endpoint Private Access	Behavior
Enabled	Disabled	• API server is accessible from the Internet (client machine to API server). • Kubernetes API requests that originate from worker nodes leave the VPC.
Enabled	Enabled	• Kubernetes API requests that originate from worker nodes use the private VPC endpoint. • API server is accessible from the Internet (client machine to API server).
Disabled	Enabled	• There is no public access to the API server from the Internet. Any commands must come from within the cluster VPC or a connected network.

End-User Communication

End users can interact with pods or applications running on the data plane through a load balancer deployed not in the control plane but in the data plane as shown in Figure 2-6. This interaction does not require a NAT or Internet gateway, regardless of the cluster configuration option.

---

[10] https://docs.aws.amazon.com/eks/latest/userguide/cluster-endpoint.html

CHAPTER 2 EKS ARCHITECTURE AND CLUSTER ACCESS CONTROL

In this setup, the load balancer acts as the frontend, handling traffic from end users, while the worker nodes serve as the backend. The load balancer routes traffic from the end users to the appropriate application pods running on the worker nodes, ensuring efficient communication without exposing the internal network.

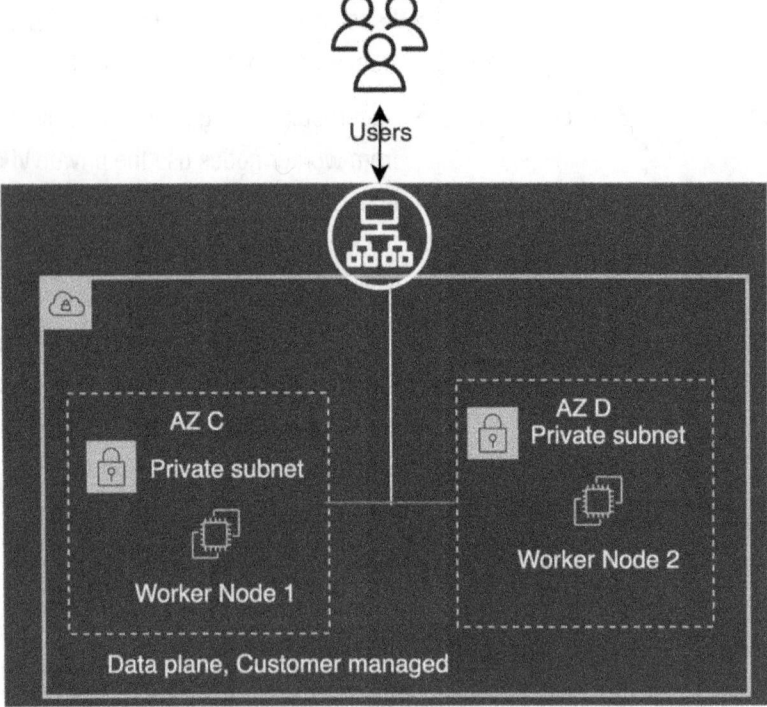

Figure 2-6. User access

Summary

There are three network access control configurations that should influence your security decisions as a cluster operator. They are the public, private, and endpoint hybrid access control configurations.

The endpoint private access clusters keep all communications private within the AWS network; the public-private option may keep administrator and service access public but will keep all communications between the data and control planes private. All API calls go through the public Internet for endpoint public access clusters. The endpoint public access clusters do not deploy VPC private endpoints in the cluster. You should not lose sight of the characteristics of these access control mechanisms as we prepare to embark on cluster deployments in the next and the subsequent chapters.

CHAPTER 3

EKS Implementations

In this chapter, we take the next step from product review to product testing. We will evaluate whether the promise of security is achievable by deploying an endpoint public access EKS cluster using Terraform code. This will give us hands-on experience and allow us to assess the actual configuration and security features in practice.

Endpoint Public Access Cluster

Before we create our first EKS cluster, it's important to take a step back to discuss the reasoning behind our tool and deployment choices.

You can deploy EKS clusters using the AWS console, an infrastructure-as-code (IaC) tool like Terraform or other command-line interface tools. I prefer Terraform to other tools. The choice of Terraform is driven by both convenience and personal preference. I'm assuming you are familiar with Terraform tool. You can still follow along with me even if you are not familiar with Terraform.

We'll begin by reviewing the structure of the code shown in Figure 3-1 and then walk through the Terraform code itself. Along the way, we'll map different sections of the code to the numbered components in Figures 3-2 and 3-3.

CHAPTER 3   EKS IMPLEMENTATIONS

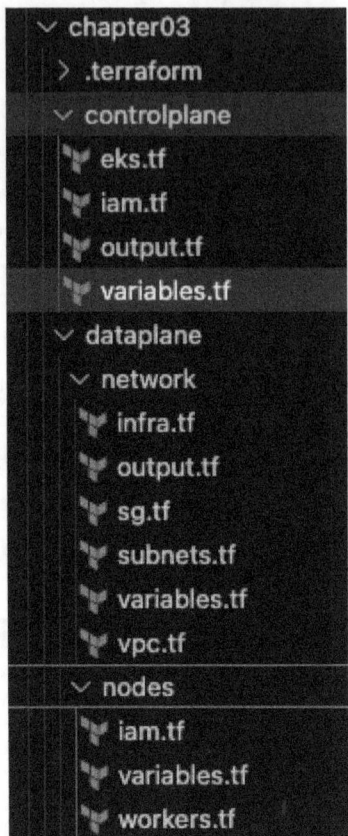

Figure 3-1. *Terraform Code Structure*

Figure 3-1 illustrates the folder structure of the code for both the data and control planes. The **controlplane** folder (referred to as a "module" in Terraform) contains the code responsible for creating the cluster's control plane.

Similarly, the **dataplane** module contains the code for the cluster's data plane, which includes two submodules, one for the **customer network** and the other for the **worker nodes**.

CHAPTER 3   EKS IMPLEMENTATIONS

The **customer network** represents the VPC managed by the AWS customer, the entity creating the cluster. The **worker nodes** are EC2 instances deployed within the customer network that will host the containerized applications.

Each module or submodule contains a **variables.tf** file that declares all the variables for the given module. For example, the **variables.tf** file for the control plane module is listed as follows:

```
variable "cluster_name" {
   default = "public-endpoint-cluster"
}
variable "cluster_version" {
  default = "1.31"
}
variable "private_subnet_ids" {}
```

where the **cluster_name** variable declares the name of the cluster and sets the default value to **public-endpoint-cluster**. Similarly, **cluster_version** declares the Kubernetes version of the cluster and sets the value to **1.31**.

The last variable, **private_subnet_ids**, represents the subnet IDs of the customer VPC where Terraform will deploy the ENIs. The ENIs enable communication from the control plane to the data plane. This variable has no default value, meaning Terraform or the cluster creator will supply the value at runtime.

We make provision for you to run simple commands required to initiate your cluster in a **script.sh** file. For example, you will find the following command for updating the kubeconfig file in the **script.sh** file accompanying the chapter03 folder:

aws eks update-kubeconfig --name public-endpoint-cluster

37

The kube config file stores the information you will need to authenticate to a cluster and make API calls. The preceding command will download data from the EKS cluster and construct an API token to automatically update the kube config file such that you can make API calls from the command line of your local laptop.

You should locate the **kube config** file in the **.kube** folder after you install the **kubectl** tool[1] on your client machine or laptop.

The initialization script also prevents character format errors if you choose to copy and execute commands directly from the book. I strongly recommend that you use the **script.sh** file where available instead of copying commands from the book directly. If you do copy commands directly from this book, ensure that the character set is consistent with the format required by your command-line tool.

Alternatively, you can format the commands from this book using a text editor like VS Code before executing them.

In the folder structure, you'll sometimes find the **pod**, pods or **deployment** folders. These folders contain manifests for deploying applications on the clusters in a given chapter.

Finally, you can clone all the codes from the book's GitHub[2] page. The code for this chapter is found in the chapter03 folder.

Control Plane Deployment

This section explains the Terraform code that will create the control plane of the endpoint public access cluster. You will find the Terraform code snippets in the **eks.tf** file under the control plane folder.

---

[1] https://kubernetes.io/docs/tasks/tools/
[2] https://github.com/Apress/AWS-EKS-Essentials

CHAPTER 3 EKS IMPLEMENTATIONS

```
resource "aws_eks_cluster" "public_endpoint_cluster" {
  name    = var.cluster_name
  version = var.cluster_version
  role_arn = aws_iam_role.cluster_role.arn
  #configure data plane subnets and eni
  vpc_config {
    subnet_ids = concat(
      var.private_subnet_ids
    )
    endpoint_public_access  = "true"
  }
  depends_on = [ aws_iam_role.cluster_role ]
}
```

The **resource "aws_eks_cluster"** specifies the type of resource Terraform should create. In this case, Terraform will create the AWS EKS cluster as per resource specification (**aws_eks_cluster**).

Terraform creates a resource if you declares a resource block given by the resource provider's name, type, and a variable name. For example, the resource block for the preceding code snippets is declared as follows:

```
resource "aws_eks_cluster" "public_endpoint_cluster" {
}
```

where the **aws_eks_cluster** combines the resource provider's name and resource type, the **public_endpoint_cluster** is the resource identifier. The general format of a resource block is given by

```
resource "<PROVIDER>_<TYPE>" "<NAME>" {
}
```

where <PROVIDER> is the resource provider such as AWS, GitHub, Google, etc., and the <TYPE> is the type of resource you want to deploy. For instance, eks_cluster, instance, and ami are resource types. The <NAME> is any identifier that follows Terraform naming convention.[3]

A resource block declares a resource of a specific type with a specific local name.[4] Terraform uses the name when referring to the resource in the same module. Resource names are scoped within a module, therefore not visible to the codes outside the module.

A resource type may require one or more arguments, optional and mandatory ones. For example, in the example code above, the **aws_eks_cluster** resource block requires three mandatory arguments, **name, version, and role_arn**, as listed below:

```
name     = var.cluster_name
version  = var.cluster_version
role_arn =aws_iam_role.cluster_role.arn
```

Besides the mandatory arguments, you can specify optional arguments such as the endpoint public access argument.

```
endpoint_public_access  = "true"
```

The argument determines the type of endpoint Terraform should create for the cluster. The "**true**" value means Terraform should deploy a public access endpoint for the cluster. The default value of the argument is true, meaning Terraform will by default create a public access endpoint for all clusters except the cluster creator explicitly set the value to false.

The **vpc_config** block of the control plane code is where Terraform creates the ENIs in the given customer's VPC subnet(s). In this example, Terraform will create the ENIs in the private subnets of the customer's VPC, much the same as the worker nodes.

---

[3] https://www.terraform-best-practices.com/naming
[4] https://developer.hashicorp.com/terraform/language/resources/syntax

CHAPTER 3 EKS IMPLEMENTATIONS

```
vpc_config {
   subnet_ids = concat(
     var.private_subnet_ids
   )
}
```

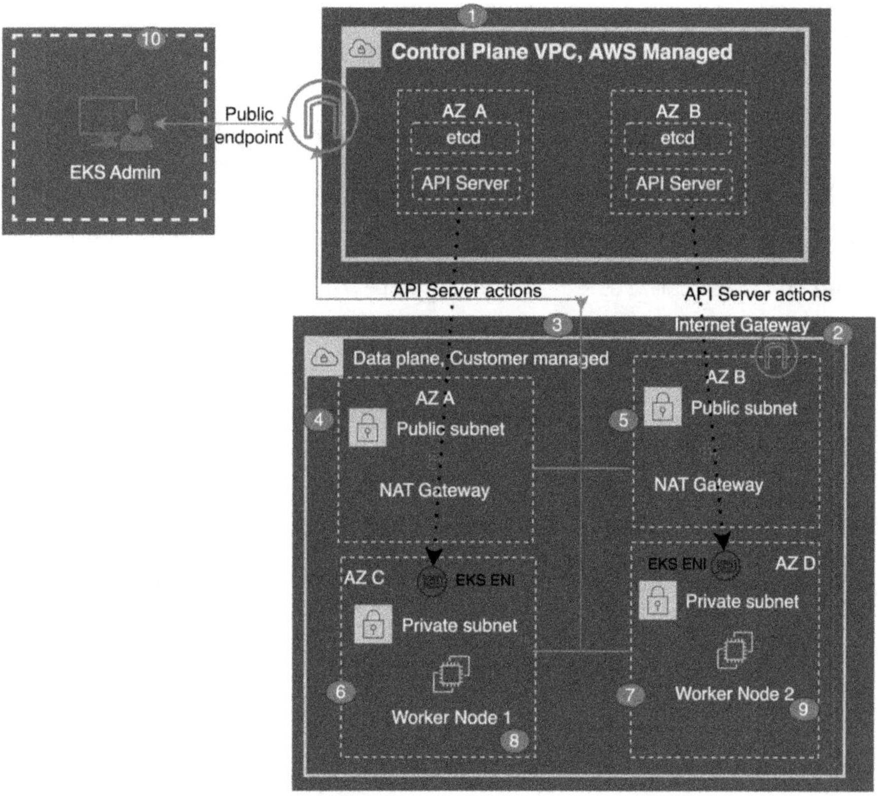

Figure 3-2. *Endpoint public access setup*

Role Assignment

Terraform cannot instruct the EKS service in AWS to create the control plane without permission. So, it must first create the necessary permissions on behalf of EKS so that the EKS service can make the necessary API calls to create the cluster. The code for this is represented by the IAM role in cluster creation code above.

role_arn = aws_iam_role.cluster_role.arn

A actual code is found in the **iam.tf** file under the control plane module as shown below.

```
#role required to create a cluster
resource "aws_iam_role" "cluster_role" {
  name = "${var.cluster_name}-role"
  assume_role_policy = <<POLICY
{
"Version": "2012-10-17",
"Statement": [
  {
    "Effect": "Allow",
    "Principal": {
      "Service": "eks.amazonaws.com"
    },
    "Action": "sts:AssumeRole"
  }
]
}
POLICY
}
```

```
# add policy to cluster role
resource "aws_iam_role_policy_attachment" "amazon_eks_cluster_
policy" {
  policy_arn = "arn:aws:iam::aws:policy/AmazonEKSClusterPolicy"
  role       = aws_iam_role.cluster_role.name
}
```

Terraform instructs AWS to create a role for the EKS service with the **aws_iam_role** resource specification in the above code. The policy section of the code creates a role with a name that refers to the cluster's name (**name = "${var.cluster_name}-role"**). You are free to choose your own name. This is followed by the trusted relationship policy allowing EKS service to assume the role as shown below:

```
assume_role_policy = <<POLICY
  {
  "Version": "2012-10-17",
  "Statement": [
    {
      "Effect": "Allow",
      "Principal": {
        "Service": "eks.amazonaws.com"
      },
      "Action": "sts:AssumeRole"
    }
  ]
}
POLICY
```

CHAPTER 3 EKS IMPLEMENTATIONS

Finally, Terraform attaches a policy to the role to grant EKS the permission to create the cluster:

```
resource "aws_iam_role_policy_attachment" "amazon_eks_cluster_policy" {
policy_arn = "arn:aws:iam::aws:policy/AmazonEKSClusterPolicy"
  role       = aws_iam_role.cluster_role.name
}
```

The **AmazonEKSClusterPolicy** is a mandatory policy for every EKS cluster.

Security Groups

EKS will automatically create a default security group to allow free flow of traffic between the data and control planes. No Terraform code is required for this except when you want to override an aspect of it. The same default security group rule will allow the EKS API server to communicate with the data plane via the cluster ENIs.

To demonstrate how to override the default outbound security group, we decided to introduce a custom security group in the **sg.tf** file under the data plane network module. The following code overrides the outbound cluster security group for Route 53 and the kubelet agents on the worker nodes. Kubelets are K8s agents that run on the nodes in the data plane to support container management. The custom outbound security group is effective only when you delete the default outbound cluster security group.

```
resource "aws_security_group_rule" "dns_port" {
    type             = "egress"
    from_port        = 53
    to_port          = 53
    protocol         = "tcp"
    cidr_blocks      = ["10.0.0.0/16"]
```

CHAPTER 3 EKS IMPLEMENTATIONS

```
    security_group_id = var.cluster_security_group_id
}
resource "aws_security_group_rule" "kube_port" {
    type              = "egress"
    from_port         = 10250
    to_port           = 10250
    protocol          = "tcp"
    cidr_blocks       = ["10.0.0.0/16"]
    security_group_id = var.cluster_security_group_id
}
```

The Data Plane VPC

Let us move on to the data plane part of the code. We want to address how the Terraform code relates to the data plane architecture.

As in Figure 3-3, the data plane portion of the EKS cluster is bounded by a VPC which is marked as 2 in the architecture. The corresponding Terraform code is in the **vpc.tf** file of the network submodule under the data plane folder.

The data plane lives in a customer VPC bounded by a CIDR range (depicted as number 2 in the architecture). The **cidr_blocks** argument specifies the IP range for the VPC; the **enable_dns_hostnames** and the **enable_dns_support** enable the hostnames and DNS support, respectively, so that the Route 53 DNS in the control plane can function as discussed earlier in Chapter 2. Lastly, the tags block creates a tag for the VPC.

```
resource "aws_vpc" "cluster_vpc" {
cidr_block =   var.cidr_blocks["cluster-network"]
enable_dns_hostnames = true
enable_dns_support   = true
```

45

CHAPTER 3   EKS IMPLEMENTATIONS

```
    tags = {
      Name = var.vpc_tag
    }
}
```

The value for the CIDR is defined in the **variables.tf** file of the module as follows:

```
variable "cidr_blocks" {
  description = "cidr blocks"
  type        = map(any)
  default = {
    private-subnet-1 = "10.0.3.0/24"
    private-subnet-2 = "10.0.4.0/24"
    public-subnet-1  = "10.0.5.0/24"
    public-subnet-2  = "10.0.6.0/24"
    cluster-network  = "10.0.0.0/16"
    internet         = "0.0.0.0/0"
  }
}
variable "vpc_tag" {
 default = "public-endpoint-cluster-vpc"
}
variable "cluster_security_group_id" {}
```

CHAPTER 3   EKS IMPLEMENTATIONS

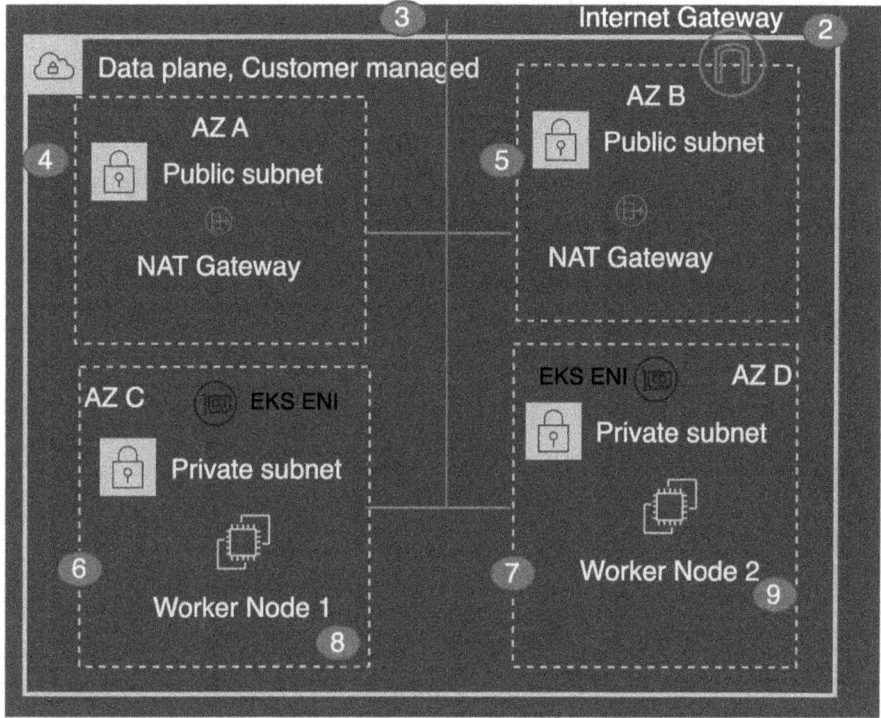

Figure 3-3. *Terraform code for data plane architecture*

An IP address range determines the logical boundary for a VPC where customers' network resource isolation begins and ends. The 10.0.0.0/16 value expresses the Internet protocol (IP) address block in the classless inter-domain address (CIDR) notation. The 10.0.3.0/24, 10.0.4.0/24, 10.0.5.0/24, and 10.0.6.0/24 are the subnets of the 10.0.0.0/16 network.

Subnets

Within a VPC are subnets represented by the numbers 4, 5, 6, and 7 in Figure 3-3. Subnets exist in availability zones where AWS resources such as nodes can be deployed. An availability zone (AZ) is a group of data centers

47

in an AWS region. It has redundant power, networking, and connectivity. A group of availability zones in a geographical location such as London, Ireland, and Ohio are referred to as a region.

The code below represents the Terraform code for the customer subnets. It consists of the data block which retrieves the availability zone for the subnets, two private and two public subnets.

```
data "aws_availability_zones" "azs" {
 state = "available"
}
resource "aws_subnet" "private_subnets" {
  vpc_id           = aws_vpc.cluster_vpc.id
  cidr_block = count.index == 0 ?    var.cidr_blocks["private-subnet-1"] :   var.cidr_blocks["private-subnet-2"]
  availability_zone = data.aws_availability_zones.azs.names[count.index]
  count = 2
  tags = {
    Name = "private-subnet-${count.index+1}"
  }
}
resource "aws_subnet" "public_subnets" {
 vpc_id      = aws_vpc.cluster_vpc.id
  cidr_block  = count.index == 0 ? var.cidr_blocks["public-subnet-1"] : var.cidr_blocks["public-subnet-2"]
  availability_zone = data.aws_availability_zones.azs.names[count.index]
  count = 2
```

```
  tags = {
    Name = "public-subnet-${count.index+1}"
  }
}
```

Network Infrastructure

Within the public subnets are the network infrastructure which comprises of the NAT, the Internet gateways, and a set of routing rules. You will find the code in the **infra.tf** file in the data plane folder.

The **aws_internet_gateway** block creates the Internet gateway, while the **aws_nat_gateway** block creates the NAT gateway. Following each resource is the creation of the routing table with the **aws_route_table** block and a route-to-route traffic to their destination.

```
"aws_internet_gateway" "internet_gw" {
  vpc_id = aws_vpc.cluster_vpc.id
  tags = {
    Name = "cluster-internet-gateway"
  }
}
#create route for internet gateway
resource "aws_route_table" "public_rt" {
  vpc_id = aws_vpc.cluster_vpc.id
  route {
    #going to internet use internet gateway
    cidr_block = var.cidr_blocks["internet"]
    gateway_id = aws_internet_gateway.internet_gw.id
  }
```

```
  tags = {
    Name = "public-rt"
  }
}
resource "aws_route_table_association" "public_rt_a" {
  #associate public route to public subnet
  subnet_id      = aws_subnet.public_subnets[count.index].id
  route_table_id = aws_route_table.public_rt.id
  count=2
}
#nat gateway eip
resource "aws_eip" "eip" {
  domain = "vpc"
  tags = {
    Name = "eip"
  }
}
#create nat gateway in the public subnet
resource "aws_nat_gateway" "natgw" {
  subnet_id     = aws_subnet.public_subnets[0].id
  allocation_id = aws_eip.eip.id
  tags = {
    Name = "nat-gateway"
  }
  depends_on = [aws_internet_gateway.internet_gw]
}
resource "aws_route_table" "private_rt" {
  #internet go to nat gateway
  vpc_id = aws_vpc.cluster_vpc.id
```

```
  route {
    cidr_block     = var.cidr_blocks["internet"]
    nat_gateway_id = aws_nat_gateway.natgw.id
  }
  tags = {
    Name = "private-rt"
  }
}
resource "aws_route_table_association" "internal_rt_a" {
  subnet_id      = aws_subnet.private_subnets[count.index].id
  route_table_id = aws_route_table.private_rt.id
  count = 2
}
```

Cluster Nodes

We now explain the code in the node's module. The code is found in the **workers.tf** file under the nodes' folder. It represents the numbers 8 and 9 of the architecture. The worker node group code is shown in the code snippet below.

```
resource "aws_eks_node_group" "nodes" {
  cluster_name    = var.cluster_name
  node_group_name = var.node_name
  node_role_arn   = aws_iam_role.worker_nodes_role.arn
  subnet_ids = var.subnet_ids
  capacity_type   = "ON_DEMAND" #or "SPOT"
  instance_types = var.instance_types
```

```
  scaling_config {
    desired_size = 2
    max_size     = 3
    min_size     = 2
  }
  update_config {
    max_unavailable = 1
  }
  labels = {
    name = var.label
  }
  tags = {
    Name = "worker-node"
  }
  depends_on = [ aws_iam_role.worker_nodes_role ]
}
```

Terraform will instruct the EKS to create two worker nodes per the above code. The required arguments for the node resource include node role represented by **nodes_role_arn** and subnets represented by **subnet_ids**. You can choose to deploy the nodes using spot instance or on-demand instance with the **capacity_type** argument.

You can scale the nodes with the **scaling_config** block configuration by specifying the appropriate values for the desired size, the maximum size, and the minimum number of nodes. The max_size argument sets the maximum number of nodes for the cluster, whereas the min_size argument sets the minimum number of nodes. The desired_size argument sets the initial number of nodes for the cluster.

```
scaling_config {
    desired_size = 2
    max_size     = 3
    min_size     = 2
}
```

Node Security

Sometimes you may want to allow access to certain services on the cluster nodes. For example, you may want SSH access or allow secure access to an application from a client. You do so by attaching additional rules to the security group of the worker nodes. For example, we created the security group rules that open the port 443 on the nodes to allow outbound calls to the Internet with the following Terraform code:

```
resource "aws_security_group_rule" "https_port" {
    type              = "egress"
    from_port         = 443
    to_port           = 443
    protocol          = "tcp"
    cidr_blocks       = ["0.0.0.0/0"]
    security_group_id = var.cluster_security_group_id
}
```

IAM

Like the control plane, the node service (EC2 service) requires the necessary permissions to make the appropriate APIs calls to create the cluster nodes. This section outlines the IAM permission requirements for the cluster nodes.

The **aws_iam_role** block creates the role with the **aws_iam_role_policy_attachment** blocks attaching the policies to the role. The Amazon EKS Worker Node permission is for the node to describe Amazon EC2 resources in the VPC.[5] It also provides permissions for the Amazon EKS Pod Identity Agent.

The Amazon EKS CNI policy provides the cluster network interface plugin with the needed permissions to modify the IP address configuration of the cluster nodes. This permission set allows the CNI to list, describe, and modify Elastic Network Interfaces (ENIs) on your behalf. The following is the IAM code:

```
#necessary roles for worker nodes
resource "aws_iam_role" "worker_nodes_role" {
  name = "${var.cluster_name}-nodes"
  assume_role_policy = jsonencode({
    Statement = [{
      Action = "sts:AssumeRole"
      Effect = "Allow"
      Principal = {
        Service = "ec2.amazonaws.com"
      }
    }]
    Version = "2012-10-17"
  })
}
#attach node role
resource "aws_iam_role_policy_attachment" "amazon_eks_worker_node_policy" {
  policy_arn = "arn:aws:iam::aws:policy/
```

---

[5] https://docs.aws.amazon.com/eks/latest/userguide/create-node-role.html

CHAPTER 3 EKS IMPLEMENTATIONS

```
AmazonEKSWorkerNodePolicy"
  role       = aws_iam_role.worker_nodes_role.name
}
resource "aws_iam_role_policy_attachment" "amazon_eks_cni_
policy" {
  policy_arn = "arn:aws:iam::aws:policy/AmazonEKS_CNI_Policy"
  role       = aws_iam_role.worker_nodes_role.name
}

resource "aws_iam_role_policy_attachment" "amazon_ec2_
container_registry_read_only" {
  policy_arn = "arn:aws:iam::aws:policy/
               AmazonEC2ContainerRegistryReadOnly"
  role       = aws_iam_role.worker_nodes_role.name
}

# Optional, only if you want SSM agent on your EKS nodes.
resource "aws_iam_role_policy_attachment" "amazon_ssm_managed_
instance_core" {
  policy_arn = "arn:aws:iam::aws:policy/
               AmazonSSMManagedInstanceCore"
  role       = aws_iam_role.worker_nodes_role.name
}
```

   The **AmazonEKSWorkerNodePolicy** and the
AmazonEKS_CNI_Policy are mandatory. However, the
AmazonEC2ContainerRegistryReadOnly is optional, and it is
for the nodes to access the elastic container registry access. Also,
the AmazonSSMManagedInstanceCorepolicy is optional. It enables the
SSM (AWS Systems Manager) agent on the nodes. The SSM agent allows
users to access the cluster nodes without SSH but with the AWS SSM agent.

main.tf File

The last file to cover here is the **main.tf** file. It is the caller file with the code that calls all the modules to create the cluster. It is like the main function in the imperative programming language.

```
provider "aws" {
  region = "us-east-1"
  profile  = "default"
}
#create eni in the dataplane (step x)
module "cluster" {
  source = "./controlplane"
  private_subnet_ids = module.vpc.private_subnet_ids
}
module "vpc" {
  source = "./dataplane/network"
  cluster_security_group_id = module.cluster.cluster_security_
  group_id
}
module "nodes" {
  source = "./dataplane/nodes"
  cluster_name = module.cluster.cluster_name
  node_name = "private-node-group"
  subnet_ids =  module.vpc.private_subnet_ids
}
```

Terraform Code Deployment

The first thing to do is to set up the EKS cluster creator account in AWS. A cluster creator is an IAM user or a role in AWS with the privilege to create an EKS cluster.

Account Setup

1. Create an AWS account.
2. Create an IAM user with Administrator Access permission.
3. Create an access key ID and secret access key for your Administrator user from the AWS console.
4. Install the AWS CLI on your local machine.
5. Use the **aws configure** command to configure the credentials on your local computer with the access key ID and secret access key. This will create a default profile for Terraform to create the cluster.
6. Install Terraform and your preferred code editor (e.g., Visual Studio Code).
7. Clone the code for this book from GitHub.[6]
8. Navigate to the directory chapter03.
9. Execute the Terraform code as follows:

   ```
   terraform init
   terraform plan
   terraform apply
   ```

Type yes if asked to see the Terraform code deployed after 15–20 minutes.

---

[6] www.apress.com/ISBN

Ensure that your AWS profile name in the .**aws/credentials** file is the same as the profile value in the Terraform code below if you encounter any permission issue. You may change the region if you want to deploy the cluster in a different region:

```
provider "aws" {
  region = "us-east-1"
  profile = "default"
}
```

Code Visualization with AWS Console

Use the AWS console to review the cluster deployment.

```
Go to AWS console ➤ EKS service, then click the cluster link.
```

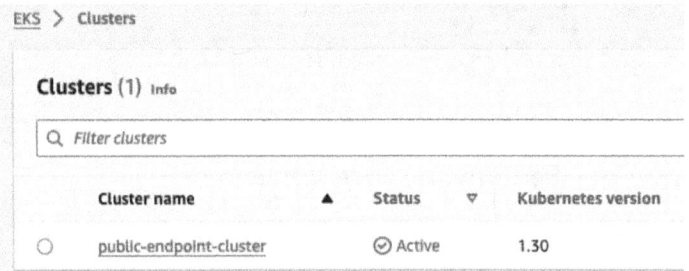

Figure 3-4. *Cluster endpoint*

Click the public-endpoint-cluster link ➤ the overview and subsequent tabs to review the cluster resources.

CHAPTER 3 EKS IMPLEMENTATIONS

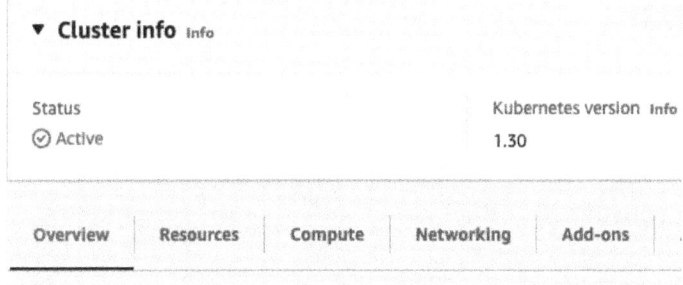

Figure 3-5. *Cluster overview tab*

Cluster Endpoint

To review the endpoint configuration, click the Networking tab and then the Manage endpoint access.

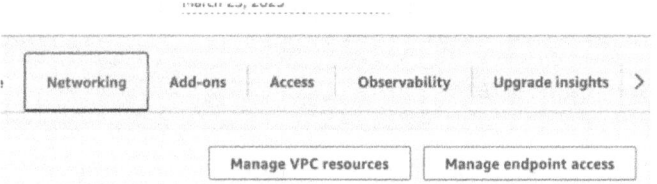

Figure 3-6. *Cluster network tab*

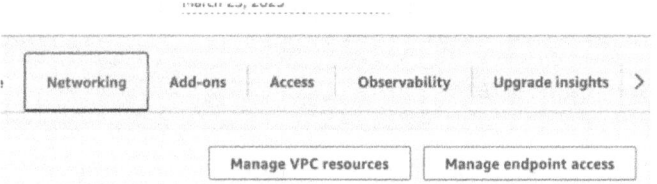

Figure 3-7. *Cluster public endpoint*

CHAPTER 3   EKS IMPLEMENTATIONS

Add-ons

By default, EKS requires network resources such as ENIs and DNS to deploy a K8s cluster on AWS. Integration of these resources needs add-ons. However, you will find no add-ons when you navigate to the Add-ons tab of the EKS console.

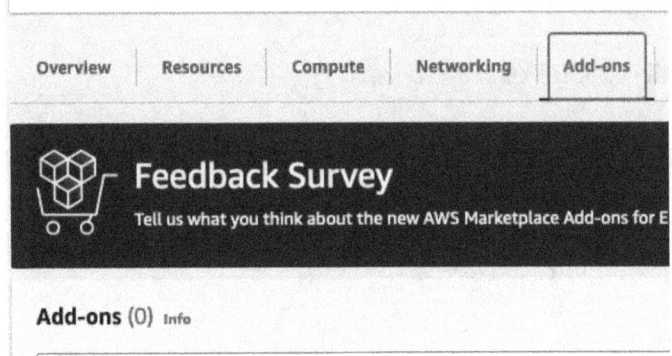

Figure 3-8. Cluster add-on tab

This does not mean add-ons were not deployed. It implies that EKS deployed self-managed add-ons. EKS will deploy self-managed add-ons if you don't explicitly specify them in your code or if you don't create the cluster with the AWS Management console.

Cluster ENIs

Find where the cluster ENIs are in AWS.

1. Navigate to the EC2 console ➤ Network & Security ➤ Network interfaces, scroll to the right to the ENIs with the Amazon EKS public-endpoint-cluster label, then click the corresponding security group of the ENI.

2. Review the inbound and the outbound rules.

CHAPTER 3   EKS IMPLEMENTATIONS

Security group IDs	Interface Type	Description
sg-0cbac75c93405141c	Elastic network interface	–
sg-0cbac75c93405141c	Elastic network interface	Amazon EKS public-endpoint-cluster

Figure 3-9. *Cluster security groups and ENIs*

Outbound rules (4)

Name	Security group rule ID	IP version	Type	Protocol	Port range
–	sgr-03980abe6f4443b74	IPv4	HTTPS	TCP	443
–	sgr-09cf84997d1b2ee88	IPv4	DNS (TCP)	TCP	53
–	sgr-003cf1f3031868339	IPv4	All traffic	All	All
–	sgr-0c911be119c439e77	IPv4	Custom TCP	TCP	10250

Figure 3-10. *Cluster security groups*

Observe that the custom outbound rules we created with the Terraform code are overridden by the wider security group rule, **sgr-003cf1f3031868339 IPv4 All traffic All 0.0.0.0/0**. You may activate the custom rule by deleting this outbound rule.

Node Security Group

```
Navigate to EC2 ➤ Instance, then click on a node ➤ security
to find the node security groups.
```

61

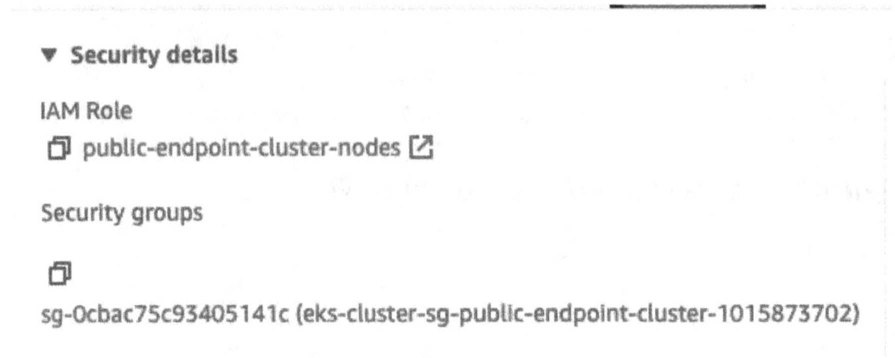

Security details

IAM Role
public-endpoint-cluster-nodes

Security groups

sg-0cbac75c93405141c (eks-cluster-sg-public-endpoint-cluster-1015873702)

Figure 3-11. Cluster security group details

Command Line Interface (CLI)

You can use the AWS CLI to retrieve similar information about the cluster as follows:

```
aws eks update-kubeconfig --name public-endpoint-cluster
aws eks describe-cluster --name public-endpoint-cluster
```

The **aws eks update-kubeconfig --name public-endpoint-cluster** command updates the .kube/config file with credentials for the endpoint public access cluster. On the other hand, the **aws eks describe-cluster --name public-endpoint-cluster** command describes the cluster. You may review the output of the command to find information about the cluster.

For Specific Query Use

```
aws eks describe-cluster --name public-endpoint-cluster --query cluster.resourcesVpcConfig.clusterSecurityGroupId
```

Testing the Cluster

Access the Cluster Nodes

```
kubectl get nodes
```

You should see the following output:

```
NAME                       STATUS   ROLES    AGE   VERSION
ip-10-0-3-14.ec2.internal  Ready    <none>   25h   v1.31.4-
                                                   eks-aeac579
ip-10-0-4-141.ec2.internal Ready    <none>   25h   v1.31.4-
                                                   eks-aeac579
```

Run an Application on the Cluster

Create the following pod manifest or YAML specification file. Give it a name such as blueapp.yml or blueapp.yaml:

```
apiVersion: v1
kind: Pod
metadata:
  name: blueapp-pod
  labels:
    app: blueapp-label
spec:
  containers:
    - name: blueapp-container
      image: cloudmanly/eks:blueapp
      ports:
        - containerPort: 8080
```

Execute the code on the K8s cluster:

```
kubectl apply -f pods/blueapp.yml
```

Check if the application is running:

```
kubectl get pod
```

You should see the following output:

```
NAME          READY   STATUS    RESTARTS   AGE
blueapp-pod   1/1     Running   0          50s
```

Cluster Security

We cannot close this chapter without discussing security. Security is going to be an integral part of most of the chapters in this book.

Identity and Access Management

Since we are operating an endpoint public access cluster, the cluster creator's credential (your AWS access key ID and the secret access key) is the only security layer protecting the cluster from compromise or unauthorized access. Anyone who again access to credentials can take over the cluster.

The current setup represents the lack of defense in depth, as the cluster depends on a single security layer, the AWS access key ID and secret access key of the cluster creator. There are no additional layers of protection in place.

To enhance security, you can configure a role with multifactor authentication (MFA) and an external ID, adding two additional layers of security to the cluster creator's access. By using AWS Roles, you assign the cluster creator temporary credentials, which are more secure than permanent access key ID and secret access key credentials.

Public Endpoint Restrictions with Web Console

Furthermore, you can enhance security by restricting access to the endpoint, limiting it from global Internet access to specific IP address blocks. This adds another security layer by reducing the attack surface to only the specified IP address ranges.

You can configure this restriction either through Terraform code or directly via the AWS Management console.[7] Use the following step with the AWS console:

Navigate to EKS ➤ Clusters, click the public-endpoint-cluster link, then click the network tab ➤ Manage endpoint access.

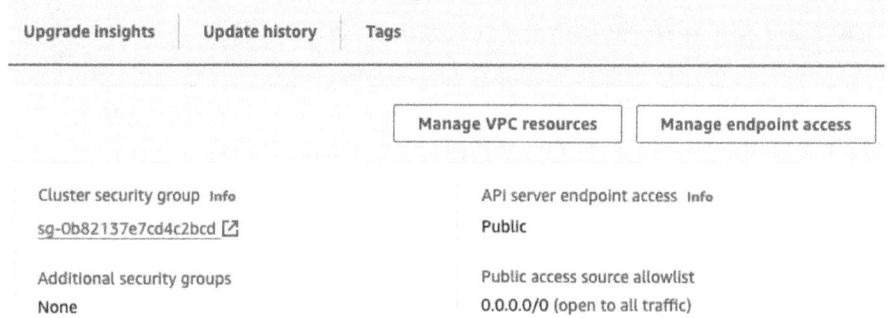

Figure 3-12. Cluster manage VPC resources

---

[7] https://aws.github.io/aws-eks-best-practices/

CHAPTER 3   EKS IMPLEMENTATIONS

Manage endpoint access: public-endpoint-cluster

Cluster endpoint access Info
Configure access to the Kubernetes API server endpoint.

○ **Public**
The cluster endpoint is accessible from outside of your VPC. Worker node traffic will leave your VPC to conne

○ **Public and private**
The cluster endpoint is accessible from outside of your VPC. Worker node traffic to the endpoint will stay wit

○ **Private**
The cluster endpoint is only accessible through your VPC. Worker node traffic to the endpoint will stay withir

▶ Advanced settings

Figure 3-13.   Cluster endpoint configuration

Click on the Advanced settings and change the CIDR block from 0.0.0.0/0 to the IP address of your laptop or any preferred public IP address range.

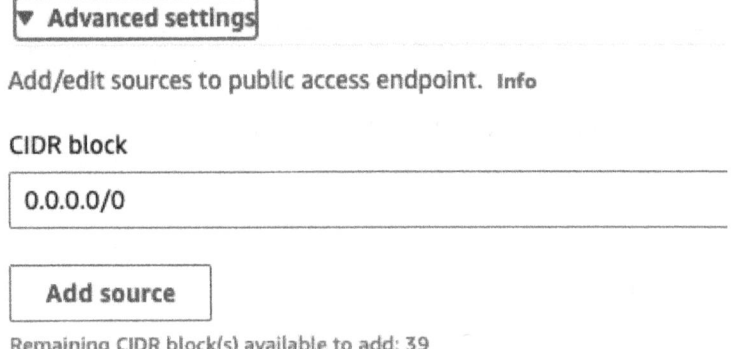

Figure 3-14.   Cluster endpoint configuration-Advanced settings

CHAPTER 3 EKS IMPLEMENTATIONS

Figure 3-15. Cluster endpoint configuration

Add additional CIDR block if needed.

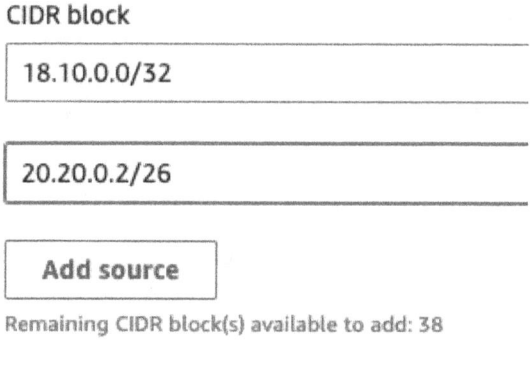

Figure 3-16. Cluster endpoint configuration

Save the configuration.

Test the configuration:

```
aws eks update-kubeconfig --name public-endpoint-cluster
```

EKS will now restrict your access to the specified IP CIDR blocks.
Test the result with the following command:

```
kubectl get nodes
```

Public Endpoint Restrictions with Code

You can use Terraform to implement the same cluster API endpoint access restrictions by adding the line **public_access_cidrs = ["181.10.0.0/32"]** to the eks.tf file:

```
resource "aws_eks_cluster" "public_endpoint_cluster" {
  name    = var.cluster_name
  version = var.cluster_version
  role_arn = aws_iam_role.cluster_role.arn
  #configure data plane subnets and eni
  vpc_config {
    subnet_ids = concat(
      var.private_subnet_ids
    )
    public_access_cidrs = ["181.10.0.0/32"]

    endpoint_public_access = "true"
  }
  depends_on = [ aws_iam_role.cluster_role ]
}
```

The **public_access_cidrs** argument restricts the endpoint to a given IP address block. You should replace 181.10.0.0/32 with the public IP address of your laptop. You can rerun the **Terraform apply** command to implement the IP address restrictions.

Public Endpoint Restrictions with CLI Command

The third alternative is through the aws eks command. You can run the following command by replacing MyIP with yours:

```
aws eks update-cluster-config \
    --region region-code \
    --name public-endpoint-cluster \
    --resources-vpc-config endpointPublicAccess=true,
    publicAccessCidrs="MyIP/32"
```

Network Security

API calls between the data and control planes of the cluster should occur over a private network to minimize the attack surface. The cluster ENIs are responsible for transmitting traffic from the control plane to the data plane. While you can deploy the ENIs in either public or private subnets, it is always recommended to deploy them in private subnets. This ensures that all or part of the API communication remains private and protected from external access.

You can review the ENIs deployment by following the steps below:

Navigate to EKS cluster, click the public-endpoint cluster ➤ Networking, then click on the Manage VPC resources.

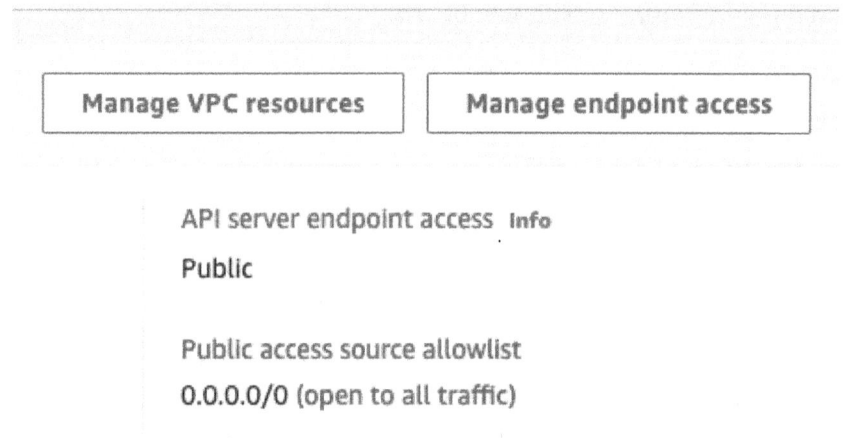

Figure 3-17. Manage endpoint access

CHAPTER 3 EKS IMPLEMENTATIONS

Review the subnets to ensure that the ENIs are deployed in the private subnets. You can change or modify the ENIs' subnets if needed.

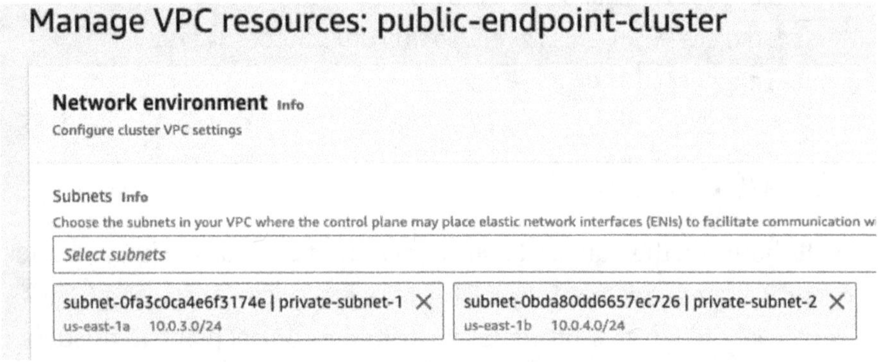

Manage VPC resources: public-endpoint-cluster

Network environment Info
Configure cluster VPC settings

Subnets Info
Choose the subnets in your VPC where the control plane may place elastic network interfaces (ENIs) to facilitate communication w

Select subnets

| subnet-0fa3c0ca4e6f3174e | private-subnet-1 ✕ | subnet-0bda80dd6657ec726 | private-subnet-2 ✕ |
us-east-1a   10.0.3.0/24   us-east-1b   10.0.4.0/24

Figure 3-18. *Cluster VPC configuration*

In production environments, ENIs are often deployed in their own subnets such that they do not coexist with the worker nodes. This is necessary to decouple the ENIs' subnets from the nodes and to reduce the odds of IPv4 exhaustion within the cluster network. We did not adopt this strategy in the current deployment. Both the nodes and the cluster ENIs are in the same subnets as shown below:

```
module "cluster" {
  source = "./controlplane"
#ENI subnet = private subnet
  private_subnet_ids = module.vpc.private_subnet_ids
}
```

The ENIs' subnets are often allocated the /28 CIDR block within the data plane VPC.[8] We should have deployed the ENIs in the **"10.0.1.0/28"** and **"10.0.2.0/28"** subnets if we were to follow the best practices.

---

[8] https://docs.aws.amazon.com/eks/latest/userguide/sec-group-reqs.html

CHAPTER 3 EKS IMPLEMENTATIONS

However, we ensured that all worker nodes are deployed in the private subnets. Deploying the nodes in the private subnets rather than the public subnets further enhances network security.

Security Group

Security group is another security control that can be tightened further. You will find two security groups in the EKS console, the cluster security group and additional security group.

Cluster security group Info
sg-0b82137e7cd4c2bcd

Additional security groups
None

Figure 3-19. *Cluster security groups*

The current cluster security group is very open. It allows all inbound traffic from the control plane to the data plane and all outbound traffic from the data plane to the control plane.

CHAPTER 3   EKS IMPLEMENTATIONS

Figure 3-20. Cluster inbound rule

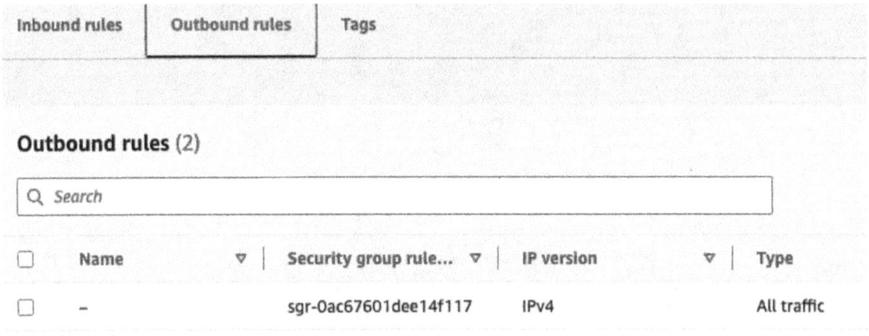

Figure 3-21. Cluster outbound rule

You can improve security by restricting access to specific CIDR blocks or protocol. You should first delete the outbound rule and leave the more specific HTTPS rule.

Click on the generic outbound rule and delete it as shown in Figure 3-22.

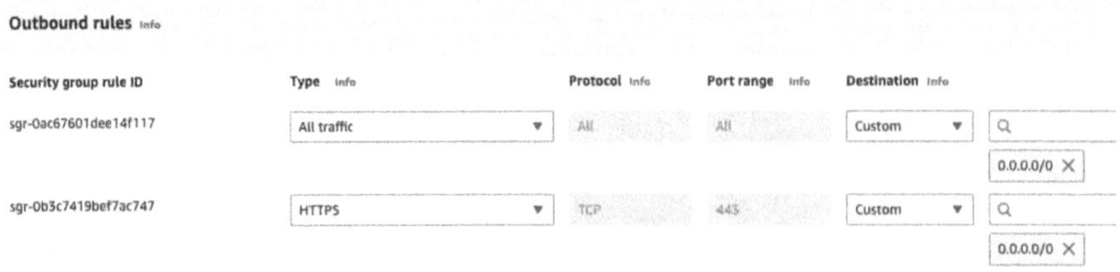

Figure 3-22. Cluster outbound rule-details

Leave the more specific HTTPS rule and click the Save changes button.

Figure 3-23. Cluster outbound rule-after deletion

Additional Security Group

By default, EKS assigns worker nodes the same open default cluster security group rules during cluster creation. You can add more specific rules to the default cluster security group before deployment. However, you cannot prevent EKS from attaching the insecure default rules to the nodes. The only way to improve security is to delete or modify the security group rules after the cluster creation.

You can associate more security group rules with the additional security group. The additional security group allows you to associate custom security groups aside the default cluster security group rules. This provides a level of flexibility, which allows cluster operators to separate the cluster security group from other security groups.[9]

We will implement additional security rules in the next chapter.

---

[9] https://aws.amazon.com/blogs/containers/enhanced-vpc-flexibility-modify-subnets-and-security-groups-in-amazon-eks/

CHAPTER 3   EKS IMPLEMENTATIONS

Cluster Stability

Kubernetes runs on three types of RESTful API versions, alpha, beta, and stable.[10] The alpha is often for testing, may contain bugs, and can be removed without any notice. All alpha API versions are disabled by default and must be explicitly enabled before use.

The API version names containing beta are safe to use, but they can be deprecated and dropped altogether within three- to nine-month notice. They are not recommended for production environments as they may cause compatibility and stability issues.

Stable API versions contain vX in their names where X is an integer. They remain available for all future releases within a Kubernetes major version and major version revision.

AWS cluster insight detects and notifies cluster operators about the usage of deprecated APIs that are due for removal. You can find this information with the following steps:

Go to EKS cluster, then click the public-endpoint cluster ➤ Upgrade insights.

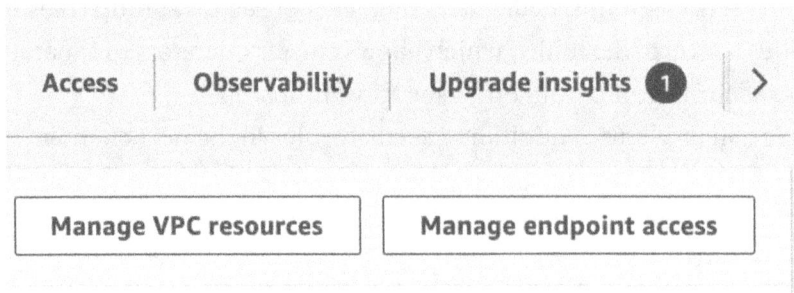

Figure 3-24. *Cluster update*

Click the Upgrade insights to see the warning.

---

[10] https://kubernetes.io/docs/reference/using-api/

CHAPTER 3   EKS IMPLEMENTATIONS

Name ▽	Insight status ▽	Version ▽	Last refresh time (UTC+02:00) ▽	Last transition time (UTC+02:00) ▼
Deprecated APIs removed in Kubernetes v1.32	⚠ Warning	1.32	an hour ago	an hour ago

Figure 3-25. *Cluster update-details*

You should find a message warning you about scheduled removal of a deprecated beta API, the **/apis/flowcontrol.apiserver.k8s.io/v1/ flowschemas** if you click the link.

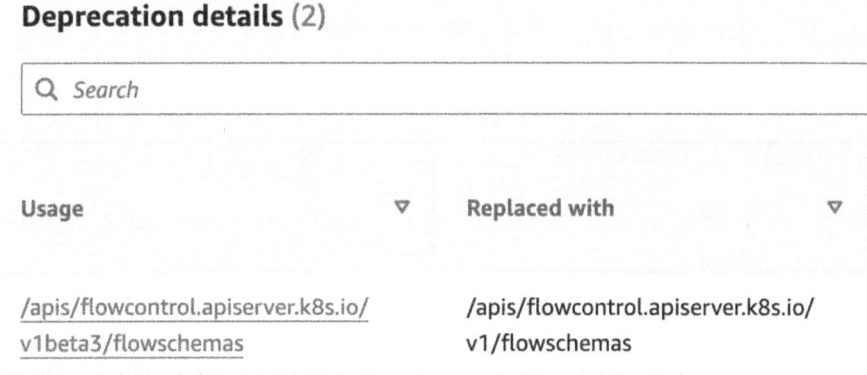

Figure 3-26. *Cluster update-deprecation details*

You may remove the deprecated API with the following steps to guarantee stability of future upgrades:

1. Update the kube config file to change the user context.

    ```
    aws eks update-kubeconfig --name public-
    endpoint-cluster
    ```

2. Find all available API versions.

   ```
   kubectl get apiservices.apiregistration.k8s.io
   ```

3. Delete the deprecated version.

   ```
   kubectl delete apiservice v1beta3.flowcontrol.apiserver.k8s.io
   ```

4. Check if the API is deleted.

   ```
   kubectl api-versions
   ```

AWS insight should remove the warning. Alternatively, you may upgrade the cluster to another version to remove the warning. The easiest way to get rid of the deprecated API is to upgrade the cluster from an outdated version to the latest version. Cluster upgrades will often install new API versions and clear warnings that may appear on the EKS console.

Cluster Deletion

Destroy your cluster and the associated resources once you are done with all your checks and tests:

```
terraform destroy
```

Type yes when asked.

Summary

We tested our first EKS cluster deployment with Terraform code focusing on an endpoint public access cluster. We reviewed the deployment and demonstrated how to make the cluster more secure with additional security layers. The security controls covered here are nonexhaustive. We will cover other security controls such as cluster identity and access management (IAM), IAM credential management, encryption, and monitoring in other chapters of the book. We believe you have acquainted yourself with EKS cluster deployment. Your experience in this chapter will be valuable for the subsequent chapters. We will deploy an endpoint private access cluster in the next chapter and examine how it further strengthens security in EKS.

CHAPTER 4

Endpoint Private Access Cluster

In Chapter 3, we deployed an EKS cluster with Terraform, focusing on the endpoint public access cluster and its security configurations. This chapter will extend the security discussion by concentrating on the endpoint private access cluster. We will show how to use IAM roles, rather than AWS access key ID and secret access key, for cluster creation, expanding on the IAM role advantages introduced earlier. Additionally, we will experiment with additional security groups and relocate the cluster ENIs to separate subnets, setting the stage for future discussions on IPv4 address management.

Cluster Creator Role Creation

Access control is crucial in AWS; one cannot create a cluster without the right permissions to the required AWS services.

The most straightforward way to control programmatic access in AWS is through access key ID and secret access key. Although AWS access key ID and secret access key are simple to create and configure, they come with operational overhead and security risks. You must rotate them regularly and safeguard them from being exposed in your code. It is quite challenging to secure a secret access key, once you configure it on a local client.

CHAPTER 4   ENDPOINT PRIVATE ACCESS CLUSTER

To further strengthen security in cluster deployments, we will switch from access key ID and secret access key to using AWS role-based access control. Roles are generally more secure and easier to manage than access key credentials. With roles, you can easily remove administrators without the need to revoke or rotate their AWS access key ID and secret access key credentials.

A breach of secret access keys can lead to lasting security risks until you rotate the keys. On the other hand, roles[1] provide short-lived tokens that generally pose a lower security risk if compromised. You can further enhance role security with MFA and external ID restrictions. While integrating these features is outside the scope, feel free to explore them on your own if you want to strengthen security even further.

The purpose of this section is to show how you can set up a role-based access control permission for a EKS cluster creator as a prelude to the actual cluster creation later in the chapter. First, we will create a role and assign it administrator permissions. Next, we will create a user, Joyce, to assume the role so that she can become the cluster creator. Finally, we will reference the profile of the role in the Terraform code to create the cluster.

Role Creation

1. Navigate to IAM ➤ Roles from the AWS IAM console(Figure 4-1).

▼ Access management
   User groups
   Users
   Roles

Figure 4-1. *IAM menu*

---

[1] https://docs.aws.amazon.com/IAM/latest/UserGuide/id_credentials_mfa_configure-api-require.html

CHAPTER 4   ENDPOINT PRIVATE ACCESS CLUSTER

2. Click Create role, then select EC2 (Figure 4-2).

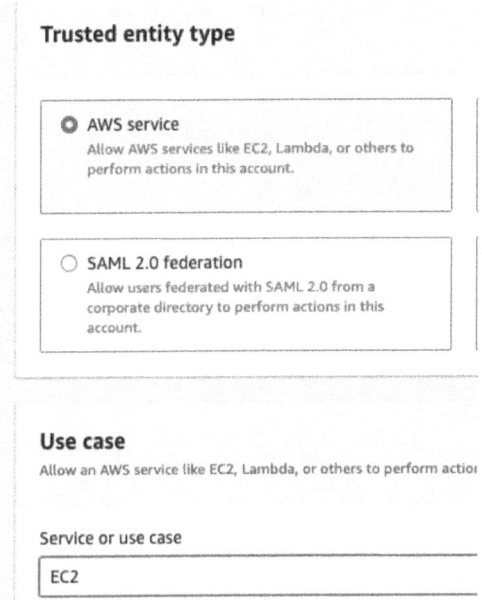

Figure 4-2. *IAM role creation*

3. Click the Next button, then select the **AdministratorAccess**.

4. Click the Next button again.

5. Name the role as EKSClusterCreatorRole.

6. Click the Create button to create the role.

Create User to Assume the Role

1. Navigate to the AWS IAM console ➤ Users ➤ Create a user.

2. Type the username (Joyce), then click Next.

81

CHAPTER 4   ENDPOINT PRIVATE ACCESS CLUSTER

3. Do not attach any permission to the user (Joyce).
4. Copy the arn of Joyce to the clipboard.
5. Create the user.
6. Naviagte to the AWS IAM console again ➤ Roles.
7. Find the EKSClusterCreatorRole you just created.
8. Click the Trust Relationships tab.
9. Edit the trust relationships to allow Joyce to assume the role.

```
{
   "Version": "2012-10-17",
   "Statement": [
   {
    "Effect": "Allow",
    "Principal": {
    "AWS": "arn:aws:iam::${ACCOUNT_ID}:user/Joyce"
    },
    "Action": "sts:AssumeRole"
    }
   ]
}
```

The trust relationship policy has two main policy elements, Version and Statement.[2] The Version element defines the version of the policy language. The current version is the 2012-10-17 version, and the former was the 2008-10-17.

---

[2] https://docs.aws.amazon.com/IAM/latest/UserGuide/reference_policies_elements_version.html

CHAPTER 4   ENDPOINT PRIVATE ACCESS CLUSTER

The statement element is the main element of the policy document. In its basic form, the Statement element consists of an array of objects, namely, Effect, Action, Resource, and sometimes Principal. The Effect block or object has two values, Allow or Deny. They determine whether permission should be granted or denied.

The Principal block specifies who can make a request for an (AssumeRole) action on an AWS resource. In other words, who is allowed to assume or use the permissions assigned to the EKSClusterCreatorRole role. This can be an IAM user or an IAM role. Principals include human users, workloads, federated users and roles.[3]

You use the Principal block to distinguish between resource-based and identity-based policies. Resource-based policies are attached to resources such as Amazon S3 buckets and Amazon DynamoDB, while identity-based policies are for identities, IAM users, groups, or roles.

The Action block specifies which actions the policy allows, which is the STS Assume Role in this case.

10. Click the Update role button to update the policy.

---

[3] https://docs.aws.amazon.com/IAM/latest/UserGuide/introduction_identity-management.html

Create EKS Describe Cluster Policy

As an AWS administrator, you need the describe policy to create and administer EKS clusters. You cannot execute certain commands if you cannot describe the cluster. Since AWS does not include this permission in the IAM administrator policy by default, you must create a custom policy that includes it and then attach that policy to the cluster administrator. Here are the steps you can follow to create the policy:

1. Navigate to the AWS IAM console ➤ Policies.

2. Click the Create policy button, then click the JSON button to open the Policy editor.

3. Delete the default policy from the editor and add the following policy:

    ```
    {
        "Version": "2012-10-17",
        "Statement": [
            {
                "Effect": "Allow",
                "Action": [
                    "eks:DescribeCluster"
                ],
                "Resource": "*"
            }
        ]
    }
    ```

4. Click the Next button.

5. Give the policy a name (e.g., eks-describe-policy).

6. Click the Create policy button.

   The EKS Describe Policy is an example of identity-based policy. It has the Effect block, the Action, and Resource, but no Principal block. This means you can attach the policy to an IAM user, group, or role but not to an AWS resource.

   The policy allows the **"eks:DescribeCluster"** action on all resources. Thus, the Effect is Allow, Action is **"eks:DescribeCluster"**, and Resource is the wildcard "*" which represents all resources.

Attach EKS Describe Cluster Policy

You may attach the describe policy with the following steps:

1. Navigate to the AWS IAM console ➤ Users ➤ Joyce.
2. Click the Permissions tab.
3. Click Add permissions ➤ Attach policies directly.
4. Select the eks-describe-policy you just created.
5. Click Next ➤ Add permissions.

Configure Role in AWS Credential File

Here are the steps for configuring roles in the AWS credential file:

1. Navigate to the AWS IAM console ➤ User. Click the user Joyce.
2. Create access key ID and secret access key for the user.

CHAPTER 4   ENDPOINT PRIVATE ACCESS CLUSTER

3. Install the AWS CLI on your local machine and configure it (see Chapter 3) or edit the **.aws/credentials** file if the AWS CLI is already installed and configured.

4. Edit the **.aws/credentials** file as follows:

```
[joyce-credentials]
aws_access_key_id = <AWS_ACCESS_KEY_ID_FOR_JOYCEe>T
aws_secret_access_key = <AWS_SECRET_ACCESS_KEY_FOR_JOYCE>.
[joyce-role]
role_arn = arn:aws:iam::${ACCOUNT_ID}:role/EKSClusterCreatorRole
source_profile = joyce-credentials
region = us-east-1
```

- The **joyce-credentials** is the reference to the IAM credential.

- The **aws_access_key_id** is the access key ID of joyce.

- The **aws_secret_access_key** is Joyce's secret access key.

- The [joyce-role] is the name of the profile. You can reference the profile in the Terraform code.

- The **role_arn** is the Amazon Resource Name of the role **EKSClusterCreatorRole**. You can find the role ARN by clicking on the EKSClusterCreator IAM role in the AWS IAM console.

- The **source_profile** specifies which credential should be used for the initial assumed role call.

- Finally, the region specifies the AWS region.

CHAPTER 4 ENDPOINT PRIVATE ACCESS CLUSTER

The Structure of the Code

It is better to understand the code for this chapter before you reference the joyce-role profile to deploy it. We will begin the review starting with the structure of the code.

The code structure as shown in Figure 4-4 is slightly different from the structure in previous chapter. The key difference here is the introduction of the bastion module. The bastion module will enable a cluster creator to access the API endpoint of the endpoint private access cluster we are about to deploy.

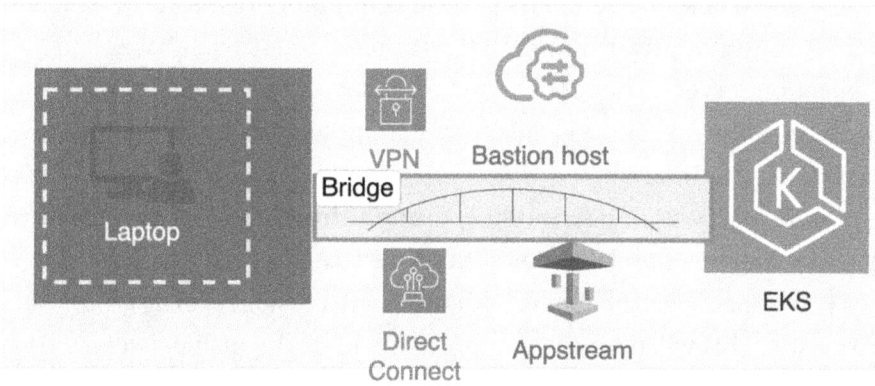

Figure 4-3. Creating a bridge

The endpoint private access clusters limit cluster access within the AWS private network. Hence, it is not possible to reach the endpoint or the EKS cluster directly from the Internet or an external network. You will need a "bridge" to connect you from the Internet or an external network to the EKS cluster as depicted in Figure 4-3.

The bridge from your laptop to the cluster includes bastion host, VPN, direct connect, SSM agent, and AppStream. The bridge secures connection between an external network and the private AWS network. The bastion host is an easy-to-implement bridge; hence, this chapter will demonstrate

87

CHAPTER 4 ENDPOINT PRIVATE ACCESS CLUSTER

the connectivity with the bastion host by deploying the bastion module Terraform code for the chapter.

The bastion module is meant to create a bastion host that will provide private access to the cluster. It creates a public EC2 instance in one of the public subnets of the customer VPC so that a cluster operator or administrator can access the cluster once she lands on the instance. As explained earlier, it is not possible to directly access an EKS cluster configured with a private endpoint from a laptop or a client machine after cluster deployment because the endpoint is not exposed to an external network.

Bastion hosts are useful for accessing endpoint private access clusters and for any other private or internal resources, such as databases and application servers. They act as a secure gateway, allowing administrators to access remote resources while maintaining security by preventing direct exposure to the Internet.

Beside the bastion host module, the **additional-sg.tf** and the **cluster-sg.tf** files are the other keynotes in the code structure (Figure 4-4). These files will respectively create the additional and cluster security groups for the cluster. This will offer us an opportunity to distinguish between the two types of security groups for the cluster. The additional security is exclusive for the cluster ENIs (the ENIs between the control plane and data plane) whereas the cluster security group is applies to all ENIs within the cluster.

Chapter 4 Endpoint Private Access Cluster

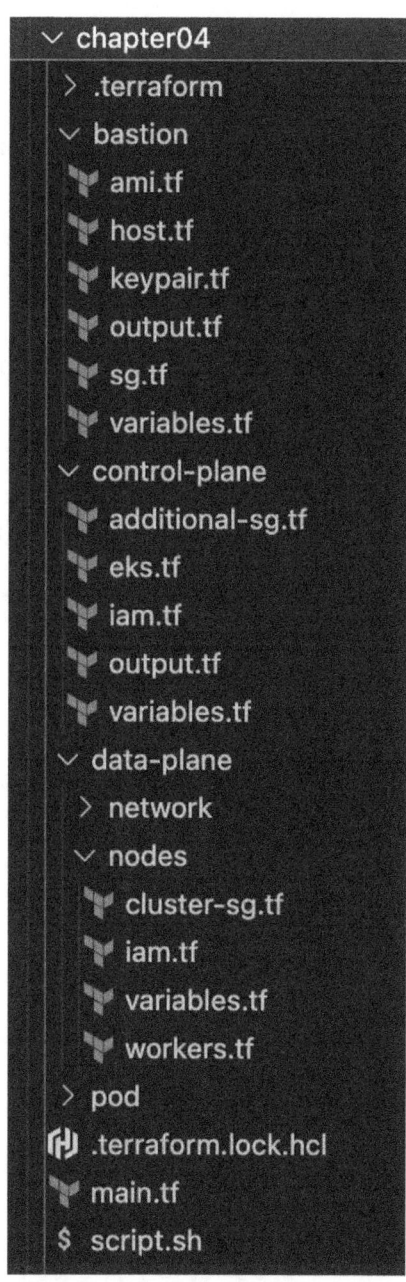

Figure 4-4. *Structure of endpoint private access cluster Terraform code*

CHAPTER 4 ENDPOINT PRIVATE ACCESS CLUSTER

Bastion Host Code

In this section, we will break down the code for setting up a **bastion host** in detail, explaining how everything works together to allow cluster creators secure access to the cluster over the bastion host. By the end of this section, you will have a clear understanding of each component involved in the configuration, from the bastion host setup to the access control mechanisms.

You should find the bastion code in the bastion module. The **host.tf** file creates the bastion instance (host) with the **aws_instance** resource for the cluster administrators. It deploys an Ubuntu instance by specifying the Ubuntu Amazon Machine Image (AMI). It then creates a secure shell (SSH) key for the cluster administrators to connect to the instance from their client computers.

```
resource "aws_instance" "instances" {
  ami           = data.aws_ami.ubuntu.id
  instance_type = var.instance-type
  key_name      = var.sshkey
  metadata_options {
    http_endpoint = "enabled"
    http_tokens   = "required"
  }
  subnet_id                   = var.subnet_id
  vpc_security_group_ids      = [aws_security_group.sg.id]
  associate_public_ip_address = true
  tags = {
    "Name" : "bastion-host"
  }
}
```

The bastion module does not create its own network. Rather, it refers to one of the public subnets of the customer network allowing instances to communicate directly with the cluster. You need a public subnet to permit remote access to the bastion host. You enable a public subnet by associating its instances with a public IP address. We implement this in Terraform with the **associate_public_ip_address** argument.

You must set the subnet ID of the bastion host instance in the **main.tf** file to one of the two public subnets. Here is how to specify it in the code:

```
module "instance" {
  source = "./bastion"
  subnet_id = module.vpc.public_subnet_ids[0]
  vpc_id = module.vpc.vpc_id
}
```

The VPC ID in the code is the runtime value for the bastion host's VPC. Because the bastion is deployed in the customer VPC, Terraform will need the VPC ID of the customer network to attach a security group to the instance. The runtime value for the VPC ID (**vpc_id**) in the preceding code is set to the customer VPC as expected.

Bastion Security Group

AWS prohibits any form of connection to an EC2 instance by default, hence the requirement for bastion host's security group. A security group configures a host-based firewall rule for an instance. It determines which traffic should be permitted and which one should be prohibited.

In our use case, the security group will open network traffic on a secure shell (SSH) port to permit free flow of traffic from the Internet to the bastion host with the Terraform code in the **sg.tf** file under the bastion module:

```
resource "aws_security_group" "sg" {
  name    = "bastion-sg"
```

CHAPTER 4   ENDPOINT PRIVATE ACCESS CLUSTER

```
vpc_id = var.vpc_id
dynamic "ingress" {
  for_each = var.ports
  content {
    from_port   = ingress.value
    to_port     = ingress.value
    protocol    = "tcp"
    cidr_blocks = [var.cidrBlocks["internet"]]
  }
}
dynamic "egress" {
  for_each = var.eports
  content {
    from_port   = egress.value
    to_port     = egress.value
    protocol    = -1
    cidr_blocks = [var.cidrBlocks["internet"]]
  }
}
}
```

The ingress part of the code admits inbound traffic to the bastion, while the egress section is for outbound calls from the bastion to the Internet.

The code uses the map variable type instead of primitive types to set the CIDR range for the security group. The value for the **var.cidrBlocks["internet"]** is **0.0.0.0/0** which refers to all IPv4 addresses. This means anyone can reach the bastion host from the Internet and can log in if they have the private SSH key.

CHAPTER 4 ENDPOINT PRIVATE ACCESS CLUSTER

The value of the variable **var.ports** is also a map declared as

```
variable "ports" {
  description = "ports"
  type        = list(any)
  default     = [22]
}
```

A map is Terraform's way of managing a list. For a single value, you can equally use a primitive variable type for the port as shown below. You would then modify the **sg.tf** code to use the primitive variable type.

```
variable "port" {
  description = "port"
  default     = "22"
}
```

Bastion Authentication

Besides the network access, you will need an SSH private key to authenticate to the bastion host. The code for the SSH key generation is found in the **keypair.tf** file. It creates 4096 bits RSA key pairs and stores the private key in a file (**key.pem**) for the cluster administrators to authenticate to the bastion host. Once on the bastion host, administrators can access the private API endpoint of the endpoint private access cluster. Terraform will automatically configure the public key of the SSH key pair on the bastion host to enable the SSH authentication.

```
resource "tls_private_key" "private-key" {
  algorithm = "RSA"
  rsa_bits  = 4096
}
```

CHAPTER 4　ENDPOINT PRIVATE ACCESS CLUSTER

```
resource "aws_key_pair" "key-pair" {
  key_name   = var.sshkey
  public_key = tls_private_key.private-key.public_key_openssh
}
resource "local_file" "exam-key" {
  content  = tls_private_key.private-key.private_key_pem
  filename = "${var.sshkey}.pem"
}
```

Network Setup

Let us move on to the network setup for the endpoint private access cluster to explain our choices for the Terraform code.

By now, it should be clear how the network setup for the endpoint private access cluster use case differs from the public one in Chapter 3 if you look at Figure 4-5.

CHAPTER 4   ENDPOINT PRIVATE ACCESS CLUSTER

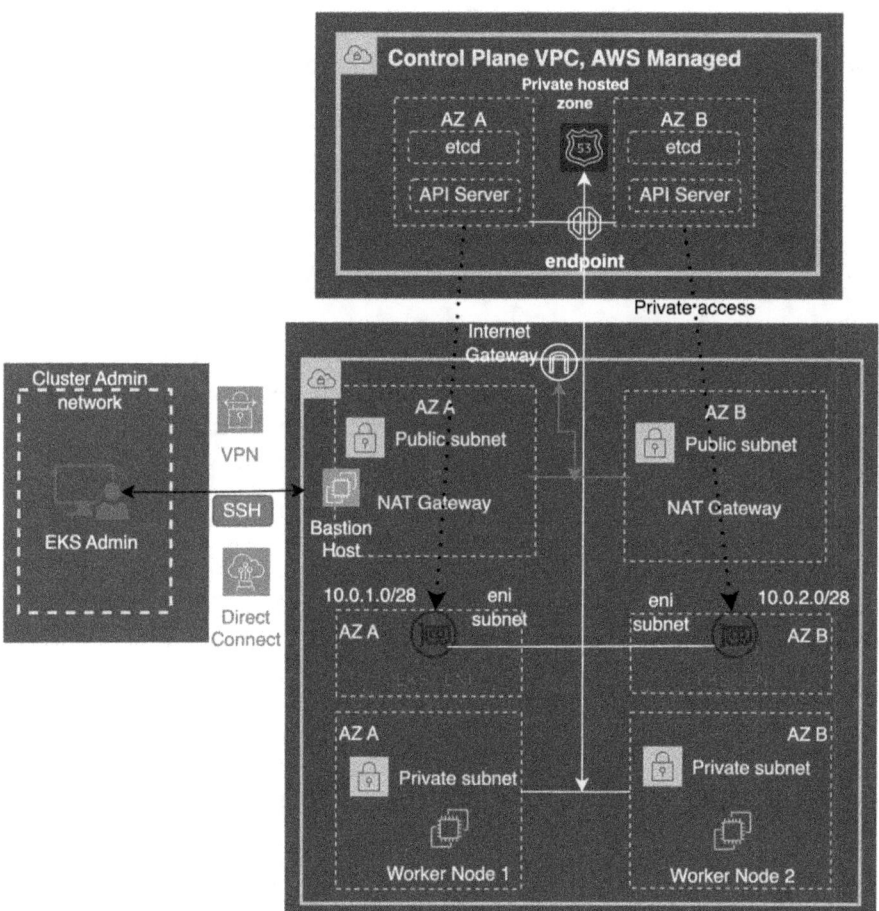

Figure 4-5. Endpoint private access cluster

The number of subnets has increased from four to six – two for cluster ENIs, two for private subnets that will host the worker nodes, and the rest for the bastion host, the network infrastructure, Internet gateway, and NAT gateway. The bastion host belongs to one of the public subnets, but the cluster creator's client machine will sit outside the cluster and connect through SSH.

The ENI subnets will be the smallest subnets within the /28 CIDR range. They separate the two cluster ENIs from the node subnets to reduce IP address exhaustion according to AWS best practices.

You should find all the subnets in the **subnets.tf** file under the network module of the data plane. As illustrated in Figure 4-5, we now have six subnets with the ENIs in the /28 private subnets. The Terraform code for this is shown below:

```
data "aws_availability_zones" "azs" {
 state = "available"
}
resource "aws_subnet" "eni_subnets" {
  vpc_id            = aws_vpc.cluster_vpc.id
  cidr_block   = count.index == 0 ? var.cidr_blocks
  ["eni-subnet-1"] : var.cidr_blocks["eni-subnet-2"]
  availability_zone = data.aws_availability_zones.azs.names
  [count.index]
  count = 2
  tags = {
    Name = "eni-subnet-${count.index+1}"
  }
}

resource "aws_subnet" "private_subnets" {
  vpc_id            = aws_vpc.cluster_vpc.id
  cidr_block   = count.index == 0 ? var.cidr_blocks["private-
  subnet-1"] : var.cidr_blocks["private-subnet-2"]
  availability_zone = data.aws_availability_zones.azs.names
  [count.index]
  count = 2
  tags = {
    Name = "private-subnet-${count.index+1}"
  }
}
```

```
resource "aws_subnet" "public_subnets" {
  vpc_id          = aws_vpc.cluster_vpc.id
  cidr_block  = count.index == 0 ? var.cidr_blocks["public-
  subnet-1"] : var.cidr_blocks["public-subnet-2"]
  availability_zone = data.aws_availability_zones.azs.
  names[count.index]
  count = 2
  tags = {
    Name = "public-subnet-${count.index+1}"
  }
}
```

EKS can create between two to four cluster ENIs in specific subnets (such as eni-subnet-1 and eni-subnet-2 in our case) to support reliable communication from the control plane to data plane.

The cluster must reference the ENI subnets to establish this communication path. The reference is found in the **eks.tf** file under the control-plane folder as follows:

```
resource "aws_eks_cluster" "private_endpoint_cluster" {
  name    = var.cluster_name
  version = var.cluster_version
  role_arn = aws_iam_role.cluster_role.arn
  #configure data plane subnets and eni
  vpc_config {
    subnet_ids = concat(
      var.eni_subnet_ids
    )
    endpoint_private_access = "true"
    endpoint_public_access  = "false"
  }
  depends_on = [ aws_iam_role.cluster_role ]
}
```

Chapter 4 Endpoint Private Access Cluster

You can control the number of ENIs for a cluster by limiting the number of subnets either in code or from the EKS console.[4] Here, we implement only two ENIs with two separate private subnets in code.

Note that EKS will delete the original ENIs and create new ones whenever you update the Kubernetes version of a cluster, so remember to check if the correct subnets are configured for your ENIs after every cluster update.

The cluster ENIs' subnets must meet the following requirements:

- ENI subnets must maintain at least six IP addresses for each ENI. However, at least 16 IP addresses are recommended which corresponds to IP/28 CIDR block (2^4).

- ENI subnets cannot reside in use1-az3, usw1-az2, and cac1-az3 availability zones or in AWS Outposts, AWS Wavelength, and AWS Local Zone.

- ENIs can reside in public or private subnets. However, private subnets are recommended.

- You can deploy self-managed nodes and Kubernetes resources to ENI subnets.

The default endpoint access is public; therefore, we must explicitly specify the type of endpoint to prevent Terraform from creating a public endpoint for the cluster. The **endpoint_private_access** argument sets the cluster endpoint to private if its value is set to "true". We also set the **endpoint_public_access** to false to avoid a hybrid scenario.

```
resource "aws_eks_cluster" "private_endpoint_cluster" {
  name    = var.cluster_name
  version = var.cluster_version
```

---

[4] https://docs.aws.amazon.com/eks/latest/userguide/network_reqs.html#network-requirements-subnets

CHAPTER 4   ENDPOINT PRIVATE ACCESS CLUSTER

```
  role_arn = aws_iam_role.cluster_role.arn
  #configure data plane subnets and eni
  vpc_config {
    subnet_ids = concat(
      var.eni_subnet_ids
    )
    endpoint_private_access = "true"
    endpoint_public_access  = "false"
  }
  depends_on = [ aws_iam_role.cluster_role ]
```

Worker Nodes

This section highlights the code for the worker nodes in the **workers.tf** file under the nodes' module. It creates two on-demand instances to run cluster applications. The code is like the one we discussed in Chapter 3 except that worker nodes do not share subnets with ENIs as shown below:

```
module "nodes" {
  source = "./data-plane/nodes"
  cluster_name = module.cluster.cluster_name
  node_name = "private-node-group"
  subnet_ids =  module.vpc.private_subnet_ids
}
```

You should find the preceding code in the main.tf file. It sets the runtime values for the subnets for the nodes to the private subnets. Detailed worker nodes code is listed as follows:

```
resource "aws_eks_node_group" "nodes" {
  cluster_name     = var.cluster_name
  node_group_name  = var.node_name
  node_role_arn    = aws_iam_role.worker_nodes_role.arn
```

```
  subnet_ids = var.subnet_ids
  capacity_type  = "ON_DEMAND" #or "SPOT"
  instance_types = var.instance_types
  scaling_config {
    desired_size = 2
    max_size     = 3
    min_size     = 2
  }
  update_config {
    max_unavailable = 1
  }
  labels = {
    name = var.label
  }
  tags = {
    Name = "worker-node"
  }
  depends_on = [ aws_iam_role.worker_nodes_role ]
}
```

Observe the **scaling_config** block which allows EKS to scale the cluster nodes.

- The desired_size represents the initial number of nodes at the time of creation. EKS attempts to maintain the desired number of nodes throughout the life of the cluster with the help of cluster autoscalers. It starts by launching the number of nodes according to desired_size specification and maintains this number of nodes if there are no scaling policies or scheduled actions attached to the cluster autoscaler.

- You can only resize the desired_size to a number within the mini_size and max_size ranges. It must be equal to or greater than the mini_size and equal to or less than the maxi_size.

- The mini_size represents the minimum number of nodes EKS can deploy. The desired_size cannot be lower than the mini_size.

- The maxi_size represents the maximum number of nodes EKS can deploy. The desired_size cannot be higher than the maxi_size.

Cluster Security Group Review

Let us take a couple of minutes to review the cluster security group code and discuss their purpose. Besides the regular cluster security group, you should find the new additional security group under the control plane module.

Additional security is an exclusive security group for cluster ENIs. You attach an additional security group to the cluster ENIs to secure communication between the control and the data planes. In contrast, the cluster security group is for all ENIs within a cluster, both worker nodes and cluster ENIs. EKS automatically creates an unrestricted default cluster security group for all cluster ENIs. You can improve the security of the cluster security group with restricted custom security group policy. Like the default security group, EKS will attach the custom cluster security group to all cluster ENIs.[5]

---

[5] https://docs.aws.amazon.com/eks/latest/userguide/sec-group-reqs.html

CHAPTER 4   ENDPOINT PRIVATE ACCESS CLUSTER

AWS recommends the rules in Table 4-1 for stricter cluster security group rules. The inbound traffic of the default security group rule is restricted to the control plane as the source, so there is little to worry about even though you can still modify it. However, the outbound rules are unrestricted and must be modified to reduce the scope and improve security.

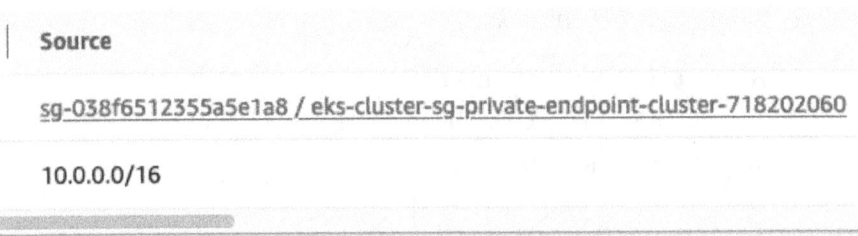

Figure 4-6. Sample source for cluster inbound rule

Table 4-1. Recommended security group rule

Rule Type	Protocol	Port	Destination	Service
Outbound	TCP	443	Cluster security group	HTTPS
Outbound	TCP	10250	Cluster security group	Kubelet
Outbound (DNS)	TCP and UDP	53	Cluster security group	DNS

The recommended rules restrict traffic to specific ports and ensure that managed and Fargate node groups can join the cluster. The rules do not necessarily apply to self-managed nodes. You are responsible for configuring the correct security group to allow self-managed nodes to join the cluster. Also, it is up to you to ensure that other resources, pods, worker nodes, and EC2 instances can communicate with the outside world when downloading updates or pulling containers from an external container registry.

CHAPTER 4   ENDPOINT PRIVATE ACCESS CLUSTER

EKS supports three types of nodes, the managed nodes, self-managed nodes, and Fargate. Managed nodes are nodes maintained by AWS and automatically provisioned by EKS on behalf of customers. EKS creates the nodes from preexisting Amazon Machine Image (AMI) and attaches them to the cluster on customers' behalf. Once provisioned, AWS takes care of the vulnerability management and notifies customers about new AMI updates whenever they become available. Customers are responsible for updating the nodes once new versions become available.

Fargate nodes are highly optimized nodes particularly useful for batch processing and workloads with sporadic traffic. They are serverless, meaning AWS takes full responsibility for everything about node management without involving customers. They handle node provisioning, configuration, patching, upgrade, updates, optimization, and scaling on customers' behalf. They offer the most secure, reliable, and sometimes cost-saving alternative to managed nodes.

Customers can create their own images and provision them as cluster nodes. Such nodes are known as self-managed nodes.[6,7,8]

---

[6] https://docs.aws.amazon.com/eks/latest/userguide/fargate.html

[7] https://docs.aws.amazon.com/eks/latest/userguide/managed-node-groups.html

[8] https://docs.aws.amazon.com/AWSEC2/latest/UserGuide/ec2-on-demand-instances.html

CHAPTER 4 ENDPOINT PRIVATE ACCESS CLUSTER

Cluster Security Group Code Review

You need the following cluster security group code to allow the worker nodes and the bastion host to communicate with the private endpoint or the API server of the cluster:

```
#inbound call from the bastion host to the private API server
resource "aws_security_group_rule" "ingress" {
    type              = "ingress"
    from_port         = 443
    to_port           = 443
    protocol          = "tcp"
    cidr_blocks       = ["10.0.0.0/16"]
    security_group_id = var.cluster_security_group_id
}
```

You will need another rule to allow the nodes to make outbound calls to the Internet to fetch containers from container registries such as Docker Hub:

```
#outbound call to the internet
resource "aws_security_group_rule" "https_port" {
    type              = "egress"
    from_port         = 443
    to_port           = 443
    protocol          = "tcp"
    cidr_blocks       = ["0.0.0.0/0"]
    security_group_id = var.cluster_security_group_id
}
```

CHAPTER 4　ENDPOINT PRIVATE ACCESS CLUSTER

You can implement stricter rules if you use a forwarding proxy to restrict IP address of the outbound call. In that case, you may change the 0.0.0.0/0 CIDR block to the specific IP block or address. For example, you may restrict outbound to specific sites with a forwarding proxy. You should find the cluster security group rule in the **sg.tf** file under the node's submodule.

Additional Security Group Code Review

An additional security group is attached to only the cluster ENIs, while a cluster security group is attached to all ENIs within a cluster. The additional security is optional and only useful when you want to segregate the security groups for the cluster ENIs from other ENIs.

This section reviews the code for the additional security group. You can find it in the **additional-sg.tf** file under the control-plane module. The code implements outbound rules for the cluster DNS and worker node's kubelets and an inbound rule for the HTTPS traffic from the control plane to the data plane. The inbound rule can replace the less restrictive inbound rule of the cluster security group.

```
resource "aws_security_group" "additional_security_group" {
  name    = "optional additional security group rules for ENIs"
  vpc_id = var.vpc_id
  ingress {
  from_port           = 443
  to_port             = 443
  protocol            = "tcp"
  cidr_blocks         = ["10.0.0.0/16"]
  }
    egress {
    from_port           = 53
    to_port             = 53
```

CHAPTER 4   ENDPOINT PRIVATE ACCESS CLUSTER

```
    protocol            = "tcp"
    cidr_blocks         = ["10.0.0.0/16"]
  }
  egress {
    from_port           = 10250
    to_port             = 10250
    protocol            = "tcp"
    cidr_blocks         = ["10.0.0.0/16"]
  }
}
```

The custom additional security rules are not effective unless you clean up the default cluster security group rules. You can clean up the rules by removing the default outbound rules attached to the ENIs. You must find the cluster ENIs after deployment and delete the default inbound and outbound security group rules. The default security groups allow all traffic as shown in Figure 4-7. To delete the rule, find the security group rule that allows all traffic and delete it once you deploy the cluster.

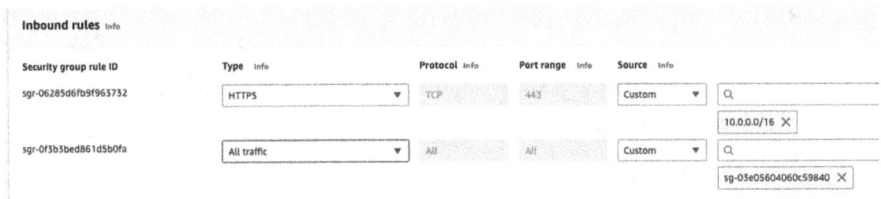

Figure 4-7. *Default security groups*

You can only remove the default inbound rule from the ENIs if you have implemented a custom inbound security rule or additional security inbound rule for the cluster ENIs; otherwise, your cluster will fail to work.

Terraform Code Deployment

Let us deploy the code so that we can review if the implementation is consistent with the theory. Follow the recipe below to deploy the Terraform code. Make sure the role is set up in your **.aws/credentials** file as explained before.

1. Download the Terraform code for chapter04.

2. Set up your aws account profile in the .aws/credentials file as follows:

    ```
    [joyce-credentials]
    aws_access_key_id = <AWS_ACCESS_KEY_ID>T
    aws_secret_access_key = <AWS_SECRET_ACCESS_KEY>.
    ```
    [joyce-role]
    ```
    role_arn = arn:aws:iam::ACCOUNT_ID:role/EKSClusterCreatorRole
    source_profile = joyce-credentials
    region = us-east-1
    ```

3. Navigate to the main.tf file.

4. Verify that profile is set to joyce-role in the **main.tf** file and the region is set appropriately as shown below. Change the profile joyce-role to a new name if you used a different profile name in your **.aws/credentials** file. Make no changes if you follow the same steps as above.

    ```
    provider "aws" {
      region  = "us-east-1"
      profile = "joyce-role"
    }
    #create vpc
    ```

CHAPTER 4 ENDPOINT PRIVATE ACCESS CLUSTER

```
module "vpc" {
  source = "./data-plane/network"
}
#create eni in the dataplane (step x)
module "cluster" {
  source = "./control-plane"
  eni_subnet_ids = module.vpc.eni_subnet_ids
  vpc_id = module.vpc.vpc_id
}
module "nodes" {
  source = "./data-plane/nodes"
  cluster_name = module.cluster.cluster_name
  subnet_ids =  module.vpc.private_subnet_ids
  cluster_security_group_id = module.cluster.cluster_security_group_id
}
module "instance" {
  source = "./bastion"
  subnet_id = module.vpc.public_subnet_ids[0]
  vpc_id = module.vpc.vpc_id
}
```

5. Execute the Terraform code.

    ```
    terraform init
    terraform apply
    ```

6. Type yes when asked.

7. You should see the following while you wait for deployment to complete:

CHAPTER 4 ENDPOINT PRIVATE ACCESS CLUSTER

```
module.cluster.aws_eks_cluster.private_endpoint_
cluster: Still creating... [10s elapsed]
15s [id=i-0354d7f78b2fa5a9a]
module.vpc.aws_nat_gateway.natgw: Still creating...
[20s elapsed] ...
```

8. You should find the following output once the deployment is complete:

    `Apply complete! Resources: xx added, 0 changed, 0 destroyed.`

    The statistics recount the number of resources added, changed, and destroyed. xx is the number of new resources that were added, 0 changed, and 0 destroyed in this case.

9. Update the cluster context.

    `aws eks update-kubeconfig --name private-endpoint-cluster --profile joyce-role`

10. Test if cluster nodes are running.

    `kubectl get nodes`

The command will time out because public endpoint access is disabled.

Cluster Review

We want to validate the consistency of the EKS deployment with the theory explained in the first half of this chapter.

CHAPTER 4 ENDPOINT PRIVATE ACCESS CLUSTER

Cluster Security Group

We will navigate the AWS console to review if the cluster security group was attached to all cluster ENIs. There are seven ENIs, including the bastion host's ENIs. Six of the ENIs belong to the cluster and one for the bastion host.

Bastion Security Group Validation

1. Navigate to EC2 ➤ Instances. Click the bastion-host instance (Figure 4-8).

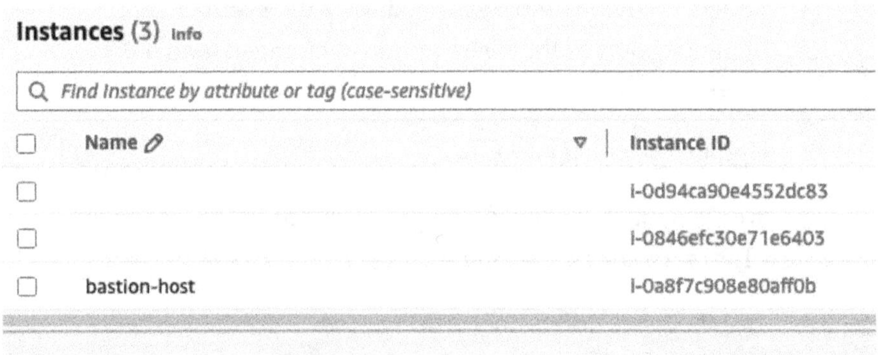

Instances (3) Info	
Name	Instance ID
	i-0d94ca90e4552dc83
	i-0846efc30e71e6403
bastion-host	i-0a8f7c908e80aff0b

Figure 4-8. Select "bastion-host"

2. Click the Security tab to find the security group attached to the bastion host's ENI (Figure 4-9).

CHAPTER 4   ENDPOINT PRIVATE ACCESS CLUSTER

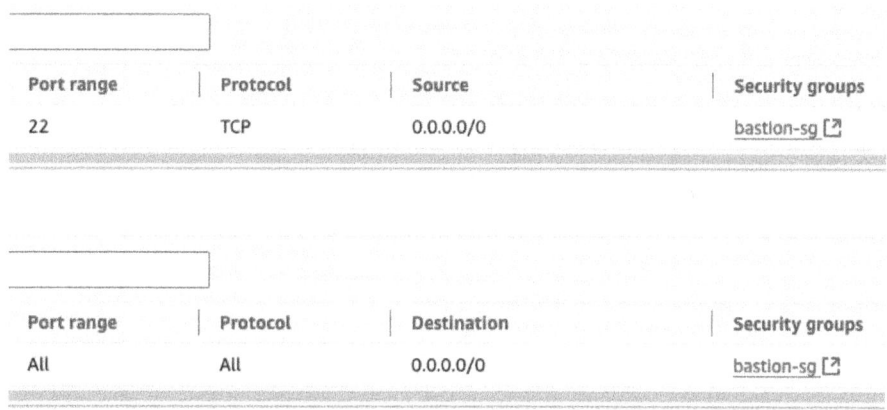

Figure 4-9. Select appropriate security group

Note that there is no cluster security group here because the bastion host is external to the cluster even though it shares the same customer VPC.

Cluster Security Group Validation

1. Navigate to EC2 ➤ Network interfaces under the Network & Security menu.

2. You should find all the ENIs of your deployment (Figure 4-10).

CHAPTER 4   ENDPOINT PRIVATE ACCESS CLUSTER

Availability Zone	Security group names
us-east-1b	optional additional security group rules for ENIs, eks-cluster-sg-private-end|
us-east-1b	eks-cluster-sg-private-endpoint-cluster-718202060
us-east-1a	–
us-east-1a	eks-cluster-sg-private-endpoint-cluster-718202060
us-east-1a	eks-cluster-sg-private-endpoint-cluster-718202060
us-east-1a	bastion-sg
us-east-1a	optional additional security group rules for ENIs, eks-cluster-sg-private-end|

Figure 4-10. Network and Security menu

The cluster ENIs have two security groups attached, the cluster security group and the additional security group. All other ENIs have only one security group attached.

3. Click the cluster security group to review the rules (Figure 4-11).

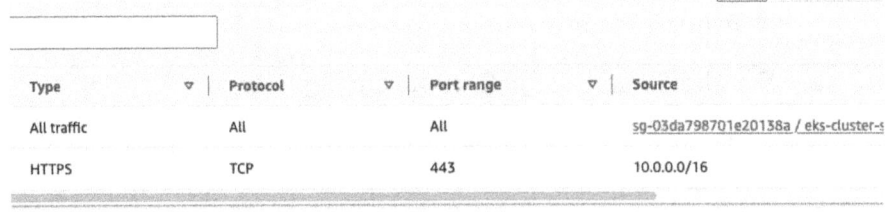

Type	Protocol	Port range	Source
All traffic	All	All	sg-03da798701e20138a / eks-cluster-s
HTTPS	TCP	443	10.0.0.0/16

Figure 4-11. Cluster security group

The default rule allows all traffic, while the custom rule restricts the traffic to HTTPS on port 443. You can delete the default rule to make access stricter.

CHAPTER 4   ENDPOINT PRIVATE ACCESS CLUSTER

4. To delete the rules, click the Edit button and remove the rule. You should end up with two rules for the cluster security group (Figures 4-12 and 4-13).

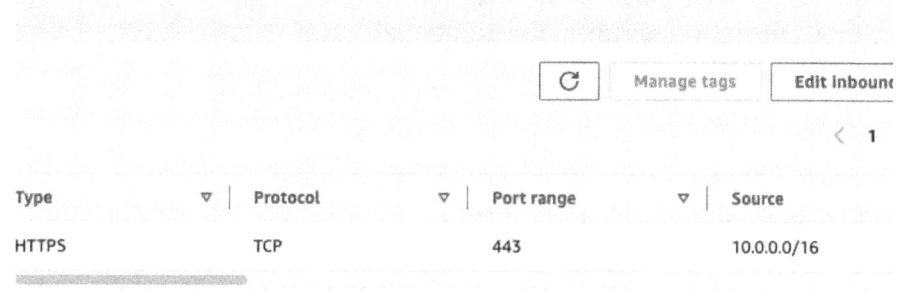

Figure 4-12. Security group rule 1

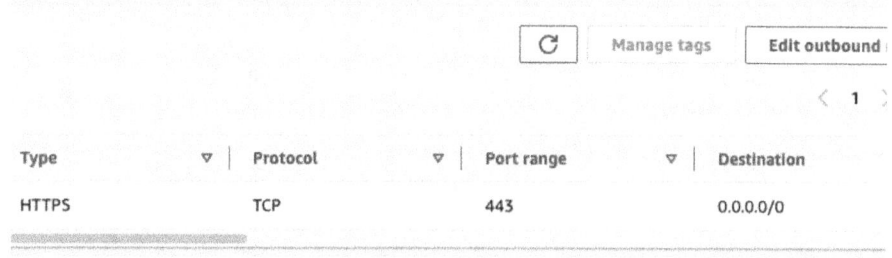

Figure 4-13. Security group rule 2

Additional Security Group Validation

1. Navigate to EC2 ➤ Network interfaces under the Network & Security menu.

2. Click the optional additional security group link to review the inbound and the outbound additional security group rules.

   The outbound rules become especially useful when

113

CHAPTER 4   ENDPOINT PRIVATE ACCESS CLUSTER

you remove the default security rules; otherwise, there is no need for them. Observe that you have two inbound rules for the cluster. You can delete the inbound cluster security group rule and leave only the inbound rule of the additional.

You can also find both cluster security group and additional security group from the EKS console from the Networking tab as follows:

Navigate to the EKS ➤ Cluster ➤ Cluster name ➤ Networking tab ➤ Cluster security group (Figure 4-14).

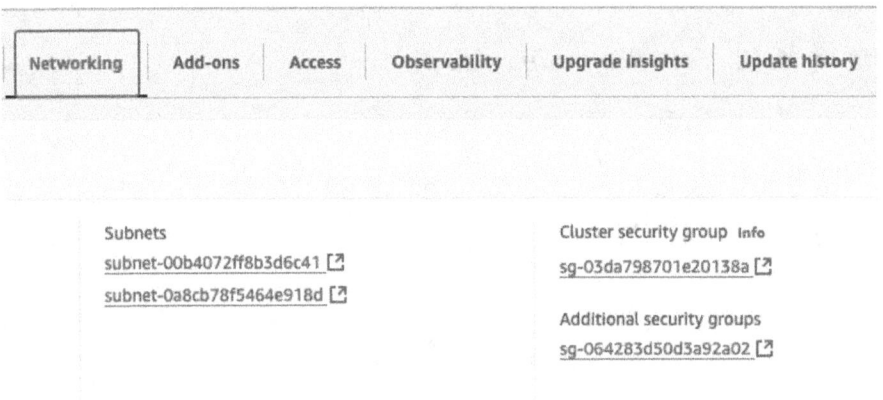

Figure 4-14. Cluster security group

Connecting to the Cluster with Bastion Host

You cannot directly access the endpoint private access cluster from your local laptop because all the resources reside in the AWS private network. You can however access the cluster by connecting to the cluster network with the bastion host deployed in this example.

We chose the bastion host implementation because of its simplicity. The Terraform code will create a private SSH key that you can use to log in to the bastion host from your laptop.

CHAPTER 4   ENDPOINT PRIVATE ACCESS CLUSTER

Alternatively, you can access the bastion host from the AWS web console as follows:

1. Navigate to the AWS console.

2. Click the bastion-host instance (Figure 4-15).

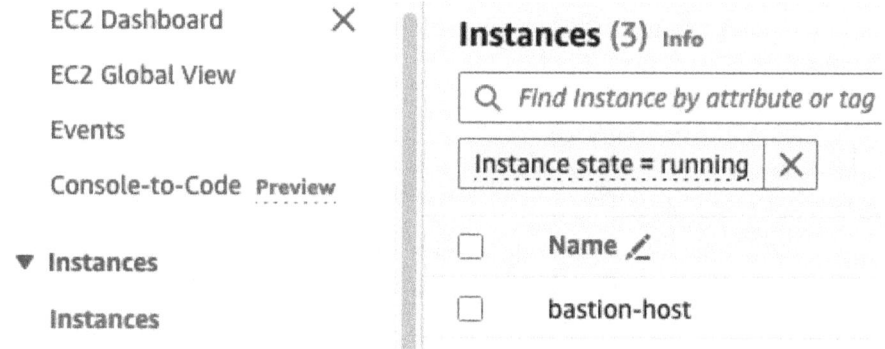

Figure 4-15. Selecting bastion-host instance

3. Click Connect ➤ EC2 Instance connect ➤ Connect button to connect to the instance (Figure 4-16).

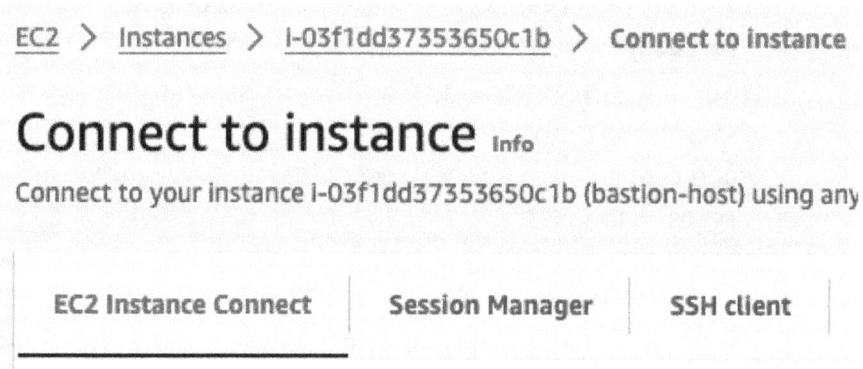

Figure 4-16. Connecting to the instance

115

CHAPTER 4 ENDPOINT PRIVATE ACCESS CLUSTER

4. Install awscli on the bastion host instance.

   ```
   sudo apt update -y && \
   sudo apt install python3-pip -y && \
   pip3 install awscli --upgrade && \
   sudo apt  install awscli -y && \
   sudo snap install kubectl --classic
   ```

5. Run AWS configure with the cluster creator's credentials (Joyce).

   ```
   aws configure
   AWS Access Key ID [None]: Joyce access key ID
   AWS Secret Access Key [None]: Joyce secret access key
   Region: Cluster region
   ```

6. Edit the .aws/credentials file and replace the content with the cluster creator's credentials and role.

   ```
   [joyce-credentials]
   aws_access_key_id = <AWS_ACCESS_KEY>..
   aws_secret_access_key = <AWS_SECRET_ACCESS_KEY>.
   ```
   [default]
   ```
   role_arn = arn:aws:iam::ACCOUNT_ID:role/EKSClusterCreatorRole
   source_profile = joyce-credentials
   region = us-east-1
   ```

7. Replace the above with your credentials.

8. While on the bastion host, update the cluster user context.

   ```
   aws eks update-kubeconfig --name private-endpoint-cluster --profile joyce-role
   ```

CHAPTER 4 ENDPOINT PRIVATE ACCESS CLUSTER

9. Test the cluster.

    kubectl get nodes

10. You should see the nodes.

```
NAME                       STATUS   ROLES    AGE   VERSION
ip-10-0-3-182.ec2.internal   Ready    <none>   19h   v1.30.0-eks-036c24b
ip-10-0-4-223.ec2.internal   Ready    <none>   19h   v1.30.0-eks-036c24b
```

11. Copy the sample pod.yml file to the bastion host.

12. Run the **kubectl apply -f pod.yml** command.

13. Run **kubectl get pods** to see the application running.

Impact and Benefits of Security Controls

This section provides a brief summary the impact and benefits of some of the security controls deployed alongside the endpoint private access cluster.

Table 4-2. Benefits for security controls

	IAM Role	Bastion Host	Private Endpoint	Additional Security Group
Impact	Enhances credential security	Reduces the attack surface	Implements defense in depth	Enhances cluster network security
Benefit	Uses temporary credentials which minimizes the security risk if they are compromised	Creates a secure bridge between the external network and AWS private network	An attacker must compromise more security layers to access the cluster, e.g., bastion host, IAM credentials	Ensures least privilege access for the cluster ENIs
	Ability to add external ID and even implement MFA	Prevents Internet-wide access but restricts access to only those who have access to the bastion host	Endpoint is not visible on the Internet	To prevent misconfiguration that may affect the cluster ENIs

Summary

We have strengthened the security of our cluster with private endpoint and used the IAM role as cluster creator to improve IAM security. We sealed off our cluster from external access and allowed only bastion access to the cluster. Having access to the cluster endpoint and even the IAM credentials is not enough to access the cluster except you can access the bastion host in addition. We experimented with additional cluster security groups and moved the cluster ENIs to their own subnets. It is important to note the effects of the two kinds of security groups implemented in this chapter. The additional security group applies only to two cluster ENIs. On the other hand, the cluster security group applies to all ENIs of the cluster. The additional security group is optional but useful when you want to segregate cluster security group for cluster ENIs from the security group of other ENIs of the same cluster. We will move on to the hybrid cluster deployment in the next chapter.

CHAPTER 5

Endpoint Hybrid Access Cluster

This chapter demonstrates the endpoint "hybrid" access cluster scenario. We will deploy a hybrid EKS cluster and illustrate how both private and public endpoints can coexist in the same cluster. We will show how you can restrict access to internal and external services or users in the same cluster. The endpoint hybrid access cluster makes it possible to access the Kubernetes API server from both AWS private and the public networks depending on your needs. The hybrid approach is beneficial when you have a good mix of external and internal access requirements, for example, when your security requirements mandate private endpoint access, but you have an external service such as Jenkins CI/CD pipeline that must access the cluster over the public Internet. You cannot implement this scenario in the endpoint private access cluster if there is no private network connectivity between the external service and the cluster. The only straightforward solution in such scenarios is to configure a public endpoint access for the external services or users while maintaining the private endpoint for internal services or users.

Cluster Creator Role Creation

As a first step in the cluster deployment, you must set up the cluster creator's access permissions. This is covered in Chapter 4, but you can follow the same recipe here if you have not done so previously.

Create a Role

1. Navigate to the AWS IAM console ➤ Roles.

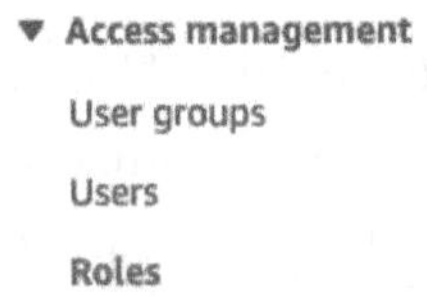

▼ Access management
    User groups
    Users
    Roles

Figure 5-1. Access management

2. Click Create role, then select EC2.

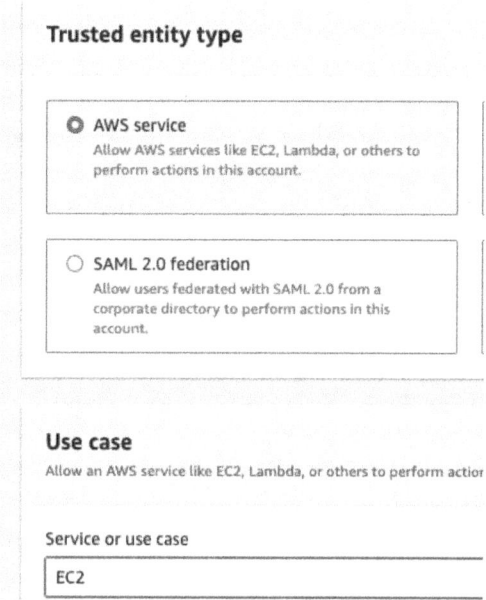

Figure 5-2. *Trusted entity type*

3. Click the Next button, then select the **AdministratorAccess**.

4. Click the Next button again.

5. Name the role as EKSClusterCreatorRole.

6. Click the Create button to create the role.

Create User to Assume the Role

Here are the steps for assuming a role:

1. Navigate to the AWS IAM console ➤ Users ➤ Create a user.

2. Type the username (Joyce), then click Next.

3. Do not attach any permission to the user (Joyce).

CHAPTER 5 ENDPOINT HYBRID ACCESS CLUSTER

4. Copy the arn of Joyce to clipboard.
5. Create the user.
6. Navigate to the AWS IAM console again ➤ Roles.
7. Find the EKSClusterCreatorRole you just created.
8. Click the Trust Relationships tab.
9. Edit the trust relationships to allow Joyce to assume the role.

```
{
   "Version": "2012-10-17",
   "Statement": [
   {
    "Effect": "Allow",
    "Principal": {
    "AWS": "arn:aws:iam::${ACCOUNT_ID}:user/Joyce"
    },
     "Action": "sts:AssumeRole"
    }
  ]
}
```

10. Click the Update role button to update the policy.

Create EKS Describe Cluster Policy

Here are the steps for creating EKS describe policy:

1. Navigate to IAM ➤ Policies.
2. Click the Create policy button, then click the JSON button to open the Policy editor.

CHAPTER 5　ENDPOINT HYBRID ACCESS CLUSTER

3. Delete the default policy from the editor and add the following policy:

```
{
    "Version": "2012-10-17",
    "Statement": [
        {
            "Effect": "Allow",
            "Action": [
                "eks:DescribeCluster"
            ],
            "Resource": "*"
        }
    ]
}
```

4. Click the next button.

5. Give the policy a name (e.g., eks-describe-policy).

6. Click the Create policy button.

Attach EKS Describe Cluster Policy

1. Navigate to IAM ➤ Users ➤ Joyce.

2. Click the Permissions tab.

3. Click Add permissions ➤ Attach policies directly.

4. Select the eks-describe-policy you just created.

5. Click Next ➤ Add permissions.

Configure Role in AWS Credential File

1. Navigate to IAM ➤ User, then click the user Joyce.

2. Create an access key ID and secret access key for the user.

3. Install the AWS CLI on your local machine and configure it (see Chapter 3) or edit the **.aws/credentials** file if the AWS CLI is already installed and configured.

4. Edit the **.aws/credentials** file as follows:

   [joyce-credentials]
   aws_access_key_id = **${ACCESS_KEY_ID}**
   aws_secret_access_key = **${SECRET_ACCESS_KEY}**

   [joyce-role]
   role_arn = arn:aws:iam::**${ACCOUNT_ID}**:role/EKSClusterCreatorRole
   source_profile = joyce-credentials
   region = us-east-1

   - The **joyce-credentials** is the reference to the IAM credential.

   - The **aws_access_key_id** is the access key ID of joyce.

   - The **aws_secret_access_key** is Joyce's secret access key.

- The [joyce-role] is the name of the profile. You can reference the profile in the Terraform code.

- The **role_arn** is the Amazon Resource Name of the role **EKSClusterCreatorRole**. You can find the role ARN by clicking the EKSClusterCreator IAM role.

- The **source_profile** specifies which credential should be used for the initial assumed role call.

- Finally, the region specifies the AWS region.

The Structure of the Code

The code's structure as shown in Figure 5-3 remains the same as in Chapter 4. We have the same bastion host for private access, cluster security group, and additional security.

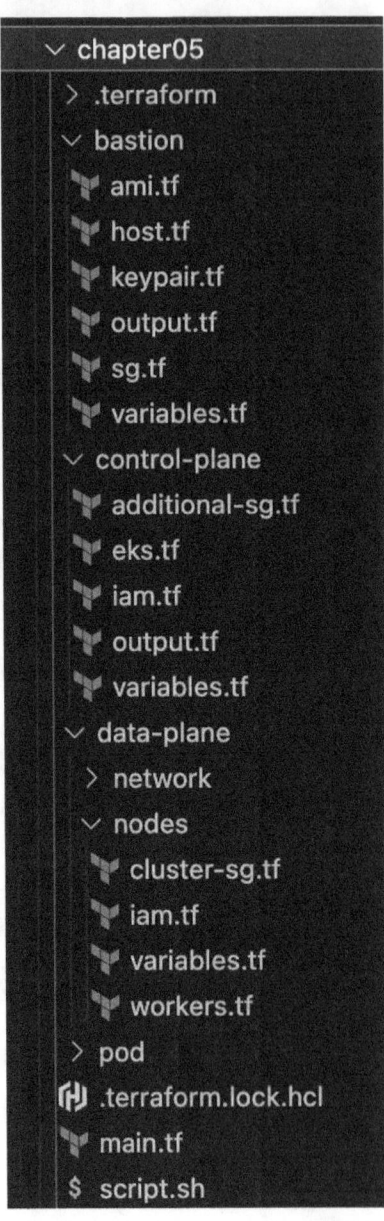

Figure 5-3. *Structure of the Terraform code for the endpoint hybrid access cluster*

CHAPTER 5 ENDPOINT HYBRID ACCESS CLUSTER

Bastion Host Code

The bastion host module remains the same as in the previous chapter. It creates an EC2 instance and SSH key pairs to enable private access to the cluster. However, with the hybrid setup the cluster operator will have two entry points to the cluster either through the private or public access endpoints depending on the restrictions conferred on the public endpoint. By default, the cluster creator or operator can access the cluster in both ways if you configure no restrictions on the public endpoint (see the "Network Setup" section for the Terraform code).

```
resource "aws_instance" "instances" {
  ami           = data.aws_ami.ubuntu.id
  instance_type = var.instance-type
  key_name      = var.sshkey
  metadata_options {
    http_endpoint = "enabled"
    http_tokens   = "required"
  }
  subnet_id                   = var.subnet_id
  vpc_security_group_ids      = [aws_security_group.sg.id]
  associate_public_ip_address = true
  tags = {
    "Name" : "bastion-host"
  }
}
```

Bastion Security Group

The bastion security group remains the same as before. It allows external users to access the cluster from the Internet through SSH on port 22.

```
resource "aws_security_group" "sg" {
  name    = "bastion-sg"
  vpc_id = var.vpc_id
  dynamic "ingress" {
    for_each = var.ports
    content {
      from_port   = ingress.value
      to_port     = ingress.value
      protocol    = "tcp"
      cidr_blocks = [var.cidrBlocks["internet"]]
    }
  }
  dynamic "egress" {
    for_each = var.eports
    content {
      from_port   = egress.value
      to_port     = egress.value
      protocol    = -1
      cidr_blocks = [var.cidrBlocks["internet"]]
    }
  }
}
```

Network Setup

Unlike the endpoint private access cluster, the endpoint hybrid access clusters have two entry points for both services and cluster administrators. Administrators and services can access the cluster both ways either through private or public endpoints as shown in Figure 5-4.

CHAPTER 5 ENDPOINT HYBRID ACCESS CLUSTER

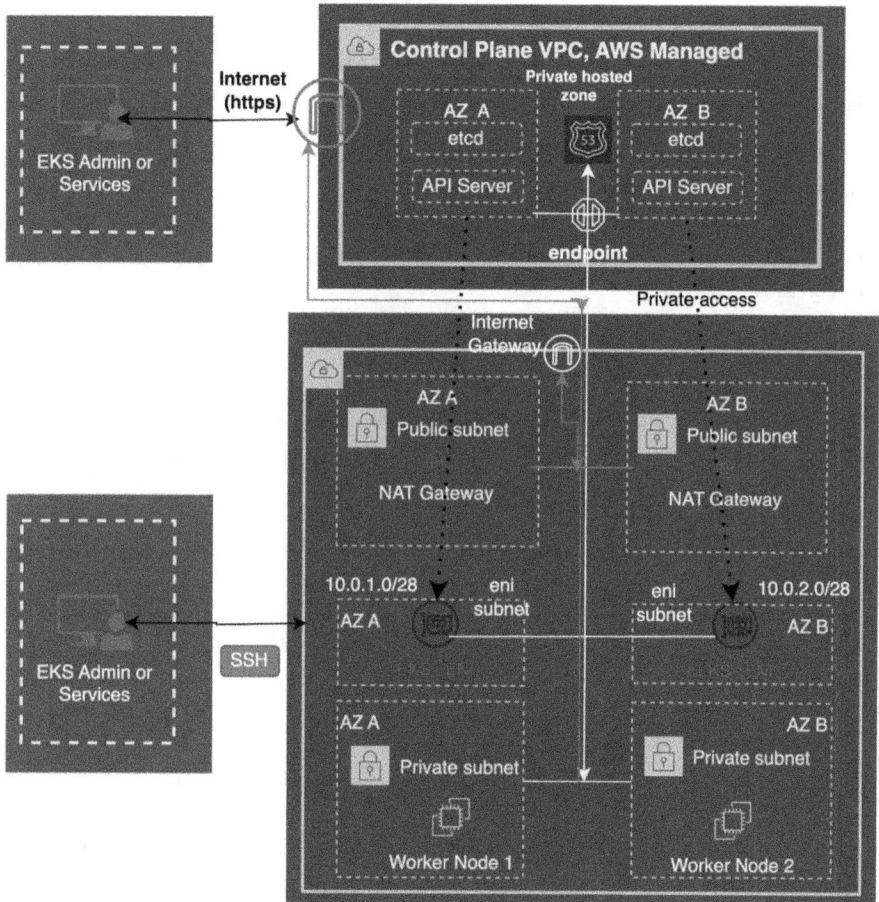

***Figure 5-4.** Endpoint hybrid access cluster*

All public Internet access goes through the public Internet, whereas the internal access ends up on the private AWS network.

The other important resources apart from the endpoints are the subnets. We have six subnets as before, two for cluster ENIs, two for private subnets that will host the worker nodes, and the rest for the bastion host, the network infrastructure, Internet gateway, and NAT gateway.

CHAPTER 5 ENDPOINT HYBRID ACCESS CLUSTER

The subnets that host the ENIs will be the smallest subnets with the /28 CIDR range. They separate the two cluster ENIs from the node subnets to reduce IP address exhaustion in accordance with the AWS best practices. You should find all the subnets in the **subnets.tf** file under the network module of the data plane as shown below:

```
data "aws_availability_zones" "azs" {
 state = "available"
}
resource "aws_subnet" "eni_subnets" {
   vpc_id            = aws_vpc.cluster_vpc.id
   cidr_block   = count.index == 0 ? var.cidr_blocks
   ["eni-subnet-1"] : var.cidr_blocks["eni-subnet-2"]
   availability_zone = data.aws_availability_zones.azs.
   names[count.index]
   count = 2
   tags = {
     Name = "eni-subnet-${count.index+1}"
   }
}
resource "aws_subnet" "private_subnets" {
   vpc_id            = aws_vpc.cluster_vpc.id
   cidr_block   = count.index == 0 ? var.cidr_blocks["private-subnet-1"] : var.cidr_blocks["private-subnet-2"]
   availability_zone = data.aws_availability_zones.azs.
   names[count.index]
   count = 2
   tags = {
     Name = "private-subnet-${count.index+1}"
   }
}
```

```
resource "aws_subnet" "public_subnets" {
  vpc_id            = aws_vpc.cluster_vpc.id
  cidr_block  = count.index == 0 ? var.cidr_blocks["public-
  subnet-1"] : var.cidr_blocks["public-subnet-2"]
  availability_zone = data.aws_availability_zones.azs.
  names[count.index]
  count = 2
  tags = {
    Name = "public-subnet-${count.index+1}"
  }
}
```

The Control Plane Module

The default endpoint access is public; therefore, we must explicitly specify the type of endpoint to ensure that Terraform creates both endpoints.

We do so with the **endpoint_private_access** argument to enable the private endpoint and the **endpoint_public_access** to configure the public endpoint as follows:

```
resource "aws_eks_cluster" "private_endpoint_cluster" {
  name     = var.cluster_name
  version  = var.cluster_version
  role_arn = aws_iam_role.cluster_role.arn
  #configure data plane subnets and eni
  vpc_config {
    subnet_ids = concat(
      var.eni_subnet_ids
    )
    endpoint_private_access = "true"
    endpoint_public_access  = "true"
```

```
    #public_access_cidrs = ["193.16.23.22/32"]
  }
  depends_on = [aws_iam_role.cluster_role ]
}
```

We have commented out the **public_access_cidrs** argument for now. We will uncomment it after deployment to test how you can restrict access for the public part of a hybrid endpoint cluster. The **public_access_cidrs** is an array of public IP addresses. It does not accept private IP addresses.

Worker Nodes

This section highlights the code for the worker nodes in the **workers.tf** file under the nodes' module. You have two instances to run user applications as before. We chose spot instances instead of on-demand instances. Spot instances use available spare EC2 capacity, making them cheaper than the on-demand instances.[1] They fall into the category of unused EC2 instance resources that enjoy steep discounts. You can lower your Amazon EC2 costs significantly with spot instances.

However, AWS can interrupt spot instances at any time; hence, spot instances are mainly useful for workloads that can be interrupted, for example, batch processing workloads such as noncritical ETL jobs, test servers, containerized workloads with good autoscaling strategy, and distributed high-performance computing workloads that support up- and downscaling. However, spot instances are not suitable for mission-critical workloads such as proxy server, load balancer, database server, email server, and LDAP servers.

---

[1] https://docs.aws.amazon.com/AWSEC2/latest/UserGuide/using-spot-instances.html

```
resource "aws_eks_node_group" "nodes" {
  cluster_name    = var.cluster_name
  node_group_name = var.node_name
  node_role_arn   = aws_iam_role.worker_nodes_role.arn
  subnet_ids = var.subnet_ids
  capacity_type  = "SPOT"
  instance_types = var.instance_types
  scaling_config {
    desired_size = 2
    max_size     = 3
    min_size     = 2
  }
  update_config {
    max_unavailable = 1
  }
  labels = {
    name = var.label
  }
  tags = {
    Name = "worker-node"
  }
  depends_on = [aws_iam_role.worker_nodes_role ]
}
```

Cluster Security Group Code Review

This section will run through the cluster security group. You need the following cluster security group to allow the bastion host to communicate with the private endpoint or the API server of the cluster. The code remains the same as in Chapter 4:

```
#inbound call from the bastion host to the private API server
resource "aws_security_group_rule" "ingress" {
    type              = "ingress"
    from_port         = 443
    to_port           = 443
    protocol          = "tcp"
    cidr_blocks       = ["10.0.0.0/16"]
    security_group_id = var.cluster_security_group_id
}
```

You will need an alternative rule to allow the nodes to make outbound calls to the Internet to fetch containers from container registries such as Docker Hub:

```
#outbound call to the internet
resource "aws_security_group_rule" "https_port" {
    type              = "egress"
    from_port         = 443
    to_port           = 443
    protocol          = "tcp"
    cidr_blocks       = ["0.0.0.0/0"]
    security_group_id = var.cluster_security_group_id
}
```

You should find the cluster security group rule in the **sg.tf** file under the node's submodule.

Additional Security Group Code Review

This section reviews the code for the additional security group. You can find it in the **additional-sg.tf** file under the control-plane module. The code implements outbound rules for the cluster DNS and worker node's kubelets. There are no ingress rules here because the cluster security group takes care of it.

CHAPTER 5 ENDPOINT HYBRID ACCESS CLUSTER

```
resource "aws_security_group" "additional_security_group" {
  name  = "optional additional security group rules for ENIs"
  vpc_id = var.vpc_id
   egress {
    from_port      = 53
    to_port        = 53
    protocol       = "tcp"
    cidr_blocks    = ["10.0.0.0/16"]
   }
   egress {
    from_port      = 10250
    to_port        = 10250
    protocol       = "tcp"
    cidr_blocks    = ["10.0.0.0/16"]
   }
}
```

To reiterate, the additional security group is attached to only the cluster ENIs, while the cluster security group is attached to all ENIs within a cluster. It is not effective unless you clean up the default cluster security group rules.

Terraform Code Deployment

Let us deploy the code and review the implementation. You should follow the recipe below to execute the Terraform code for this chapter. Make sure the role is configured in your **.aws/credentials** file as explained earlier.

1. Download the Terraform code for chapter05.

2. Go to the location of the **main.tf** file.

CHAPTER 5   ENDPOINT HYBRID ACCESS CLUSTER

3. Verify that the profile is set to joyce-role or your profile name in the **main.tf** file and the region is set appropriately.

4. Change the profile joyce-role to a new name if you used a different profile name in your **.aws/credentials** file.

```
provider "aws" {
region = "us-east-1"
profile = "joyce-role"
}
#create vpc
module "vpc" {
  source = "./data-plane/network"
}
#create eni in the dataplane (step x)
module "cluster" {
  source = "./control-plane"
  eni_subnet_ids = module.vpc.eni_subnet_ids
  vpc_id = module.vpc.vpc_id
}
module "nodes" {
  source = "./data-plane/nodes"
  cluster_name = module.cluster.cluster_name
  subnet_ids =  module.vpc.private_subnet_ids
  cluster_security_group_id = module.cluster.cluster_security_group_id
}
module "instance" {
  source = "./bastion"
```

CHAPTER 5 ENDPOINT HYBRID ACCESS CLUSTER

```
    subnet_id = module.vpc.public_subnet_ids[0]
    vpc_id = module.vpc.vpc_id
}
```

5. Execute the Terraform code.

   ```
   terraform unit
   terraform apply
   ```

6. Type yes when asked.

7. You should see the following while you wait for deployment to complete:

   ```
   module.cluster.aws_eks_cluster.private_endpoint_cluster: Still creating... [10s elapsed]
   15s [id=i-0354d7f78b2fa5a9a]
   module.vpc.aws_nat_gateway.natgw: Still creating... [20s elapsed] ...
   ```

8. You should find the following output once the deployment is complete:

   ```
   Apply complete! Resources: 33 added, 0 changed, 0 destroyed.
   ```

   The statistics recount the number of resources added, changed, and destroyed. 33 resources were added, 0 changed, and 0 destroyed in this case.

9. Update the cluster context.

   ```
   aws eks update-kubeconfig --name hybrid-endpoint-cluster --profile joyce-role
   ```

139

CHAPTER 5   ENDPOINT HYBRID ACCESS CLUSTER

10. Verify the number of running nodes.

    ```
    kubectl get nodes
    ```

    The command should output the nodes.

Troubleshooting the Cluster

You can access if the cluster is up and running or fix issues with the following steps:

1. Update the cluster context.

   ```
   aws eks update-kubeconfig --name hybrid-endpoint-cluster --profile joyce-role
   ```

2. Display information about the cluster.

   ```
   aws eks describe-cluster --name hybrid-endpoint-cluster --profile joyce-role
   ```

   The **aws eks describe-cluster** command displays information about the cluster. The information includes cluster name, when it was created, network configuration, and more. The input for the commands is the cluster name and the AWS IAM user profile.
   You can use the information to troubleshoot the cluster.

3. Verify the number of running nodes.

   ```
   kubectl get nodes
   ```

CHAPTER 5   ENDPOINT HYBRID ACCESS CLUSTER

This command displays the running nodes if the cluster is configured properly. You can use the command to retrieve information about other cluster objects such as pods and deployments. The inputs for the kubectl get command are the object type and the namespace, for example, kubectl get pods -n kube-system. The default namespace is used if no namespace is specified.

4. Display pods in the kube-system namespace.

    ```
    kubectl get pods -n kube-system
    ```

    This will output the following system pods:

NAME	READY	STATUS	RESTARTS	AGE
aws-node-pzmkr	2/2	Running	0	60m
aws-node-vv9c2	2/2	Running	0	60m
coredns-789f8477df-g7kt7	1/1	Running	0	66m
coredns-789f8477df-vcrqw	1/1	Running	0	66m
kube-proxy-9s9wc	1/1	Running	0	60m
kube-proxy-s2c9v	1/1	Running	0	60m

5. Describe cluster pods.

    ```
    kubectl describe pods -n kube-system
    ```

    The command will display information about the pods running in the kube-system namespace. The kube-system namespace is where system pods reside. An alternative command is **kubectl logs [pod name]**. You use the kubectl logs if you know the name of the object.

6. You can describe your nodes with the kubectl describe command.

   ```
   kubectl describe nodes
   ```

   You use the kubectl describe command to describe objects to find more information about them, especially if they are in an error state. The kubectl describe nodes command will display a lot of information about nodes, including node roles, labels, creation timestamp, CPU, and more.

7. You can log information about an object such as pods with the kubectl logs command as follows:

   ```
   kubectl logs aws-node-pzmkr -n kube-system
   ```

   The command requires the name of the object. The default namespace is used if no namespace is specified.

8. Check the permission of the cluster creator.

   ```
   kubectl auth can-i list nodes
   ```

   You use the kubectl auth can-i command to check user permissions, which actions the current user can perform. The above command verifies if a user can list nodes or not. The verb "list" represents the action, and the "nodes" is the resource or object name.
   The general format is given by

   ```
   kubectl auth can-i VERB [Type ➤ OBJECT NAME ➤ RESOURCE]
   ```

CHAPTER 5   ENDPOINT HYBRID ACCESS CLUSTER

9. Verify if the current user can perform all actions.

    ```
    kubectl auth can-i "*" "*"
    ```

    The "Yes" output means the cluster creator has access to all resources.

10. You may examine logs in case the cluster fails or objects are not deployed.

    ```
    kubectl auth can-i VERB [Type ➤ OBJECT NAME ➤ RESOURCE]
    ```

11. You can also use the AWS console to review and troubleshoot your cluster. You can use CloudWatch Logs to troubleshoot a cluster.

Cluster Review

We want to validate the consistency of the EKS deployment against the theory introduced in the first half of this chapter in this section.

Cluster Security Group Cleanup

The default cluster security group grants unrestricted access to the cluster nodes. You should clean up the security group to enforce least privileged access.

We want to clean up the security group before we connect to the cluster access. You can find both the cluster security group and additional security group from the EKS console under the Networking tab as follows:

```
Navigate to the EKS ➤ Cluster ➤ Cluster name ➤ Networking
tab, then click the Cluster security group link.
```

143

CHAPTER 5 ENDPOINT HYBRID ACCESS CLUSTER

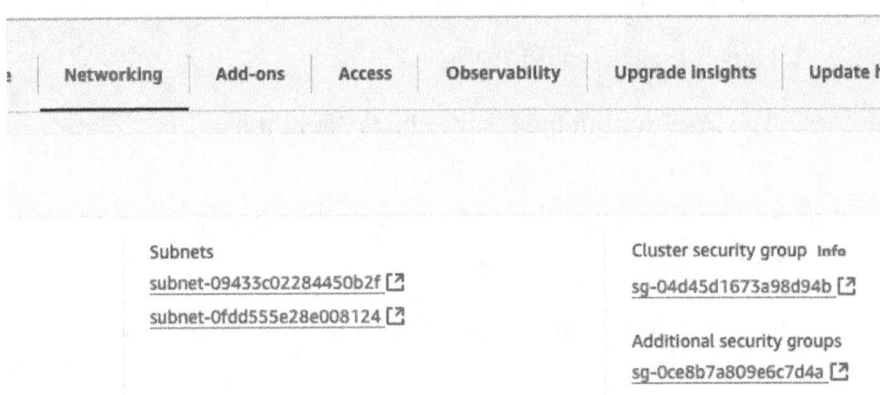

Figure 5-5. EKS Networking

This will take you to the security group console.

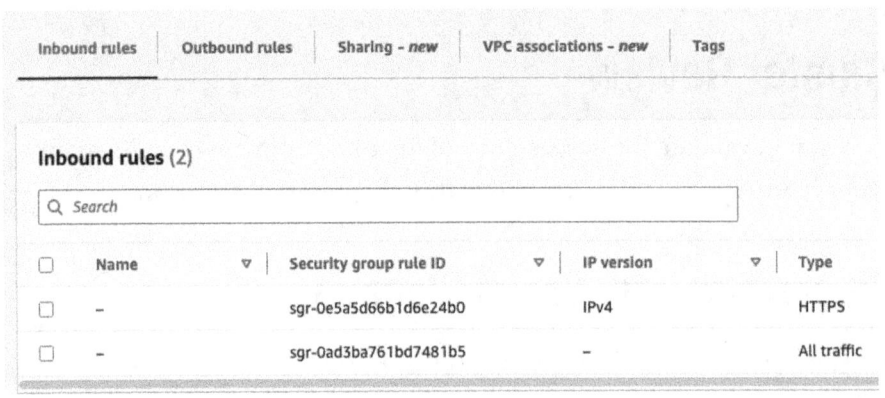

Figure 5-6. Cluster inbound rule

Click the default security group and follow the steps below to delete the default security rules:

1. Click the Inbound tab.

2. Click the Edit inbound rules button.

3. Delete the default inbound security rule, sg-04d45d1673a98d94b.

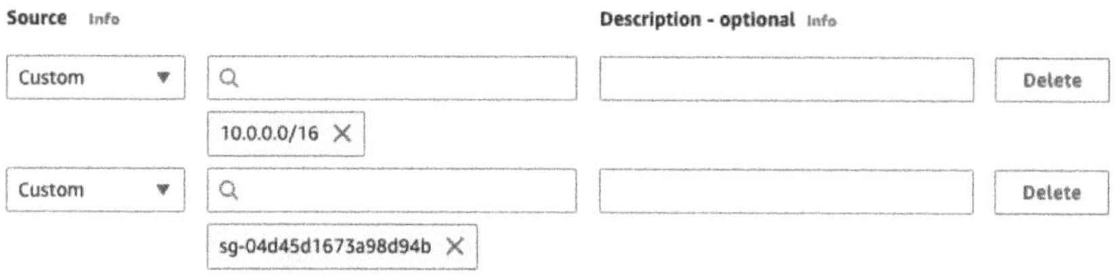

CHAPTER 5   ENDPOINT HYBRID ACCESS CLUSTER

Figure 5-7. AWS security group console

4. Save the changes.

5. Repeat the same steps for the outbound default security group rule.

Additional Security Group Review

We want to review the additional security group to validate if it is configured as planned.

Navigate to the EKS ➤ Cluster ➤ Cluster name ➤ Networking tab, then click the Additional cluster security group link.

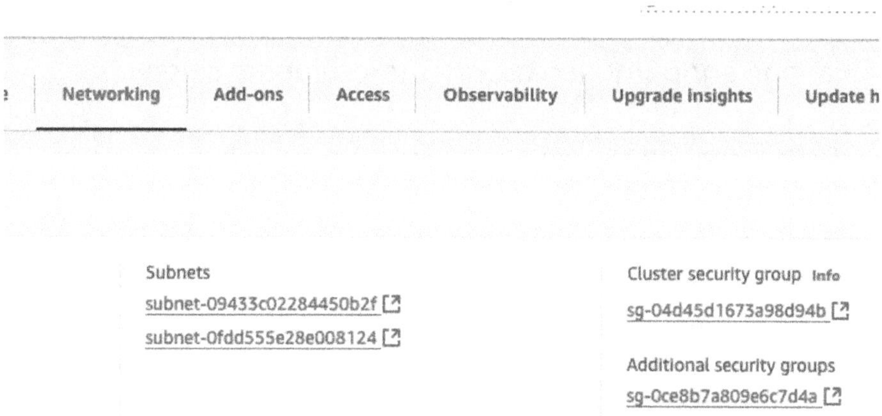

Figure 5-8. AWS EKS console

145

CHAPTER 5   ENDPOINT HYBRID ACCESS CLUSTER

You should find empty inbound rules and two outbound rules as shown in Figure 5-9.

IP version	Type	Protocol	Port range	Destination
IPv4	Custom TCP	TCP	10250	10.0.0.0/16
IPv4	DNS (TCP)	TCP	53	10.0.0.0/16

Figure 5-9. AWS EKS console

You do not need to change anything here since the outbound rules are configured as expected.

Connecting to the Cluster
The Endpoint Hybrid Cluster

You can utilize the following step to review the hybrid endpoint:

Navigate to the EKS console ➤ Cluster ➤ Cluster name ➤ Networking tab, then click the Manage endpoint access.

Manage endpoint access: private-endpoint-cluster

Cluster endpoint access Info
Configure access to the Kubernetes API server endpoint.

○ Public
   The cluster endpoint is accessible from outside of your VPC. Worker node traffic will leave your VPC to connect to the endpoint.

● Public and private
   The cluster endpoint is accessible from outside of your VPC. Worker node traffic to the endpoint will stay within your VPC.

○ Private
   The cluster endpoint is only accessible through your VPC. Worker node traffic to the endpoint will stay within your VPC.

▶ Advanced settings

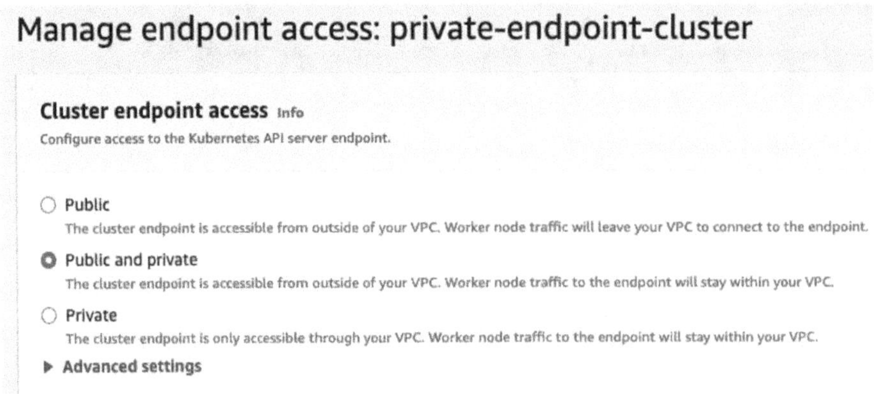

Figure 5-10. Cluster endpoint access console

You should find the public and private endpoints selected.

Public Cluster Access Test

You should be able to access the cluster from your local machine through the public endpoint. You do so by running the change context commands on your local machine as follows:

```
aws eks update-kubeconfig --name hybrid-endpoint-cluster
kubectl get nodes
```

You should see an output like this:

```
NAME                        STATUS   ROLES    AGE   VERSION
ip-10-0-3-173.ec2.internal  Ready    <none>   20m   v1.31.0...
ip-10-0-4-171.ec2.internal  Ready    <none>   20m   v1.31.0 ...
```

Run your pods locally with the following commands:

Run the **kubectl apply -f pod/blueapp.yml**
Run **kubectl get pods**

You should find the pods running on the cluster with the following output:

```
kubectl apply -f pod/blueapp.yml
pod/blueapp-pod created
kubectl get pods
NAME          READY   STATUS    RESTARTS   AGE
blueapp-pod   1/1     Running   0          26s
```

Private Cluster Access Test

This section will test the private endpoint access to verify if the cluster can handle both public and private access.

147

CHAPTER 5   ENDPOINT HYBRID ACCESS CLUSTER

Log in to the bastion host from your laptop or use the AWS web console.

1. Go to the AWS console.
2. Click the bastion-host instance.

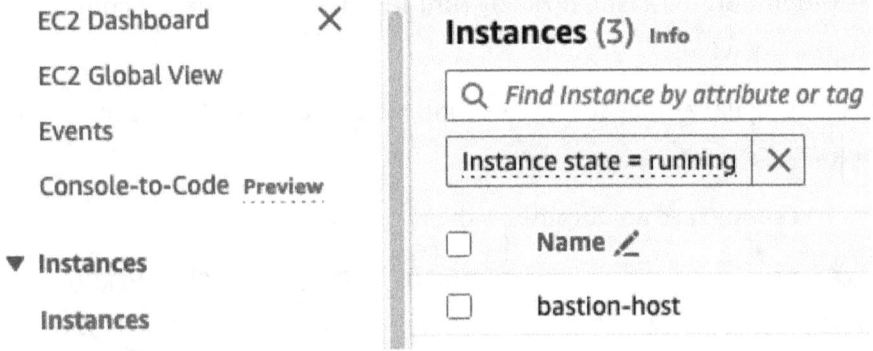

Figure 5-11. EC2 instance console

3. Click Connect ➤ EC2 Instance connect ➤ Connect button to connect to the instance.

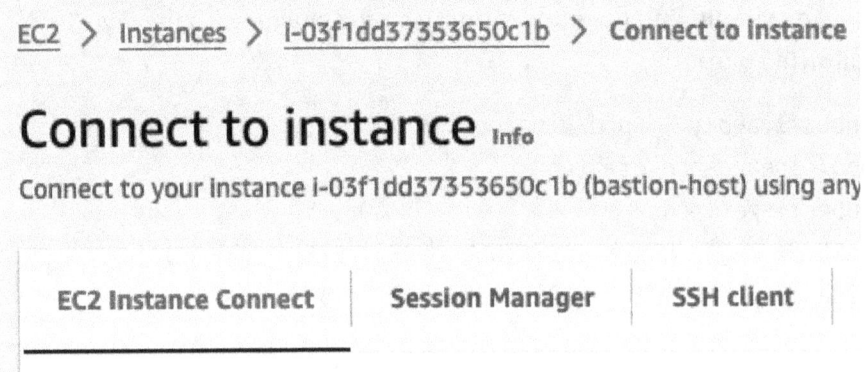

Figure 5-12. EC2 instance connection console

148

CHAPTER 5   ENDPOINT HYBRID ACCESS CLUSTER

4. Install awscli on the instance.

    ```
    sudo apt update -y && \
    sudo apt install python3-pip -y && \
    pip3 install awscli --upgrade && \
    sudo apt  install awscli -y && \
    sudo snap install kubectl --classic
    ```

5. Run AWS configure with the cluster creator's credentials (Joyce).

    ```
    aws configure
    AWS Access Key ID [None]: Joyce access key ID
    AWS Secret Access Key [None]: Joyce secret access key
    Region: Cluster region
    ```

6. Edit the .aws/credentials file and replace the content with the cluster creator's credentials and role.

    ```
    [joyce-credentials]
    aws_access_key_id = <AWS_ACCESS_KEY_ID>
    aws_secret_access_key = <AWS_SECRET_ACCESS_KEY>
    ```
    [default]
    ```
    role_arn = arn:aws:iam::<ACCOUNT_ID>:role/
    EKSClusterCreatorRole
    source_profile = joyce-credentials
    region = us-east-1
    ```

    Replace the above with your credentials and ACCOUNT_ID. Also note that the profile name is no longer joyce-role but set to **default**, meaning you don't need to append the --profile argument when

149

CHAPTER 5 ENDPOINT HYBRID ACCESS CLUSTER

you run the **aws eks update-kubeconfig** command. The **aws eks update-kubeconfig** command without the profile argument automatically falls back to the default profile.

7. Update the cluster user context.

   ```
   aws eks update-kubeconfig --name hybrid-endpoint-cluster
   ```

8. Test the cluster.

   ```
   kubectl get nodes
   ```

9. You should see the nodes.

```
NAME                       STATUS   ROLES    AGE   VERSION
ip-10-0-3-14.ec2.internal  Ready    <none>   25h   v1.31.4-eks-aeac579
ip-10-0-4-141.ec2.internal Ready    <none>   25h   v1.31.4-eks-aeac579
```

10. Copy the sample blueapp.yml file to the bastion host.

11. Run the **kubectl apply -f blueapp.yml** command.

12. Run **kubectl get pods** to see the application running.

The test shows that you can access the private endpoint of the cluster from the bastion host and public endpoint on our local laptop. Thus, we confirm the hybrid cluster deployment.

Test Public Endpoint Restrictions

We cannot complete this chapter without demonstrating why you need a hybrid cluster. Suppose you are running an external Jenkins server with a public IP address 193.16.23.22. Suppose you want to restrict external access to the Jenkins server but block all other external access, then you can do so by reconfiguring the endpoints. You can utilize the Terraform code or with the AWS console.

For Terraform code, uncomment the **public_access_cidrs** argument in the **eks.tf** file and rerun the **terraform apply** command.

For the AWS console, go to the **EKS ➤ Cluster ➤ Cluster name ➤ Networking tab, click the Manage endpoint access, then click the Advanced settings** to review the CIDR block. Edit the CIDR block and add the preferred public IP address. Save the changes and test the cluster.

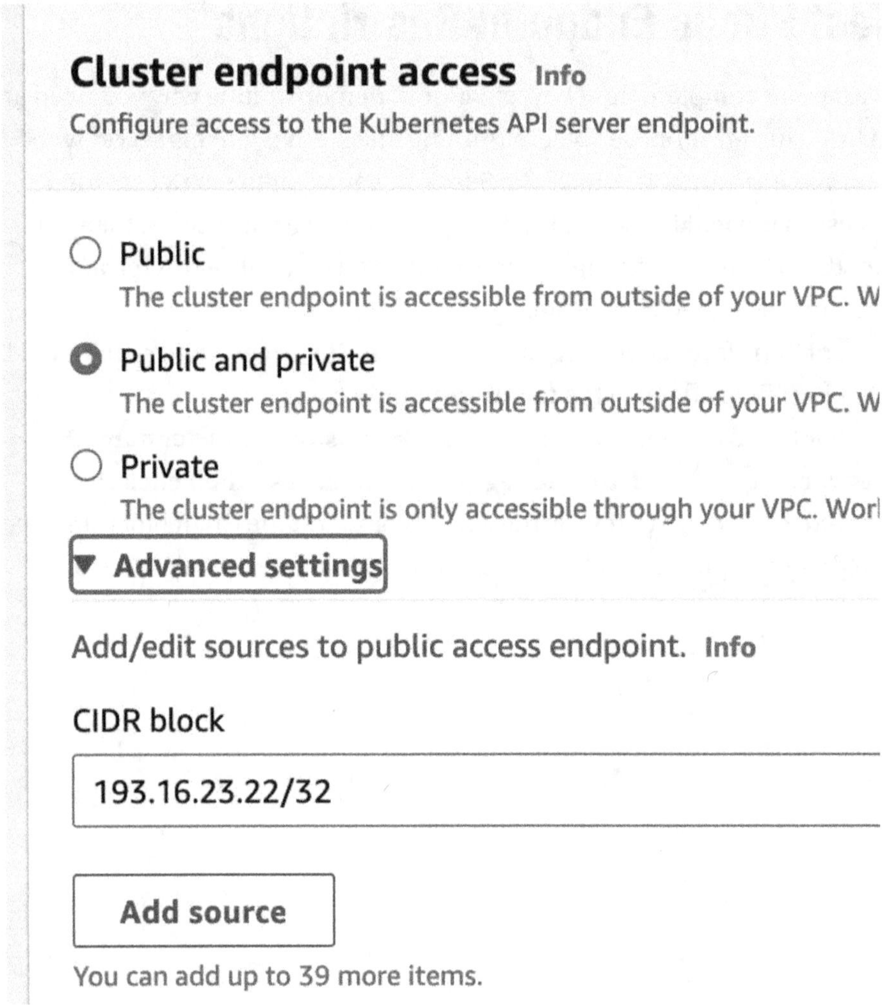

Cluster endpoint access Info
Configure access to the Kubernetes API server endpoint.

○ **Public**
The cluster endpoint is accessible from outside of your VPC. W

◉ **Public and private**
The cluster endpoint is accessible from outside of your VPC. W

○ **Private**
The cluster endpoint is only accessible through your VPC. Worl

▼ Advanced settings

Add/edit sources to public access endpoint. Info

CIDR block

193.16.23.22/32

Add source

You can add up to 39 more items.

Figure 5-13. AWS EKS endpoint access console

Now run the following commands to test the public endpoint:

```
aws eks update-kubeconfig --name hybrid-endpoint-cluster
--profile joyce-role
kubectl get nodes
```

CHAPTER 5　ENDPOINT HYBRID ACCESS CLUSTER

This should fail because of the restriction. You can replace the IP address with the public IP of your local machine and test the access again. You should be successful this time round. You can google "my IP address" to find your public IP.

Summary

We covered the public and private (hybrid) endpoint access cluster in this chapter. It is the last one of the three endpoints available in EKS. Its major merit is to enable both external and internal cluster access where necessary, especially where you have a mix of external and internal services. You can restrict the public endpoint to specific IP addresses to improve security of the cluster and to allow the external services cluster access over the public Internet. The next chapter will focus on one more component of the EKS cluster which is node.

CHAPTER 6

Cluster Nodes

So far, we have covered the EKS architecture and explored some aspects of EKS cluster security. Now, it's time to focus on the cluster nodes as we continue to dive deeper into EKS services. In this chapter, you'll learn about the three types of nodes and how to implement two of them in practice, managed nodes and self-managed nodes. Additionally, we will introduce launch templates and demonstrate how to implement them.

Node and Node Groups

EKS clusters package containers into pods and run them on one or more EC2 instances, which are referred to as nodes. Nodes belong to the data plane and provide the computing power necessary for both system and application pods to operate. They run within the customer's VPC and interact with the control plane through the cluster API server endpoint. A node can host as many pods as its resources allow, as depicted in Figure 6-1.

CHAPTER 6 CLUSTER NODES

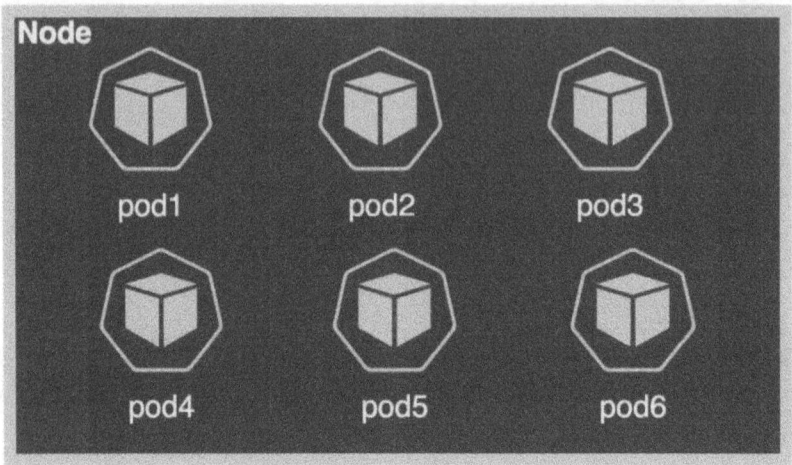

Figure 6-1. EKS node and pods

In a learning or test environment, you could deploy all your pods on a single EC2 instance, but in practice, it's always recommended to use multiple instances to take advantage of the cluster's scaling capabilities. Therefore, customers often deploy one or more EC2 instances into a group of nodes called a **node group**. A node group consists of one or more EC2 instances deployed in an EC2 Auto Scaling group. It bundles these instances together to run workloads in an EKS cluster.

Figure 6-2 illustrates how you can run multiple node groups (e.g., Node Group 1 and Node Group 2) within the same cluster, allowing for better scalability and flexibility.

CHAPTER 6 CLUSTER NODES

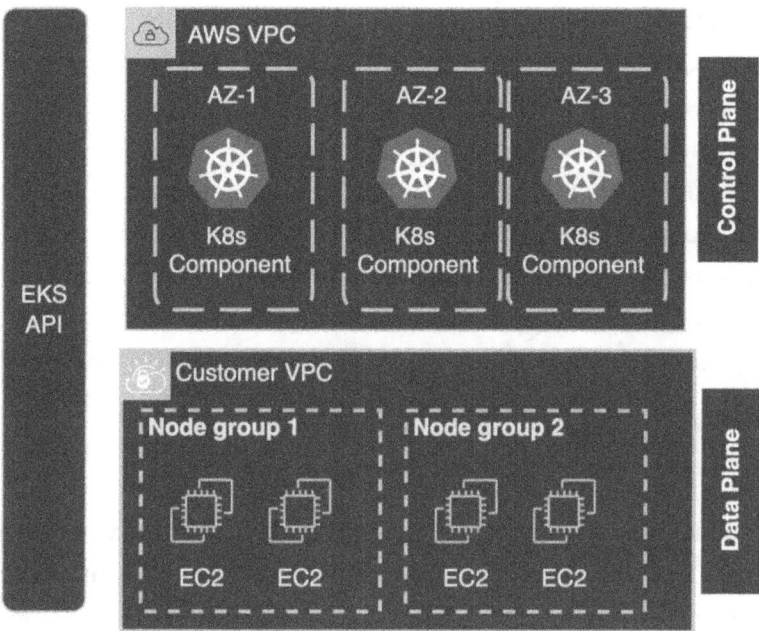

Figure 6-2. EKS node groups

Types of Nodes

EKS supports three types of nodes, the managed nodes, self-managed nodes, and Fargate. We will discuss each of the node type in the following subsections.

Managed Nodes

Managed nodes or node groups are nodes whose images are maintained by AWS on customers' behalf. You opt for a managed node when you want to share responsibilities with AWS in managing the underlying EC2 image EKS deploys for your cluster. EKS creates the nodes from a preexisting Amazon Machine Image (AMI) and attaches them to the cluster. Once provisioned, AWS takes care of image updates, fixes vulnerabilities associated with the image, creates new AMIs, and notifies customers about them. The AMI update happens once a month or whenever a new K8s version is released. The AWS's shared responsibility ends once the AMI is released, and customers are informed.

Customers are responsible for patching or upgrading the cluster nodes once AWS releases a new AMI. AWS cannot patch the cluster nodes on behalf of customers because they have no access to the customer's account that hosts the node groups. Customers can update the cluster from the EKS console or with infrastructure as code (e.g., Terraform) or command-line tools.[1]

You can choose from two types of managed nodes: **spot** or **on-demand** nodes.

On-demand nodes run standard EC2 instances. When you deploy on-demand nodes, you have full control over their lifecycle, meaning you decide when to launch, stop, reboot, or terminate the nodes. Additionally, you pay a fixed price for compute capacity by the second, with no long-term commitments. This offers flexibility without the need for up-front costs or long-term contracts.

This is completely opposite to spot instances or nodes. Spot instances have no fixed price and no availability guarantees. AWS controls when to terminate the instances. Hence, they are well suited for noncritical workloads that can sustain sporadic traffic interruptions such as data analysis, batch jobs, background processing, and test applications. They are a cost-effective alternative to on-demand nodes if you can afford unplanned interruptions to your workloads.

You can combine both spot and on-demand node groups in the same cluster to balance out reliability with cost depending on your needs.

---

[1] https://docs.aws.amazon.com/eks/latest/userguide/managed-node-groups.html

You specify node type with the **capacity_type** argument in Terraform as follows:

```
resource "aws_eks_node_group" "nodes" {
...
  #on-demand or spot
  capacity_type = "SPOT"
  scaling_config {
    desired_size = 1
    max_size     = 2
    min_size     = 1
  }
  update_config {
    max_unavailable = 1
  }
  labels = {
    name = var.tag
  }
}
```

Managed Launch Template

AWS creates a launch template for you when you use managed nodes. The default launch template specifies configuration information of the underlying EC2 instance of your node as shown below.[2] This includes the AMI ID, the instance type, a key pair, security groups, and other parameters needed to launch the EC2 instance for your node.

---

[2] https://docs.aws.amazon.com/autoscaling/ec2/userguide/launch-templates.html

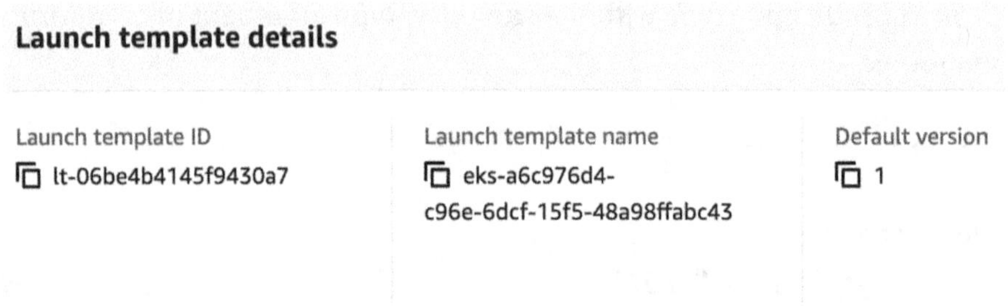

CHAPTER 6   CLUSTER NODES

Launch template details

Launch template ID
lt-06be4b4145f9430a7

Launch template name
eks-a6c976d4-c96e-6dcf-15f5-48a98ffabc43

Default version
1

Figure 6-3. *Launch template details*

Launch templates are immutable. You cannot modify them after creation. However, you can create a new one or build the latest version on top of the old one. In this case, the outdated version becomes the base for the latest version. You can then add your own layer of modifications on top of the base to create the latest version of the base template.

Launch template versioning means you can create a recent version from a base configuration or existing template whenever you want. You can also delete a version when you no longer need it.

Launch template is used by the AWS autoscaling group to upscale and downscale cluster nodes. The autoscaling group service monitors your applications and automatically adjusts capacity to maintain steady, predictable performance at the lowest possible cost. It is easy to set up application scaling for multiple resources across multiple services in minutes with AWS Auto Scaling.[3]

The autoscaling part of the Terraform script is represented as follows:

```
scaling_config {
    desired_size = 1
    max_size     = 2
    min_size     = 1
}
```

---

[3] https://aws.amazon.com/autoscaling/

The desired and min size determines the initial number of nodes, while the max size specifies how many nodes the autoscaler can scale up to. The autoscaler uses the launch template to scale nodes from the desired size to the maximum size whenever the cluster needs more nodes.

Self-Managed

Sometimes the Amazon Machine Images (AMIs) are not fit for purpose. Customers would want to package their own image to reduce operational overheads or meet certain security needs. They may create a golden image from preinstalled packages or applications to respond to the peculiar needs. It is common for organizations to opt for self-managed nodes rather than managed or Fargate nodes.

EKS does not provide the same automation support for customers who elect to use their own images to create cluster nodes (self-managed nodes). Firstly, customers will be responsible for connecting the nodes to the cluster. Secondly, they will be responsible for managing the image lifecycle. This includes image creation, vulnerability, and patch management. Lastly, customers will be responsible for creating a custom launch template to launch the nodes that will join the cluster.

Fargate

Right sizing of nodes is often difficult to come by when you deploy managed or self-managed nodes. You may miss the right number of nodes or the right size of nodes for your application pods unless you can implement a Karpenter controller or addon. The Karpenter addon can automatically launch the right compute resources to handle your cluster's application needs.[4]

---

[4] https://karpenter.sh/

Without Karpenter, Fargate nodes may be a good option. It provides on-demand, right-sized compute capacity for application pods.[5] Fargate is highly optimized and may save costs on batch processing and workloads that can sustain sporadic traffic interruptions. It is serverless, meaning AWS takes full responsibility of everything about nodes or node group management without involving customers. They handle node provisioning, patching, upgrade, optimization, and scaling on customers' behalf. Fargate offers the most secure and reliable alternative to managed and self-managed nodes.

Customers control which and how pods run on Fargate with Fargate profiles and selectors. You can add up to five selectors to each profile. Each selector contains a namespace and optional labels. EKS matches pods using a namespace and the labels that are specified in the selector. Pods that match a selector run on the Fargate nodes.

Managed Node Code Review

We want to deploy an endpoint public access cluster in this chapter and review the node part of the deployment. You should discover the default launch template and how it works together with the autoscaling group. We will move away from deploying additional security groups in this example.

To recap, EKS creates a default autoscaling group and a launch template whenever you spin up a managed node. The launch template specifies the configuration information for the managed node group.[6] The information includes the Amazon Machine Image (AMI) ID, the instance type, security groups, and all other parameters required by EKS to launch the managed node group(s).

---

[5] https://docs.aws.amazon.com/eks/latest/userguide/fargate.html
[6] https://docs.aws.amazon.com/autoscaling/ec2/userguide/launch-templates.html#:~:text=A%20launch%20template%20is%20similar,used%20to%20launch%20EC2%20instances.

CHAPTER 6   CLUSTER NODES

The launch template is referenced by the autoscaling group to scale nodes from the desired size to the maximum size whenever the cluster needs more nodes.

An example Terraform code for the nodes is listed below:

```
resource "aws_eks_node_group" "nodes" {
  cluster_name    = var.cluster_name
  node_group_name = var.node_name
  node_role_arn   = aws_iam_role.nodes_assume_role_policy.arn
  #cluster will deploy t3.medium instance by default
  instance_types = [var.instance_type]
  subnet_ids = var.subnets_id
  scaling_config {
    #set the minimum and desired number to 1 respectively
    desired_size = 1
    max_size     = 2
    min_size     = 1
  }
  update_config {
    max_unavailable = 1
  }
  labels = {
    name = var.tag
  }
  depends_on = [aws_iam_role_policy_attachment.amazon_eks_worker_node_policy]
}
```

The preceding code sets the minimum and the desired size to one and the maximum size to two, respectively. This means the number of nodes cannot go below one, and the cluster can only scale from one

163

CHAPTER 6 CLUSTER NODES

node to a maximum of two. We also set the instance type to t3.small with the **instance_types** argument. The default instance type is t3.medium if nothing is specified.

Managed Node Deployment

This section provides step-by-step instructions to execute the Terraform code for this chapter so that we can review the nodes and their launch template.

1. Navigate to the folder chapter06.

2. Verify if the profile is set to **default** in the **main.tf** file and the region is set appropriately.

3. Make changes to your **.aws/credentials** file to set the cluster creator's credentials to default as follows:

   ```
   [joyce-credentials]
   aws_access_key_id = ${access_key_id}
   aws_secret_access_key = ${secret_access_key}
   ```

   [default]
   ```
   role_arn = arn:aws:iam::${ACCOUNT_ID}: role/EKSClusterCreatorRole
   source_profile = joyce-credentials
   region = us-east-1
   ```

4. Execute the Terraform code.

   ```
   terraform init
   terraform apply
   ```

5. Type yes when asked.

6. You can change context and retrieve the nodes as follows:

```
#Update user context
aws eks update-kubeconfig --name public-endpoint-cluster
#Get nodes
kubectl get nodes
```

Managed Node Deployment Review

Let us review how EKS created the node and which launch template was used. You can navigate to the launch template from the EKS console as follows:

Navigate to the EKS, click the cluster name ➤ node-groups ➤ Autoscaling group name link, then click again the autoscaling group link.

You should see detailed information about the autoscaling group – the launch template ID, the AMI ID, instance type, storage key pair, version, and more. You should find the node capacity under the group details. This is displayed in Figure 6-4. It consists of the desired, minimum, and maximum capacity as specified in the Terraform code.

CHAPTER 6   CLUSTER NODES

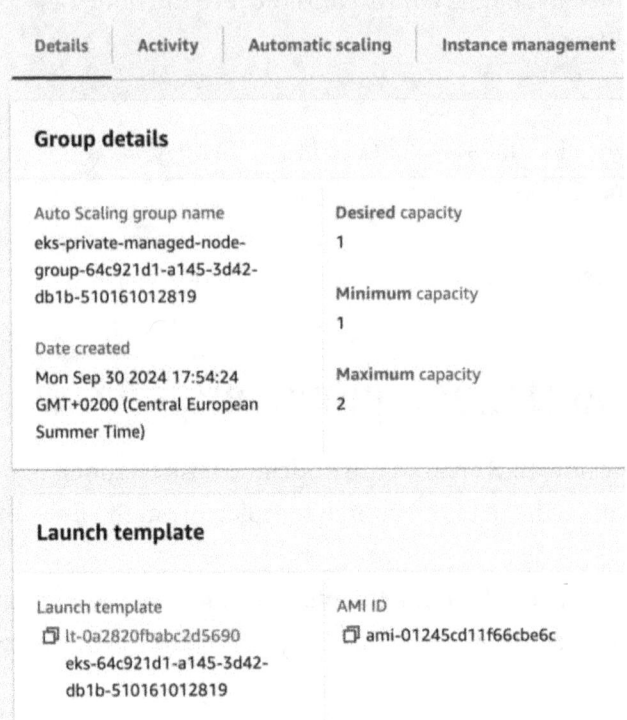

Figure 6-4. *Autoscaling group configuration*

- The desired capacity represents the initial number of nodes at the time of creation. EKS attempts to maintain the desired number of nodes throughout the life of the cluster. In this case, EKS will maintain a node group with one instance throughout the cluster's life.

- The minimum capacity depicts the minimum number of nodes EKS can deploy – one in this example.

- The maximum capacity depicts the maximum number of nodes EKS can deploy – two in this case. That is the cluster can scale up to two nodes in the node group.

CHAPTER 6   CLUSTER NODES

You can click the link for the launch template ID to switch to the launch template page. You should find the same page from the **EC2 ➤ Launch Templates**.

You should find the launch template details with the launch template ID, name, and the default version number as shown in Figure 6-5.

Launch template details

Launch template ID	Launch template name	Default version
lt-06be4b4145f9430a7	eks-a6c976d4-c96e-6dcf-15f5-48a98ffabc43	1

Figure 6-5. *Launch template details*

You should also find the AMI ID, the instance type, security group IDs, and the availability zone as shown in Figure 6-6.

Instance details	Storage	Resource tags	Network interfaces	Advanced details

AMI ID	Instance type	Availability Zone
ami-0a590d6ae1d449080	t3.small	-

Security groups	Security group IDs
-	sg-0d9ba332fe10823b1

Figure 6-6. *Sample launch template*

Custom Launch Templates

We want to switch from the default launch template to a custom launch template so that we can specify custom requirements for our nodes. You can customize nodes with a launch template according to your operational or security needs.

However, you should be aware that custom launch templates may introduce additional operational overheads during nodes or cluster upgrades. You cannot initiate automatic node group update from the AWS console when you deploy your cluster with a custom launch template. That means you cannot just click a button on the AWS console to apply the latest security patches to your nodes.[7]

In addition, custom launch templates will deprive you of receiving automatic update information about your node groups from AWS. Hence, you must monitor update information yourself and modify your custom launch template to handle the current updates whenever they become available.

Conversely, custom template allows you to set the properties of your nodes such as AMI ID, the instance type, volume size, and security group IDs with AMI ID being the most important for node update. You must deploy the correct AMI ID to keep up with regular updates. You should first retrieve the AMI ID you want to deploy and specify it in your launch template. You can update the AMI ID when a recent version is published.

To do that, you could retrieve the latest version of an AMI ID with the following AWS CLI command:

```
aws ssm get-parameter --name /aws/service/eks/optimized-ami/$EKS_VERSION/amazon-linux-2/recommended/image_id --region $AWS_REGION --query "Parameter.Value" --output text
```

The preceding AWS Systems Manager (SSM) service command requires the K8s version number and the AWS region for amazon-linux-2 instances. The command may return the latest AMI ID of a given K8s version. For example, the following command returns the AMI ID for K8s version 1.31 in the us-east-1 region as **ami-0eddf4b3eca8324cc**:

---

[7] https://docs.aws.amazon.com/eks/latest/userguide/update-managed-node-group.html

```
aws ssm get-parameter --name /aws/service/eks/optimized-
ami/1.31/amazon-linux-2/recommended/image_id --region us-east-1
--query "Parameter.Value" --output text
```

You can retrieve the same information from the AWS console with the following steps:

Navigate to EC2 ➤ AMIs, select public images, then search for k8s_1.31.

Version **1.31** is the K8s version you want to deploy. You should find a list of image IDs with creation dates if you scroll to the right side of the page. You can choose the latest AMI ID according to the creation date.

Name	AMI name	AMI ID
	ubuntu-eks-pro/k8s_1.31/imag...	ami-029dd0b240825b984
	ubuntu-eks/k8s_1.31/images/h...	ami-074009be02e315f3d
	ubuntu-eks-pro/k8s_1.31/imag...	ami-0f4ff42c3f6b706d6

Figure 6-7. Sample AMI images

We will use the **ami-0dcb2d7d97bcda689** and **ami-0eddf4b3eca8324cc** AMI IDs to demonstrate how to update nodes from one version to another in the custom template example. You should find the custom template example in the **chapter06-launch-template** folder under the **node** module. The **launch-template.tf** file contains the Terraform code below:

```
resource "aws_launch_template" "launch_template" {
  name = "custom-launch-template"
```

CHAPTER 6   CLUSTER NODES

```
#######################################
#optimized ami for k8s version 1.31 is ami-0eddf4b3eca8324cc
/* start with K8s version 1.30 image ID ami-0dcb2d7d97bcda689
and change it
to k8s version 1.31 after cluster upgrade
*/
  image_id = "ami-0dcb2d7d97bcda689"
  block_device_mappings {
     device_name = "/dev/sdf"
     ebs {
       volume_size = 50
     }
  }
  ebs_optimized = true
  metadata_options {
    http_endpoint                = "enabled"
    http_tokens                  = "required"
    http_put_response_hop_limit = 1
    instance_metadata_tags       = "enabled"
  }
  network_interfaces {
   associate_public_ip_address = false
  }
#user data encoding
user_data = filebase64("${path.module}/user-data.sh")
  tag_specifications {
    resource_type = "instance"
     tags = {
        name = "instance-with-custom-launch-template"
     }
  }
}
```

CHAPTER 6 CLUSTER NODES

A launch template has many configurations. Notwithstanding, the two most important configurations are the user data and the AMI ID (image ID). The AMI ID enables you to update nodes from your Terraform code when a new AMI update becomes available. Terraform refers to the AMI ID as an image ID. An image ID is an optional argument but most important if you want to update images from your Terraform code.

By default, EKS will deploy an optimized AMI ID that corresponds to the K8s version of the cluster if you do not specify any image ID in your Terraform code. You can change the default behavior by specifying your own AMI ID.

The following activity will demonstrate how to implement a custom launch template with two AMI IDs starting with the image ID for K8s version 1.30 (**ami-0dcb2d7d97bcda689**) and upgrading to the image ID for K8s version 1.31 (**ami-0eddf4b3eca8324cc**). You can start from version 1.31 and upgrade it to version 1.32.

Terraform Code Execution

1. Make sure the image ID is set to **ami-0dcb2d7d97bcda689** in the custom launch template.

2. Deploy the Terraform code in the chapter06-launch-template.

   ```
   cd chapter06-launch-template
   terraform init
   terraform apply
   ```

3. Update context.

   ```
   aws eks update-kubeconfig --name public-endpoint-cluster
   ```

CHAPTER 6 CLUSTER NODES

4. Retrieve the version of the node.

   kubectl get nodes

   The output should state the K8s version of the nodes as

NAME	STATUS	ROLES	AGE	VERSION
ip-10-0-4-204.ec2.internal	Ready	<none>	13m	v1.30.4-eks-a737599

5. You should find the launch template and the image ID when you go to **EKS, click the cluster name, then click the compute tab.** Note that AWS provides no update information even though the AMI ID is a version below the current Kubernetes version.

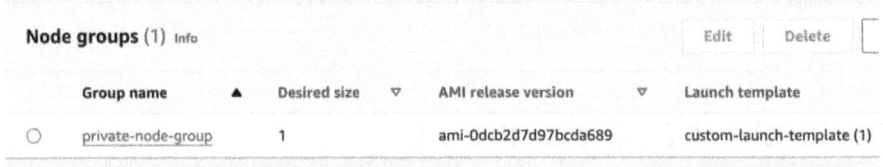

Figure 6-8. EKS node group console

6. Replace the image ID in the custom launch template file in the Terraform code with the image ID for K8s version 1.31.

   image_id = "**ami-0eddf4b3eca8324cc**"

7. Apply the changes.

   terraform apply

8. Verify the version of the nodes from the EKS console or with kubectl.

   kubectl get nodes

CHAPTER 6   CLUSTER NODES

You should notice the updated version as **ami-0eddf4b3eca8324cc and a new launch template**.

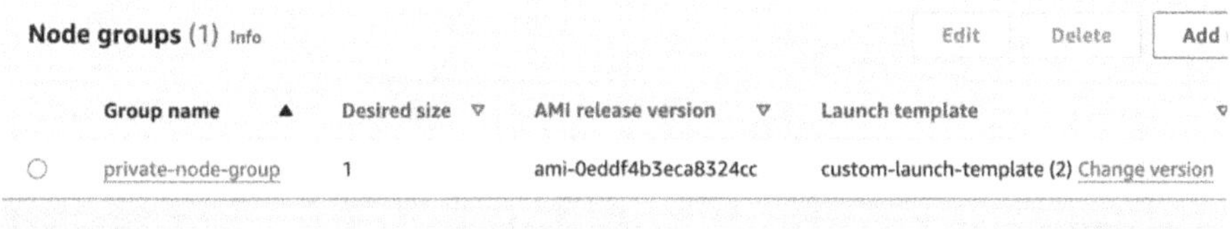

Figure 6-9. EKS node group console

Custom Launch Template Instantiation

This section explain how you can instantiate a custom template. You must first create the template and call the custom launch template in the worker node code with the launch template block to override the default template. The block requires the ID or the name of the launch template and the version. You may specify the **$Latest** value to instruct EKS to deploy the latest launch template for your cluster. You can also specify a specific version number for EKS to deploy.

```
resource "aws_eks_node_group" "nodes" {
  cluster_name = var.cluster_name
  node_group_name = var.node_name
  node_role_arn  = aws_iam_role.nodes_role.arn
  subnet_ids = var.subnets_id
  capacity_type  = "ON_DEMAND"
  instance_types = ["t3.small"]
  launch_template {
  id = aws_launch_template.launch_template.id
  version = "$Latest"
  }
  scaling_config {
     desired_size = 1
```

173

```
      max_size = 3
      min_size = 1
   }
   update_config {
      max_unavailable = 1
   }
   labels = {
      name = var.tag
   }
   depends_on = [ aws_iam_role.nodes_role ]
}
```

User Data File

You will find a reference to the encoded user data file in the launch template as follows:

`user_data = filebase64("${path.module}/user-data.sh")`

The **user-data.sh** file contains information about startup commands and bootstrap script for the node groups. You will find the script in the **user-data.sh** file as follows:

```
MIME-Version: 1.0
Content-Type: multipart/mixed; boundary="==MYBOUNDARY=="

--==MYBOUNDARY==
Content-Type: text/x-shellscript; charset="us-ascii"

#!/bin/bash
/etc/eks/bootstrap.sh public-endpoint-cluster \
  --kubelet-extra-args '--max-pods=120' \
  --use-max-pods false

--==MYBOUNDARY==
```

The file has an extremely strict format, so be careful if you decide to edit it. The most important part of the file is the **/etc/eks/bootstrap.sh public-endpoint-cluster** command, where **public-endpoint-cluster** is the name of the cluster. The primary purpose of the **bootstrap.sh** script is to allow the nodes created with custom templates to join the cluster.

You can specify additional optional arguments in the script such as the **kubelet-extra-args** argument which determines the pod density of the nodes. We will discuss pod density in the next chapter. The user data does more than just joining a node to a cluster and modifying the node's pod density. You can include custom commands or scripts to install additional packages or configuration files on the nodes.

Self-Managed Node Deployment

You create a self-managed node if you use your own AMI or modify the Amazon AMI to include your specific requirements. The first step in this process is to create your own AMI and use it to create your cluster node groups.

You can create your own AMI from scratch or from an Amazon-based image. We will demonstrate the latter with the AWS console and the Packer tool afterwards.

Creating AMI with AWS Console

1. Navigate to AWS console ➤ Images ➤ AMI.
2. Select Public images.

CHAPTER 6   CLUSTER NODES

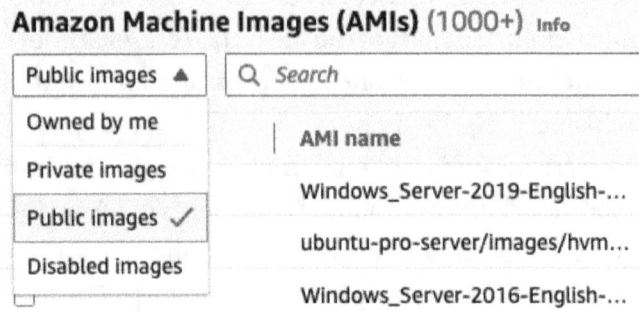

Figure 6-10. Amazon Machine Image console

3. Search for amazon-eks-node-1.30 or k8_1.30 or K8s_1.31 from the search box.

4. Select the first AMI.

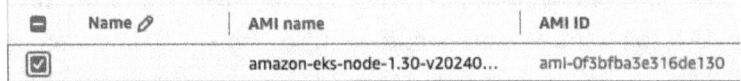

Figure 6-11. Amazon Machine Image console image selection

5. Click the Launch instance from AMI.

6. Type a name.

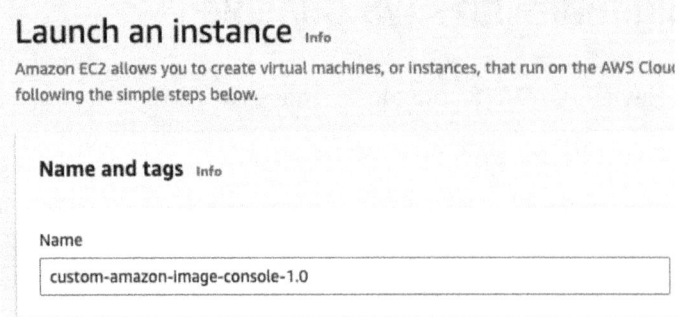

Figure 6-12. Launch template console - Launch an instance

176

CHAPTER 6   CLUSTER NODES

7. Select instance type.

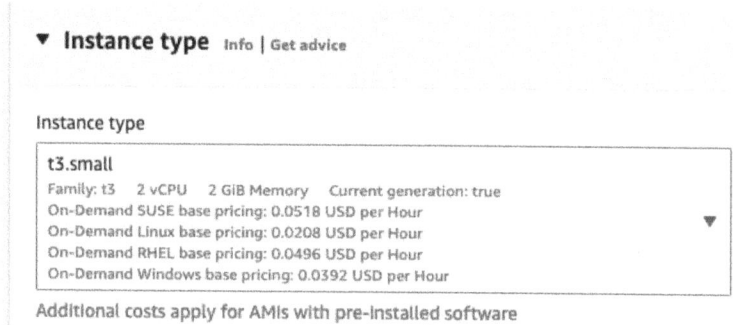

Figure 6-13. Amazon Machine Image console - instance type

8. Select your SSH keys or proceed without keys. You select SSH keys if you want to log in to the instance with SSH and install packages before you create the image.

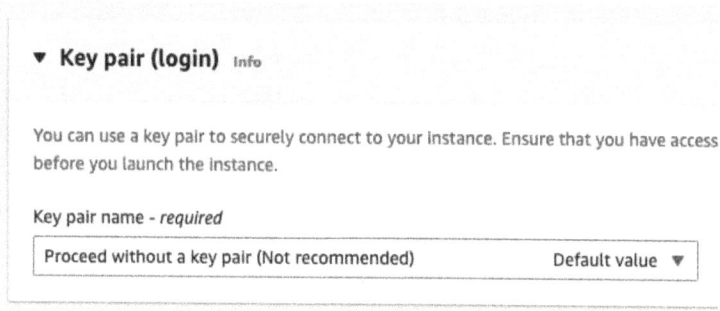

Figure 6-14. Launch template console - key pair (login)

177

CHAPTER 6   CLUSTER NODES

9. Click Launch and wait for the instance to finish initialization.

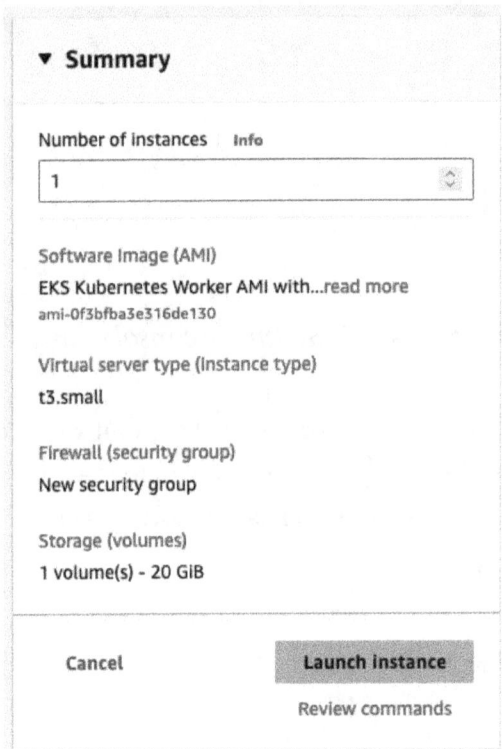

Figure 6-15. Launch template console - summary

10. Select the instance and create an image from the instance.

CHAPTER 6   CLUSTER NODES

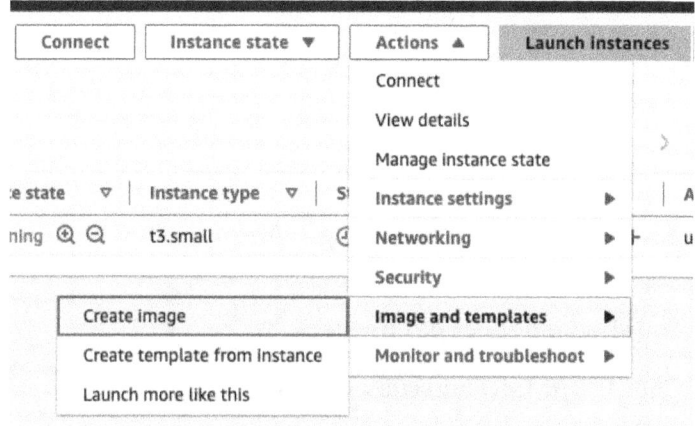

Figure 6-16. *Launch template console - Action*

11. Type the name of the image and click Create.

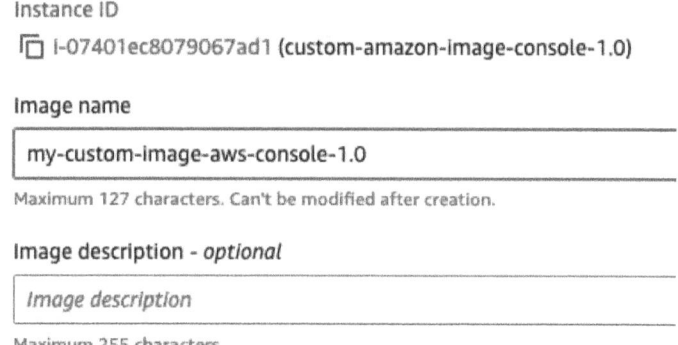

Figure 6-17. *Launch template console - Instance ID*

12. Terminate the instance from the EC2 console.
13. Navigate to AMI and select owned by me.

179

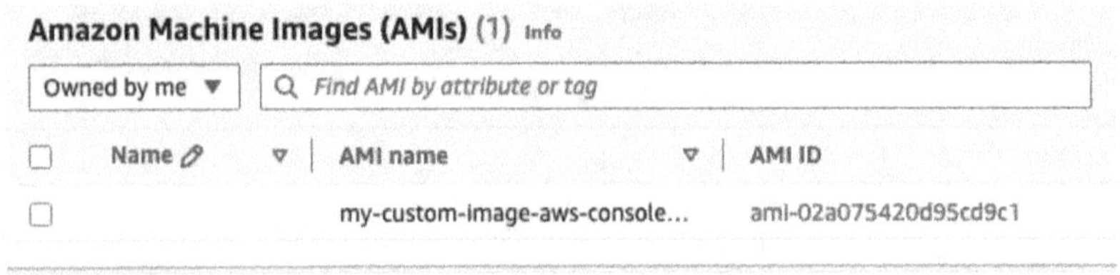

CHAPTER 6 CLUSTER NODES

Amazon Machine Images (AMIs) (1) Info		
Owned by me ▼	Q Find AMI by attribute or tag	
☐ Name	AMI name	AMI ID
☐	my-custom-image-aws-console...	ami-02a075420d95cd9c1

Figure 6-18. *Amazon Machine Image console*

14. You should notice your image.

15. Click the AMI ID and copy the AMI ID.

16. Modify the code in the chapter06-self-managed folder to use the new image ID as follows:

```
resource "aws_launch_template" "launch_template" {
 name = "self-managed-launch-template"
#My AWSconsole image
image_id = "ami-02a075420d95cd9c1"
  block_device_mappings {
     device_name = "/dev/sdf"
     ebs {
       volume_size = 50
     }
   }
   ebs_optimized = true
   metadata_options {
     http_endpoint              = "enabled"
     http_tokens                = "required"
     http_put_response_hop_limit = 1
     instance_metadata_tags     = "enabled"
   }
   network_interfaces {
    associate_public_ip_address = false
   }
```

```
      user_data = filebase64("${path.module}/user-data.sh")
        tag_specifications {
          resource_type = "instance"
          tags = {
            name = "test"
          }
        }
      }
```

17. Execute the Terraform code to deploy the self-managed nodes.

Creating Image with Packer

Packer is a community tool for creating identical machine images for multiple platforms from a sole source configuration. It is lightweight and runs on every major operating system. It can create machine images for multiple platforms in parallel making it highly efficient.[8]

Packer communicates with AWS during image creation. The straightforward way to enable communication is to create a public subnet for Packer by attaching an Internet gateway to the default VPC and configuring the main route table to allow Internet access.

1. Create an Internet gateway.

---

[8] https://developer.hashicorp.com/packer/docs/intro

CHAPTER 6 CLUSTER NODES

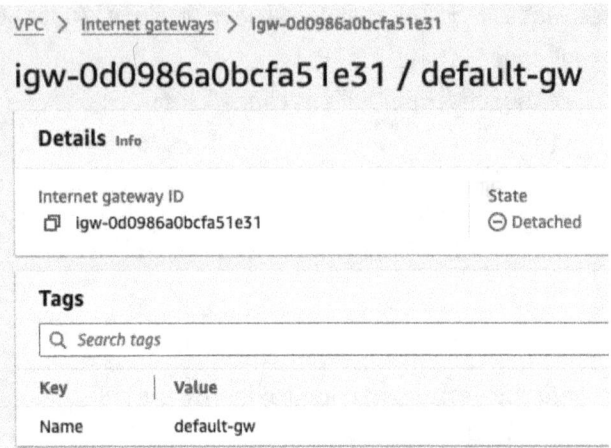

Figure 6-19. *VPC Internet gateway console*

    2. Attach the gateway to the default VPC.

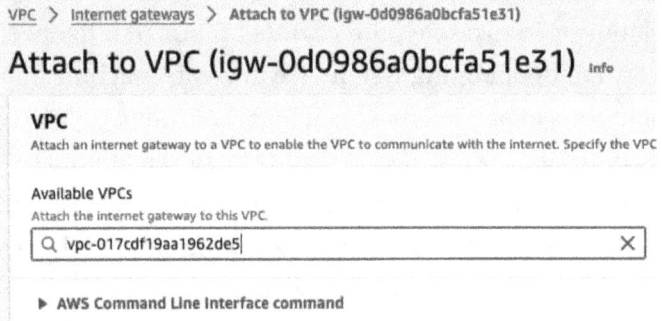

Figure 6-20. *VPC Internet gateway - attachmenet*

    3. Configure the route table to use the Internet gateway.

CHAPTER 6   CLUSTER NODES

```
VPC > Route tables > rtb-0c1fc9e3254e056e7 > Edit routes
```

Edit routes

Destination	Target
172.31.0.0/16	local
	Q local
Q 0.0.0.0/0 ×	Internet Gateway
	Q igw-0d0986a0bcfa51e31

Figure 6-21. *VPC route table console*

4. Install Packer.[9]

5. Create a Packer configuration file for the image.

   ```
   packer {
     required_plugins {
       amazon = {
         version = ">= 1.2.8"
         source  = "github.com/hashicorp/amazon"
       }
     }
   }
   packer {
     required_plugins {
       vagrant = {
         version = "~> 1"
         source = "github.com/hashicorp/vagrant"
       }
     }
   }
   ```

---
[9] https://developer.hashicorp.com/packer/tutorials/docker-get-started/get-started-install-cli

```
source "amazon-ebs" "amazon-2" {
  ami_name      = "custom-amazon-image-packer-1"
  instance_type = "t3.small"
  region        = "us-east-1"
  source_ami    = "ami-00ec84c1189958713"
  ssh_username  = "root"
}

build {
  name = "custom-amazon-build"
  sources = [
    "source.amazon-ebs.amazon-2"
  ]

  post-processor "vagrant" {}
  post-processor "compress" {}
}
```

6. Save the configuration as **eks-amazon-image-1.pkr.hcl**.

7. Build the image.

   ```
   packers build eks-amazon-image-1.pkr.hcl
   ```

8. Navigate to AWS AMI to find the newly created image.

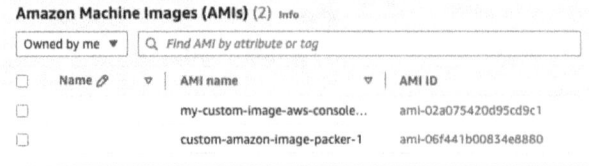

Figure 6-22. Amazon Machine Image console

9. Modify the launch template code to use the new image ID.

   ```
   resource "aws_launch_template" "launch_template" {
    name = "self-managed-launch-template"
   #my packer image
   image_id = "ami-06f441b00834e8880"
     block_device_mappings {
        device_name = "/dev/sdf"
        ebs {
          volume_size = 50
        }
     }
     ...
   ```

10. Apply the change.

    ```
    terraform apply -auto-approve
    ```

11. Verify the changes with the **kubectl get nodes** command.

12. Do not forget to delete the Internet gateway and the instances created by Packer after the deployment.

Graceful Node Group Update

In both custom launch template examples before this section, we demonstrated how to upgrade nodes from K8s version 1.30 to 1.31 by changing the AMI ID in code. Changing an old AMI ID to a new one and running the terraform apply command results in downtime for applications running on the nodes.

This could be impactful for high availability applications that demand little or no downtime. You could avoid the downtime for such applications by adopting the graceful update strategy. The steps for the strategy are as follows:

- Create a new node group with the latest AMI version.
- Migrate the application pods from the old node group to the new node group with the latest AMI.
- Terminate the old node group once the migration is successful.

Demonstration of Graceful Update Strategy

1. Destroy the launch template cluster.

    terraform destroy

2. Deploy the cluster in the chapter06-graceful-upgrade folder.

    terraform init
    terraform apply

3. Update context.

    aws eks update-kubeconfig --name public-endpoint-cluster

4. Verify the node version.

    kubectl get nodes

    This should return the node as **ip-10-0-4-100.ec2.internal**.

CHAPTER 6   CLUSTER NODES

5. Deploy pods on the node group.

   `kubectl apply -f pod/deployment.yml`

6. Verify if pods are running.

   `kubectl get pods`

7. Taint the node group to disable pod schedule. Taint determines how pods should be scheduled. It allows existing pods or pods with specific labels to run on a node. We will defer discussion on the tainted nodes to a later stage in the book.

   `kubectl taint nodes` **`ip-10-0-4-100.ec2.internal`** `dedicated=for-special-pods:NoSchedule`

8. Verify if the node is tainted.

   `kubectl describe nodes | grep Taints`

9. Uncomment the code for the node group 2 in the **main.tf** file.

   ```
   module "node-group-2" {
     source = "./dataplane/node-group-2"
     cluster_name = module.eks.cluster_name
     subnets_id = module.vpc.private_subnet_ids
   }
   ```

10. Deploy the new module.

    ```
    Terraform init
    terraform apply
    ```

11. Verify the number of nodes and note the two node versions.

    ```
    kubectl get nodes
    ```

12. Verify which node is running the pods.

    ```
    kubectl get pods -o wide
    ```

13. Drain the pods from the old node group to the new node group. Leave out the daemonsets.

    ```
    kubectl drain ip-10-0-4-100.ec2.internal --ignore-daemonsets=true
    ```

14. Verify if pods are moved to the new node group.

    ```
    kubectl get pods -o wide
    ```

15. Comment out the node group 1 in the **main.tf** file.

    ```
    /*
    module "node-group-1" {
      source = "./dataplane/node-group-1"
      cluster_name = module.eks.cluster_name
      subnets_id = module.vpc.private_subnet_ids
    }
    */
    ```

16. Delete the old node group.

    ```
    terraform apply -auto-approve
    ```

17. Verify if pods are running on the latest node.

    ```
    kubectl get pods -o wide
    kubectl get nodes
    ```

EKS will be responsible for doing all the steps explained above if you use managed node without any customization.[10]

Cluster Upgrade Tips

There are a few things you should know before you upgrade a cluster or nodes. You should first gather information about the cluster. Valuable information includes K8s cluster version, API, and node versions.

Version upgrade is incremental, meaning you cannot skip versions. For example, you cannot upgrade from K8s version 1.29 to 1.31. You must go from 1.29 to version 1.30 and then 1.31.

To upgrade your node, find a suitable AMI ID from the AWS console or use the following command:

```
aws ssm get-parameter \
--name /aws/service/eks/optimized-ami/version/amazon-linux-2/recommended/image_id \
--region region \
--query "Parameter.Value" --output text
```

Replace the region, the K8s version, and the ami-type with your own. The ami-type is **amazon-linux-2-arm64/recommended** in this example, but you can choose from one of the following options:

- amazon-linux-2023/x86_64/standard for Amazon Linux 2023 (AL2023) x86–based instances

- amazon-linux-2023/arm64/standard for AL2023 ARM instances

---

[10] https://docs.aws.amazon.com/eks/latest/userguide/managed-node-update-behavior.html

CHAPTER 6   CLUSTER NODES

- amazon-linux-2 for Amazon Linux 2 (AL2) x86-based instances

- amazon-linux-2-arm64 for AL2 ARM instances, such as AWS Graviton-based instances

Finally, don't forget to update addons and API versions. We will touch on these two later in the book.

Summary

Yet again we come to the end of another eventful chapter covering the twist and turns of creating and managing EKS node groups. We reviewed the three types of node groups and deployed two of them, managed and self-managed node groups, without touching Fargate since it is out of scope for this book. We implemented self-managed nodes with custom images created with Packer and AWS console. Finally, we demonstrated how to upgrade self-managed nodes with and without downtime. You can create and manage your cluster nodes the way you want so long as you know what to do. You can rely on AWS for the heavy lifting if you decide to maintain the default launch template, or you can perform the heavy lifting yourself if you have legitimate requirements that cannot be fulfilled by managed AWS node.

CHAPTER 7

EKS IP Address Management

Here comes Javi ready to test a single node cluster running on a t3.small instance. He only wants to run 12 replicas of the same application, each consuming less than 1MB of memory. The 2GB of memory and 2 vCPUs of the t3.small instance is more than enough to run the workload.

With the deployment at hand, he soon realized that only 9 out of the 12 pod replicas were deployed. Javi could not understand why 12 pods, each requiring 1MB, could not fit on an instance with 2GB of RAM. "Something is definitely wrong!" he exclaimed.

This is not the lack of computing resources; there must be another reason. Convinced it was not a lack of computing resources, he suspected another issue and reached out to Reena, the EKS operator, for assistance.

IP address exhaustion might be the probable cause, Reena suspected. She explained that memory and CPU resources alone are not sufficient for running workloads on an EKS cluster – network resources, such as IP addresses, are equally critical. It is always important to ensure that there are enough IP addresses before you deploy workloads on your EKS cluster, Reena advised.

To avoid falling into the same trap as Javi and to prevent unforeseen issues, it is essential to understand IP address management before deploying large workloads.

CHAPTER 7 EKS IP ADDRESS MANAGEMENT

This chapter focuses on networking and IP address management for EKS cluster nodes. You will explore how to manage IP addresses using the AWS VPC Container Network Interface (CNI) plugin. Most importantly, you will learn how the AWS CNI plugin enhances IP address capacity on nodes through IP prefixes.

Node IP Addressing

We will start by explaining how EKS manages IP addresses on nodes to optimize resource usage. A shortage of IP addresses limits a node's ability to run pods, resulting in wastage of compute resources, memory, and vCPU. In EKS clusters, having ample memory and vCPU is ineffective without sufficient IP addresses. EKS provisions pods on a node not only based on its memory and vCPU capacity but also on its ability to allocate adequate IP addresses and computing resources.

Like a physical server, each node has one or more network interface cards, which correspond to the primary Elastic Network Interface (ENI) in AWS. AWS assigns an IP address to each primary ENI. However, a single primary IP address or even two is not sufficient to distinguish traffic for the numerous pods that can run on a node.

To address the IP addressing capacity limitation, AWS introduced secondary IP addresses. As illustrated in Figure 7-1, AWS increases an instance's IP address capacity by attaching one or more secondary ENIs to the primary ENI of cluster nodes. It allocates a fixed number of IP addresses to each secondary ENI, which are then made available for use by the pods running on the node. This approach ensures that nodes have sufficient IP addresses to support their workloads.

CHAPTER 7 EKS IP ADDRESS MANAGEMENT

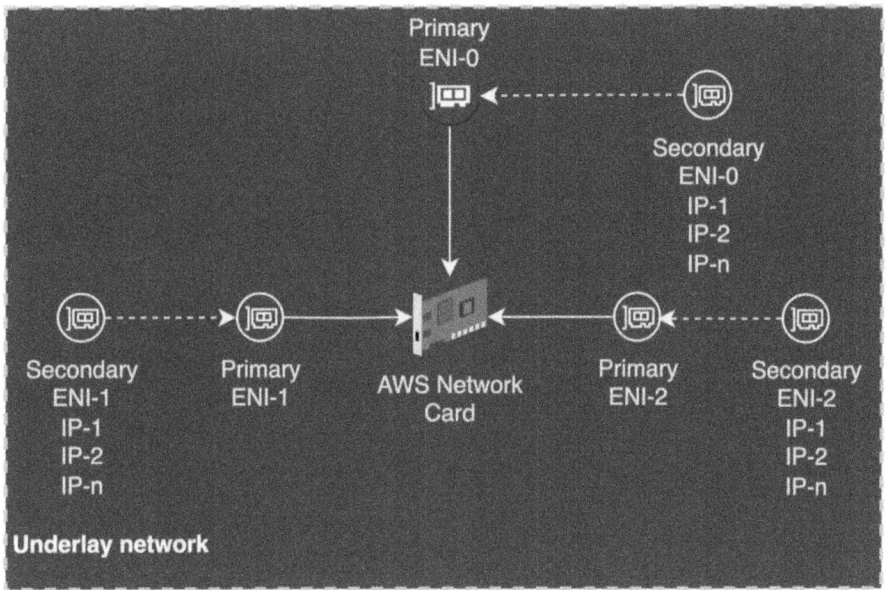

Figure 7-1. AWS network interface card

The number of primary and secondary ENIs depends on the instance type. As shown in Table 7-1, the t3.small instance type has a maximum of three primary ENIs and four IP addresses per ENI, making twelve IP addresses in total. This means the t3.small instance can consume a maximum of twelve IP addresses from its host subnet – three IPs for the primary ENIs and three IPs for each secondary ENI.

Since EKS assigns an IP address per pods, the t3.small cannot host more than 12 pods no matter how small the pods might be.

Table 7-1. Network interfaces for EC2 instances

Instance Type	No. of Network Card	Max. Network Interfaces (Primary ENIs)	IP Addresses per Interface	Number of Pods
t3.micro	1	2	2	4
t3.small	1	3	4	11
t3.medium	1	3	6	17
m6idn.32xlarge	2	16	50	786

When you launch an instance such as t3.small, AWS EC2 service creates primary ENIs depending on the cluster's node configuration and assigns each ENI a primary IP address from the host subnet. It then attaches secondary ENIs to the respective primary ENIs, assigns an IP address to each of the secondary ENIs, and reserves the remaining IP addresses for future use.

Cluster Deployment and Review

It's often easier to grasp AWS concepts through practical demonstration. Let's deploy the cluster for this chapter and examine how primary and secondary network interfaces function within EKS.

1. Deploy the Terraform code in chapter07.

   ```
   cd chapter07
   terraform init
   terraform apply
   ```

CHAPTER 7   EKS IP ADDRESS MANAGEMENT

2. Update context.

   aws eks update-kubeconfig --name public-endpoint-cluster

3. Retrieve the version of the node.

   Kubectl get nodes

4. Examine the network interface of the worker node.

   Navigate to EC2, click the instance, scroll down and click the Networking tab, scroll down again to find the two primary ENIs with device indexes 0 and 1.

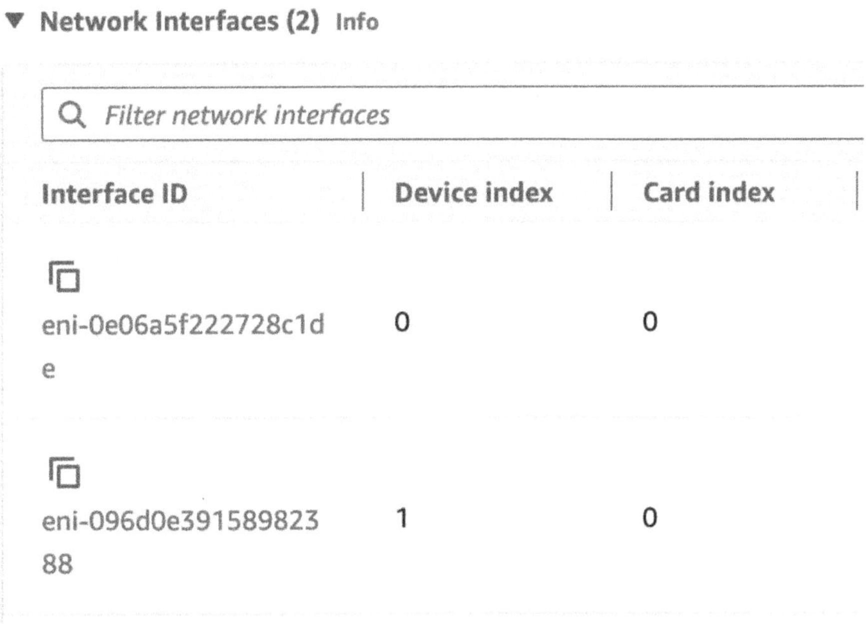

▼ **Network Interfaces (2)** Info

Interface ID	Device index	Card index
eni-0e06a5f222728c1de	0	0
eni-096d0e39158982388	1	0

Figure 7-2. Network interface

CHAPTER 7   EKS IP ADDRESS MANAGEMENT

Observe that the EC2 service created only two primary ENIs initially.

5. Scroll to the right to find the IP addresses of the primary ENIs, which are 10.0.4.182 and 10.0.4.83 in this case.

Description	Public IPv4 address	Private IPv4 address
–	–	10.0.4.182
aws-K8S-i-0065191b0…	–	10.0.4.83

Figure 7-3. Network interface - IP Address of primary ENIs

6. Examine the secondary ENIs.

   Click on one of the link of the primary ENIs to reveal the corresponding secondary ENIs and their IP addresses.

CHAPTER 7   EKS IP ADDRESS MANAGEMENT

▼ IP addresses

Private IPv4 address
🗐 10.0.4.182

Private IPv4 DNS
🗐 ip-10-0-4-182.ec2.internal

Public IPv4 address
-

Public IPv4 DNS
-

Secondary public IPv4 addresses
-

Secondary private IPv4 addresses
🗐 10.0.4.113
🗐 10.0.4.65
🗐 10.0.4.125

Figure 7-4. *Secondary network interface*

The primary ENIs with the IP address 10.0.4.182 has a secondary ENI with three IP addresses, 10.0.4.113, 10.0.4.65, and 10.0.4.125.

7. Scroll down to find the secondary ENI attached to the primary ENI (eni-attach-02a1b3f6449351046).

▼ Network interface attachment

Attachment status
⊘ Attached

Attachment ID
🗐 eni-attach-02a1b3f6449351046

Delete on termination
True

Network card index
0

Figure 7-5. *Network interface attachment*

8. Repeat the same for the second primary ENI.

CHAPTER 7   EKS IP ADDRESS MANAGEMENT

▼ IP addresses

Private IPv4 address
🗐 10.0.4.83

Private IPv4 DNS
🗐 ip-10-0-4-83.ec2.internal

Public IPv4 address
-

Public IPv4 DNS
-

Secondary public IPv4 addresses
-

Secondary private IPv4 addresses
🗐 10.0.4.230
🗐 10.0.4.120
🗐 10.0.4.127

Figure 7-6. Secondary network interface

9. Delete one of the primary ENIs.

   Click the link for one of the primary ENIs and attempt to delete the interface by clicking the Delete network interface button.

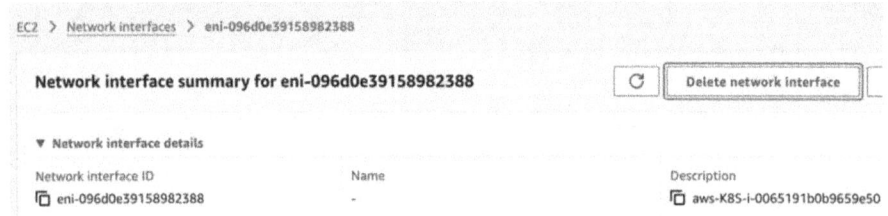

Figure 7-7. Attempt primary ENI deletion

You should see a disabled deletion button.

The litmus test for primary and secondary ENIs lies in whether you can delete them from a node or not. Primary ENIs have permanent attachment to a node. You cannot create or detach them once a node is launched.[1] In contrast, secondary ENIs are ephemeral, meaning you can attach or detach them from a node, whether the node is in a running or stopped state.

You can attach ENIs as cold, hot, or warm depending on the status of the node. You attach an ENI as cold when a node is in stopped state. You can attach an ENI to a node as hot when the node is running and active, for example, after cluster deployment or after you add a new node to the cluster. Hot attachment is important when you do not want to lose capacity or add a new node to the cluster.

Furthermore, you can attach ENIs as warm when the instance is in a stop state. You must stop the instance, attach an ENI, and reboot the instance afterward. You may lose capacity during warm attachment.

AWS attaches primary ENIs in their cold state and secondary in either hot or warm state. The different mode of attachments allows for efficient management of network interfaces in varying node conditions.

The VPC Container Network Interface

Secondary IP addresses play a crucial role in facilitating communication among pods within an EKS cluster. EKS utilizes these secondary IP addresses to establish an overlay network, enabling seamless pod-to-pod communication across the cluster. An overlay network operates on top of an underlying host network (known as the underlay network), abstracting the network infrastructure to simplify internal pod communication.

By default, the Amazon VPC Container Network Interface (VPC CNI) plugin or addon is responsible for the overlay network. It relies on secondary IP addresses to facilitate pod-to-pod communication on the overlay network, enabling pods to use the same IP address as the host VPC network.[2]

---

[1] https://docs.aws.amazon.com/AWSEC2/latest/UserGuide/network-interface-attachments.html
[2] https://github.com/aws/amazon-vpc-cni-k8s

The VPC CNI plugin manages the secondary IP addresses and their assignment on the overlay network. It supports security groups for pods. That means it can restrict pod communications within the overlay network.

The VPC CNI plugin can increase the default number of secondary IP addresses that a node can support, allowing for better scalability. It also accelerates pod launches and efficiently manages IP address allocation, improving the overall performance and responsiveness of the cluster. Additionally, the plugin offers various other features to optimize network management and pod connectivity.

The VPC CNI plugin automates IP address management for pods with its Local IP Address Management (L-IPAM) daemon (IPAMD). IPAMD creates and attaches secondary ENIs to nodes and makes their IPs available for pods. It does so by allocating a pool of IP addresses or prefixes known as warm pools from the IP range of the node's subnet. The IPAMD maintains the warm pool of IP addresses or prefixes on each node for assignment to pods as they are scheduled.[3]

Pod Density

This section will explain how to compute the pod density of a node. Pod density refers to the total IP address capacity of a node. It determines how many pods can run on a given node. Default pod density is given by the formula

```
Default pod density = ENI*(IP-1) + 2
```

---

[3] https://aws.amazon.com/blogs/containers/amazon-vpc-cni-increases-pods-per-node-limits/

where ENI is the maximum number of network interfaces of an instance type and IP is the number of IP addresses per interface. The -1 indicates the IP address consumed by the primary ENIs. As shown in Figure 7-8, the primary ENIs consumed three private IPv4 addresses, and the secondary ENIs consumed nine addresses.

Figure 7-8. Primary and secondary IP addresses

The +2 indicates the number of IP addresses reserved for host network mode or system pods such as the kube-proxy and VPC CNI pods. Host network mode pods run on the primary ENI's IP addresses and share the same network namespace as the host.[4]

As an example, t3.small instances have a maximum of three ENIs and four IP addresses per ENI, one for primary and three for each secondary ENI. Hence, the default pod density for t3.small instances = 3 * (4-1) + 2 = 11 pods.

This means you can deploy a maximum of nine application pods on t3.small if the instance has enough resources and two host network mode pods, making 11 in total.

---

[4]https://aws.github.io/aws-eks-best-practices/networking/vpc-cni/

CHAPTER 7   EKS IP ADDRESS MANAGEMENT

An M5 instance has a maximum of three ENIs and ten IPs per ENI. This implies 3 * (10-1) + 2 = 29 default IP addresses.

You can retrieve pod density information for an instance with the following AWS CLI command:

```
aws ec2 describe-instance-types \
    --filters "Name=instance-type,Values=t3.*" \
    --query "InstanceTypes[].{ \
        Type: InstanceType, \
        MaxENI: NetworkInfo.MaximumNetworkInterfaces, \
        IPv4addr: NetworkInfo.Ipv4AddressesPerInterface}" \
 --output table
```

Replace the t3.* with your own instance type.

Pod Density Demonstration

We will examine how pod density could constrain your pod deployments with an example. We will deploy a pod on the cluster you provisioned for this chapter and examine the IP address constraint on the node.

1. Execute pods on the cluster.

    ```
    kubectl apply -f pod/deployment.yml
    ```

    The content of the deployment.yml manifest is as follows:

    ```
    apiVersion: apps/v1
    kind: Deployment
    metadata:
      name: nginx-deployment
      labels:
        app: nginx
    ```

CHAPTER 7 EKS IP ADDRESS MANAGEMENT

```
spec:
  replicas: 7
  selector:
    matchLabels:
      app: nginx
  template:
    metadata:
      labels:
        app: nginx
    spec:
      containers:
      - name: nginx
        image: nginx:1.14.2
        ports:
        - containerPort: 80
```

2. Observe the output in the AWS console.

   Navigate to **EC2 ➤ instances ➤ Networking tab**.

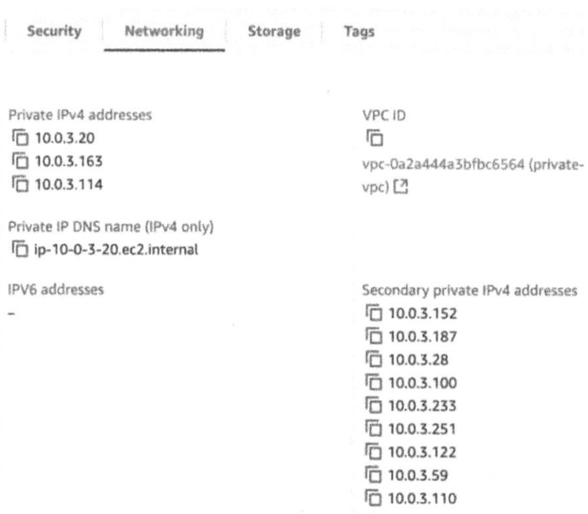

Figure 7-9. *Primary and secondary IP addresses-Networking*

CHAPTER 7   EKS IP ADDRESS MANAGEMENT

The number of secondary IP addresses has increased from six to nine and primary ENIs from two to three.

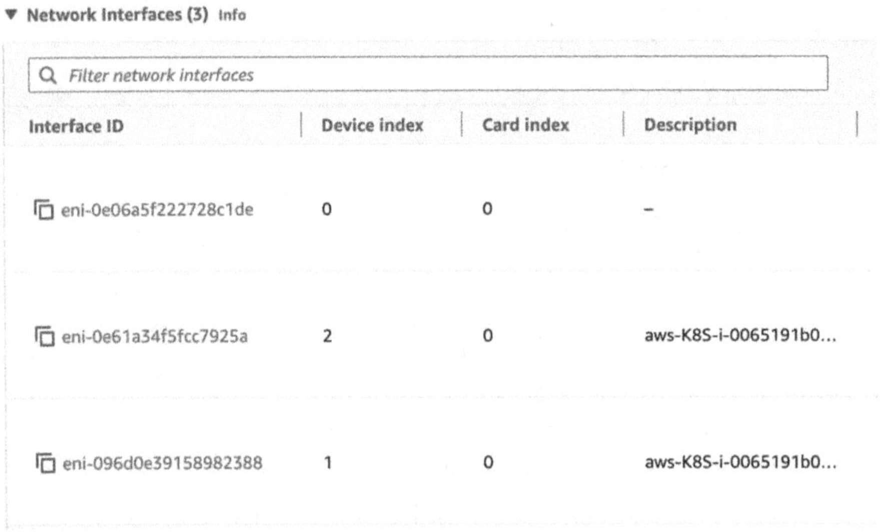

Interface ID	Device index	Card index	Description
eni-0e06a5f222728c1de	0	0	–
eni-0e61a34f5fcc7925a	2	0	aws-K8S-i-0065191b0...
eni-096d0e39158982388	1	0	aws-K8S-i-0065191b0...

Figure 7-10. *Network interface IDs*

3. Verify if all the pods are running.

   kubectl get pods

   You should find all the seven pods in the running state.

   ```
   NAME                                READY   STATUS
   nginx-deployment-d556bf558-4rvj8    1/1     Running
   nginx-deployment-d556bf558-bzqp5    1/1     Running
   nginx-deployment-d556bf558-cjl99    1/1     Running
   nginx-deployment-d556bf558-g2drq    1/1     Running
   nginx-deployment-d556bf558-jrzm4    1/1     Running
   nginx-deployment-d556bf558-kcrfg    1/1     Running
   nginx-deployment-d556bf558-mk6gw    1/1     Running
   ```

CHAPTER 7   EKS IP ADDRESS MANAGEMENT

4. Increase the number of replicas in the yaml file to nine.

   ```
   apiVersion: apps/v1
   kind: Deployment
   metadata:
     name: nginx-deployment
     labels:
       app: nginx
   spec:
     replicas: 9
     selector:
       matchLabels:
         app: nginx
     template:
       metadata:
         labels:
           app: nginx
       spec:
         containers:
         - name: nginx
           image: nginx:1.14.2
           ports:
           - containerPort: 80
   ```

5. Redeploy the pod and observe the results.

   ```
   kubectl apply -f pod/deployment.yml
   ```

6. Verify if all the pods are running.

   ```
   kubectl get pods
   ```

CHAPTER 7   EKS IP ADDRESS MANAGEMENT

7. You should find some pending pods even though you have enough IPs.

NAME	READY	STATUS
nginx-deployment-d556bf558-4rvj8	1/1	Running
nginx-deployment-d556bf558-bzqp5	1/1	Running
nginx-deployment-d556bf558-cjl99	1/1	Running
nginx-deployment-d556bf558-cv6l6	0/1	Pending
nginx-deployment-d556bf558-g2drq	1/1	Running
nginx-deployment-d556bf558-jrzm4	1/1	Running
nginx-deployment-d556bf558-kcrfg	1/1	Running
nginx-deployment-d556bf558-mk6gw	1/1	Running
nginx-deployment-d556bf558-qg4nm	0/1	Pending

8. Log in to one of the running pods.

   `kubectl exec -it nginx-deployment-d556bf558-4rvj8 sh`

   where `nginx-deployment-d556bf558-4rvj8` is the name of one of the running pods.

9. Find the total memory consumption.

   `cat /sys/fs/cgroup/memory.current`
   2555904 bytes = 2.56MB

10. Find the CPU usage.

    `cat /sys/fs/cgroup/cpu.stat`
    usage_usec 24153
    user_usec 24153
    system_usec 0
    core_sched.force_idle_usec 0
    nr_periods 0

```
nr_throttled 0
throttled_usec 0
nr_bursts 0
burst_usec 0
```

You could infer the root cause of the pending pods from the above analysis which could still be the IP address constraints even though we have not exhausted all secondary IPs.

Pod Density with Prefix

As you observed from the preceding demonstration, the private IP addresses are the major bottleneck for resource management in EKS. Since private IP addresses are free of charge, it does not make sense to constrain valuable compute resources whatsoever because of lack of private IPs.

As demonstrated earlier, private IP addresses are a significant bottleneck for resource management in EKS. Since private IP addresses incur no additional cost, it is inefficient to limit valuable compute resources due to a shortage of IPs. You can maximize the available IP addresses to ensure that EKS clusters fully utilize their compute capacity, memory, and vCPU without being restricted by IP address constraints.

Realizing the significant waste of resources brought about by the secondary IP addressing management scheme, AWS released the VPC CNI version 1.9 in 2021 to address the shortcomings. They introduced the IP address prefix assignment mode literally removing IP address restriction on nodes. With prefix assignments, the number of pods per node is no longer constrained by the number of interfaces and the number of IPs per interface.

However, not all instances support the new prefix assignment mode. The prefix assignment is only applicable for AWS Nitro System instances. The AWS Nitro System is a lightweight hypervisor for the next-generation AWS EC2 instances. It enables AWS to innovate faster, further reduce cost for customers, and improve security and pod density.[5]

The VPC CNI prefix assignment mode allows you to run more pods per node on AWS Nitro-based EC2 instance types. You achieve this by assigning a /28 IPv4 address prefix to the ENIs of a given instance type if the VPC CIDR block has enough IP address space.

With the IP address prefix, a t3.small instance will leapfrog from 11 pods or IP addresses to 146. The computation is given by

- **Maximum number of interfaces * ((No.of IPs per interface -1) * 16 IPs per prefix) + 2**
- **= 3 ENIs * ((4-1) * 16 IPs per prefix) + 2**
- **= 146** pods per t3.small instance type[6]

In theory, a t3.small instance can run 146 pods if they have enough compute resources or K8s best practices support it. K8s scalability guide recommends a maximum number of 110 pods per node, and in most cases, this will be the maximum enforced by the CNI unless a cluster creator decides otherwise.

Prefix Assignment Mode Demonstration

Let us demonstrate how we can increase the number of IPs for the same t3.small node from 12 to 146 to run as many pods as possible.

---

[5] https://aws.amazon.com/ec2/nitro/
[6] https://github.com/aws/amazon-vpc-cni-k8s/blob/master/misc/eni-max-pods.txt

CHAPTER 7   EKS IP ADDRESS MANAGEMENT

You should find the code for this demonstration in the chapter07-prefix folder. The three key things to pay attention to in the code are the instance type, CNI addon, and the user data.

- Prefix assignment requires an AWS Nitro instance type.

    The AWS Nitro System is a collection of hardware and software components that enable high performance, high availability, and high security. It provides bare metal capabilities that eliminate virtualization overhead. Nitro instances support workloads that require full access to host hardware.[7]

- VPC CNI addon.

    The VPC CNI addon takes care of the address management. It increases the number of IPs on a node beyond the maximum set by the secondary IP address allocation scheme. You must deploy the VPC CNI addon and set the prefix delegation mode to true as in the following code snippet:

```
resource "aws_eks_addon" "vpc_cni_addon" {
  cluster_name = aws_eks_cluster.public_endpoint_cluster.name
  addon_name   = "vpc-cni"
   configuration_values = jsonencode({
     env = {
       ENABLE_PREFIX_DELEGATION = "true"
       WARM_PREFIX_TARGET = "1"
     }
   })
}
```

---

[7] https://docs.aws.amazon.com/ec2/latest/instancetypes/ec2-nitro-instances.html

Setting the ENABLE_PREFIX_DELEGATION argument to true triggers prefix IP address assignment mode.

- User data configuration.

The user data script is responsible for configuring the maximum number of pods per node to keep up with the K8s best practices. The following user data script specifies a maximum of 120 pods for the t3.small node outside the K8s limit but within the upper limit of 146 IPs and 10 pods above the K8s threshold:

```
MIME-Version: 1.0
Content-Type: multipart/mixed;
boundary="==MYBOUNDARY=="
--==MYBOUNDARY==
Content-Type: text/x-shellscript; charset="us-ascii"
#!/bin/bash
/etc/eks/bootstrap.sh public-endpoint-cluster \
    --kubelet-extra-args '--max-pods=120' \
    --use-max-pods false
--==MYBOUNDARY==
```

Verification

Use the following steps to verify the deployment:

1. Deploy the cluster in the chapter07-prefix folder.

   ```
   cd chapter07-prefix
   terraform init
   terraform apply
   ```

CHAPTER 7   EKS IP ADDRESS MANAGEMENT

2. Update user context after Terraform script execution.

   ```
   aws eks update-kubeconfig --name public-
   endpoint-cluster
   ```

3. Find CNI version.

   ```
   kubectl describe daemonset aws-node --namespace kube-
   system | grep amazon-k8s-cni: | cut -d : -f 3
   ```

4. Verify the /28 prefix configuration.

   ```
   aws ec2 describe-instances --filters "Name=tag-
   key,Values=eks:cluster-name" \
     "Name=tag-value,Values=public-endpoint-cluster" \
     --query 'Reservations[*].Instances[].{InstanceId:
   InstanceId, Prefixes: NetworkInterfaces[].
   Ipv4Prefixes[]}'
   ```

5. Find cluster nodes.

   ```
   kubectl get nodes
   ```

6. Use the node's name to find the maximum number of IPs per node according to K8s best practices.

   ```
   kubectl describe node ip-10-0-3-114.ec2.internal | grep
   'pods\|PrivateIPv4Address'
   ```

7. Verify if you can run more pods than nine with the deployment.yml file in the pod folder.

   ```
   kubectl apply -f pod/deployment.yml
   ```

8. Get the number of nodes running.

   ```
   kubectl get pod
   ```

CHAPTER 7   EKS IP ADDRESS MANAGEMENT

9. Scale the number of pods to 30.

   ```
   kubectl scale deployment nginx-deployment --replicas 30
   ```

10. You should find 30 pods in running state on the same instance which failed to run 9 pods in the last demonstration.[8]

    ```
    NAME                                    READY   STATUS
    nginx-deployment-d556bf558-65p8g        1/1     Running
    nginx-deployment-d556bf558-6h58n        1/1     Running
    nginx-deployment-d556bf558-7tx2f        1/1     Running
    nginx-deployment-d556bf558-9l4mf        1/1     Running
    nginx-deployment-d556bf558-bmdzx        1/1     Running
    nginx-deployment-d556bf558-cbggc        1/1     Running
    nginx-deployment-d556bf558-cgkdn        1/1     Running
    nginx-deployment-d556bf558-cprq2        1/1     Running
    nginx-deployment-d556bf558-fndnm        1/1     Running
    nginx-deployment-d556bf558-gfdbr        1/1     Running
    nginx-deployment-d556bf558-jgmm4        1/1     Running
    nginx-deployment-d556bf558-jldvq        1/1     Running
    nginx-deployment-d556bf558-kqjdt        1/1     Running
    nginx-deployment-d556bf558-lssv6        1/1     Running
    nginx-deployment-d556bf558-m9292        1/1     Running
    nginx-deployment-d556bf558-mck7q        1/1     Running
    nginx-deployment-d556bf558-nrbpm        1/1     Running
    nginx-deployment-d556bf558-plsrt        1/1     Running
    nginx-deployment-d556bf558-pzbvt        1/1     Running
    nginx-deployment-d556bf558-qmpfj        1/1     Running
    nginx-deployment-d556bf558-qp2mq        1/1     Running
    ```

---

[8] https://docs.aws.amazon.com/eks/latest/userguide/managing-vpc-cni.html

```
nginx-deployment-d556bf558-rbll2    1/1    Running
nginx-deployment-d556bf558-t4qgs    1/1    Running
nginx-deployment-d556bf558-t7mzm    1/1    Running
nginx-deployment-d556bf558-vjxzh    1/1    Running
nginx-deployment-d556bf558-x4vvv    1/1    Running
nginx-deployment-d556bf558-x5q79    1/1    Running
nginx-deployment-d556bf558-xmd2w    1/1    Running
nginx-deployment-d556bf558-xwgvg    1/1    Running
nginx-deployment-d556bf558-zmmz5    1/1    Running
```

Summary

Every EKS node consists of one or more primary ENIs. Attached to each ENI is a secondary ENI. Each secondary ENI can host one or more IP addresses determined by the instance type. The secondary IP addressing scheme is wasteful as it constrains memory and vCPU resources. Unlike the secondary IP address scheme, the prefix assignment mode virtually removes the IP address constraints in EKS. It is the modern way of managing IP addresses in EKS. However, implementation of the prefix assignment mode requires AWS Nitro System instances and addons. That means clusters deployed with old non-nitro instances can only implement secondary IP addresses. This chapter has demonstrated how to manage IP addresses efficiently on AWS Nitro system instances with prefix assignment mode. We showed how the IP address prefix overcomes the default IP address limitations with AWS "Nitro nodes" and VPC CNI addon. The next chapter will focus on addons. We will discuss diverse kinds of addon and how they extend cluster capabilities.

CHAPTER 8

EKS Addons

There are many occasions where you would want to extend the capabilities of your EKS cluster to make the cluster more efficient as we saw in Chapter 7. In Chapter 7, we were able to extend the pod density of a t3.small instance from 12 IP addresses to 120 addresses with the help of the VPC CNI plugin. Plugins, also known as addons, are software designed to support or extend the operational capabilities of EKS clusters. These include observability, efficient networking, autoscaling, and service integration. The type of addons and how they operate will be an important learning and a foundation for more advanced topics such as service mesh, service integration, persistent storage, and more. This chapter begins an extensive discussion about addons and ends with addon deployment and upgrades. The goal here is to offer a high-level introduction to the topic to complete the discussion on the EKS cluster components. Further application of addons will follow later in the book. You should learn about diverse kinds of addons and when to use them after going through the chapter.

Controllers

In this section, we will study the fundamentals of addons and controllers in EKSs and explain why they are essential. As a cluster, running uncoordinated can lead to instability, affecting its performance, scalability, and its survival. To prevent cluster instability, K8s must continuously manage and control the states of all objects to keep them coordinated.

CHAPTER 8 EKS ADDONS

EKS clusters rely on addons and controllers for cluster synchronization, automating and enforcing the desired state of their cluster resources. Controllers continuously monitor the cluster objects, comparing their current states with the desired states. They take corrective actions to reconcile the differences if they find any discrepancies between the current and the desired state of an object.

The desired state may be specified by a cluster operator, administrator or a developer in a specification or a YAML file for a controller to enforce. This could be anything from how many pods should run on a cluster to how much memory the pod should consume.

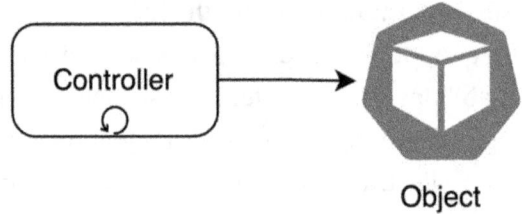

Figure 8-1. *Controller and K8s object*

Figure 8-1 illustrates how a controller monitors an object to maintain its desired state. A controller is like a thermostat in an electric iron. It monitors the temperature of the iron and either reduces or increases it to ensure that the iron stays within the desired temperature.

K8s object controllers are themselves monitored and managed by the controller manager. A controller manager is a K8s component that oversees the activities of object controllers. It is a control loop that monitors and regulates the state of a K8s cluster. It subscribes to information about the current state of the cluster and objects within it and triggers object controllers to move the cluster toward the desired state.

It has no direct contact with cluster objects themselves; instead, it engages object controllers to synchronize object states.

CHAPTER 8 EKS ADDONS

The object controllers interact with cluster objects via API server to keep them coordinated. They handle various automated activities at the cluster or pod level. Examples of object controllers are endpoint controller, replication controller, namespace controller, service accounts controller, deployment, stateful set, and daemon set controllers.[1]

Figure 8-2 attempts to group controllers into two main categories. They are the intrinsic (built-in) and extrinsic (non-native) controllers. We explain the grouping in the sections that follow.

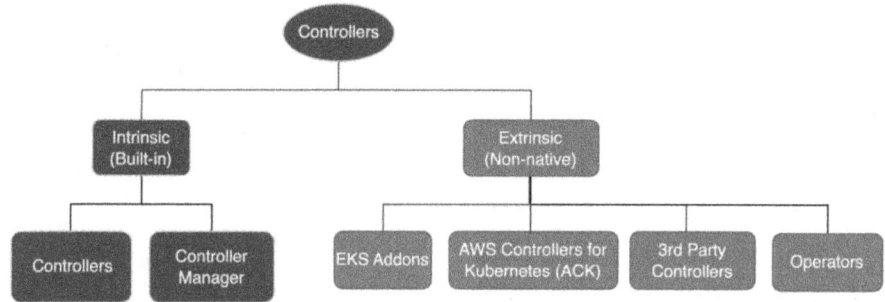

Figure 8-2. *Cluster controllers*

Intrinsic Controllers

Intrinsic controllers are built-in controllers designed to manage the states of native K8s objects. Built-in means they are an integral part of the K8s codebase, or they are K8s native. They are installed in every K8s cluster by default and do not require any additional installation to activate them.

---

[1] https://kubernetes.io/docs/reference/command-line-tools-reference/kube-controller-manager/

217

CHAPTER 8 EKS ADDONS

There are two kinds of intrinsic controllers, controllers for K8s objects (controllers or K8s controllers) and controller manager. Object controllers control the state of K8s objects such as deployment, replica set, services, secrets, daemon set, jobs[2] extensions.[3]

Intrinsic controllers includes intrinsic extensions. Intrinsic extensions are controlled by the addon manager (a kind of object controller). The addon manager manages the desired state of extensions.[4] It maintains all the extensions present in the cluster in one place to make sure that they are always operating in their desired states.

An addon is an application-independent software that provides supporting operational capabilities to cluster applications. For example, the Web UI addon can display applications running on a cluster and allow administrators to create, scale, or modify individual K8s objects (such as deployments, jobs, daemon sets, etc.).

The other intrinsic controller is the controller manager. It is the mother of all controllers. It manages all other intrinsic controllers such as namespaces, jobs, and replica set controllers in K8s.

Extrinsic Controllers

Extrinsic controllers are controllers with independent codebase maintained by AWS or a third-party. They are not bootstrap with K8s cluster and do require additional configuration or installation to activate them. The four types of extrinsic controllers are the EKS addons, AWS controllers for Kubernetes (ACK), operators, and third-party controllers. Let us discuss each type in the subsequent subsections.

---

[2] https://www.linkedin.com/pulse/kubernetes-api-objects-list-down-abdullah-shaukat
[3] https://kubernetes.feisky.xyz/v/en/setup/addon-list/addon-manager
[4] The Kubernetes Workshop: Learn how to build and run highly scalable workloads on Kubernetes, Zachary Arnold, Sahil Dua, Wei Huang, Faisal Masood, Melony Qin, and Mohammed Abu Taleb

EKS Addon Controllers

EKS add-on controllers are designed to manage the states of AWS EKS cluster add-on. They integrate with the K8s API to control AWS-specific objects. Available addons are Amazon EBS, EFS, VPC CNI plugin, CoreDNS, Kube-proxy, and S3 CSI.[5] The rest are CSI snapshot controller, AWS Distro for OpenTelemetry, GuardDuty agent, CloudWatch Observability agent, and Pod Identity Agent.

The descriptions of each add-on from AWS documentations are shown in Table 8-1.

Table 8-1. AWS addon documentation

Addons	Description
Amazon VPC CNI plugin	Provide native VPC networking for EKS clusters
CoreDNS	A flexible, extensible DNS server that can serve as the Kubernetes cluster DNS
Kube-proxy	Maintain network rules on each Amazon EC2 node
Amazon EBS CSI driver	Provide Amazon EBS storage for EKS clusters
Amazon EFS CSI driver	Provide Amazon EFS storage for EKS clusters
Mountpoint for Amazon S3 CSI driver	Provide Amazon S3 storage for EKS clusters
Node monitoring agent	Detects additional node health issues
CSI snapshot controller	Enable the use of snapshot functionality in compatible CSI drivers, such as the Amazon EBS CSI driver

(*continued*)

---

[5] https://docs.aws.amazon.com/eks/latest/userguide/workloads-add-ons-available-eks.html

CHAPTER 8   EKS ADDONS

Table 8-1. (*continued*)

Addons	Description
AWS Distro for OpenTelemetry	Secure, production-ready, AWS supported distribution of the OpenTelemetry project
Amazon GuardDuty agent	Security monitoring service that analyzes and processes foundational data sources including AWS CloudTrail management events and Amazon VPC flow logs. Amazon GuardDuty also processes features, such as Kubernetes audit logs and runtime monitoring
Amazon CloudWatch Observability agent	Monitoring and observability service provided by AWS. This add-on installs the CloudWatch Agent and enables both CloudWatch Application Signals and CloudWatch Container Insights with enhanced observability for Amazon EKS
EKS Pod Identity Agent	Ability to manage credentials for your applications, like the way that EC2 instance profiles provide credentials to EC2 instances

EKS addons extend the operational capabilities of K8s clusters to support observability, efficient networking, autoscaling, storage, and service integration. They enable K8s applications and objects to interact with underlying AWS network, compute, and storage resources.[6]

AWS keeps add-ons in dedicated private container image registries known as the Amazon container image registries for Amazon EKS add-ons.[7] You can find a dedicated registry for various AWS regions.

---

[6] https://docs.aws.amazon.com/eks/latest/userguide/eks-add-ons.html
[7] https://docs.aws.amazon.com/eks/latest/userguide/add-ons-images.html

They include the 602401143452.dkr.ecr.eu-west-1.amazonaws.com registry in the eu-west-1 region and the 602401143452.dkr.ecr.sa-east-1.amazonaws.com registry in the us-east-1 region.

Figure 8-3 illustrates how K8s controllers and EKS addon controllers manage the state of both K8s and AWS objects. It also shows how EKS addon controllers facilitate interaction between applications running on a K8s cluster and AWS resources outside the cluster. The AWS addons act as a bridge, connecting K8s objects with AWS services and resources. It enables communication between K8s objects and AWS resources or services.

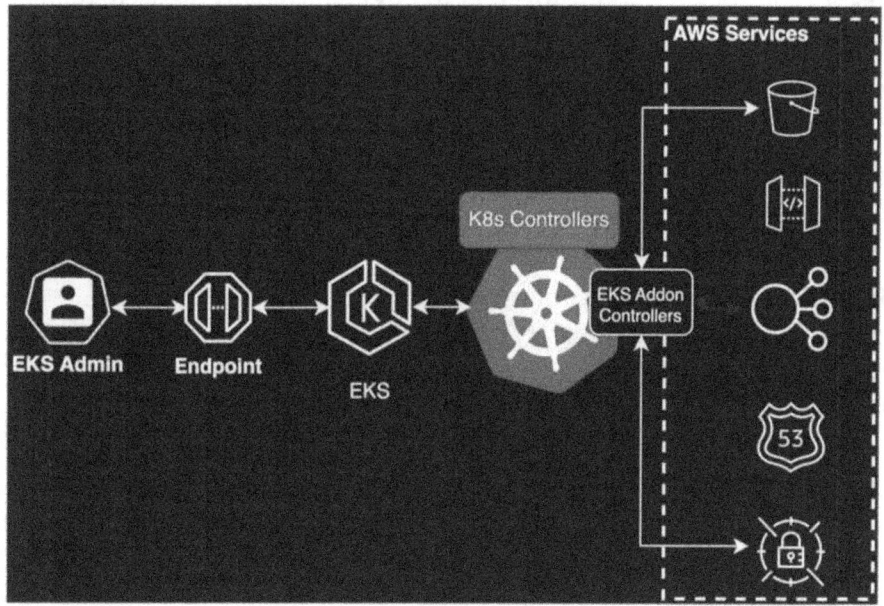

Figure 8-3. Cluster controllers and AWS services

AWS Controllers for Kubernetes

K8s applications often require several supporting resources like databases, message queues, and object storages to function. Traditionally, such resources may be provisioned by an administrator on behalf of developers. The developers must then integrate their applications with the backend resources manually or through another automation tool. Provisioning and integrating resources separately could be time-consuming and increase operation workloads.

AWS controller for Kubernetes (ACK) enables developers to define and integrate AWS resources directly with the same code and tools. There is no need to employ another administrator or tool to connect backend resources to an application. A developer can provision an application and all its resources with the same K8s manifest if the cluster deploys ACK controllers.

ACK is a collection of K8s custom resource definitions (CRDs) and custom controllers working together to extend the ability of K8s to manage AWS resources.

For example, developers can integrate the following ACK specification for S3 bucket into their manifests to create S3 buckets for applications without support from a system administrator or an operational team. The developer engineer has an end-to-end responsibility of applications and backend systems. This saves previous time and reduces dependencies on system administrators and other external tools. The following is an example of ACK specification for an S3 bucket:

```
apiVersion: s3.services.k8s.aws/v1alpha1
kind: Bucket
metadata:
  name: ack-s3
  namespace: default
spec:
  name: ack-s3
```

AWS objects use ACK controllers to maintain their desired state. Hence, you must configure or install a corresponding ACK controller from the publicly available AWS ACK elastic container registry gallery[8] before you can run an ACK object on a K8s cluster.

---

[8] https://gallery.ecr.aws/aws-controllers-k8s/

ACK controllers improve the developer experience, enabling them to leverage and adopt a growing range of AWS services.

Operators

Another kind of extrinsic controllers are operator controllers. They are custom (non-native) controllers that use K8s API extensions to maintain the states of custom objects on a K8s cluster. Unlike ACK controllers, operator controllers are vendor agnostic. They support any objects developed with K8s's custom resource APIs.

A custom resource is an extension of the K8s API that is often extrinsic to default K8s installation.[9] Once a custom resource is installed, developers can create and access its objects in the manner as the built-in K8s objects like pods and deployments.

With operators, you can define and create your own objects aside the core K8s objects and deploy them seamlessly on a K8s cluster. Operator controllers may be designed to maintain the state of objects that automate operational tasks such as backup, patching, updates, performance, and availability monitoring.

Third-Party Addon Controllers

Finally, you can implement third-party addons or controllers to control the state of third-party objects. Third-party objects are developed by third-party vendors to address specific needs. For example, you can control network objects on a K8s cluster with a third-party network interface such as calico or cilium.

---

[9] https://kubernetes.io/docs/concepts/extend-kubernetes/api-extension/custom-resources/

With extrinsic controllers, K8s no longer orchestrates core objects but any object created with K8s resource object definition (CRD) and has a corresponding controller installed on the cluster as depicted in Figure 8-4.

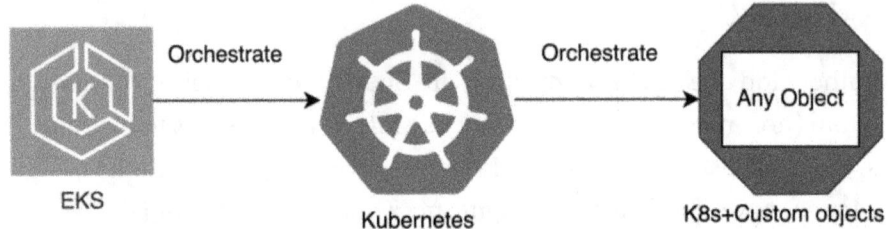

Figure 8-4. Custom objects

Self-Managed Addons

We want to crown the discussion on controllers by looking at how to manage addon updates. K8s cannot interact with the AWS services without controllers. It maintains and deploys basic controllers or addons necessary to create EKS clusters by default.

Where EKS sources the basic controllers depend on the deployment tool and the addon configurations. For example, EKS will deploy AWS-managed controllers if you deploy the cluster with AWS EKS tools; otherwise, it will deploy a self-managed controller if the third-party deployment tool does not explicitly specify an AWS-managed addon in code or in the configuration file.

The AWS shared responsibility model does not apply to self-managed addons. Customers are responsible for maintaining and updating self-managed add-ons. On the contrary, AWS will be responsible for managed addons. AWS recommends managed addons since they have less operational overheads in terms of updates and maintenance. AWS will keep you updated with information and patches whenever they become available.

Addon Implementation

We will spend some time in this section explaining the code for this chapter and illustrate how you can deploy and update managed addons in EKS. Before we review the code and deploy it, let's find the available managed addon versions for VPC CNI and kube-proxy so that we can differentiate the versions we would like to deploy.

EKS deploys the kube-proxy addon on each Amazon EC2 node to maintain network rules on your nodes and enable network communication to your pods.[10] You can use the following AWS CLI command to find the add-on versions for the VPC CNI plugin:

```
aws eks describe-addon-versions --kubernetes-version 1.31
--addon-name vpc-cni \
    --query 'addons[].addonVersions[]. {Version: addonVersion,
      Defaultversion: compatibilities[0].defaultVersion}'
    --output table
```

```
-----------------------------------------
|           DescribeAddonVersions       |
+----------------+----------------------+
| Defaultversion |       Version        |
+----------------+----------------------+
|  False         |  v1.18.5-eksbuild.1  |
|  False         |  v1.18.4-eksbuild.1  |
|  False         |  v1.18.3-eksbuild.3  |
|  True          |  v1.18.3-eksbuild.2  |
|  False         |  v1.17.1-eksbuild.1  |
|  False         |  v1.16.4-eksbuild.2  |
+----------------+----------------------+
```

---

[10] https://docs.aws.amazon.com/eks/latest/userguide/managing-kube-proxy.html#:~:text=The%20kube%2Dproxy%20add%2Don,proxy%20in%20the%20Kubernetes%20documentation

CHAPTER 8 EKS ADDONS

The command returns all VPC CNI add-on versions. EKS will deploy the v1.18.3-eksbuild.2 version if you do not specify any version when you configure the addon in your Terraform code. You can repeat the same command for the kube-proxy addon by replacing the name of the addon as follows:

```
aws eks describe-addon-versions --kubernetes-version 1.31
--addon-name kube-proxy \
    --query 'addons[].addonVersions[].{Version: addonVersion,
    Defaultversion: compatibilities[0].defaultVersion}'
    --output table
```

DescribeAddonVersions	
Defaultversion	Version
False	v1.31.0-eksbuild.5
True	**v1.31.0-eksbuild.2**
False	v1.30.3-eksbuild.9
False	v1.30.3-eksbuild.5
False	v1.30.3-eksbuild.2
False	v1.29.7-eksbuild.9
False	v1.29.7-eksbuild.5
False	v1.29.7-eksbuild.2
False	v1.28.8-eksbuild.5

Code Review

You should find the addon code in the **addons.tf** file in the folder chapter08. The first resource is for the VPC CNI addon, and the second is for the kube-proxy addon as shown below:

```
resource "aws_eks_addon" "vpc_cni_addon" {
  cluster_name = var.cluster_name
  addon_name   = "vpc-cni"
  #addon_version = "v1.18.5-eksbuild.1"
   configuration_values = jsonencode({
     env = {
     ENABLE_PREFIX_DELEGATION = "true"
     WARM_PREFIX_TARGET = "1"
   }
 })
}

resource "aws_eks_addon" "eks_kube_proxy_addon" {
 cluster_name =  var.cluster_name
  addon_name   = "kube-proxy"
  #addon_version = "v1.31.0-eksbuild.5"
  resolve_conflicts_on_create = "OVERWRITE"
  resolve_conflicts_on_update = "OVERWRITE"
}
```

We have commented out the addon_version arguments in the script so that EKS can deploy the selected default versions for each addon. The selected default versions are few versions behind the current cluster versions. We will uncomment the version arguments so that EKS can deploy the latest addons and take the opportunity to demonstrate how to upgrade addons.

CHAPTER 8 EKS ADDONS

The uncommented Terraform code should look as follows:

```
resource "aws_eks_addon" "vpc_cni_addon" {
  resource "aws_eks_addon" "vpc_cni_addon" {
  cluster_name = var.cluster_name
  addon_name    = "vpc-cni"
  addon_version = "v1.18.5-eksbuild.1"
    configuration_values = jsonencode({
      env = {
      ENABLE_PREFIX_DELEGATION = "true"
      WARM_PREFIX_TARGET = "1"
    }
  })
}
resource "aws_eks_addon" "eks_kube_proxy_addon" {
 cluster_name =  var.cluster_name
  addon_name    = "kube-proxy"
  addon_version = "v1.31.0-eksbuild.5"
  resolve_conflicts_on_create = "OVERWRITE"
  resolve_conflicts_on_update = "OVERWRITE"
}
```

Deployment and Validation

1. Deploy the **commented** version of the Terraform code in the folder chapter08.

   ```
   cd chapter08
   terraform init
   terraform apply
   ```

CHAPTER 8   EKS ADDONS

2. Update context.

   aws eks update-kubeconfig --name public-endpoint-cluster

3. Retrieve the version of the node.

   kubectl get nodes

4. Find the addons from the EKS console.

   Go to EKS console, click the name of the cluster, then click the addon tab to find the available managed addons.

CHAPTER 8   EKS ADDONS

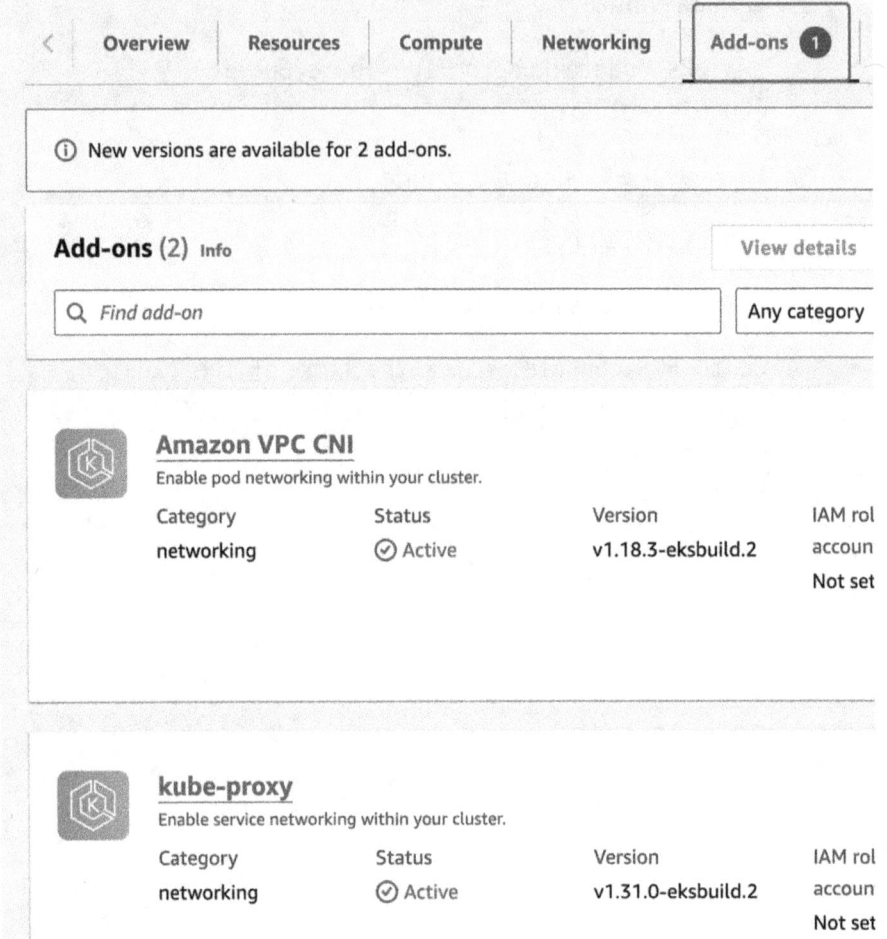

Figure 8-5. *Plugins or addons*

5. You should find the upgraded version information on the right side of the page. This indicates that the deployed version is not the latest version.

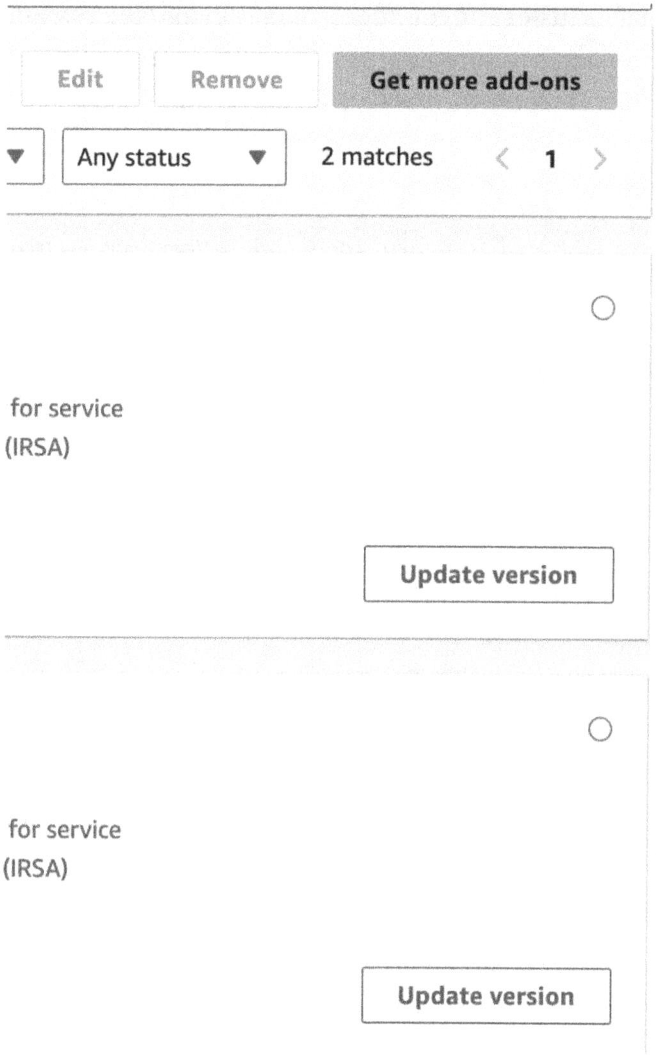

CHAPTER 8 EKS ADDONS

Figure 8-6. Addon update

You can verify the deployed version with the following command:

```
aws eks describe-addon --cluster-name <cluster-name>
--addon-name <addon name> --query addon.addonVersion
--output text
```

Replace the cluster and the addon names to find the version of the vpc-cni addon deployed on the current cluster. For example, the following command should return the vpc-cni addon version deployed by the cluster:

```
aws eks describe-addon --cluster-name public-endpoint-cluster
--addon-name vpc-cni --query addon.addonVersion --output text
```

Version Upgrade

You can automate addon upgrade by uncommenting the version arguments in the code and by rerunning the **terraform apply** command:

```
resource "aws_eks_addon" "vpc_cni_addon" {
  cluster_name = aws_eks_cluster.public_endpoint_cluster.name
  addon_name   = "vpc-cni"
  addon_version = "v1.18.5-eksbuild.1"
   configuration_values = jsonencode({
     env = {
     ENABLE_PREFIX_DELEGATION = "true"
     WARM_PREFIX_TARGET = "1"
    }
  })
}

resource "aws_eks_addon" "eks_kube_proxy_addon" {
 cluster_name = aws_eks_cluster.public_endpoint_cluster.name
  addon_name   = "kube-proxy"
  addon_version = "v1.31.0-eksbuild.5"
  resolve_conflicts_on_create = "OVERWRITE"
  resolve_conflicts_on_update = "OVERWRITE"
  depends_on = [aws_eks_cluster.public_endpoint_cluster]
}
```

CHAPTER 8 EKS ADDONS

Wait for the deployment to complete and return to the EKS console to verify if the addon was updated. You can also perform the same task manually as follows:

1. Go to the EKS console.

2. Click the upgrade cluster and a version higher than the current minor version.

3. Click the Add-ons tab.

Figure 8-7. Add-ons

4. Click the Update version button for the VPC CNI addon.

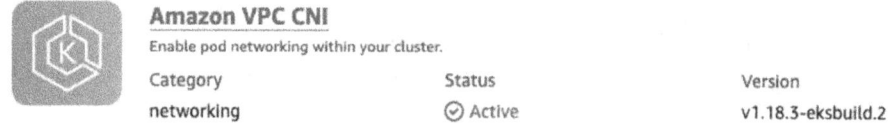

Figure 8-8. Amazon VPC CNI add-ons

5. Choose the latest version and click Save changes.

233

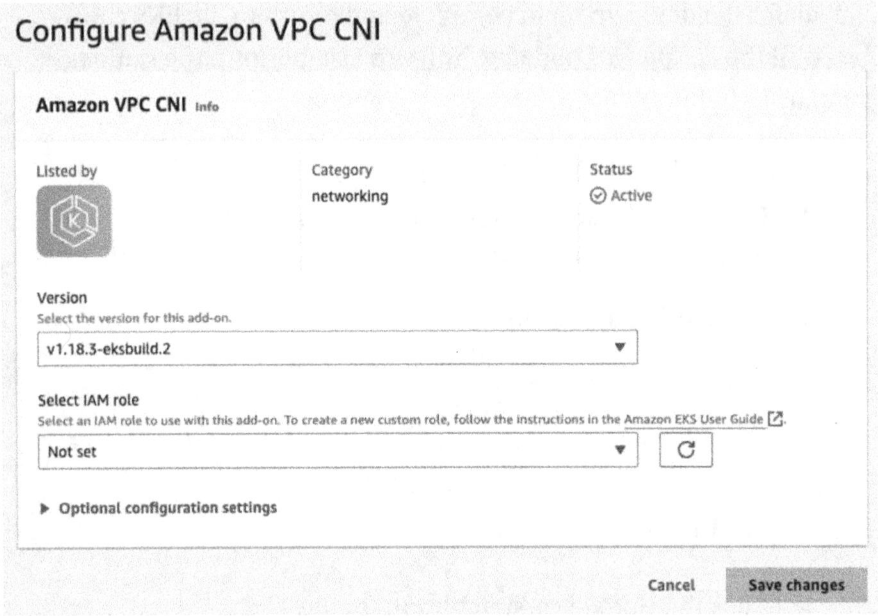

CHAPTER 8 EKS ADDONS

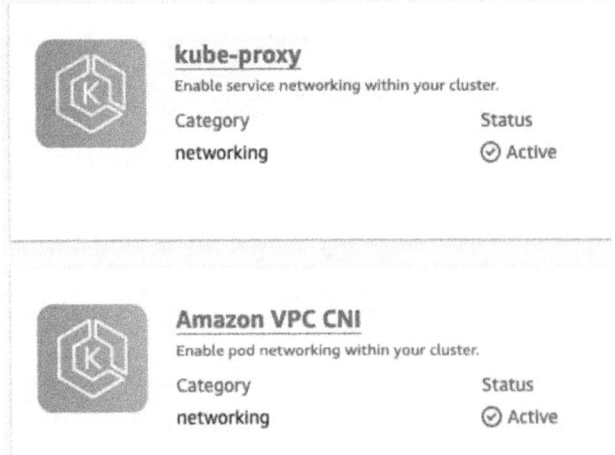

Figure 8-9. VPC CNI add-on upgrade

6. You should wait for the update to be completed. You should see the output as shown in Figure 8-10.

Figure 8-10. Other Add-ons

CHAPTER 8 EKS ADDONS

Controller and Deployment

You can list the built-in K8s controllers with the following command if you are interested in finding built-in controllers:

kubectl get sa -n kube-system

You should see the following output:

attachdetach-controller
aws-cloud-provider
aws-node
certificate-controller
clusterrole-aggregation-controller
coredns
cronjob-controller
daemon-set-controller
default
deployment-controller
disruption-controller
eks-vpc-resource-controller
endpoint-controller
endpointslice-controller
endpointslicemirroring-controller
ephemeral-volume-controller
expand-controller
generic-garbage-collector
horizontal-pod-autoscaler
job-controller
kube-proxy
legacy-service-account-token-cleaner
namespace-controller
node-controller

235

CHAPTER 8 EKS ADDONS

```
persistent-volume-binder
pod-garbage-collector
pv-protection-controller
pvc-protection-controller
replicaset-controller
replication-controller
resourcequota-controller
root-ca-cert-publisher
service-account-controller
service-controller
statefulset-controller
tagging-controller
ttl-after-finished-controller
ttl-controller
validatingadmissionpolicy-status-controller
```

The command retrieves and displays controllers in the kube-system namespace.

ACK Controller Deployment

Let us go through how to deploy an extrinsic controller. We deployed an ACK controller for an AWS S3 bucket with the following steps:

1. Create the environment variable for the installation.

   ```
   export ACK_SYSTEM_NAMESPACE=ack-system \
   export PROFILE=default      \
   export AWS_REGION=us-east-1 \
   export SERVICE=s3 \
   export RELEASE_VERSION=$(curl -sL https://api.github.com/repos/aws-controllers-k8s/${SERVICE}-controller/releases/latest | jq -r '.tag_name | ltrimstr("v")')
   ```

2. Log in to the helm registry.

   ```
   aws ecr-public get-login-password --region $AWS_REGION
   --profile $PROFILE | helm registry login --username AWS
   --password-stdin public.ecr.aws
   ```

3. Install the S3 controller.

   ```
   helm install --create-namespace -n $ACK_SYSTEM_
   NAMESPACE ack-$SERVICE-controller \ oci://public.ecr.
   aws/aws-controllers-k8s/$SERVICE-chart
   --version=$RELEASE_VERSION --set=aws.region=$AWS_REGION
   ```

4. Review the output.

   ```
   NOTES:
   s3-chart has been installed.
   This chart deploys "public.ecr.aws/aws-
   controllers-k8s/s3-
   controller:1.0.17".
   Check its status by running:
   kubectl --namespace ack-system get pods -l "app.
   kubernetes.io/instance=ack-s3-controller"
   ```

5. Validate the controller installation.

   ```
   kubectl --namespace ack-system get pods -l "app.
   kubernetes.io/instance=ack-s3-controller"
   ```

   This should output something like this:

   ```
   ack-s3-controller-s3-chart-6b686d6d76-8675s
   ```

6. Create the bucket YAML file.

   ```
   apiVersion: s3.services.k8s.aws/v1alpha1
   kind: Bucket
   ```

```
metadata:
  name: ack-s3
  namespace: default
spec:
  name: ack-s3
```

7. Create an S3 bucket.

   ```
   kubectl apply -f pod/s3.yml
   ```

8. Verify the object creation.

   ```
   kubectl get Bucket
   ```

   This should output the bucket object as ack-s3.

The controller will need a service account to access the actual AWS service. We will discuss service accounts later in Chapter 15.

Summary

This chapter introduced a high-level discussion of addons or controllers and how they work in EKS. Controllers are meant to maintain the state of a K8s cluster and extend the capabilities of its APIs. They work to bring the cluster to its desired state or near desired state as determined by the cluster administrators or developers. You can find two main groups of controllers. They are the intrinsic and extrinsic controllers. Intrinsic controllers are integrated into the K8s codebase, while extrinsic controllers are external to the K8s codebase. Extrinsic controllers may provide unparalleled developer experience. They enable developers to leverage and adopt a growing range of AWS services. We will return to the application of controllers in Chapter 14 and beyond. The next chapter will focus on identity and access management in EKS.

CHAPTER 9

Identity and Access Management

We have covered identity and access management (IAM) for cluster creators in EKS. However, we are yet to manage multiple cluster operators or administrators. This chapter will expand the access control discussion from managing a single cluster administrator to handling multiple cluster administrators, using the deprecated aws-auth ConfigMap method for access control.

Until recently, AWS relied on the aws-auth ConfigMap access control method to authorize administrative access to EKS clusters. The authentication in aws-auth ConfigMap occurs in AWS IAM, while the authorization takes place in K8s. This requires cluster administrators to switch between AWS IAM and K8s APIs and configuration files when managing multiple cluster operators. The switching and editing of configurations make the access control method complicated and error prone especially when you have many operators.

AWS has since deprecated the aws-auth ConfigMap access control method and replaced it with the new cluster access control method. However, the aws-auth ConfigMap method remains the default access control method in EKS. For this reason, we cannot discuss the new access control method without delving into the old.

Chapter 9 Identity and Access Management

We will spend the rest of this chapter treating the old cluster access control method before we advance to the new one in Chapter 10. We will highlight how AWS simplifies access control in AWS IAM as compared to access control with K8s and develop from there to implementing and validating the aws-auth ConfigMap access control method.

IAM in EKS

Figures 9-1 and 9-2 show two sets of access control traffic flows. Figure 9-1 represents the flow for AWS IAM. In Figure 9-1, both authentication and authorization occur at one place, in the AWS IAM. In contrast, the aws-auth ConfigMap access control traffic flow in Figure 9-2 involves two different services, the AWS IAM and the K8s RBAC service.

Figure 9-1. *The EKS new access control method*

As illustrated in Figure 9-2, the **kubectl** command makes an API call to the EKS cluster's endpoint with an access token created from the caller's credentials in step 1.

EKS forwards the request to the AWS IAM service for authentication in step 2. The IAM service verifies the token associated with the call and returns a response back to the EKS service. EKS requests for authorization in step 3 if the authentication is successful.

K8s finds which group is associated with the principal or the caller in its RBAC database and denies or grants the principal access to the cluster in step 4.

CHAPTER 9   IDENTITY AND ACCESS MANAGEMENT

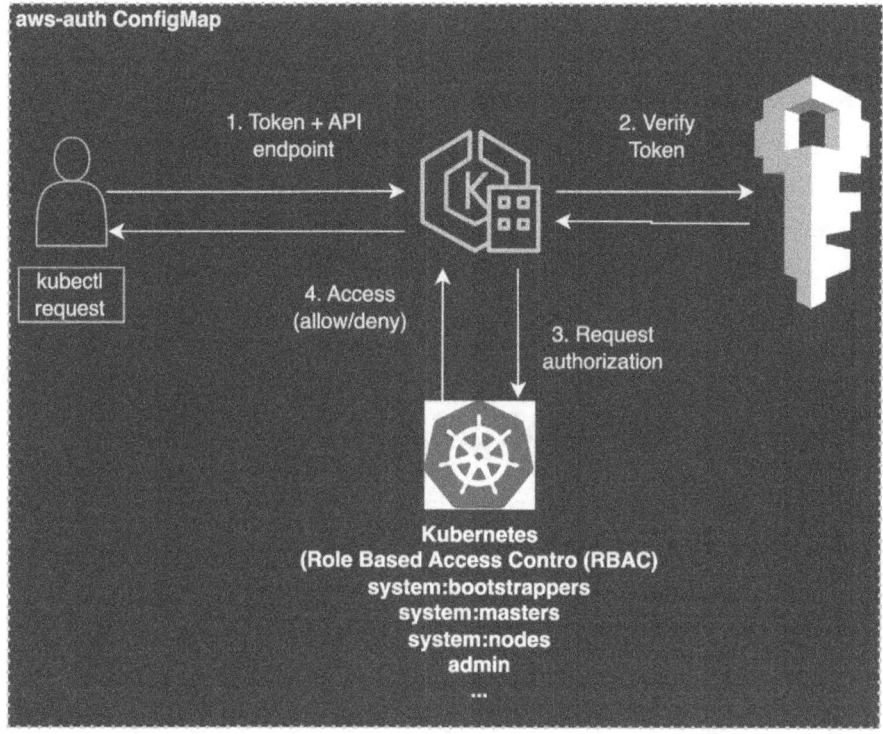

Figure 9-2. *The old aws-auth ConfigMap access control method*

The access control flow in Figure 9-2 represents the old aws-auth ConfigMap method. The old method tightly couples the permissions of the cluster creators to the cluster. Thus, it grants permanent and irrevocable access to the cluster creator.[1] The worst part of this for organizations is that cluster creators may retain their access even when they leave the organization.

---

[1] https://aws.amazon.com/blogs/containers/a-deep-dive-into-simplified-amazon-eks-access-management-controls/

CHAPTER 9   IDENTITY AND ACCESS MANAGEMENT

This situation has led to the recommendation to use IAM roles to create EKS clusters instead of IAM users. Using an AWS IAM role provides a layer of indirection to control who could assume the role. This way, you can revoke the cluster creators' access by removing their ability to assume a role in the account.

The good news is that we can now revoke a cluster creator's access with the new cluster access method before or after cluster creation regardless of the type of IAM principal that created the cluster.

The aws-auth ConfigMap Authentication

We previously utilized access credentials to create or access the EKS service. Basically, access credentials, roles, or secret access key and access key IDs are meant for resource creation. However, authentication to API endpoints and subsequent access to the K8s cluster components and objects does not depend solely on the same cluster creator's credentials. Rather, cluster access depends on bearer tokens derived from the cluster creator's access credentials and the cluster's certificate authority (CA).

We will step into the cluster access process in this section for you to experience how the aws-auth ConfigMap is implemented in practice. The following recipe will construct an access token and show how you can access the cluster with the token.

Cluster Access Demonstration

1. Navigate to the folder chapter09.

2. Deploy the Terraform code in the chapter09 folder.

3. Navigate to the AWS console ➤ EKS.

4. Click the cluster ➤ Overview.

CHAPTER 9   IDENTITY AND ACCESS MANAGEMENT

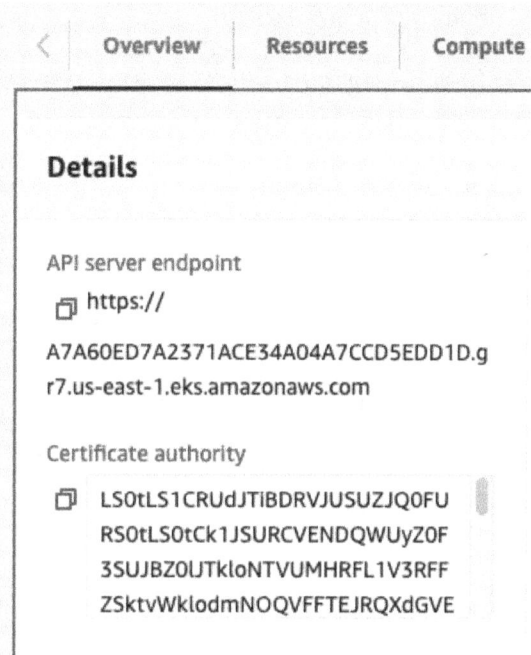

Figure 9-3. *EKS cluster overview console*

5. Copy the API server endpoint of the cluster.

   https://xxx.gr7.us-east-1.eks.amazonaws.com

6. Store the API endpoint in the **API_SERVER** variable.

   API_SERVER=https://xxx.gr7.us-east-1.eks.amazonaws.com

7. Copy the certificate authority of the cluster and save it in a file, **cacert.crt**.

8. Convert the cacert.crt file to the PEM file format with a base64 tool.

   base64 -i cacert.crt -d > ca.crt

9. Install the jq tool.

243

CHAPTER 9   IDENTITY AND ACCESS MANAGEMENT

10. Create an authentication token.

    ```
    TOKEN=$(aws --region us-east-1 eks get-token --cluster-name public-endpoint-cluster | jq -r .status.token)
    ```

11. Connect to the API endpoint with an authentication token and certificate authority.

    ```
    curl --cacert ca.crt $API_SERVER/ -H "Authorization: Bearer $TOKEN"
    ```

12. Find the identity of the API caller.

    ```
    kubectl auth whoami --server $API_SERVER \
    --certificate-authority ca.crt \
    --token $TOKEN
    ```

13. Verify the caller again.

    ```
    kubectl auth whoami
    ```

    The **auth whoami** command returns the context of the aws-auth ConfigMap configuration. We explain the content of the file as follows:

    - *Username*: A string which identifies the end user.

    - *UID*: A unique string which identifies the end user. It is more consistent and unique than username.

    - *Groups*: A set of strings, each of which indicates the user's membership in a named logical collection of users. The membership group for cluster creators is **system:masters**. Members of this group have unrestricted access to the K8s API.

CHAPTER 9 IDENTITY AND ACCESS MANAGEMENT

- *Extra fields*: A map of strings to list of strings which holds additional information authorizers may find useful.

- The **system:authenticated** group presents all authenticated users.[2]

Using the Kube Config File

You do not need to go through this struggle to access the cluster after deployment. You can use the aws eks update-kubeconfig --name <cluster_name> command to achieve the same.

AWS automatically stores all the information you will need to construct the access token in the **.kube/config** file when you run the aws eks update-kubeconfig --name <cluster_name> command. You should find the file completed with the cluster certificate and token generation commands when you open the **.kube/config** file. The content of the file should resemble the following:

```
apiVersion: v1
clusters:
- cluster:
    certificate-authority-data: jSUluWmcwYkk2ME4OU2NYWjBS
    SnUzRUlRRTdzSWUoRXlhTGZQN1lNTHExCjJ5c1VPMWF4MzdHNnJ5
    SSt9LdzNTNE1qMzF4MkxkZGQ1OTlHd29vT1NtRm1wMkE1Tm
...
    server: https://xxx.gr7.us-east-1.eks.amazonaws.com
  name: arn:aws:eks:us-east-1:${ACCOUNT_ID}:cluster/public-endpoint-cluster
```

---

[2] https://kubernetes.io/docs/reference/access-authn-authz/authentication/

CHAPTER 9 IDENTITY AND ACCESS MANAGEMENT

```
contexts:
- context:
    cluster: arn:aws:eks:us-east-1:${ACCOUNT_ID}:cluster/
    public-endpoint-cluster
    user: arn:aws:eks:us-east-1:${ACCOUNT_ID}:cluster/public-
    endpoint-cluster
  name: arn:aws:eks:us-east-1:${ACCOUNT_ID}:cluster/public-
  endpoint-cluster
current-context: arn:aws:eks:us-east-1:${ACCOUNT_ID}:cluster/
public-endpoint-cluster
kind: Config
preferences: {}
users:
- name: arn:aws:eks:us-east-1:${ACCOUNT_ID}:cluster/public-
endpoint-cluster
  user:
    exec:
      apiVersion: client.authentication.k8s.io/v1beta1
      args:
      - --region
      - us-east-1
      - eks
      - get-token
      - --cluster-name
      - public-endpoint-cluster
      - --output
      - json
      command: aws
      env:
      - name: AWS_PROFILE
        value: default
```

CHAPTER 9 IDENTITY AND ACCESS MANAGEMENT

The **kube config** file provides access to the cluster without creating your own token from scratch. It has an entry for each cluster, the DNS name, the TLS certificate, and a command for generating bearer tokens. You can manually create the entry or use the **update kube config** command to do so.

You can run the `kubectl auth whoami` command to find information about your user. The command retrieves your access permission with a token constructed with the information in the .kube/**config** file.

You can read the **kubeconfig** configuration with the following command:

`kubectl config view` or

`kubectl config view -o template --template='{{ index."current-context"}} '`

You may modify the ConfigMap directly using kubectl tool as follows:

`kubectl edit cm aws-auth -n kube-system`

The aws-auth ConfigMap Access Control Approach

The aws-auth ConfigMap handles the authorization part of the K8s cluster access, while AWS IAM handles the authentication. It implements role-based access control (RBAC) for the cluster administrators. AWS IAM Authenticator for K8s depends on configuration information from the aws-auth ConfigMap to enable cluster access for IAM principals.[3]

EKS assigns the IAM principal that created the cluster, the **system:masters** RBAC group. The principals in this group have unrestricted access to the cluster. Further, the cluster creator's membership in the group

---

[3] https://docs.aws.amazon.com/eks/latest/userguide/auth-configmap.html

CHAPTER 9 IDENTITY AND ACCESS MANAGEMENT

is not visible in the **kube config** file. Consequently, you cannot revoke the cluster creator's access by editing the configuration.

However, you can edit the aws-auth ConfigMap configuration to grant access to new cluster creator administrators. We will learn how to do this with a demonstration later in the chapter.

K8s RBAC Roles

Planning access control is one of the cardinal jobs of administrators. To understand who will do what and which roles should be assigned to which users or group of users are daily preoccupations of IAM administrators. To plan such activities, administrators should first understand which roles the system provides and how to allocate them. This section discusses the standard K8s RBAC roles and how to apply them to manage administrators.

With your cluster deployed, you can retrieve K8s's RBAC groups with the following command:

1. Switch context to the default user.

    ```
    aws eks update-kubeconfig --name <cluster_name>
    ```

2. Retrieve the available roles with one of the following two commands:

    ```
    kubectl get clusterroles   or
    kubectl get clusterroles | grep -v '^system'
    ```

CHAPTER 9 IDENTITY AND ACCESS MANAGEMENT

Table 9-1. *Mapping of K8s RBAC groups to EKS roles*

K8s Groups	EKS Roles	Privileges
system:masters	cluster-admin	Cluster-wide super admin
admin	Admin	Full access within a namespace
edit	edit	Perform basic actions like deploying pods, viewing and observing nonsensitive objects within a given namespace
view	view	Read-only within a namespace

Table 9-1 maps the standard K8s RBAC group to the EKS roles. The **system:masters** group is the most powerful group in the cluster. Members of this group have unrestricted access to the cluster.

The K8s admin group is the second most powerful role. It is not an administrator of the entire cluster but an administrator of a cluster namespace. Namespaces group cluster resources for a group of users.

A namespace administrator has full access to a namespace and can control who accesses the namespace. Similarly, K8s limits the edit and the view groups access to a namespace. An administrator with such roles can either edit or view resources in a given namespace.

Role Assignment Demonstration Role

Let us demonstrate how to assign distinct roles to users using the aws-auth ConfigMap access control method.

We will create a test user, Alice, and assign her different privileges from the RBAC groups in Table 9-1 and test her access to the cluster. We will assign her the cluster admin, cluster reader (view), and the namespace admin roles and test her access in each case.

CHAPTER 9   IDENTITY AND ACCESS MANAGEMENT

Create the Test User, Alice

- Create a user Alice.

  ```
  aws iam create-user --user-name alice
  ```

- Create a policy file policy.json with the following content:

  ```
  {
      "Version": "2012-10-17",
      "Statement": [
          {
              "Effect": "Allow",
              "Action": [
               "eks:DescribeCluster"
              ],
              "Resource": "*"
          }
      ]
  }
  ```

  The eks:DescribeCluster permission is mandatory for all cluster administrators.

- Create an IAM policy with the policy.json file.

  ```
  aws iam create-policy --policy-name <policy-name> --policy-document file://policy.json
  ```

  Replace <policy-name> with a chosen name, for example, eks-describe-policy.

CHAPTER 9   IDENTITY AND ACCESS MANAGEMENT

- Copy the policy arn from step 3, for example, **arn:aws:iam::${ACCOUNT_ID}:policy/eks-describe-policy**.

- Attach the policy to Alice so that she can read or describe the cluster.

```
aws iam attach-user-policy --policy-arn
arn:aws:iam::${ACCOUNT_ID}:policy/eks-describe-policy
--user-name alice
```

Configure aws-auth ConfigMap
Example 1: Making Alice Cluster Administrator

1. Generate an access key ID and secret access key for Alice.

   ```
   aws iam create-access-key --user-name alice
   ```

2. Create an entry in the **.aws/credentials** file for Alice.

   ```
   [alice]
   region = us-east-1
   aws_access_key_id = ${access_key_id}
   aws_secret_access_key = ${secret_access_key}
   ```

3. Switch user context.

   ```
   aws eks update-kubeconfig --name public-endpoint-cluster --profile alice
   ```

4. Test if Alice can access the cluster.

   ```
   kubectl get nodes
   ```

251

CHAPTER 9 IDENTITY AND ACCESS MANAGEMENT

The **get nodes** command should fail because Alice has no access to the cluster.

5. Change user context to the default cluster creator.

   ```
   aws eks update-kubeconfig --name public-endpoint-cluster
   ```

6. Make Alice a cluster-wide administrator.

   ```
   eksctl create iamidentitymapping \
   --region us-east-1 \
   --cluster public-endpoint-cluster \
   --arn arn:aws:iam::${ACCOUNT_ID}:user/alice \
   --group system:masters \
   --no-duplicate-arns
   ```

7. Switch user context to Alice.

   ```
   aws eks update-kubeconfig --name public-endpoint-cluster --profile alice
   ```

8. Test if Alice can access the cluster.

   ```
   kubectl get nodes or
   kubectl get services
   ```

   You should find all the nodes and services.

9. Find the identity mapping.

   ```
   eksctl get iamidentitymapping --cluster public-endpoint-cluster
   ```

10. Create a test namespace.

    ```
    kubectl create ns test-ns
    ```

CHAPTER 9 IDENTITY AND ACCESS MANAGEMENT

Note that you can assign permission to a role instead of an IAM user with the following eksctl command:

```
eksctl create iamidentitymapping --cluster <cluster-name>
--region=eu-central-1 --arn arn:aws:iam::ACCOUNTID:role/
myIAMrole
--group system:masters --username creatorAccount
```

Example 2: Making Alice Default Namespace Admin

1. Switch user context to the default cluster administrator.

   ```
   aws eks update-kubeconfig --name public-endpoint-cluster
   ```

2. Map the Alice user to the admin group.

   ```
   eksctl create iamidentitymapping \
   --region us-east-1 \
   --cluster public-endpoint-cluster \
   --arn arn:aws:iam::${ACCOUNT_ID}:user/alice \
   --group admin \
   --no-duplicate-arns
   ```

   The **--no-duplicate-arns** attribute prevents duplicated entries in the config file.

3. Unlike the system:masters group, you must bind Alice to the admin group and namespace to grant her the required access. Bind Alice to the admin group and default namespace.

253

CHAPTER 9   IDENTITY AND ACCESS MANAGEMENT

```
kubectl create rolebinding admin-binding \
--clusterrole=admin \
--group admin \
 --namespace=default
```

4. Switch user context to Alice.

   ```
   aws eks update-kubeconfig --name public-endpoint-cluster --profile alice
   ```

5. Verify if Alice can access the cluster.

   ```
   kubectl get services
   ```

6. Verify if Alice can create deployments.

   ```
   kubectl auth can-i create deployments
   ```

7. Verify if Alice can retrieve nodes.

   ```
   kubectl get nodes
   ```

   This should fail because Alice has no access to the system nodes.

8. Find the identity mapping.

   ```
   eksctl get iamidentitymapping --cluster public-endpoint-cluster
   ```

This command will return the content of the aws-auth ConfigMap file with duplicated entries for user Alice if the **--no-duplicate-arns** attribute was not used.

CHAPTER 9   IDENTITY AND ACCESS MANAGEMENT

Manual Editing of aws-auth ConfigMap

Manual editing is another way of granting administrators access to a K8s cluster. You can do this in two ways: by using the edit view command or with any suitable editor.

1. Switch user context to the default cluster creator.

   aws eks update-kubeconfig --name public-endpoint-cluster

2. Open the aws-auth ConfigMap file for editing.

   kubectl edit configmap aws-auth -n kube-system

   Notice the absence of the cluster creator user in the file.

3. Press i to insert the mapUsers section. Add Alice's arn to the userarn and specify the username as alice and groups as **system masters** as follows:

   apiVersion: v1
   data:
     mapRoles: |
       - groups:
         - system:bootstrappers
         - system:nodes
         rolearn: arn:aws:iam::ACCOUNTID:role/test-cluster-nodes
         username: system:node:{{EC2PrivateDNSName}}
     mapUsers: |
       - userarn: arn:aws:iam::${ACCOUNT_ID}:user/alice
         username: alice
         groups:
           - system:masters

255

CHAPTER 9 IDENTITY AND ACCESS MANAGEMENT

```
kind: ConfigMap
metadata:
  creationTimestamp: ".."
  name: aws-auth
  namespace: kube-system
  resourceVersion: "816"
  uid: 0de5b298-9aaf-481f-
```

Press the Esc button and type the :wq! command to save the changes to the ConfigMap file.

4. Switch user context to Alice.

   ```
   aws eks update-kubeconfig --name public-endpoint-cluster --profile alice
   ```

5. Test if Alice can access the cluster.

   ```
   kubectl get nodes
   ```

   You should see all the cluster nodes.

6. Verify if Alice can create deployments.

   ```
   kubectl auth can-i create pods
   ```

7. View nodes.

   ```
   kubectl get services
   ```

   You should see all the services.

Adding Cluster Editor Role

1. Switch user context to the default cluster creator.

   ```
   aws eks update-kubeconfig --name public-endpoint-cluster
   ```

CHAPTER 9 IDENTITY AND ACCESS MANAGEMENT

2. Open the aws-auth ConfigMap file for editing.

    ```
    kubectl edit configmap aws-auth -n kube-system
    ```

3. Press i and edit the aws-auth ConfigMap file as follows:

    ```
    apiVersion: v1
    data:
      mapRoles: |
        - groups:
          - system:bootstrappers
          - system:nodes
          rolearn: arn:aws:iam::ACCOUNTID:role/public-endpoint-cluster-nodes
          username: system:node:{{EC2PrivateDNSName}}
      mapUsers: |
        - userarn: arn:aws:iam::${ACCOUNT_ID}:user/alice
          username: alice
          groups:
            - edit
    kind: ConfigMap
    metadata:
      creationTimestamp: ".."
      name: aws-auth
      namespace: kube-system
      resourceVersion: "16237"
      uid: 515138aa-d0b0-4925-8d24
    ```

    Just change the system:masters to edit. Press the Esc button and type the **:wq!** command to save the changes to the ConfigMap file.

257

CHAPTER 9 IDENTITY AND ACCESS MANAGEMENT

4. Switch user context to Alice.

   ```
   aws eks update-kubeconfig --name public-endpoint-cluster --profile alice
   ```

5. Verify the configuration with the following commands:

   ```
   kubectl get svc
   kubectl get nodes
   kubectl auth can-i create deployments
   ```

   You should observe restrictions on Alice's access to the cluster.

Using Custom Groups

You can create a custom group if the default groups do not meet your needs. We will create a custom **readonly** group and demonstrate how to grant access with a custom group.

1. Switch user context to the default cluster creator.

   ```
   aws eks update-kubeconfig --name public-endpoint-cluster
   ```

2. Open the aws-auth ConfigMap file for editing.

   ```
   kubectl edit configmap aws-auth -n kube-system
   ```

3. Press i and edit the aws-auth ConfigMap file as follows:

   ```
   apiVersion: v1
   data:
     mapRoles: |
       - groups:
   ```

CHAPTER 9 IDENTITY AND ACCESS MANAGEMENT

```
      - system:bootstrappers
      - system:nodes
      rolearn: arn:aws:iam::${ACCOUNT_ID}:role/public-
      endpoint-cluster-nodes
      username: system:node:{{EC2PrivateDNSName}}
    mapUsers: |
      - userarn: arn:aws:iam::${ACCOUNT_ID}:user/alice
        username: alice
kind: ConfigMap
metadata:
  creationTimestamp: ".."
  name: aws-auth
  namespace: kube-system
  resourceVersion: "16237"
  uid: 515138aa-d0b0-4925-8d24-3c0a
```

Replace the account ID with yours. Assign no group to Alice. Press the Esc button and type the **:wq!** to save the changes to the ConfigMap file.

4. Create a file **readonly-binding.yml** with the following content:

```
kind: ClusterRole
apiVersion: rbac.authorization.k8s.io/v1
metadata:
  name: readonly-role
rules:
- apiGroups: [""]
  resources: ["nodes", "namespaces", "pods"]
  verbs: ["get", "list"]
```

259

```yaml
    - apiGroups: ["apps"]
      resources: ["deployment", "daemonsets"]
      verbs: ["get", "list","watch"]
---
apiVersion: rbac.authorization.k8s.io/v1
kind: ClusterRoleBinding
metadata:
  name: readonly-role-binding
subjects:
- kind: User
  name: alice
  apiGroup: rbac.authorization.k8s.io
roleRef:
  kind: ClusterRole
  name: readonly-role
  apiGroup: rbac.authorization.k8s.io
```

The ClusterRole section defines the custom readonly permissions, while the ClusterRoleBinding section attaches the cross-namespace role for the user.

5. Run the `kubectl apply -f readonly-binding.yml` command to apply the changes.

6. Switch user context to Alice.

7. Verify if Alice can read the nodes.

    `kubectl get nodes`

8. You should see all the nodes because Alice is authorized to read nodes, namespaces, and pods in the cluster, in addition to deployment and daemonsets in the app namespace.

CHAPTER 9 IDENTITY AND ACCESS MANAGEMENT

9. Verify the configuration.

```
kubectl auth can-i get pods
kubectl auth can-i create pods
kubectl run nginx --image=nginx
```

Manual Editing of aws-auth ConfigMap with Code Editor

You can use a code editor to edit the aws-auth ConfigMap file just like the kubectl edit command. We want to present a few examples in this section.

1. Switch user context to the default cluster creator.

   ```
   aws eks update-kubeconfig --name public-endpoint-cluster
   ```

2. Read the aws-auth ConfigMap file.

   ```
   kubectl get configmap -n kube-system aws-auth -o yaml > aws-auth.yml
   ```

3. Open the aws-auth.yml file.

   ```yaml
   apiVersion: v1
   data:
     mapRoles: |
       - groups:
         - system:bootstrappers
         - system:nodes
         rolearn: arn:aws:iam::${ACCOUNT_ID}:role/public-endpoint-cluster-nodes
   username: system:node:{{EC2PrivateDNSName}}
   kind: ConfigMap
   ```

CHAPTER 9   IDENTITY AND ACCESS MANAGEMENT

```
metadata:
  creationTimestamp: ".."
  name: aws-auth
  namespace: kube-system
  resourceVersion: "..."
  uid: ...
```

Notice the absence of the cluster creator user in the file.

4. Edit the file to add Alice to the **system masters** group.

```
apiVersion: v1
data:
  mapRoles: |
    - groups:
      - system:bootstrappers
      - system:nodes
      rolearn: arn:aws:iam::${ACCOUNT_ID}:role/test-cluster-nodes
      username: system:node:{{EC2PrivateDNSName}}
  mapUsers: |
    - userarn: arn:aws:iam::${ACCOUNT_ID}:user/alice
      username: alice
      groups:
        - system:masters
kind: ConfigMap
metadata:
  creationTimestamp: ".."
  name: aws-auth
  namespace: kube-system
  resourceVersion: "816"
  uid: 0de5b298-9aaf-481f-
```

262

CHAPTER 9 IDENTITY AND ACCESS MANAGEMENT

Make sure there is another configuration for Alice on the file.

5. Delete the existing aws-auth ConfigMap configuration.

   ```
   kubectl delete -f aws-auth.yml
   ```

6. Create a new configuration with the changes.

   ```
   kubectl apply -f aws-auth.yml
   ```

7. Switch user context to Alice.

   ```
   aws eks update-kubeconfig --name public-endpoint-cluster --profile alice
   ```

8. Test if Alice can access the cluster.

   ```
   kubectl get services
   ```

9. Verify if Alice can create deployments.

   ```
   kubectl auth can-i create deployments
   ```

10. View nodes.

    ```
    kubectl get nodes
    ```

    You should see all the nodes.

Adding Cluster Editor Role

1. Switch user context to the default cluster creator.

   ```
   aws eks update-kubeconfig --name public-endpoint-cluster
   ```

CHAPTER 9   IDENTITY AND ACCESS MANAGEMENT

2. Edit the aws-auth ConfigMap file to add Alice to the edit group.

   ```
   apiVersion: v1
   data:
     mapRoles: |
       - groups:
         - system:bootstrappers
         - system:nodes
         rolearn: arn:aws:iam::ACCOUNTID:role/public-
         endpoint-cluster-nodes
         username: system:node:{{EC2PrivateDNSName}}
     mapUsers: |
       - userarn: arn:aws:iam::${ACCOUNT_ID}:user/alice
         username: alice
         groups:
           - edit
   kind: ConfigMap
   metadata:
     creationTimestamp: ".."
     name: aws-auth
     namespace: kube-system
     resourceVersion: "16237"
     uid: 515138aa-d0b0-4925-8d24
   ```

3. Run kubectl delete -f aws-auth.yml.

4. Run kubectl apply -f aws-auth.yml.

5. Verify the configuration with the following commands:

   ```
   kubectl get svc
   kubectl auth can-i create deployments
   kubectl get nodes
   ```

Summary

We have gone through a recipe for editing the aws-auth ConfigMap to demonstrate how difficult it can be to manage cluster administrators with the old cluster access control method. The aws-auth ConfigMap is deprecated and no longer the access control method of choice for EKS clusters. The new EKS access control method will take the center stage in the next chapter.

CHAPTER 10

The New Cluster Access Management

This chapter builds on the chapter before but focuses on the new EKS cluster access management method. The goal is to explain the merit of the new EKS cluster access management method and illustrate how it simplifies cluster administration.

As we noticed in the chapter before, access to a K8s cluster in EKS rests on the behind-the-scenes mapping between an IAM principal such as a cluster administrator and K8s role-based access control (RBAC) groups such as the system masters group. The behind-the-scenes mapping is created with the aws-auth ConfigMap object.[1] Configuring the aws-auth ConfigMap could be complicated and error prone and could demand switching between AWS and K8s APIs, eventually increasing the operational overhead for the cluster administration.

In the old aws-auth ConfigMap approach, the cluster creator is comparable to the AWS account root user. They have unrestricted and irrevocable access to the cluster and do not appear in the aws-auth ConfigMap configuration file that maps the IAM principals to K8s RBAC groups.

---

[1] https://aws.amazon.com/blogs/containers/a-deep-dive-into-simplified-amazon-eks-access-management-controls/

CHAPTER 10   THE NEW CLUSTER ACCESS MANAGEMENT

AWS introduced the new EKS cluster access management method to simplify EKS cluster administration. It offloads K8s access management to the new AWS/EKS IAM automating the behind-the-scenes mapping between AWS IAM principals and K8s RBAC groups.

You can automatically associate an IAM principal with predefined AWS-managed K8s policies known as access policies, and EKS will do all the behind-the-scenes mapping between the policies and K8s RBAC groups. This relieves cluster administrators from manually editing the K8s RBAC configuration files to map AWS principals to K8s RBAC groups.

Unlike the aws-auth ConfigMap approach, no user has irrevocable or permanent access to the cluster. Cluster creators do not have automatic access to the cluster, and their entitlement can be revoked before or after the cluster creation. You can refine the access rights of cluster creators as you wish in the new EKS cluster access management paradigm.

The rest of this chapter will introduce in detail the new EKS cluster access control management method. We will also implement a few scenarios to show how the method eases cluster administration.

Access Entries and Policy Association

This section introduces the steps involved in creating cluster administrators with the new EKS cluster access management method. The new EKS cluster access management method encompasses a three-step process, the creation of the IAM principal in the "EKS IAM" (access entry), the association of the EKS principal with access policies or custom K8s permissions (access policy association), and automated behind-the-scenes mapping.

The access entry step is where a cluster administrator registers an AWS IAM principal in the AWS/EKS access entry IAM service. Think of the AWS/EKS access entry IAM as a "mini" or miniature IAM for an EKS cluster.

The second step is the access policy step where a cluster administrator attaches policies to the registered AWS/EKS IAM principal to access the K8s components and objects. Consider this step as the cluster binding step. The binding step involves the attachment of access policies to an IAM principal.[2]

Finally, the EKS completes the policy assignment with the automated behind-the-scenes mapping between the access policy and K8s RBAC groups.

Figure 10-1 illustrates the three-step process, including the behind-the-scenes mapping. A cluster administrator creates an access entry for a principal in step 1, assigns a policy or permission to the principal in step 2, and EKS does the behind-the-scenes mapping in step 3.

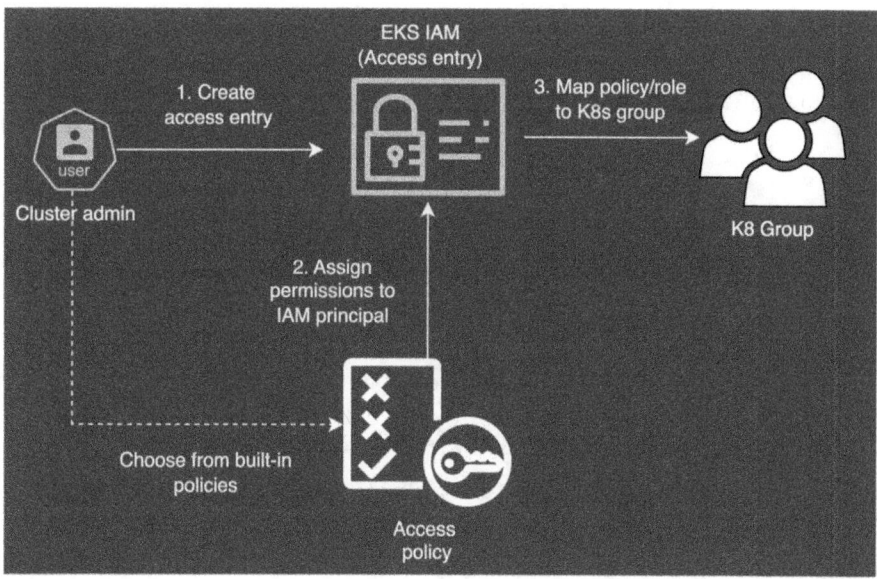

Figure 10-1. The new cluster access management process

---

[2] https://aws.amazon.com/blogs/containers/a-deep-dive-into-simplified-amazon-eks-access-management-controls/

CHAPTER 10   THE NEW CLUSTER ACCESS MANAGEMENT

Built-In Access Entry Policy

The new EKS cluster access control method simplifies access management further with managed access policies for cluster administrators to choose from and assign them to the access entry principals in the AWS/EKS IAM.

You find these managed access policies with the following command:

```
aws eks list-access-policies
```

The command should produce the following results:

```
{
    "accessPolicies": [
        {
            "name": "AmazonEKSAdminPolicy",
            "arn": "arn:aws:eks::aws:cluster-access-policy/
            AmazonEKSAdminPolicy"
        },
        {
            "name": "AmazonEKSAdminViewPolicy",
            "arn": "arn:aws:eks::aws:cluster-access-policy/
            AmazonEKSAdminViewPolicy"
        },
        {
            "name": "AmazonEKSClusterAdminPolicy",
            "arn": "arn:aws:eks::aws:cluster-access-policy/
            AmazonEKSClusterAdminPolicy"
        },
        {
            "name": "AmazonEKSEditPolicy",
            "arn": "arn:aws:eks::aws:cluster-access-policy/
            AmazonEKSEditPolicy"
        },
```

CHAPTER 10   THE NEW CLUSTER ACCESS MANAGEMENT

```
    {
        "name": "AmazonEKSViewPolicy",
        "arn": "arn:aws:eks::aws:cluster-access-policy/
        AmazonEKSViewPolicy"
    },
    {
        "name": "AmazonEMRJobPolicy",
        "arn": "arn:aws:eks::aws:cluster-access-policy/
        AmazonEMRJobPolicy"
    },
    {
        "name": "AmazonSagemakerHyperpodClusterPolicy",
        "arn": "arn:aws:eks::aws:cluster-access-policy/
        AmazonSagemakerHyperpodClusterPolicy"
    },
    {
        "name": "AmazonSagemakerHyperpodControllerPolicy",
        "arn": "arn:aws:eks::aws:cluster-access-policy/
        AmazonSagemakerHyperpodControllerPolicy"
    },
    {
        "name": "AmazonSagemakerHyperpodSystem
        NamespacePolicy",
        "arn": "arn:aws:eks::aws:cluster-access-policy/
        AmazonSagemakerHyperpodSystemNamespacePolicy"
    }
  ]
}
```

Use the following command if you want to format the output:

```
aws eks list-access-policies --output table
```

CHAPTER 10 THE NEW CLUSTER ACCESS MANAGEMENT

Table 10-1 maps the output of the access policies to the default K8s RBAC groups.[3] It leaves out the Sage maker and the EMR policies since they are out of scope for this discussion.

Table 10-1. Managed policies

Default K8s Roles	Privileges	AWS EKS Policy	Administrators
Cluster-admin	Cluster-wide super user	AmazonEKSClusterAdminPolicy	Cluster Creators
Admin	Full access within a namespace	AmazonEKSAdminPolicy	Namespace administrators
Edit	Read/write within a namespace	AmazonEKSEditPolicy	Namespace editor
View	Read-only within a namespace	AmazonEKSViewPolicy	Security auditor
Custom	Cluster developer	Custom policy	Developers/administrators

Cluster administrators can assign any of the policies in Table 10-1 to a cluster administrator depending on their security or least privilege needs. They can also create custom policies if the managed policies cannot meet their security requirements.

Apart from the **AmazonEKSClusterAdminPolicy** policy, all other policies in the table are scoped to a namespace. K8s uses namespaces to segment access to resources. A namespace administrator manages resources and access to the namespace. Think of namespace as a project assigned to a team. The namespace administrator becomes the project

---

[3] https://docs.aws.amazon.com/eks/latest/userguide/access-policies.html#access-policy-permissions

administrator and manages the project for the rest of the team. You can create multiple namespaces and assign each of them to specific administrators.

Access Management Authentication Modes

The new EKS cluster access management method is backward compatible. You can configure both the old aws-auth ConfigMap method and the new method side by side in the same cluster. This is especially useful for those who had an old cluster at the time when the new cluster access management method was introduced or those with an old configuration base and want to have a gradual transition.

Alternatively, you can choose to configure a specific access method per your requirements. Thus, you can choose from hybrid or specific implementation of the cluster access management method. You can do so with the following three modes of operation, the API, API_AND_CONFIG_MAP, and CONFIG_MAP.[4]

The API_AND_CONFIG_MAP authentication mode enables support for both the new cluster access and the old aws-auth ConfigMap methods. However, the API authentication mode supports only the new EKS cluster access management method. Similarly, the CONFIG_MAP authentication mode supports only the old aws-auth ConfigMap access management method.

EKS allows cluster administrators to switch authentication modes after cluster creation with the following commands:

```
aws eks update-cluster-config \
  --name <CLUSTER_NAME> \
  --access-config authenticationMode=API
```

---

[4] https://aws.amazon.com/blogs/containers/a-deep-dive-into-simplified-amazon-eks-access-management-controls/

or

```
aws eks update-cluster-config \
  --name <CLUSTER_NAME> \
  --access-config authenticationMode=API_AND_CONFIG_MAP
```

The first command implements only the new cluster access management method, whereas the second command implements both the old and the new method. Switching an authentication mode may be irreversible. For example, you can switch from CONFIG_MAP to API_AND_CONFIG_MAP and then from API_AND_CONFIG_MAP to API.

However, you cannot reverse the order by switching back to CONFIG_MAP or API_AND_CONFIG_MAP from API. Also, you cannot revert to CONFIG_MAP from API_AND_CONFIG_MAP.[5]

The New Cluster Access Management Implementation

We will deploy the EKS cluster for this section and show how to implement various access scenarios with the new cluster access management method. We will assign Alice the cluster creator, namespace admin, and cluster reader permissions and test the outcome of each assignment with the new cluster access management method.

Before then we will review the Terraform code to explain the major changes. You will find the changes in the **eks.tf** file as shown in the code snippet below. We set the authentication mode to API and the ConfigMap modes to allow both cluster access management modes (the old and the new versions).

---

[5] https://aws.amazon.com/blogs/containers/a-deep-dive-into-simplified-amazon-eks-access-management-controls/

We set the bootstrap cluster creator admin permission to true to grant the cluster creator full access to the cluster. The bootstrap cluster creator admin permission argument when set to false revokes the cluster creator's access to the cluster except for creation of administrators.

```
resource "aws_eks_cluster" "public_endpoint_cluster" {
  name     = var.cluster_name
  role_arn = aws_iam_role.eks_assume_role.arn
  version = var.cluster_version
  vpc_config {
    subnet_ids = concat(
      var.enis_subnet_ids
    )
    endpoint_public_access  = "true"
  }
  access_config {
    authentication_mode = "API_AND_CONFIG_MAP"
    bootstrap_cluster_creator_admin_permissions = "true"
  }
  depends_on = [aws_iam_role.eks_assume_role]
}
```

It is possible to configure the authentication mode after cluster creation with the following command:

aws eks update-cluster-config --name cluster-name --access-config authenticationMode=API_AND_CONFIG_MAP

Granting Cluster Creator Access to Alice

The following recipe will grant the cluster creator permission to Alice, an IAM user:

CHAPTER 10 THE NEW CLUSTER ACCESS MANAGEMENT

1. Deploy the cluster in the chapter10 folder and switch context to the default cluster creator.

   ```
   aws eks update-kubeconfig --name <CLUSTER_NAME>
   ```

2. List available access entries for the current user (cluster creator).

   ```
   aws eks list-access-entries --cluster-name public-endpoint-cluster
   ```

3. Create a user Alice if you have not done so in Chapter 9.

   ```
   aws iam create-user --user-name alice
   ```

4. Create a policy file policy.json with the following content:

   ```
   {
       "Version": "2012-10-17",
       "Statement": [
           {
               "Effect": "Allow",
               "Action": [
                "eks:DescribeCluster"
               ],
               "Resource": "*"
           }
       ]
   }
   ```

   The eks:DescribeCluster permission is mandatory for all cluster administrators.

CHAPTER 10   THE NEW CLUSTER ACCESS MANAGEMENT

5. Create an IAM policy with the policy.json file above.

   ```
   aws iam create-policy --policy-name <policy-name>
   --policy-document file://policy.json
   ```

   Replace <policy-name> with a chosen name, for example, eks-describe-policy.

6. Copy the policy arn in step 5, for example, **arn:aws:iam::${ACCOUNT_ID}:policy/eks-describe-policy**.

7. Attach the policy to Alice to enable her to describe the cluster.

   ```
   aws iam attach-user-policy --policy-arn
   arn:aws:iam::${ACCOUNT_ID}:policy/eks-describe-policy
   --user-name alice
   ```

8. List all users in your account.

   ```
   aws iam list-users
   ```

9. Copy the arn of the user Alice.

   arn:aws:iam::${ACCOUNT_ID}:user/alice.

10. Create access entry for alice.

    ```
    aws eks create-access-entry --cluster-name <CLUSTER_NAME> --principal-arn <IAM_PRINCIPAL_ARN>
    ```

    Replace the CLUSTER_NAME with the name of your cluster and the IAM_PRINCIPAL_ARN with the arn of Alice. For example:

    ```
    aws eks create-access-entry --cluster-name public-endpoint-cluster --principal-arn arn:aws:iam::${ACCOUNT_ID}:user/alice
    ```

CHAPTER 10   THE NEW CLUSTER ACCESS MANAGEMENT

You should see the following output:

```
{
    "accessEntry": {
        "clusterName": "<cluster_name>",
        "principalArn": "arn:aws:iam::ACCOUNT_ID:user/alice",
        "kubernetesGroups": [],
        "accessEntryArn": "arn: aws:eks:us-east-1: ACCOUNT_ID: access-entry/<cluster_name>/user/ACCOUNT_ID/alice/b2ca1843-...",
        "createdAt": "..",
        "modifiedAt": "..",
        "tags": {},
        "username": "arn:aws:iam::ACCOUNT_ID:user/alice",
        "type": "STANDARD"
    }
}
```

11. View the available access policies you can attach to Alice.

    ```
    aws eks list-access-policies --output table
    ```

12. Assign the cluster creator policy to Alice.

    ```
    aws eks associate-access-policy \
    --cluster-name <CLUSTER_NAME> \
    --principal-arn <PRINCIPAL_ARN>\
    --policy-arn <POLICY_ARN> \
    --access-scope type=<TYPE>
    ```

For example:

```
aws eks associate-access-policy \
--cluster-name public-endpoint-cluster \
--principal-arn arn:aws:iam::${ACCOUNT_ID}:user/alice \
--policy-arn arn:aws:eks::aws:cluster-access-policy/
```
AmazonEKSClusterAdminPolicy \
```
--access-scope type=cluster
```

The **access-scope type = cluster** argument grants Alice access to all namespaces of the cluster. You should have a similar output as before.

13. Create a profile for Alice in your **.aws/credentials** file.

    ```
    [alice]
    region = <AWS_REGION>
    aws_access_key_id = <ACCESS_KEY_ID>
    aws_secret_access_key = <SECRET_ACCESS_KEY>
    ```

14. Switch user context.

    ```
    aws eks update-kubeconfig --name <CLUSTER_NAME>
    --profile alice
    ```

15. Verify if Alice can access the cluster pods and nodes and create a namespace.

    ```
    kubectl get pods -A
    kubectl get nodes
    kubectl create ns test-ns
    ```

Alice should be able to run any of the commands successfully because she is now a cluster administrator.

CHAPTER 10 THE NEW CLUSTER ACCESS MANAGEMENT

Create Cluster Admin

This scenario makes Alice the default namespace administrator.

1. Switch context back to the original cluster creator.

   ```
   aws eks update-kubeconfig --name <CLUSTER_NAME>
   ```

2. Remove the cluster creator access for Alice.

   ```
   aws eks disassociate-access-policy --cluster-name <CLUSTER_NAME> \
       --principal-arn arn:aws:iam::${ACCOUNT_ID}:user/alice \
       --policy-arn arn:aws:eks::aws:cluster-access-policy/AmazonEKSClusterAdminPolicy
   ```

   Replace the cluster name and the principal arn with yours.

3. Downgrade Alice permission to a namespace admin.

   ```
   aws eks associate-access-policy \
   --cluster-name <CLUSTER_NAME> \
   --principal-arn arn:aws:iam::${ACCOUNT_ID}:user/alice \
   --policy-arn arn:aws:eks::aws:cluster-access-policy/**AmazonEKSAdminPolicy** \
   --access-scope type=cluster
   ```

4. List the policy associated with Alice.

   ```
   aws eks list-associated-access-policies --cluster-name <CLUSTER_NAME> \
     --principal-arn arn:aws:iam::${ACCOUNT_ID}:user/alice
   ```

You should find the following output:

```
{
    "associatedAccessPolicies": [
        {
            "policyArn": "arn:aws:eks::aws:cluster-
            access-policy/**AmazonEKSAdminPolicy**",
            "accessScope": {
                "type": "cluster",
                "namespaces": []
            },
            "associatedAt": "...",
            "modifiedAt": "..."
        }
    ],
    "clusterName": "public-endpoint-cluster",
```

5. Switch context back to Alice's profile.

   ```
   aws eks update-kubeconfig –name <CLUSTER_NAME>
   --profile alice
   ```

6. Test the access.

   ```
   kubectl get nodes
   ```

   This should fail with the error message server (Forbidden): nodes are forbidden User "arn:aws:iam::${ACCOUNT_ID}:user/alice" cannot list resource "nodes" in API group "" at the cluster scope. This is because Alice is no longer a cluster administrator.

7. Test the access.

   ```
   kubectl get pods -A
   ```

CHAPTER 10   THE NEW CLUSTER ACCESS MANAGEMENT

You should find all the pods listed as follows:

NAMESPACE	NAME	READY	STATUS	RESTARTS	AGE
kube-system	aws-node-f5hmv	2/2	Running	0	22m
kube-system	coredns-789f8477df-42h5c	1/1	Running	0	24m
kube-system	coredns-789f8477df-8kqk7	1/1	Running	0	24m
kube-system	kube-proxy-75x6f	1/1	Running	0	22m

Namespace Access

This scenario makes Alice a namespace administrator in a specific namespace other than the default namespace. The name of the namespace is test-ns.

1. Switch context back to the cluster creator.

   ```
   aws eks update-kubeconfig --name <CLUSTER_NAME>
   ```

2. Create the **test-ns** namespace.

   ```
   kubectl create ns test-ns
   ```

3. Disassociate the EKS Admin Policy from Alice.

   ```
    aws eks disassociate-access-policy --cluster-name public-endpoint-cluster \
        --principal-arn arn:aws:iam::
          552247556312:user/alice \
        --policy-arn arn:aws:eks::aws:cluster-access-
          policy/AmazonEKSAdminPolicy
   ```

4. Assign Alice AmazonEKSAdminPolicy within the test-ns namespace.

282

```
aws eks associate-access-policy --cluster-name
<CLUSTER_NAME> \
  --principal-arn arn:aws:iam::${ACCOUNT_
    ID}:user/alice \
  --policy-arn arn:aws:eks::aws:cluster-access-
    policy/AmazonEKSAdminPolicy \
  --access-scope type=namespace,namespaces=test-ns
```

5. Switch context back to Alice's profile.

   ```
   aws eks update-kubeconfig –name <CLUSTER_NAME>
   --profile alice
   ```

6. Test the permission.

   ```
   kubectl get nodes
   ```

   This permission will only work when Alice tries to access pods in an existing test* namespace. You should get the error message server (Forbidden): nodes are forbidden User "arn:aws:iam::${ACCOUNT_ID}:user/alice" cannot list resource "nodes" in API group "" at the cluster scope.

7. Test the permission.

   ```
   kubectl get pods -n test-ns
   ```

   This should be successful displaying **No resources found in test-ns namespace**.

CHAPTER 10   THE NEW CLUSTER ACCESS MANAGEMENT

Granting Custom Permissions with K8s RBAC

This scenario grants a custom developer permission to Alice through Kubernetes groups.

1. Switch context back to the cluster creator.

   ```
   aws eks update-kubeconfig --name <CLUSTER_NAME>
   ```

2. Remove the namespace admin access from Alice.

   ```
   aws eks disassociate-access-policy --cluster-name <CLUSTER_NAME> \
       --principal-arn arn:aws:iam::${ACCOUNT_ID}:user/<username> \
       --policy-arn arn:aws:eks::aws:cluster-access-policy/AmazonEKSAdminPolicy
   ```

3. Create cluster role binding.

   ```
   kubectl create clusterrolebinding readonly \
   --clusterrole=readonly-role \
   --group=readonly-group
   ```

4. Define the role permissions and binding with the following YAML file:

   ```
   kind: ClusterRole
   apiVersion: rbac.authorization.k8s.io/v1
   metadata:
     name: readonly-role
   rules:
   - apiGroups: [""]
     resources: ["nodes", "namespaces", "pods"]
   ```

CHAPTER 10   THE NEW CLUSTER ACCESS MANAGEMENT

```
  verbs: ["get", "list"]
- apiGroups: ["apps"]
  resources: ["deployment", "daemonsets"]
  verbs: ["get", "list","watch"]
```

5. Execute the binding command.

   ```
   kubectl apply -f rolebinding.yaml
   ```

6. Remove access entry for Alice.

   ```
   aws eks delete-access-entry --cluster-name <CLUSTER_NAME> \
    --principal-arn arn:aws:iam::${ACCOUNT_ID}:user/alice
   ```

7. Create a new access entry for Alice with the readonly-group. Replace the ARN with that of Alice's.

   ```
   aws eks create-access-entry --cluster-name <CLUSTER_NAME> \
     --principal-arn <IAM_PRINCIPAL_ARN> \
     --kubernetes-groups readonly-group
   ```

8. Switch context to Alice's profile.

   ```
   aws eks update-kubeconfig --name <CLUSTER_NAME> -profile alice
   ```

9. Test the following commands:

   ```
   kubectl auth can-i get pod, it should be yes.
   kubectl get pods -A
   kubectl get nodes
   kubectl get deployment
   ```

285

CHAPTER 10   THE NEW CLUSTER ACCESS MANAGEMENT

All the commands should be successful except the kubectl get deployment command because it was not configured in the policy.

Assigning Permissions to IAM Roles

This scenario assigns IAM permission to a role rather than an IAM user. This is useful when you want to assign the same permission to several users.

1. Switch context to the cluster creator.

2. Create a policy file and save it as eks-describe-policy.json.

   ```
   {
       "Version": "2012-10-17",
       "Statement": [
           {
               "Effect": "Allow",
               "Action": [
               "eks:DescribeCluster"
               ],
               "Resource": "*"
           }
       ]
   }
   ```

3. Create an IAM policy with the policy file.

   ```
   aws iam create-policy --policy-name eks-describe-policy --policy-document file://eks-describe-policy.json
   ```

CHAPTER 10   THE NEW CLUSTER ACCESS MANAGEMENT

4. Create a trusted relationship policy file (trust.json).

```
{
  "Version": "2012-10-17",
  "Statement": [
      {
      "Effect": "Allow",
      "Principal": { "AWS": "arn:aws:iam::${ACCOUNT_
      ID}:user/alice" },
      "Action": "sts:AssumeRole"

      }
  ]
}
```

5. Create a role with a trusted relationship policy.

```
aws iam create-role --role-name my-test-eks-role
--assume-role-policy-document file://trust.json
```

6. Copy the role arn.

```
arn:aws:iam::${ACCOUNT_ID}:role/my-test-eks-role
```

7. Attach the EKS cluster describe policy above (my-role-policy) to the role.

```
aws iam attach-role-policy --role-name my-test-eks-role --policy-arn arn:aws:iam::${ACCOUNT_ID}:policy/eks-describe-policy
```

8. Create a new profile for Alice in the .aws/credentials file.

```
[alice]
region = us-east-1
aws_access_key_id = <ACCESS_KEY_ID>
aws_secret_access_key = <SECRET_ACCESS_KEY>
```

CHAPTER 10   THE NEW CLUSTER ACCESS MANAGEMENT

```
[alice-role]
 role_arn = arn:aws:iam::${ACCOUNT_ID}:role/my-
 test-eks-role
 source_profile = alice
 region = us-east-1
```

9. Add entry for the role so that the users who assume the role will become the cluster administrator.

```
aws eks create-access-entry \
--cluster-name public-endpoint-cluster \
--principal-arn arn:aws:iam::${ACCOUNT_ID}:role/my-
test-eks-role
```

10. Create permission with the role arn.

```
aws eks associate-access-policy \
--cluster-name public-endpoint-cluster \
--principal-arn arn:aws:iam::${ACCOUNT_ID}:role/my-
test-eks-role \
--policy-arn arn:aws:eks::aws:cluster-access-policy/
AmazonEKSClusterAdminPolicy \
--access-scope type=cluster
```

11. Switch context.

```
aws eks update-kubeconfig --name public-endpoint-
cluster --profile alice-role
```

12. Test the following commands:

```
kubectl auth can-i get pod
kubectl get pods -A
kubectl get nodes
```

CHAPTER 10　THE NEW CLUSTER ACCESS MANAGEMENT

The above test should be successful because we assigned EKS cluster creator privilege to the role. You can find the access entry from the **AWS console ➤ EKS ➤ Access tab**.

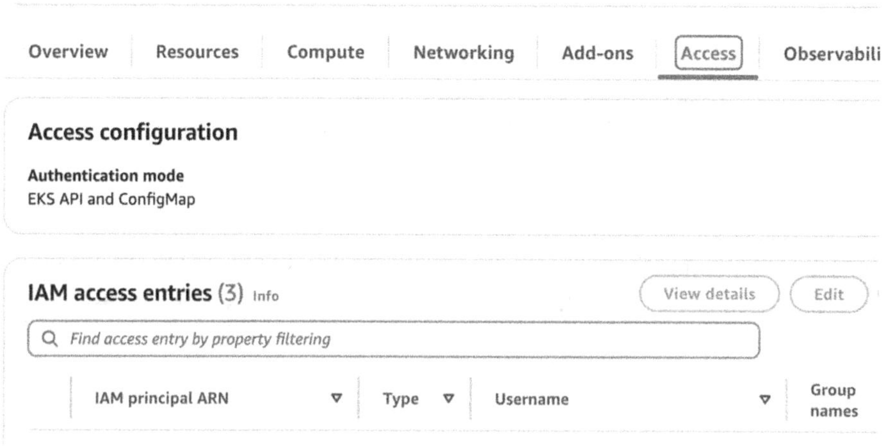

Figure 10-2. EKS access console

You can also use the same console to create cluster administrators.

Creating Access Entry with EKS Console

You can configure users from the EKS console if you want to avoid the command line.

1. Go to the EKS console.
2. Click the name of the cluster.
3. Click the Access tab.
4. Click the access entry.
5. Select your IAM principal.
6. Click the Next button.

7. Choose an access policy.

8. Choose access scope.

9. Click the Next button and create access.

Disable Cluster Creator

With the new EKS cluster access management method, you can create a cluster with no cluster creator access, and yet the cluster creator can manage administor privileges.

You can do so by disabling the bootstrap cluster creator admin permissions in the eks.tf file as follows:

```
access_config {
    authentication_mode = "API_AND_CONFIG_MAP"
    bootstrap_cluster_creator_admin_permissions = "false"
}
```

The access_config block specifies the authentication mode and sets the bootstrap cluster creator permission to false. This means the cluster creator will have no access to the K8s services or objects except access entry.

1. Delete the cluster.

    ```
    terraform destroy -auto-approve
    ```

2. Recreate the cluster.

    ```
    terraform apply -auto-approve
    ```

3. Switch context.

    ```
    aws eks update-kubeconfig --name public-endpoint-cluster
    ```

4. Test access.

   ```
   kubectl get nodes
   ```

   Access should fail with the following error message:

   18056 memcache.go:265] couldn't get the current server API group list: the server has asked for ... because the cluster creator has no permissions.

5. Verify your permission as a cluster creator.

   ```
   aws eks list-access-entries --cluster-name public-endpoint-cluster
   
   {
       "accessEntries": [
           "arn:aws:iam::${ACCOUNT_ID}: role/public-
               endpoint-cluster-nodes"
       ]
   }
   ```

6. Retrieve the nodes.

   ```
   kubectl get nodes
   ```

   This should fail because the cluster administrator role is disabled with the **bootstrap_cluster_creator_admin_permissions = "false"** argument as in the eks.tf file.

Summary

Navigating the complex landscape of the old aws-auth ConfigMap was undoubtedly challenging. But the new cluster access management method has no doubt reduced the complexities. Understanding the intricate interplay between IAM and K8s RBAC groups is a critical piece of the

CHAPTER 10   THE NEW CLUSTER ACCESS MANAGEMENT

puzzle, as you master the new cluster access management method. The new access management method automates mapping between EKS IAM and K8s RBAC groups, relieving administrators from complex and error-prone configuration file editing. This chapter marks the end of discussion on the essential concepts in EKS. The chapters that follow will dive into K8s concepts and later advanced EKS concepts.

PART 2

CHAPTER 11

Kubernetes

We began this book with a brief history of Kubernetes (K8s), how it all started, and how we got here. We introduced Figure 11-1 to illustrate the relationship between Amazon Elastic Kubernetes Service (EKS) and the K8s orchestrator. Since then, we have concentrated all our energy on EKS, its architecture, components, security, and functionalities. It is now time to shift our attention to K8s and explore its core strength which is running containerized applications. K8s excels at orchestrating, scaling, and managing containers, providing a robust platform for deploying modern, cloud-native applications efficiently.

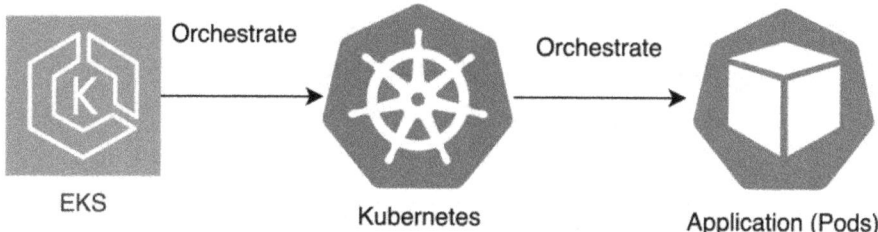

Figure 11-1. *Relationship between EKS and K8s*

Part 2 of this book will focus primarily on K8s, starting with its core components and learning how to identify them within EKS clusters. We will achieve this by examining an EKS deployment to discover and explain each Kubernetes component in detail. This hands-on exercise is designed to provide a deeper understanding of the inner workings of Kubernetes to give you practical experience with its architecture and operations.

CHAPTER 11   KUBERNETES

Key Benefits of Kubernetes

K8s automates application deployment, scaling, and operation. By continuously monitoring application states, it simplifies application management, making sure that they are consistently updated, running efficiently, and aligned with the desired configurations. This automation reduces operational complexity and enhances reliability.[1] K8s decides how and where the applications should run. It maintains their lifecycles based on a given policy.

Some of the benefits of K8s are as follows:[2]

- *Efficiency*: Optimizes hardware, system, and applications' resource usage.

- *Reliability*: Minimizes downtime ensuring that application services are always available.

- *Portability*: Runs diverse workload and on various platforms, including stateless, stateful, and data-processing workloads.

- *Flexibility*: Runs on various platforms, from physical machines to cloud infrastructure.

- *Security*: Provides robust security features including secure communications between multiple services.

- *Auto-healing*: Enables automated recovery from failures.

---

[1] https://medium.com/@rphilogene/what-is-kubernetes-what-you-need-to-know-as-a-developer-674af25e3947

[2] Hands-On Kubernetes, Service Mesh and Zero-Trust: Build and manage secure applications using Kubernetes and Istio by Swapnil Dubey and Mandar J. Kulkarni

CHAPTER 11   KUBERNETES

- *Capability to scale*: Can scale applications horizontally (scaling up and down) and vertically (scaling in and out).

- *Extensibility*: You can add more features to a K8s cluster without impacting the already present applications.

- *Support for batch executions*: Supports batch and cron jobs execution.

- *Rollbacks and rollouts*: You can choose to roll back and roll out your application in stages before production. This can allow you to test the latest version of a service on a section of users and before allowing it for all once you are satisfied with the test.

- *Storage and config management*: Provides the capability to use various storage solutions – SSD or HDD, Google Cloud Storage, AWS S3, or Azure Storage.

- *Configuration management*: Supports effective management of general and secret configurations.

- *Open source community*: Benefits from a large community of developers and users who contribute to its continuous improvement.

Kubernetes Architecture

Figure 11-2 provides a visual representation of the K8s architecture. It highlights the core components and illustrates how they interact with one another. The diagram serves as a reference architecture for understanding the relationships between components such as the API server, controller manager, scheduler, etcd, and kubelet, along with their roles in orchestrating containerized applications.

The control plane is the most intelligent part of the cluster. It is responsible for making global decisions, such as scheduling pods to appropriate nodes, managing the cluster's overall state, and coordinating tasks to ensure efficient operation and resource utilization.[3] The control plane is also responsible for detecting and responding to cluster events such as failures. It consists of the API server, etcd, scheduler, and the controller manager.

We will briefly recap each of the core K8s components, providing an overview of their roles and functions within the cluster in the consequent sections.

The API Server Component

The API server is the most vital component of the control plane. It is the communication gateway and hub for both internal cluster components and external clients such as the kubectl command-line tool.

The API server facilitates communication by exposing K8s's RESTful API to cluster components and clients. It is the communication hub for all internal and external interactions within the K8s cluster. All communications, whether initiated through the GUI, CLI, or API calls, pass through the API server. It is the central interface, processing requests and guaranteeing that the cluster's components remain interconnected and responsive.

When a client sends a request to the cluster, the API server first validates it to verify that the request is well formed and authorized. Once validated, it processes the request, executes the necessary actions, and coordinates with other K8s components to render the request.

---

[3] https://kubernetes.io/docs/concepts/overview/components/

The ETCD Component

The **etcd** component is a distributed database for storing cluster information, including manifests, metadata, and state information. K8s relies on the information in the **etcd** database to respond effectively to cluster events such as network issues, node failures, storage disruptions, or deployment problems. By maintaining a consistent and reliable record of the cluster's state, **etcd** plays a key role in ensuring the stability and resiliency of K8s operations.[4]

etcd stores every user object under a key with the name **/registry/object/namespace/object-name**. For instance, the key name for a pod with the name "**blueapp-pod**" deployed in the default namespace will be stored as **/registry/pods/default/blueapp-pod**.

All requests to **etcd** pass through the API server for validation, processing, and execution. For security purposes, the API server is the sole component authorized to directly interact with the **etcd** datastore. This ensures controlled access and protects the integrity of the cluster's critical data.

---

[4] The Kubernetes Workshop: Learn how to build and run highly scalable workloads on Kubernetes, Zachary Arnold, Sahil Dua, Wei Huang, Faisal Masood, Melony Qin, and Mohammed Abu Taleb

CHAPTER 11   KUBERNETES

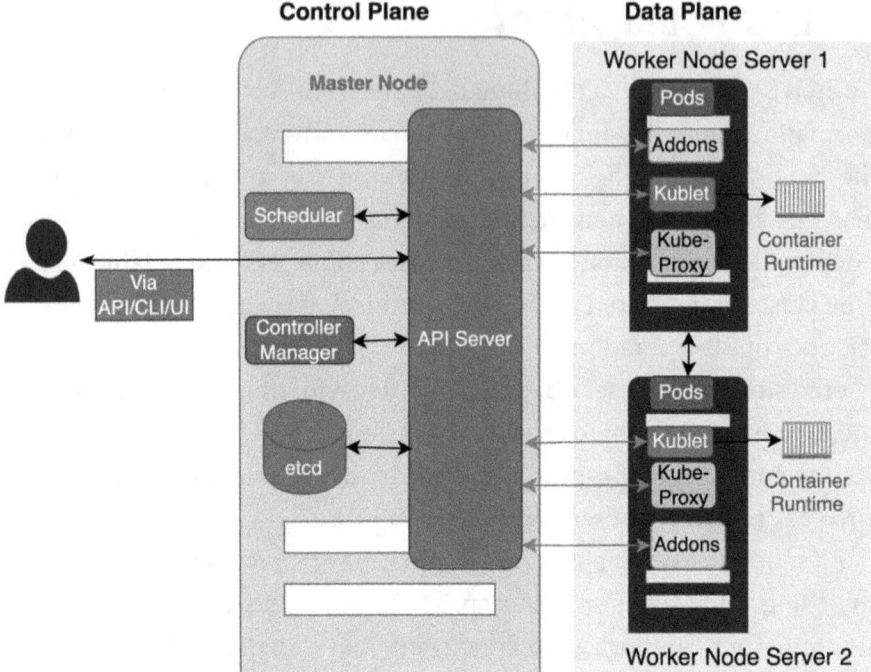

Figure 11-2. Kubernetes cluster

Scheduler Component

The scheduler is responsible for assigning the most suitable node to an incoming application or pod (workload). It relies on decision-making algorithms and a comprehensive understanding of the cluster's state to optimally place workloads.

The decision-making algorithm considers resource availability, hardware/software/policy constraints, affinity, and anti-affinity specifications before deciding on the correct node to provide a workload. Others include data locality, inter-workload interference, tolerations, and deadlines.[5] The scheduler helps maximize efficiency and maintain balance across the cluster.

---

[5] https://kubernetes.io/docs/concepts/overview/components/

The Controller Manager Component

You may notice several controllers when you run the `kubectl get --raw='/readyz?verbose'` or the `kubectl sa -ns kube-system` command. The controller manager keeps the cluster in its desired state. It controls the individual object and component controllers in the cluster.

The **controller manager** orchestrates the various object-specific controllers to maintain the cluster's desired state. For example, the **node controller** monitors the health of nodes and responds appropriately if a node becomes unavailable. Similarly, the **ReplicaSet controller** ensures that the actual number of pod replicas matches the desired count specified for the cluster. These controllers work collaboratively under the coordination of the controller manager to ensure the stability and resilience of the cluster.

The Kubelet Component

The kubelet maintains the desired state of containers. Running on the worker nodes of the data plane, the kubelet manages the lifecycle of containers within application pods on those nodes. It interacts with the control plane to receive instructions and see to it that containers are running as specified in the pod definitions.

Kubelet communicates with the underlying container runtime (Docker containerd, podman, or Windows container) to start a container and ensure that their desired state is maintained.[6]

---

[6] The Kubernetes Workshop: Learn how to build and run highly scalable workloads on Kubernetes, Zachary Arnold, Sahil Dua, Wei Huang, Faisal Masood, Melony Qin, and Mohammed Abu Taleb

CHAPTER 11   KUBERNETES

Kubelet is responsible for starting pods. It takes as input pod specifications and verifies that the actual running pod meets the container definitions inside the specifications. It monitors the health of containers. In addition, it regularly updates the API server about the status of containers.[7]

The Kube-proxy Component

Kube-proxy is a distributed network router that runs on every node. Its main function is to route inbound traffic to a service endpoint of an application.

It maintains network rules that allow communication between pods and network sessions inside or outside of a cluster. Kube-proxy forwards traffic to applications directly or may rely on the operating system packet filtering layer to do the same.

Kube-proxy can balance the traffic in a round-robin manner by leveraging the underlying Linux iptables/IPVS technology when multiple containers serve one application.

Addon

Addons are auxiliary components used to extend the capabilities of the cluster. It provides additional functionalities such as monitoring, logging, networking, and security enhancements. Addons enhance the overall flexibility and utility of K8s by enabling features beyond its core functionalities (see Chapter 8). You can find addons on both data and control planes. CoreDNS is an example of control plane addon, while network plugins like Calico is an example of data plane addons.

---

[7] Hands-On Kubernetes, Service Mesh and Zero-Trust: Build and manage secure applications using Kubernetes and Istio by Swapnil Dubey and Mandar J. Kulkarni

Pods

A pod encapsulates one or more containers and represents a single instance of a running process within a cluster. It is the smallest deployable unit in Kubernetes, created and managed to run applications or services. Pods provide an abstraction that includes the container(s), storage resources, unique network IP, and configurations necessary for the application to function.

Kubernetes Component Illumination

This section demonstrates how to deploy a K8s cluster and discover its components. Through this exercise, you will explore the roles and interactions of key components. You will gain a deeper understanding of the cluster's architecture and functionality.

To proceed with deploying the **Terraform** code and discovering the cluster components, follow these steps:

1. Navigate to the chapter11-k8s folder.
2. Deploy the cluster in the folder.
3. List all nodes.

    ```
    kubectl get nodes
    ```

4. Inspect control plane components and addons. The components and addons live in the kube-system namespace.

    ```
    kubectl get pods -n kube-system
    ```

5. Examine the etcd component.

    ```
    kubectl describe pod etcd -n kube-system
    ```

CHAPTER 11   KUBERNETES

6. Find the status of the K8s cluster components.

   ```
   kubectl get cs or
   kubectl get componentstatus
   ```

   You should find the health of three controls of the K8s components.

NAME	STATUS	MESSAGE
etcd-0	Healthy	ok
scheduler	Healthy	ok
controller-manager	Healthy	ok

   The output indicates that three components are healthy. Note that not all components are displayed by this command. For example, the health of the cluster API server component is not displayed here.

7. Verify the API server component.

   ```
   kubectl describe services
   ```

   The command should output information about the API server component as follows:

Name:	kubernetes
Namespace:	default
Labels:	**component=apiserver**
provider=kubernetes	

   The API server component is the most important component of the entire cluster.

8. Run the component status (cs) command.

   ```
   kubectl get cs
   ```

CHAPTER 11   KUBERNETES

This should produce more detailed results. Use the kubectl get --raw='/readyz?verbose' alternative command if you encounter issues with the **cs** command. The **cs** command was deprecated in K8s version 1.19+.

[+]ping ok
[+]log ok
[+]**etcd ok**
...
[+]poststarthook/start-kube-**apiserver-admission-initializer** ok
[+]poststarthook/generic-apiserver-start-informers ok
[+]poststarthook/priority-and-fairness-config-consumer ok
[+]poststarthook/priority-and-fairness-filter ok
[+]poststarthook/storage-object-count-tracker-hook ok
[+]poststarthook/start-apiextensions-informers ok
[+]poststarthook/start-apiextensions-**controllers** ok
[+]poststarthook/crd-informer-synced ok
[+]poststarthook/start-service-ip-repair-**controllers** ok
[+]poststarthook/rbac/bootstrap-roles ok
[+]poststarthook/**scheduling/bootstrap-system-priority-classes** ok
[+]poststarthook/priority-and-fairness-config-producer ok
[+]poststarthook/start-system-namespaces-**controller** ok
...

9. Find controllers.

   kubectl get sa -n kube-system

CHAPTER 11 KUBERNETES

Output of some of the K8s controllers:

```
attachdetach-controller
aws-cloud-provider
aws-node
certificate-controller
clusterrole-aggregation-controller
coredns
cronjob-controller
daemon-set-controller
default
deployment-controller
disruption-controller
eks-vpc-resource-controller
endpoint-controller
endpointslice-controller
endpointslicemirroring-controller
ephemeral-volume-controller
expand-controller
generic-garbage-collector
horizontal-pod-autoscaler
job-controller
kube-proxy
legacy-service-account-token-cleaner
namespace-controller
node-controller
persistent-volume-binder
pod-garbage-collector
pv-protection-controller
pvc-protection-controller
replicaset-controller
```

```
replication-controller
resourcequota-controller
root-ca-cert-publisher
service-account-controller
service-controller
statefulset-controller
tagging-controller
ttl-after-finished-controller
...
```

10. Run K8s configuration dump.

    ```
    kubectl cluster-info dump > clusterinfo.dump
    ```

    The **kubectl cluster-info dump** command can collect a massive amount of information about a cluster. You may dump the cluster information in a file and use keywords to find your K8s components.

    You can find more information about the API server component under ServiceList of the dump.

    ```
    {
      "kind": "ServiceList",
      "apiVersion": "v1",
      "metadata": {
          "resourceVersion": "37311"
      },
      "items": [
          {
        "metadata": {
            "name": "kubernetes",
             "namespace": "default",
              ....
    ```

CHAPTER 11   KUBERNETES

```
    "labels": {
        "component": "apiserver",
        "provider": "kubernetes"
                }
            },
    .....
    }
```

11. Find information about kubelet from the dump or use the kubectl describe command.

    `kubectl describe nodes`

    You should notice components such as kubelet and kube-proxy under system info.

    ```
    System Info:
      .....
      OS Image:                    Amazon Linux 2
      Operating System:            linux
      Architecture:                amd64
      Container Runtime Version:   containerd://1.7.2
      Kubelet Version:             v1.31.5-eks-5e0fdde
      Kube-Proxy Version:          v1.31.5-eks-5e0fdde
    ```

12. You can dump performance metrics information with the following command:

    `kubectl get --raw /metrics >metrics`

    Performance metrics provide insights into the performance and health of K8s clusters. They tell administrators about what is happening inside the cluster. The information includes the availability, utilization, and overall operation of resources spanning nodes, pods, and containers managed within a K8s environment.[8]

13. Clean up resources.

    ```
    terraform destroy
    ```

Summary

We began this chapter with an introduction to Kubernetes and continued with the functions of each of the components and how they communicate with each other to make the cluster run. We ended with hands-on illumination to discover and interact with components. It should be clear to you which planes you can find K8s components in by now. The next chapter will begin to run containerized applications on K8s.

---

[8] https://kubernetes.io/docs/concepts/cluster-administration/system-metrics/

CHAPTER 12

Running Apps on K8s

As an application orchestrator, Kubernetes (K8s) excels when it runs applications. The time spent on K8s cluster deployments and configurations will be worthless if we do not spend a fraction of it on applications that depend on them. K8s does not run applications in their native binary or executable file format but in the modern open container initiative file format. This calls for an intermediate step to package applications into a format executable by K8s. We do that with container images. This chapter will introduce application packaging for K8s clusters. We will present recipes for packaging applications into container images such that K8s clusters can execute them. We will discuss container image packaging, image registration, and deployment on K8s clusters.

Container Packaging

Traditionally, application development ends once developers package an application into web archive (war), java archive (jar), or executable file (exe) format and ship it to the operations team for deployment. The operations (ops) team takes over from the developers, installs application dependencies, creates configuration files, and an environment before they deploy the package. This approach could be time-consuming, cause undue delays in product delivery, and may result in high operational costs.

CHAPTER 12   RUNNING APPS ON K8S

Containers were introduced to improve software delivery. They allow developers to package applications into a self-contained and portable format. The package includes all dependencies and configuration files necessary to deploy the application in any environment, cutting off the need for a dedicated ops team, reducing delays and high operational cost.

Containers use the union file system (UFS) or the modern open container initiative (OCI) file system to package applications and their dependencies into stand-alone and portable artifacts for deployment across multiple platforms. The only requirement for the platform is to install a container runtime environment that can unpack and execute the containerized package in the bundled file system (OCI or UFS).

A UFS is a type of file system that can merge or overlay multiple directories or files into a single object consisting of base and upper layers. It creates a read-only or an immutable package that prevents any alteration to the original file or folder content. Examples of UFS file system types are aufs, Btrfs, overlay, overlay2, and device mapper.

The overlay file system of containers is a layered file system representing a bundle of application code, executables, dependencies or libraries, and configuration files stacked together on a stripped-down operating system which forms the base layer of the container artifact as shown in Figure 12-1.

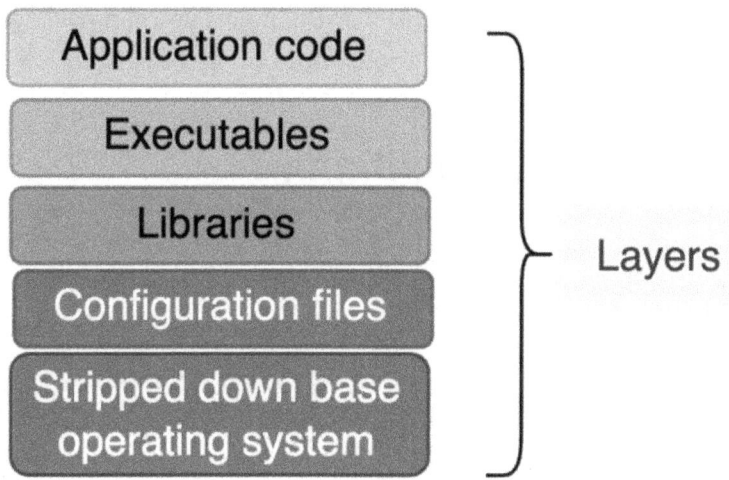

Figure 12-1. Layers of container image

This layered file system is known as the container image. An image is a stack of files/directories represented as a single object. Inside of the image is a stripped-down operating system (OS), files, and dependencies required to run an application.[1] You can describe a container image as a collection of loosely connected read-only layers where each layer comprises of one or more files.

K8s run only containerized applications. An application must first be packaged into a container image to run on a K8s node. The node requires a container runtime environment to unpack and execute the code in the container image.

Creating a container image for a K8s cluster involves a couple of steps. It involves installation of a container runtime environment on a local machine, creation of a configuration file, building of the image, storage of the image in a container registry, and making the image accessible to the cluster. We will spend the rest of the chapter on containers and container images.

---

[1] Docker deep dive: Zero to Docker in a single book, Nigel Poulton

CHAPTER 12   RUNNING APPS ON K8S

The following sections will introduce you to how you can package, register, and deploy containerized applications on a K8s cluster.

Containerized Applications

The application packaging format for K8s clusters isn't a binary but a pod. A pod is a collection of one or more containers. It is a group of one or more containers, with shared storage, network resources, and a specification detailing how to run the containers in their encapsule.[2]

The containers inside the pod are processes that spring up when a container runtime environment unpacks and executes a container image. Containers are fast to start and ultra-portable. Moving container workloads from a private data center to a public cloud or even on a developer laptop involves little to no effort.

A container is analogous to a virtual machine.[3] A major difference is that containers do not require their own full-blown operating system. Rather, they share the host's operating system, freeing up massive amounts of computing resources, CPU, RAM, and storage. The net effect of running a container is reduced overhead of OS patching, maintenance costs, and sometimes even licensing costs.

Application containers live in the data plane. They are kept healthy by kubelets. As shown in Figure 12-2, kubelets communicate with the container runtime to ensure that pods and their containers are running as specified by a controller in the control plane. The container runtime is responsible for managing the execution and the lifecycle of containers.[4] The actual container architecture and detailed discussion is out of scope. However, we will introduce how to install and package container images in the following sections.

---

[2] https://kubernetes.io/docs/concepts/workloads/pods/
[3] Docker deep dive zero to docker in a single book, Nigel Poulton
[4] https://kubernetes.io/docs/concepts/overview/components/

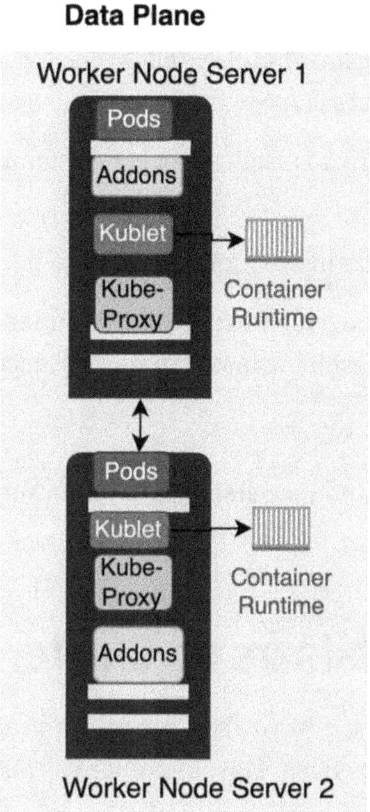

CHAPTER 12 RUNNING APPS ON K8S

Figure 12-2. Kubelet and container runtime in the data plane

Docker Desktop Installation

This section runs through the steps involved in installing a container runtime environment on a local machine. A runtime environment is required for building and creation of a container image. The following steps should take you through the installation of Docker desktop. Docker is the most popular software platform for building, testing, and deploying containers. Other platforms are LXC, Hyper-V, and podman.

1. Google install Docker Desktop. You may find the following link: https://docs.docker.com/desktop/install/mac-install/.

2. Follow the link to install a Docker container on your Mac.

3. Repeat similar instructions if you have Windows.

4. Once installed, run the following command on your terminal to test if the installation was successful:

   ```
   docker version
   ```

5. You should find the version of your docker installation.

Running Containers on Cluster

To get started, let us test how you can run an application on an EKS cluster with the following steps. This is just to prepare us for the examples ahead.

1. Deploy the cluster in the folder chapter12.

2. Update the user context.

   ```
   aws eks update-kubeconfig --name public-endpoint-cluster
   ```

3. Run the Hello World application on the cluster.

   ```
   kubectl run hello-world --image=hello-world
   ```

4. Check if pod is running.

   ```
   kubectl get pod
   ```

You should get this output:

```
NAME          READY   STATUS      RESTARTS      AGE
hello-world   0/1     Completed   1 (14s ago)   42s
```

This pod is expected to crash after a few seconds, so do not be alarmed if it does happen. The Hello World container is one of many publicly available containers you can deploy on your cluster. You can build your own container and make it available to your cluster or run a third-party public container on your cluster.

Containers are stored in a container registry. A container registry is like the GitHub platform for containers. You can make the container public or private on the container registry platform. You can also create your own private container registry exclusive to you or your organization. Examples of container registries are Docker Hub and AWS Elastic Container Registry (ECR).

Custom Container Image

The hello-world container was executed from a public registry. You can package your own container image and make it available for deployment if you do not want to use a publicly available container or if you want to run your application as a container.

You can follow these steps to build your own container image from an Ubuntu base:

1. Go to the chapter12 folder.
2. Find the Dockerfile file in the apps folder.

The Dockerfile is the configuration file for creating container images. It contains all the commands the Docker container image builder could call to assemble an image using the OCI file system. The content of the file is as follows:

```
FROM --platform=linux/amd64 ubuntu:latest
RUN apt update -y
RUN apt -y install curl
RUN apt -y install default-jdk
RUN apt -y install lynx
WORKDIR /tmp
RUN curl -O https://archive.apache.org/dist/tomcat/tomcat-10/v10.1.8/bin/apache-tomcat-10.1.8.tar.gz
RUN tar xzvf apache-tomcat-10*tar.gz
RUN mv apache-tomcat-10*/  tomcat/
RUN mkdir /opt/tomcat/
RUN mv tomcat/ /opt/
COPY index.html /opt/tomcat/webapps/ROOT
WORKDIR /opt/tomcat/
EXPOSE 8080
RUN chmod +x /opt/tomcat/bin/catalina.sh
CMD ["/opt/tomcat/bin/catalina.sh", "run"]
```

The image file system is layers of files stacked on top of each other beginning with the FROM command. The FROM command initializes a new build stage and sets the base image for subsequent commands.[5]

The base image is any valid Docker base image. They are lightweight, stripped down, or hardened virtual machines designed for containerized applications. The base image in this example is an Ubuntu Docker image.

---

[5] https://docs.docker.com/reference/dockerfile/#from

The optional **--platform=linux/amd64** flag specifies the platform for your container image. You can optionally tag the FROM command with the version of the base image as **ubuntu:latest.** If you omit it, the image builder assumes the latest tag by default or returns an error if it cannot find any valid tag value.

The ADD, COPY, and RUN commands add discrete layers on top of the base layer. The COPY command copies files or directory to the image, the ADD command adds local, remote files or directories to the image, and the RUN command executes commands of the base operating system.[6] Each of these commands generates a layer on top of the base operating system.

The CMD command specifies what command or script to execute within the container once the container starts. It adds no layer to the base image.

Once you build the layers in the Dockerfile, the Docker builder automatically adds a thin read/write layer on top of the stack where it writes all runtime changes such as creation of a new file, modifying an existing file, and deleting a file. The changes you make at the runtime do not alter the container images because they are immutable.[7] All updates and upgrades within a container do not translate into upgrades of the image that created the container.

Building Container Images

Let us use this section to go through the recipe for building your own image from the Dockerfile in the chapter12 folder.

1. Go to the folder with Dockerfile.

2. Build the image.

    ```
    docker build -t image_name .
    ```

---

[6] https://docs.docker.com/reference/dockerfile/
[7] https://docs.docker.com/guides/

CHAPTER 12   RUNNING APPS ON K8S

3. Replace the image_name with test-app and any valid name.

4. Go to the Docker desktop image registry to find the image in your local container registry.

5. Verify if the image was created and exists in your local registry.

   ```
   docker images test-app
   ```

6. You should find the following output:

   ```
   REPOSITORY        TAG       IMAGE ID
   test-app          latest    e7a1e26cf8c0
   CREATED           SIZE
   7 minutes ago     999MB
   ```

The size shows the size of the image, 999MB in this case. The latest represents the image tag or the version, and the e7a1e26cf8c0 is the image ID.

Finding the Layers

We will step into the image to find the layers that constitute the image. You may list the layers of a container image with the command

```
docker inspect test-app
```

This should produce the following output:

```
[
...
    {
        "Id": "sha256:e7a1e26cf8c02ade43a86fc7521f6a4ca32515d12
d4fc897fc8528f554c173cc",
```

```
            "RepoTags": [
                "test-app:latest"
            ],
...
            "Name": "overlay2"
        },
        "RootFS": {
            "Type": "layers",
            "Layers": [
                "sha256:42d3f8788282c6e48bac7236609753b240db3
                53465dc55cb77c21f2391720dd9",
                "sha256:bb0ea3f4226dba1113d9edd01612a00ab4003
                49f63fc68b05eb7dd40fd2043e1",
                "sha256:1a833e7f301fb820e9f01b988136ffc60cd6
                cef9a165417ce4df9648acaee8a3",
                "sha256:d2a7e45c4da8c680ccfe122eaaf3c692fe4538
                42686072a68d9d423e3e0c8fac",
                "sha256:8773792d3ead94471370b31e734cbd0dd32518
                daca8913233c3c4d4722308da7",
                "sha256:5f70bf18a086007016e948b04aed3b82103a36
                bea41755b6cddfaf10ace3c6ef",
                "sha256:63752b82f042d4db9651c9a244c31fe8203562
                cdd5c7af36c52ffd2fa90bb9f4",
                "sha256:f912cb9b12d48ed7d27961404aad2aa910ea6
                be92ad2e5d901abd86ddabe1bc1",
                "sha256:d94544ef760c7ff9fef44f5959d316e8e763d
                49438ea62e89e1378f45655fb35",
                "sha256:79901162c57f151272b708e4a512ababdfab6
                8fb2cdc453e2553ed2b7f151a9a",
                "sha256:a4ace41e99aac5cea5e82679e4d036e768dda3
                05930413f46a01764e961f3b3f",
```

```
                    "sha256:31bfefc26d1e74f62cab40dcb6b458916246e
                    420183dceaeabd940d419e4c2d1",
                    "sha256:25fc26f928d544814d5c935d80d0696f63b80
                    2d22335a8b14beb1eea98ad8616",
                    "sha256:202c4e6d0f40925af45ed3455cf7b37df311f
                    6c029b3e790b6b778b56a6a7cbc",
                    "sha256:5f70bf18a086007016e948b04aed3b82103a3
                    6bea41755b6cddfaf10ace3c6ef"
                ]
        },
...
    }
]
```

The list reveals the name of the image and the file type and bunch of numbers representing the hash values of each layer that constitute the image. The name of the image is test-app, and the version is the latest. The file type is overlay2.

You can explore the image further with the following steps:

1. Make a new directory.

   ```
   mkdir layers
   ```

2. Change the directory.

   ```
   cd layers
   ```

3. Create a Docker image archive.

   ```
   docker save --output testapp.tar test-app
   ```

4. Extract the archive.

   ```
   tar -vxf testapp.tar
   ```

CHAPTER 12   RUNNING APPS ON K8S

You should see the following output:

```
x blobs/sha256/d94544ef760c7ff9fef44f5959d316e8e763d4
9438ea62e89e1378f45655fb35
x blobs/sha256/e7a1e26cf8c02ade43a86fc7521f6a4ca32515d
12d4fc897fc8528f554c173cc
x blobs/sha256/f4d316a9ae4c05f388449d886a05b3dc3e6bfc
4ee993b5fe8e8995fe67c11835
x blobs/sha256/f912cb9b12d48ed7d27961404aad2aa910ea6be
92ad2e5d901abd86ddabe1bc1
x index.json
x manifest.json
x oci-layout
x repositories
```

5. List the layers.

   ```
   cat manifest.json | jq
   cat index.json | jq
   ```

6. Explore layers further.

   ```
   cd blobs/sha256
   ```

7. Open a layer in the list of layers.

   ```
   cat 011499334b78984209eeaed3e800e2f5d9789ffe21d7db5
   185a0a432ec84b499 | jq
   ```

323

Image Optimization

Sometimes you would want to optimize a docker image so that it can run faster and use less computing resources. You can do so with techniques such as using minimal base images, multistage builds, and reducing the number of layers. Other techniques are caching, Dockerignore, and keeping application data outside the image.[8]

We want to discuss image optimization with layers. Image size may depend on the number of layers. The simplest way to reduce the size is to reduce the number of layers by combining two or more commands in the container build file (DockerFile). Instead of executing individual RUN commands such as this:

```
RUN apt update -y
RUN apt -y install curl
RUN apt -y install default-jdk
RUN apt -y install lynx
```

you can combine the RUN commands to reduce the number of image layers as follows:

```
FROM --platform=linux/amd64 ubuntu:latest
RUN apt update -y && \
    apt -y install curl && \
    apt -y install default-jdk && \
    apt -y install lynx
WORKDIR /tmp
RUN curl -O https://archive.apache.org/dist/tomcat/tomcat-10/v10.1.8/bin/apache-tomcat-10.1.8.tar.gz && \
    tar xzvf apache-tomcat-10*tar.gz && \
    mv apache-tomcat-10*/  tomcat/ && \
```

---

[8] https://devopscube.com/reduce-docker-image-size/

```
    mkdir /opt/tomcat/ && \
    mv tomcat/ /opt/
COPY index.html /opt/tomcat/webapps/ROOT
WORKDIR /opt/tomcat/
EXPOSE 8080
RUN chmod +x /opt/tomcat/bin/catalina.sh
CMD ["/opt/tomcat/bin/catalina.sh", "run"]
```

By combining the RUN command with the AND (&&) operator, you reduce the number of image layers and the eventual image size. The multistage build, caching, and the rest are out of scope.

Running Custom Containers on EKS

The custom image we created earlier is stored in a local image registry. Local registries are not accessible by EKS clusters. EKS clusters cannot execute local images unless you publish them in a public or private registry such as the Docker Hub image registry or AWS Elastic Container Registry (ECR).

Images in the public registries are open to everyone and require no authentication to download and run it on a cluster. On the other hand, the private registry mandates authentication to grant access to an image. In this case, you must configure EKS with an authentication credential or key to make the access possible. We will experiment with both private and public registries in the following subsections.

CHAPTER 12 RUNNING APPS ON K8S

Docker Hub Public Registry

We will build and push our custom container image to a public registry in Docker Hub to make it accessible to our cluster with the following recipe:

1. Create a Gmail or GitHub account.

2. Go to the Docker Hub container image registry.

    https://hub.docker.com/

3. Click the Sign up button.

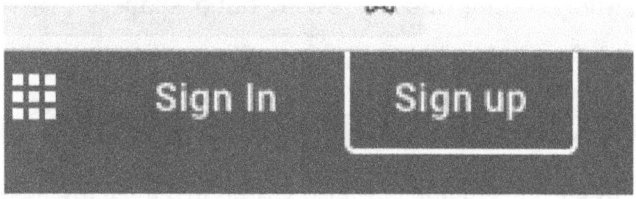

Figure 12-3. *Docker Hub registration*

4. Use your Gmail or GitHub account to sign up.

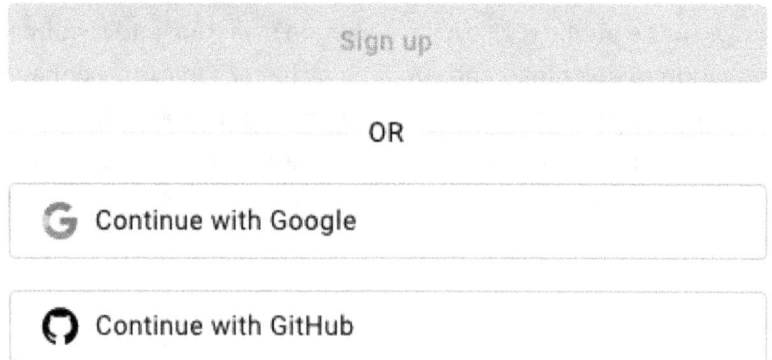

Figure 12-4. *Docker Hub registration and IdP login page*

CHAPTER 12 RUNNING APPS ON K8S

5. Type your Docker Hub username and click Sign up.

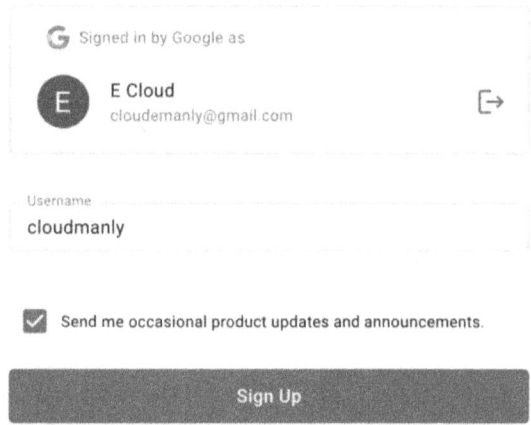

Figure 12-5. Docker Hub registration with Google IdP

6. Click the Repository tab.

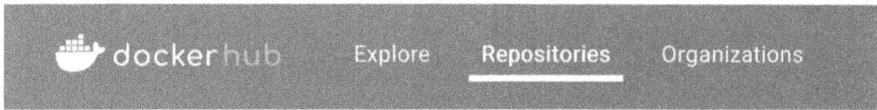

Figure 12-6. Docker Hub home page

CHAPTER 12　RUNNING APPS ON K8S

7. Click Create repository, then choose public registry and your preferred repository name.

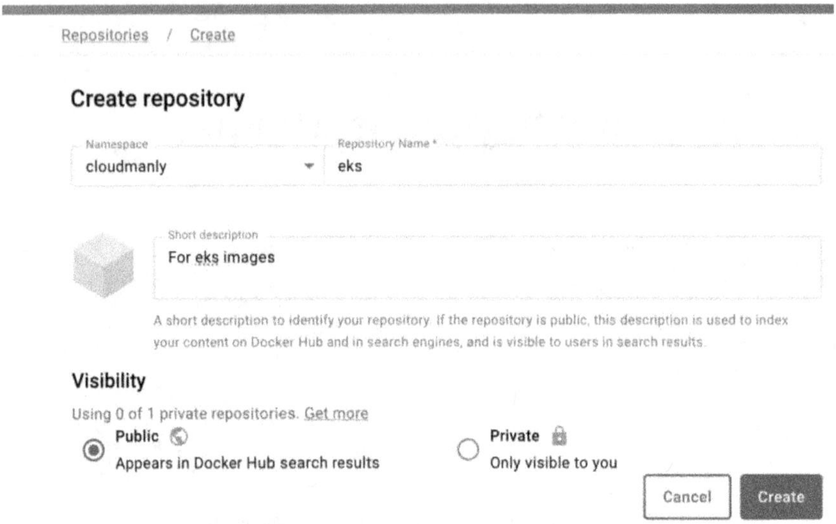

Figure 12-7. Creating public container registry

8. Configure access to the registry from your local machine.

    ```
    docker login -u yourusername
    ```

9. Type your password.

10. Use the Dockerfile in Chapter12.

    ```
    FROM --platform=linux/amd64 ubuntu:latest
    RUN apt update -y && \
        apt -y install curl && \
        apt -y install default-jdk && \
        apt -y install lynx
    WORKDIR /tmp
    RUN curl -O https://archive.apache.org/dist/tomcat/
    ```

```
    tomcat-10/v10.1.8/bin/apache-tomcat-10.1.8.tar.gz && \
        tar xzvf apache-tomcat-10*tar.gz && \
        mv apache-tomcat-10*/  tomcat/ && \
        mkdir /opt/tomcat/  && \
        mv tomcat/ /opt/
    COPY index.html /opt/tomcat/webapps/ROOT
    WORKDIR /opt/tomcat/
    EXPOSE 8080
    RUN chmod +x /opt/tomcat/bin/catalina.sh
    CMD ["/opt/tomcat/bin/catalina.sh", "run"]
```

11. Build the image with the Docker Hub registry tag.

    ```
    docker build -t cloudmanly/eks:blueapp .
    ```

    Replace cloudmanly/eks with the name of your repository.

12. Push the image to the registry.

    ```
    docker push cloudmanly/eks:blueapp
    ```

Run the Image on EKS

Create a pod definition file for the container and save it as blueapp-pod.yml. It is possible to specify multiple containers, but we will specify a single container in this example to simplify the discussion:

```
apiVersion: v1
kind: Pod
metadata:
  name: blueapp-pod
  labels:
    app: blueapp-label
```

```
spec:
  containers:
    - name: blueapp-container
      image: cloudmanly/eks:blueapp
      ports:
        - containerPort: 8080
```

We break down the pod definition as follows:

- apiVersion: Kubernetes API version required for the object (Pod in this case)

- kind: Specifies the kind of Kubernetes object which is a Pod in this case

- metadata: Specifies the metadata or information that uniquely identifies the object

- spec: Specification of our pod, such as container name, ports, image name, and volumes

The apiVersion, kind, spec, and metadata are mandatory fields in the manifest. They apply to all Kubernetes object types. However, the layout of spec depends on the object type.

Execute the custom container after cluster deployment with the following steps:

1. Update user context.

   ```
   aws eks update-kubeconfig --name public-endpoint-cluster
   ```

2. Execute the pod definition file.

   ```
   kubectl apply -f blueapp-pod.yml
   ```

3. Check if the pods are running.

   ```
   kubectl get pods
   ```

4. Log in to the pod.

   ```
   kubectl exec --stdin --tty blueapp-pod /bin/bash
   ```

5. Update the pod and install net-tools.

   ```
   apt update && apt install net-tools
   ```

6. Find the IP address of the pod by running

   ```
   ifconfig
   ```

7. Note the IP address of your pod, 10.0.0.83 in my case.

8. Open the website of the application in the container.

   ```
   lynx localhost:8080
   ```

   Press q | and y to exit the app | type exit to exit the pod.

The update you just did will not affect the underlying image if someone else decides to run the same container on another cluster or when you decide to rerun the container.

In case you have any issues with running the pod, use the `kubectl log blueapp` command to troubleshoot the pod. You should also check the platform of your worker nodes, whether it supports ARM or AMD. Modify the Dockerfile to use the correct platform, rebuild, and rerun the container. It is better to execute the remove and the prune commands before you rebuild your image. The two commands will remove any existing image from your local registry and make it ready for a brand-new one:

```
docker rm -vf $(docker ps -aq)
docker system prune -a
```

CHAPTER 12   RUNNING APPS ON K8S

Private Repository

The Docker Hub public repository makes images available to everyone on the Internet. Organizations often want to keep their images private in a private repository and grant exclusive access to members of the organization.

You can use a private Docker Hub repository or AWS Elastic Container Registry (ECR) to store private images and make them available to your EKS cluster. The first step is to create a container registry in your AWS account, then build and push the image to the registry. The second step is to grant EKS access to the registry to pull and run the image.

We will demonstrate this with the AWS ECR private registry.

1. Create an AWS ECR registry.

    ```
    aws ecr create-repository \
        --repository-name docker-images \
        --region us-east-1 \
        --tags '[{"Key":"env","Value":"test"},
        {"Key":"team","Value":"DevOps"}]'
    ```

2. Copy the URI of the registry.

3. Log in to the registry.

    ```
    aws ecr get-login-password --region us-east-1 | docker login --username AWS --password-stdin ACCOUNTID.dkr.ecr.us-east-1.amazonaws.com/docker-images
    ```

    Replace the ACCOUNTID with yours. We piped the `aws ecr get-login-password --region us-east-1` to the docker login so that you can use docker commands as in the previous section to administer the ECR. The command should output a message such as **Login Succeeded**.

CHAPTER 12 RUNNING APPS ON K8S

4. Build the blueapp image for the ECR as before.

   docker build -t **ACCOUNTID.dkr.ecr.us-east-1. amazonaws.com/docker-images**:blueapp.

5. Push the image to ECR.

   docker push **ACCOUNTID.dkr.ecr.us-east-1. amazonaws.com/docker-images**:blueapp

You should find the repository and the image created in the AWS ECR console.

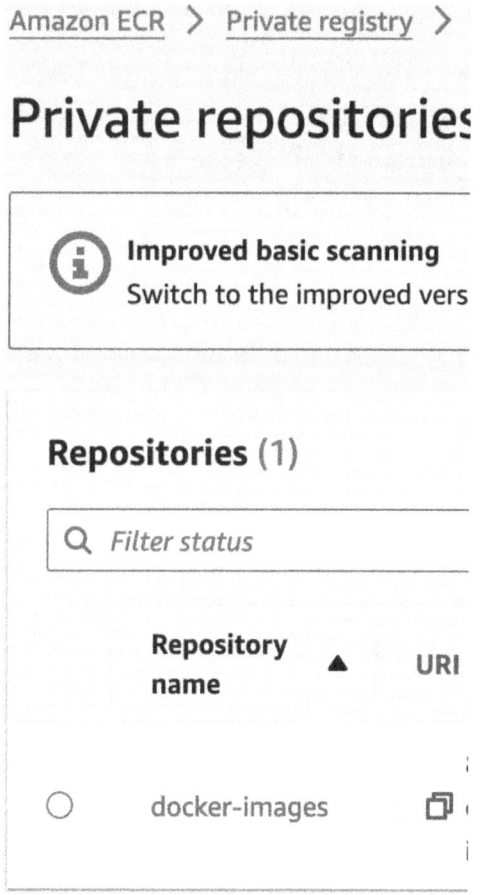

Figure 12-8. Docker Hub repository

CHAPTER 12   RUNNING APPS ON K8S

Running ECR Image on EKS

You need to set up a proper access control to instruct EKS to pull and run an image from a private ECR repository. There are two ways to grant this access, through an IAM or a service account policy. The easy and straightforward approach is the use of the IAM policy.

We will introduce an IAM policy example in this chapter and defer the service account approach for now.

You must grant ECR access to the workers to enable them to pull and run an image from a private ECR repository. The access is already granted in the **iam.tf** file under the node module as follows:

```
resource "aws_iam_role_policy_attachment" "amazon_ec2_container_registry_read_only" {
  policy_arn = "arn:aws:iam::aws:policy/AmazonEC2ContainerRegistryReadOnly"
  role       = aws_iam_role.nodes_assume_role_policy.name
}
```

You should now create a pod definition file that references the registry.

1. Create Pod manifest to reference the private ECR repository.

   ```
   apiVersion: v1
   kind: Pod
   metadata:
     name: blueapp-pod
     labels:
       app: blueapp-label
   spec:
     containers:
       - name: blueapp-container
         image: ACCOUNTID.dkr.ecr.us-east-1.amazonaws.com/
   ```

docker-images:blueapp
         ports:
           - containerPort: 8080

   Replace the ACCOUNTID with yours and save the specification in the pod-ecr.yml file.

2. Execute the pod definition file.

   ```
   Kubectl create -f pod-ecr.yml
   ```

3. Check if the pods are running.

   ```
   kubectl get pods
   ```

4. Log in to the pod.

   ```
   kubectl exec --stdin --tty blueapp-pod /bin/bash
   ```

5. Open the website of the application.

   ```
   lynx localhost:8080
   ```

   Everything should work as before.

Summary

We began this chapter with an introduction to containers and continued with its packaging and execution on a K8s cluster. We went through how to package an application into a container image and run it on K8s and also how to handle a container registry, both public and private. A private registry involves authorization for worker nodes to be able to access the registry. Building and publishing container images is a daily preoccupation of developers. Developers should not just build images but find ways of optimizing them using techniques such as minimal base images, multistage builds, and combination of commands in the Dockerfile configuration file. They can also use other techniques such as caching and Dockerignore. We will continue the discussions in the next chapter focusing on pods as we begin to tackle individual K8s objects.

CHAPTER 13

The Pod Object

Kubernetes (K8s) objects are entities that can persist in a K8s cluster. You create cluster objects by describing their desired states in either a YAML or JSON file format for a cluster to run. We refer to the file as an object manifest or specification file. The object manifest may contain the object kind and the mandatory arguments the cluster required for the object creation. A good understanding of object specification files could help you make the right choices and to avoid simple mistakes so that you can spend less time on troubleshooting when you begin to deploy objects or pods on a cluster. It would be beneficial to arm yourself with a good understanding of what should go into object specification files as you venture into more application deployments on K8s clusters.

We plan to focus on pod specification in this chapter. We will deploy a cluster, retrieve its manifest, and discuss arguments that define the desired state of the pod.

Pod Specification

Pods wrap applications to make them suitable for K8s to manage. They are the smallest deployable units that can be created and managed by K8s.[1] The mandatory parameters of a pod specification are given as follows:

---

[1] https://kubernetes.io/docs/concepts/workloads/pods/

```
apiVersion: v1
kind: Pod
metadata:
  name: pod-name
spec:
  containers:
    - name: container-name-1
      image: container-image-1
    - name: container-name-2
      image: container-image-2
```

- apiVersion: Specifies the compatible K8s API version for the pod. A pod cannot run if a cluster does not support its API version. The three API versions are Alpha, Beta, and Stable.

- kind: Specifies the type of object the K8s should create on a node. For example, Pod, Deployment, Secrets, Service Accounts, Roles, Role Bindings, Cluster Roles, Cluster Role Bindings, Ingress, Ingress Classes, Network Policies, Endpoints, etc.

- metadata: Identifies and describes an object. For example, name, labels, namespace, and annotation.

- spec: Specifies the container for a pod and declares the desired state and object characteristics.

Pod Parameter Experiment

Pod specifications go beyond the four basic parameters described above. Let us use the following steps to find more information about pod specification:

CHAPTER 13   THE POD OBJECT

1. Go to the chapter13 folder.

2. Deploy the cluster.

   ```
   terraform init
   terraform apply
   ```

3. Update the kube config context.

   ```
   aws eks update-kubeconfig --name public-endpoint-cluster
   ```

4. Deploy the blueapp pod.

   ```
   kubectl create -f pods/blueapp.yml
   ```

5. Extract the pod configuration file.

   ```
   kubectl describe pod blueapp-pod
   ```

The command should output the following:

Name:	blueapp-pod
Namespace:	default
Priority:	0
Service Account:	default
Node:	ip-10-0-4-225.ec2…
Start Time:	Tue, 09 …
Labels:	app=blueapp-label
Annotations:	\<none\>
Status:	Running
IP:	10.0.4.251
IPs:	
IP:	10.0.4.251

CHAPTER 13 THE POD OBJECT

Containers:
  blueapp-container:
    Container ID: containerd://b285bee...
    Image: cloudmanly/eks:blueapp
    Image ID: docker.io/cloudmanly/..
    Port: 8080/TCP
    Host Port: 0/TCP
    State: Running
    Started: Tue, 09 ...
    Ready: True
    Restart Count: 0
    Environment: <none>
    Mounts:
/var/run/secrets/kubernetes.io/serviceaccount from kube-api-access-kwfdw (ro)

Conditions:
  Type   Status
  PodReadyToStartContainers   True
  Initialized   True
  Ready   True
  ContainersReady   True
  PodScheduled   True

Volumes:
  kube-api-access-kwfdw:
    Type: Projected (a volume that contains injected data from multiple sources)
    TokenExpirationSeconds: 3607
    ConfigMapName: kube-root-ca.crt
    ConfigMapOptional: <nil>
    DownwardAPI: true

QoS Class: BestEffort
Node-Selectors: <none>

Tolerations: node.kubernetes.io/not-ready:NoExecute op=Exists for 300s   node.kubernetes.io/unreachable:NoExecute op=Exists for 300s
Events:
```
  Type    Reason     Age    From              Message
  ----    ------     ----   ----              -------
  Normal  Scheduled  65s    default-scheduler
  Normal  Pulling    62s    kubelet           Pulling image
  "cloudmanly/eks:blueapp"
  Normal  Pulled     38s    kubelet           Successfully
  pulled image "cloudmanly/eks:blueapp" in 24.717s (24.717s
  including waiting). Image size: 392795805 bytes.
  Normal  Created    38s    kubelet           Created container
  blueapp-container
  Normal  Started    37s    kubelet           Started container
  blueapp-container
```

Let us go through the various fields in the pod specification.

Name

Name is also known as pod ID. It is a pod's unique identifier within a namespace.

Namespace

A namespace is a container for isolating and controlling access to resources within a cluster. Through namespaces you can grant access to different teams in an organization to work on separate projects in the same cluster.[2]

---

[2] https://www.vmware.com/topics/kubernetes-namespace

CHAPTER 13   THE POD OBJECT

Organizations that use a single cluster for multiple environments such as development, testing, and production can use namespaces to sandbox the development and testing environments from the production environment such that production code is not affected by changes made to codes in the development or test namespaces.

Cluster administrators can set policy-driven resource limits on namespaces by defining resource quotas for CPU or memory utilization. This can ensure that every project or namespace has the resources it needs to run and that no one namespace can consume all available resources.

A namespace can reduce API search space to lower latency and improve overall performance of applications within the cluster. With multiple namespaces for different projects, the K8s API will have fewer items to search when performing operations.

K8s cannot isolate resources such as nodes, Storage Class, and Persistent Volume within a namespace.[3] A resource is an API endpoint that represents a cluster object. For instance, /api/v1/pods, /api/v1/pods/{pod_name}, and /api/v1/deployments/{deployment_name} are examples of pod and deployment resources.

A resource name can be unique within a namespace but not across namespaces. You can retrieve API resources with the following commands:

```
kubectl api-resources -o wide or
kubectl api-resources -o wide -n test-ns
```

The test-ns namespace must exist in your cluster before you can run the second command.

Finally, namespaces cannot be nested in K8s clusters.

---

[3] https://kubernetes.io/docs/concepts/overview/working-with-objects/namespaces/

CHAPTER 13 THE POD OBJECT

Initial Namespace

K8s create four initial namespaces out of the box for you: default, kube-node-lease, kube-system, and kube-public.[4]

You cannot deploy objects on a K8s cluster without a namespace. Because of this, K8s includes the default namespace so that users can create objects without having to create their own namespace. The default namespace is particularly relevant if there is no need to isolate resources.

The kube-node-lease namespace holds Lease objects associated with each node. Node leases allow the kubelet to send heartbeats so that the control plane can detect node failure.

The kube-public namespace is readable by all clients, authenticated and unauthenticated clients. It is created for cluster-wide resources that should be publicly visible and readable. You deploy a resource into this namespace if you want every object in the cluster to read your resource. Lastly, the kube-system namespace is reserved for K8s system objects such as daemon sets.

A daemon set manages pods on nodes. It ensures that all or some nodes run a copy of a pod. It pushes pods to nodes when they are added to the cluster and removes them when they are removed from the cluster. As nodes are removed from the cluster, those pods are garbage collected. Deleting a daemon set will clean up the pods it created.[5]

Namespace Demonstration

Let's run through how you can access and create namespaces in your cluster. You can access the initial namespaces with one of the following commands:

```
kubectl get namespaces -A or
kubectl get ns -A
```

---

[4] https://kubernetes.io/docs/concepts/overview/working-with-objects/namespaces/

[5] https://kubernetes.io/docs/concepts/workloads/controllers/daemonset/

CHAPTER 13   THE POD OBJECT

The command should output the following:

```
NAME               STATUS      AGE
default            Active      6m12s
kube-node-lease    Active      6m12s
kube-public        Active      6m12s
kube-system        Active      6m12s
```

Use the following command to create your own namespace:

```
kubectl create ns <namespace name>
e.g kubectl create ns test-ns
```

Use the following command to deploy a pod into your custom namespace:

```
kubectl create -f pod/blueapp -n <namespace name>
e.g. kubectl create -f pod/blueapp -n test-ns
```

Use the following command to retrieve applications from a custom namespace:

```
Kubectl get blueapp-pod -n test-ns
```

Priority

Pod priority indicates the importance of a pod relative to other pods. The K8s scheduler will prioritize important pods over less important ones. If a pod cannot be scheduled, the scheduler will try to preempt or evict a lower priority pod to make room for the new one.[6]

---

[6] https://kubernetes.io/docs/concepts/scheduling-eviction/pod-priority-preemption/

Service Account

A service account grants a pod permission to interact with services such as S3 bucket. A service account is created for service, not end users or human beings. It is used to identify and authenticate cluster objects, pods, system components, and entities inside and outside the cluster, including the API server.[7]

Node

Nodes run pods in a cluster. The node parameter shows the node in the cluster where a pod was scheduled. Knowing which node a pod was scheduled on can help you with troubleshooting if something should go wrong with the pod deployment.

Label

Labels are key/value pair identifiers you can attach to K8s objects to make your specification meaningful and relevant for users. You can organize objects into groups with labels to allow users to write efficient search queries to find and apply changes to them.[8]

As an example, you organize your objects based on teams with labels as shown below. In this example, we express the object specification using labels to communicate the environment, the team, and project to end users:

```
metadata:
  labels:
    environment: test
    team: operations
    project: Bagan
```

---

[7] https://kubernetes.io/docs/concepts/security/service-accounts/
[8] https://kubernetes.io/docs/concepts/overview/working-with-objects/labels/

Teams can filter pods that are assigned to them if they know the labels and even apply changes to the objects.

K8s internally maintains the mappings of labels to corresponding objects using optimized data structures to make queries faster.

Annotations

Annotations are only for information purposes. They are not even as useful as labels which are implemented to filter or apply policy to an object. Annotations are metadata information for libraries that cannot be used for filtering or object selection. They have fewer constraints than labels. You can store any kind of data in annotations, including unstructured information.[9]

Annotations are not entirely useless constructs. They shine when you want to integrate with external tools or services, for example, integration with a load balancer and CI/CD pipeline. Annotations can integrate AWS load balancer with your applications for end users to interact with them.

Status

This property shows the state of a pod. They are[10]

- *Pending*: The pod is waiting to get scheduled on a node or for at least one of its containers to initialize.
- *Running*: The pod has been assigned to a node and has one or more running containers.
- *Succeeded*: All the pod's containers exited without errors.

---

[9] The Kubernetes Workshop: Learn how to build and run highly scalable workloads on Kubernetes by Zachary Arnold, Sahil Dua, Wei Huang
[10] https://www.datadoghq.com/blog/debug-kubernetes-pending-pods/

- *Failed*: One or more of the pod's containers terminated with an error.

- *Unknown*: Usually occurs when the Kubernetes API server cannot communicate with the pod's node.

QoS

Kubernetes classifies pods and allocates them into a specific quality of service (QoS) class based on the resource requests of their containers and how those requests relate to resource limits. K8s uses QoS classes to decide which pods to evict from nodes and which ones are experiencing resource pressure.

The three QoS classes are guaranteed, burstable, and best effort. When a node runs out of resources, K8s will first evict the best effort pods running on that node, followed by burstable, and lastly the guaranteed pods. When this eviction is due to resource pressure, only pods exceeding resource requests are candidates for eviction.[11]

Node Selectors

The node selector parameter assigns labels to nodes such that the K8s scheduler can deploy pods on a specific node. In other words, you add the node selector field to a pod specification to target nodes so that K8s will schedule pods onto those nodes.

For example, the node selector labels in the following pod specification will enforce the scheduler to deploy the **node-selector-pod** on a node in the east-us region and with SSD storage:

---

[11] https://kubernetes.io/docs/tasks/configure-pod-container/quality-service-pod/

```
apiVersion: v1
kind: Pod
metadata:
    name: node-selector-pod
spec:
  containers:
    - name: blueapp
      image: blueapp
    nodeSelector:
        region: us-east-1
        disktype: ssd
```

Tolerations

Toleration and taint work together to place a pod on a node. You apply taint to nodes and toleration to pods.

Each taint consists of three parts:

- *Key*: Unique identifier for the taint
- *Value*: An optional value associated with the taint key
- *Effect*: Indicates how the taint affects pod scheduling

The effect of a taint has three values:

- *NoSchedule*: Prevents new pods from being scheduled on the tainted node
- *PreferNoSchedule*: Avoid placing new pods on a tainted node unless necessary
- *NoExecute*: Evicts or removes existing pods that do not tolerate the taint

Taints mark nodes with specific attributes for certain workloads or prevent certain pods from being placed on the nodes. Unlike node affinity, taint allows nodes to repel pods. On the contrary, toleration allows a tainted node to accept a pod that otherwise must be repelled. It is an exception to the rule. Toleration grants an exception to pods that must be repelled on a tainted node.

In short, tolerations allow pods with certain markings to run on a tainted node. Toleration specifies key/value pairs for a pod to indicate which tainted node the pod can run on.

K8s automatically adds a toleration with **node.kubernetes.io/not-ready** and **node.kubernetes.io/unreachable** keys by default to nodes and set their durations for only 300 seconds (about 10 minutes).[12] The scheduler is always responsible for assigning a pod to its matching taints on a node.

Events

Events record pod activities. K8s generates a lot of events related to the pods or deployments of a workload, the scheduling, and more. They help to understand what is happening in a cluster. You can filter events based on a namespace, all namespaces, or based on specific resources.

How to List Events

You can list events with the following commands.

List recent events in the default namespace:

```
kubectl events
```

List recent events in all namespaces:

```
kubectl events --all-namespaces
```

---

[12] https://kubernetes.io/docs/concepts/scheduling-eviction/taint-and-toleration/

List recent events for the specified pod, then wait for more events and list them as they arrive:

`kubectl events --for pod/blueapp-pod --watch`

List recent events in YAML format:

`kubectl events -o yaml`

List recent only events of type "Warning" or "Normal":

`kubectl events --types=Warning,Normal`

Summary

This chapter introduced pod specifications, their arguments to build the foundation for application deployment, and how to handle manifest in YAML file format. The manifest dictates the desired state of pods or cluster objects, their description, and lifecycle. The extensive review was meant to build a solid foundation for the chapters ahead as you prepare yourself for more application deployments on K8s clusters. The next chapter will introduce the service object and how to use it to expose pods to the outside world.

CHAPTER 14

The Service Object

Pods in Kubernetes (K8s) are private by default, meaning they are not directly accessible to end users. To expose them to the outside world, you need to use a **service object**. The service object provides a stable way to expose pods, enabling external users to access the applications running within them. This chapter introduces the K8s service object and demonstrates how it facilitates external access to pods. By the end of this chapter, you will understand how to configure and use service objects to make your applications accessible to end users.

Pod Deployment

To deploy the application for this chapter and explore the different ways of accessing it, follow these steps:

1. Navigate to the folder chapter14.

2. Deploy the cluster.

   ```
   cd chpater14
   terraform init
   terraform apply
   ```

3. Update the kube config context.

   ```
   aws eks update-kubeconfig --name public-endpoint-cluster
   ```

CHAPTER 14   THE SERVICE OBJECT

4. Deploy the blueapp pod.

   ```
   kubectl create -f pods/blueapp.yml
   ```

5. Verify the state of the pod; if not, wait for the pod to be created.

   ```
   kubectl get pod
   ```

K8s supports internal access to pods without a service object. However, a service object may be required to expose pods or applications to end users. The following sections will show some of the ways you can expose pods to end users.

K8s supports internal access to pods without the need for a service object. Pods within the same cluster can communicate with each other directly using their internal IPs. However, service objects become necessary when you need to expose pods or applications to end users (either within or outside the cluster).

The following sections will cover various methods for exposing pods to end users, demonstrating how service objects can facilitate external access to applications running within the cluster.

Internal Access to Application

We will start with the **kubectl exec** command. The kubectl exec command can enable cluster administrators to access pods internally. The **kubectl exec** command connects you to a pod or container and allows you to run commands and the applications running inside it.

We will connect to the blue app container with the **kubectl exec** command and run the **lynx** command-line browser in the container to access the blueapp application on port 8080. The blueapp application runs a Tomcat web application server on port 8080.

CHAPTER 14 THE SERVICE OBJECT

Let's connect to the pod with the **kubectl exec** command:

```
kubectl exec -it blueapp-pod -- /bin/bash
```

The **/bin/bash** argument of the exec command specifies the type of shell that will be enabled for access. You can specify any shell (sh, csh, zsh) if the container supports it.

Once inside the container, you can open the application with the **lynx** command-line browser by executing the following command:

```
lynx localhost:8080
```

You can type **q** to quit the browser and the **exit** command to exit the container. This is quite an unusual way of accessing an application. It requires complex commands and the access right of a cluster administrator.

The usual way of exposing an application to end users is through a proxy, port forwarder, or K8s service objects. Proxies or port forwarding tunnels traffic through the K8s API server to a pod allowing external users to communicate with the applications running inside the pod.

Access to the API server is required to proxy or forward the traffic. The API server then becomes a temporary gateway between your local port or proxy and the K8s cluster.

Port Forwarding and Proxy

The kubectl port-forward and kubectl proxy are the two commands for tunneling external traffic to a pod. Kubectl proxy is a TCP (Layer 4) tunnel, while kubectl port-forward is an HTTP (Layer 7) tunnel.[1]

---

[1] https://kubernetes.io/docs/tasks/access-application-cluster/port-forward-access-application-cluster/

CHAPTER 14   THE SERVICE OBJECT

The two commands are useful for developers and cluster administrators to quickly access or test a cluster application directly from their local machines when a new feature is deployed or when they want to debug or troubleshoot an application. They are the quickest way to interact with your application, making development and debugging faster and more accurate.

You can use port forwarding to securely connect to internal services such as backend databases and safely interact with APIs that are only meant to be used within the K8s cluster.[2]

Port Forwarding Example

Let's create a port forwarding tunnel for the blueapp application.

1. Check if the pod is running from the previous deployment and note down the pod's name (blueapp).

    kubectl get pods

2. Execute the port forwarding command.

    kubectl port-forward pods/blueapp-pod 8080

3. Test the blueapp in your local browser.

    http://localhost:8080

---

[2] https://medium.com/@90mandalchandan/port-forwarding-in-kubernetes-a-guide-using-kubectl-845dde6244d4

4. Your browser should display the blue app as follows:

Figure 14-1. Application display

Using a Proxy

Let's create a new tunnel with the kubectl proxy to test the differences between the port forwarding and the proxy commands.

1. Stop the port forwarding command.

   CTRL + C

2. Run the kubectl proxy command.

   kubectl proxy --port=8080

3. Test the application from your local browser with the following options:

   localhost:8080

CHAPTER 14 THE SERVICE OBJECT

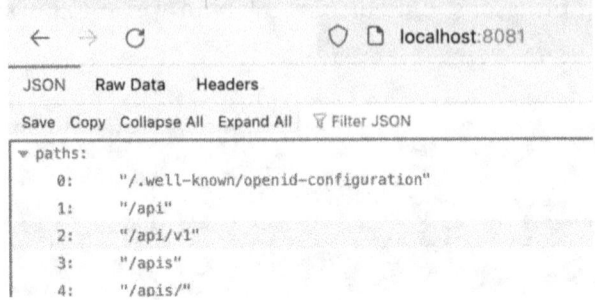

Figure 14-2. Application API display-1

```
localhost:8080/api
```

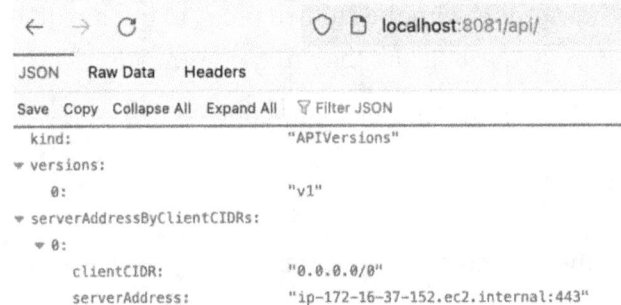

Figure 14-3. Application API display-2

```
localhost:8080/api/pods
```

```
←  →  C                    localhost:8081/api/pods
JSON   Raw Data   Headers
Save  Copy  Collapse All  Expand All  ▽ Filter JSON
   kind:         "Status"
   apiVersion:   "v1"
   metadata:     {}
   status:       "Failure"
   message:      "the server could not find the requested resource"
   reason:       "NotFound"
   details:      {}
   code:         404
```

Figure 14-4. Application API display-3

CHAPTER 14   THE SERVICE OBJECT

Using the Service Objects

Port forwarding and local proxies are useful for debugging, testing, or temporary access to K8s applications. Services and ingress controllers are rather the preferred means of exposing pods to the outside world for end users' access because they support efficient and reliable traffic management.

Even though you can combine services with proxies or port forwarders as before, such setup is not recommended as they are for temporary access, testing, or debugging purposes only.

A service acts as a proxy between a pod or a group of pods and the external world.[3] They map service ports to application port(s). Services are independent from pods, so developers do not need to change an application code to deploy a service.

K8s provides diverse service types such as ClusterIP, NodePort, LoadBalancer, and ExternalName, each serving specific communication purposes within and outside a cluster.[4] Table 14-1 explains some of the service types.

---

[3] https://kubernetes.io/docs/concepts/services-networking/service/
[4] https://edgedelta.com/company/blog/kubernetes-services-types#:~:text=ClusterIP%20assigns%20internal%20IP%20addresses,addresses%20for%20external%20traffic%20distribution

CHAPTER 14 THE SERVICE OBJECT

Table 14-1. *Service types*

Service Type	Port Range	Use Case
ClusterIP	Any IP inside the cluster	For inter-service interactions within the cluster
NodePort	30000–32767	Exposes applications to external clients via specific ports on worker nodes
LoadBalancer	Any public IP inside the cluster	Like NodePort, but with the added benefit of using the cloud providers' load-balancing capabilities
ExternalName	No specific port range. It creates DNS records that point to an external DNS name	Used to map a service to a DNS name outside of the cluster, facilitating easy access to the service
Headless Services	No specific port range	They facilitate content delivery, data retrieval, and integration between various platforms

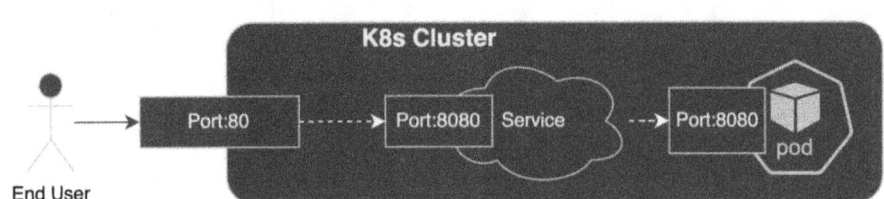

Figure 14-5. *Service object*

Figure 14-5 illustrates the traffic flow from an end user to an application inside a pod. It shows how you can implement a service object to expose an application to the outside world. You expose an external port

CHAPTER 14　THE SERVICE OBJECT

(80) to a service for an end user to reach the application. The end user sends a request to the application on the external port (80). The browser forwards the request to the service on port 8080; the service object in turn forwards the request to the application on the same port.

Even though services are supposed to expose pods to the public, not all service types are public by default. For example, Cluster IP service type is always private. You can only access the service through proxy, port forwarding, or direct access to cluster nodes.

On the other hand, service types such as Node Port can become public depending on where you deploy it on the cluster. For example, a Node Port service is public if you deploy it in a public subnet of a cluster; otherwise, it remains private within the cluster.

Node Port Service Type Example

A Node Port service exposes a set of pods to the outside world. It allows external traffic to reach services running inside a cluster.

When you create a Node Port service, K8s assigns a static port known as NodePort on each node in the cluster. It then maps this NodePort to the service port of a pod so that the Node Port can forward traffic and end user to the corresponding service port. NodePort is assigned a special port range between 30000 and 32767.

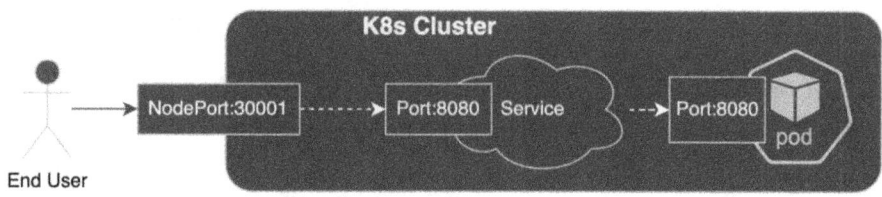

Figure 14-6. Service object

CHAPTER 14 THE SERVICE OBJECT

NodePort allows external access only when it is deployed on a public network. You cannot reach pods that run on a private network, even if you deploy a NodePort in the network. You still need port-forward or proxies to forward traffic before you can reach the service.

```
kubectl port-forward svc/blueapp-svc 30001 or
kubectl -proxy=30001 svc/blueapp-svc
```

You will need to deploy the service below prior to the port forwarding:

```
kind: Service
apiVersion: v1
metadata:
  name: blueapp-svc
  labels:
     svc: blueapp-svc-label
spec:
  type: NodePort
  selector:
     app: blueapp-label
  ports:
  - port: 8082 #service port, can be any port
    nodePort: 30001 #nodport between 30000-32767
    name: app-port
    targetPort: 8080 #your app or container/pod or port
```

You would normally place a load balancer in front of a Node Port or deploy it in a public subnet to avoid the port forwarding.

Node Port Service Type and Public Network

Let's deploy the code in the chapter14-pub and if we can access Node Port service directly from a public subnet.

CHAPTER 14   THE SERVICE OBJECT

The most meaningful change to the code is the **map_public_ip_on_ launch = true**. It is a line in the subnets.tf file. It makes the private subnet public by associating a public IP address. The second most important change to the code is calling of the subnet module in the **main.tf** file. The main.tf file ensures that the nodes are deployed in public subnets. You need both changes in the code to support the external access through the Node Port.

```
resource "aws_subnet" "public_subnets" {
  vpc_id           = aws_vpc.cluster_vpc.id
  cidr_block   = count.index == 0 ? var.cidr_blocks["public-
                   subnet-1"] : var.cidr_blocks["public-subnet-2"]
  availability_zone = data.aws_availability_zones.azs.
                      names[count.index]
  count = 2
  map_public_ip_on_launch = true
  tags = {
    Name = "public-subnet-${count.index+1}"
  }
}

module "nodes" {
  source = "./dataplane/nodes"
  cluster_name = module.cluster.cluster_name
  security_group_id =   module.cluster.cluster_security_
                        group_id
  subnet_ids =  module.vpc.public_subnet_ids
}
```

CHAPTER 14 THE SERVICE OBJECT

Finally, we open the Node Port on the nodes with the following security group rule in the **sg.tf** file:

```
resource "aws_security_group_rule" "nodeport" {
  type              = "ingress"
  from_port         = 30001
  to_port           = 30001
  protocol          = "tcp"
  cidr_blocks       = ["0.0.0.0/0"]
  security_group_id =    var.security_group_id
}
```

Now deploy the code and execute the following commands:

1. Update user context.

    aws eks update-kubeconfig --name public-endpoint-cluster

2. Deploy the blueapp application.

    kubectl apply -f pods/blueapp.yml

3. Check if the pod is running.

    kubectl get pods

4. Deploy the Node Port service.

    kubectl apply -f pods/svc-nodeport.yml

    The Node Port service has the following manifest:

    kind: Service
    apiVersion: v1
    metadata:
      name: blueapp-svc
      labels:

```
      svc: blueapp-svc-label
spec:
  type: NodePort
  selector:
    app: blueapp-label
  ports:
  - port: 8082 #service port, can be any port
    nodePort: 30001 #nodport between 30000-32767
    name: app-port
    targetPort: 8080 #your app or container/pod or port
```

It specifies the object kind as service and the service type as NodePort, meaning the cluster will deploy the NodePort service.

5. Test if the service is running.

   ```
   kubectl get service
   ```

   You should find the following output:

NAME	TYPE	CLUSTER-IP	EXTERNAL-IP	PORT(S)	AGE
blueapp-svc	NodePort	172.20.1.45	<none>	8080:30001/TCP	13s
kubernetes	ClusterIP	172.20.0.1	<none>	443/TCP	7m34s

6. Retrieve the public IP address of the worker nodes from the AWS EC2 service console or with the following AWS CLI command:

   ```
   aws ec2 describe-instances --query 'Reservations[*].Instances[*].[InstanceId, PublicIpAddress]' --output table
   ```

CHAPTER 14   THE SERVICE OBJECT

7. Test the blueapp with the curl command.

   ```
   curl http://PublicIP:30001
   ```

8. Open the blueapp in your browser with the public IP address.

   ```
   http://PublicIP:30001
   ```

Your browser should display the application.

Figure 14-7. Application display with public NodePort IP load

Testing Cluster IP Service

You can repeat the same steps for the Cluster IP service type to test the external access to the application as follows:

1. Delete the Node Port service.

   ```
   kubectl delete -f pods/svc-nodeport.yml
   ```

2. Deploy the default Cluster IP service.

   ```
   kubectl apply -f pods/svc-clusterip.yml
   ```

   The Cluster IP service manifest is listed as follows:

   ```
   kind: Service
   apiVersion: v1
   metadata:
     name: blueapp-svc
   ```

364

CHAPTER 14   THE SERVICE OBJECT

```
    labels:
      svc: blueapp-svc-label
  spec:
    selector:
      app: blueapp-label
    ports:
    - port: 8081 #cluster IP service port, can be any port
      name: app-port
      targetPort: 8080 #your app or container/pod or port
```

Observe that the service object has no service type. K8s deploys the default Cluster IP service if no service type is specified.

3. Test if the service is running.

   Kubectl get svc

4. Retrieve the public IP address of the worker nodes from the AWS EC2 service console or from the AWS CLI.

   ```
   aws ec2 describe-instances --query 'Reservations[*].
   Instances[*].[InstanceId, PublicIpAddress]'
   --output table
   ```

5. Try to access the application from your browser on port 30001 or on port 8081.

   http://PublicIP:30001 or http://PublicIP:8081

   None of them should work.

6. Port-forward traffic to the Cluster IP service type.

   Kubectl port-forward svc/blueapp-svc 8081

7. Access the site with your browser at localhost:8081.

Figure 14-8. Application display

You should be successful this time.

Unlike the Node Port, connection to the Cluster IP service through the public node IPs and the local port 8081 failed. You could not expose the default Cluster IP service to the outside world even on a public node. The Cluster IP service is always private and useful for internal communication only.

It is an internal load balancer for the cluster. It is implemented when no other service is specified in a service object manifest. It is useful for communication between internal services or microservices, backend database access within the cluster, communication between pods in different namespaces, and more.

Load Balancers

We use load balancers for an industry-grade external access to cluster applications. Local proxies and port forwarding lack a sustained way of distributing traffic for production-grade applications. User experience, enhanced security, and service availability are improved drastically with load balancers. We introduce an industrial way of end-user access in this section.

Load balancing is a better way of exposing pods to the outside world than a port forwarding tunnel or Node Port services. End users may access a pod by sending a request to a load balancer. The load balancer forwards the request to a cluster service object which in turn pushes the request to the container running inside the pod. Finally, the application receives the request, renders it, and sends a response to the end user as shown in Figure 14-9.

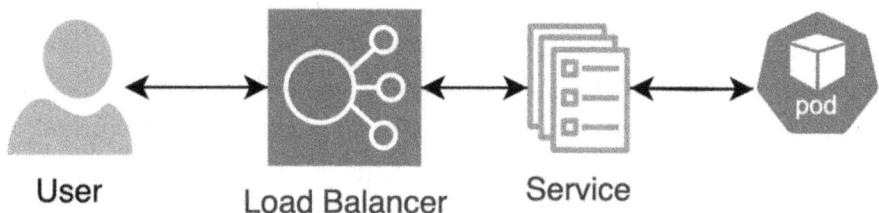

Figure 14-9. End-user access via load balancer

An added benefit of load balancers is even traffic distribution to registered targets such that no single target is overburdened while other target nodes remain idle. Moreover, through session or cookie affinity, load balancers such as AWS Elastic Load Balancers (ELBs)[5] can keep the same traffic source for the same target or node in a session to ensure flow consistency. Traffic from a particular client always routes to a specific target.

The AWS Elastic Load Balancer

It is now time to shift our attention to AWS Elastic Load Balancers (ELBs). AWS ELBs support multiple targets, EC2 instances, containers, and IP addresses. They can scale up and down (add or remove instances) as incoming traffic changes over time. They can serve as the single point of contact for clients to enhance availability of applications. AWS ELBs can monitor the health of registered targets and route traffic only to the healthy ones.

---

[5] https://docs.aws.amazon.com/elasticloadbalancing/

CHAPTER 14   THE SERVICE OBJECT

The four types of ELBs are classic, network, gateway, and application load balancers. The choice of a load balancer depends on application needs. For example, AWS recommends an application load balancer (ALB) for flexible application management, network load balancer (NLB) for an extreme performance application, and applications that mandate static IP addresses.

Furthermore, AWS recommends classic load balancers (CLBs) for an existing application that runs on EC2-Classic network or an EC2 instance. Even though EC2-Classic network or instances are no longer supported, classic load balancers are still available on the EC2-VPC platform, the non-classic (VPC based) EC2 instances.[6] It is a legacy, less intelligent but cost-effective load balancer.

While other ELBs have many targets, the only target for classic load balancers is EC2 instances. CLB can only route traffic to workloads running on EC2 instances.

Other considerations when choosing a load balancer include security and the type of traffic you want to process. If you want to inspect traffic, route traffic-based HTTP/HTTPS path, header, or method, then an application load balancer is necessary. Again, if you want to route general-purpose remote procedure calls (gRPC) or web socket protocols, then ALB is the preferred choice.

Also, if you are interested in advanced security features such as web application firewall and identity management, then ALB is the preferred choice. As an application load balancer, ALB can only process the application layer or the layer 7 traffic (URL, heads, API method, etc.).

ALB is the most suitable for containerized applications. It gives you more control over routing, using different paths to distribute the workload over pods. ALB can schedule a group of pods to handle user updates and others to handle authentication. Its path-based routing can assign specific user actions to a pod or a group of pods.

---

[6] https://www.zehntech.com/aws-is-retiring-the-classic-load-balancer-whats-next/

CHAPTER 14   THE SERVICE OBJECT

In contrast, if you want to inspect or route traffic based on IP address and port numbers, then NLB is the preferred choice. NLB allows security groups that can restrict access to specific IP addresses or ports. Consequently, NLB should be your preferred choice if you want security group support. NLB is preferred when you don't want to differentiate pods in traffic distributions.[7] NLB can only process TCP/IP layer 3/4 traffic (ports or IP addresses).

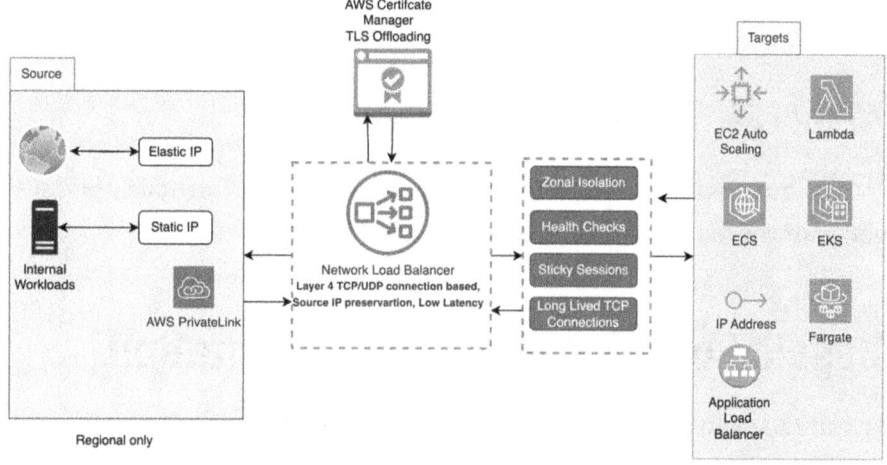

Figure 14-10. *Network load balancer*

Figures 14-10 and 14-11 summarize the features of NLB and ALB. ALB is included in the target group for NLB, meaning ALB can be an internal load balancer (LB) for NLB but not the other way round.

---

[7]https://aws.amazon.com/elasticloadbalancing/?nc=sn&loc=1

CHAPTER 14   THE SERVICE OBJECT

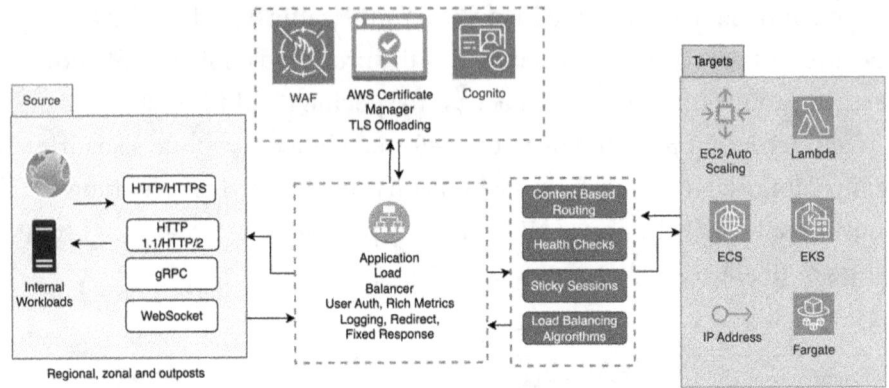

Figure 14-11. Application load balancer

Last but not least, if you are interested in third-party virtual appliances, then gateway load balancer is your preferred choice.

Classic Load Balancer Implementation

We want to expose the blueapp application through the classic load balancer with the following recipe:

1. Initialize the terraform in chapter14-alb.

    ```
    terraform init
    ```

2. Deploy the cluster.

    ```
    terraform apply -auto-approve
    ```

3. Update user context.

    ```
    aws eks update-kubeconfig --name public-endpoint-cluster
    ```

4. Execute the application YAML file.

    ```
    kubectl apply -f pods/clb.yml
    ```

CHAPTER 14   THE SERVICE OBJECT

5. Check if the pod is running.

   kubectl get pods

6. Test if service is running.

   kubectl get svc

7. Wait for about five to ten minutes for the load balancer to deploy.

8. Use curl or a local web browser to access the URL of the load balancer.

   curl -v k8s-default-blueapp-dd41-0f5906.elb.us-east-1.amazonaws.com

9. Open the link to your browser.

Figure 14-12. Application display with CLB load balancer endpoint

10. Delete the manifest.

    kubectl delete -f pods/clb.yml

The application manifest below creates a pod and specifies the classic load balancer as the service type. The manifest is divided into two sections with three hyphens. The first section is the pod specification, and the second section is the service specification. The service specification section contains a line for the service type specified as load balancer.

371

CHAPTER 14 THE SERVICE OBJECT

The **type:LoadBalancer** service type refers to the AWS classic load balancer. The classic load balancer is the default load balancer. EKS will deploy the CLB except your manifest explicitly states otherwise.

```
---
kind: Pod
apiVersion: v1
metadata:
  name: blueapp-pod
  labels:
    app: blueapp
spec:
  containers:
    - name: blueapp
      image: cloudmanly/eks:blueapp
      ports:
        - containerPort: 8080
---
apiVersion: v1
kind: Service
metadata:
  name: blueapp-svc
spec:
  selector:
    app: blueapp
  ports:
  - protocol: "TCP"
    port: 80
    targetPort: 8080
    type: LoadBalancer
```

Network Load Balancer

This example exposes the same blueapp to end users through the AWS network load balancer. The first section of the manifest creates the pod, while the second section creates the service.

The annotations section specifies the characteristics of the load balancer. It informs EKS which load balancer to deploy. For example, service.beta.kubernetes.io/aws-load-balancer-nlb-target-type specifies the type of the load balancer as the AWS Network Load Balancer (NLB). You create annotation inside the pod specification and the service type inside the service specification.

```
---
kind: Pod
apiVersion: v1
metadata:
  name: blueapp-pod
  labels:
    app: blueapp
  annotations:
    service.beta.kubernetes.io/aws-load-balancer-type: external
    service.beta.kubernetes.io/aws-load-balancer-nlb-
    target-type: ip
    service.beta.kubernetes.io/aws-load-balancer-scheme:
    internet-facing
spec:
  containers:
    - name: blueapp
      image: cloudmanly/eks:blueapp
      imagePullPolicy: Always
      ports:
        - containerPort: 8080
```

CHAPTER 14   THE SERVICE OBJECT

```
---
apiVersion: v1
kind: Service
metadata:
  name: blueapp-svc
spec:
  selector:
    app: blueapp
  ports:
  - protocol: "TCP"
    port: 80
    targetPort: 8080
  type: LoadBalancer
```

1. Deploy the application and the load balancer.

   ```
   kubectl apply -f pods/nlb.yml
   ```

2. Check if the pods are running.

   ```
   kubectl get pods
   ```

3. Test if service is running.

   ```
   kubectl get service
   ```

4. Wait for five to ten minutes for the load balancer to deploy.

5. Use curl to open the load balancer's url.

   ```
   curl -v k8s-default-blueapp-dd41-0f.elb.us-east-1.amazonaws.com
   ```

6. Open the link in your browser.

Figure 14-13. Application display with network load balancer endpoint

7. Delete the application.

   kubectl delete -f pods/nlb.yml

Application Load Balancer

You cannot deploy an ALB with only pod annotations because the ALB is a custom object in EKS. K8s/EKS native objects are managed by controllers that maintain their desired states. Controllers for standard or native objects are bootstrapped with the cluster. Hence, there is no need to install additional controllers.

AWS Application Balancer (ALB) is not a standard resource or object in K8s/EKS, meaning it has no bootstrapped controller.[8] For this reason, ALB relies on a custom AWS ALB ingress controller to route traffic to applications.

---

[8] https://aws.amazon.com/blogs/opensource/kubernetes-ingress-aws-alb-ingress-controller/

CHAPTER 14   THE SERVICE OBJECT

An ingress is a resource that manages external or internal HTTP(S) access to a service within a cluster. It routes HTTP and HTTPS traffic through a single-entry point to different services inside a cluster. The entry point is backed by ingress rules which determine the destination of an incoming traffic.[9]

An ingress controller connects ALB to K8s services to decouple the ingress controller from the K8s service objects. It enables a single ingress to serve multiple services. Figure 14-14 depicts the flow from an ALB to an ingress controller and to a service object.

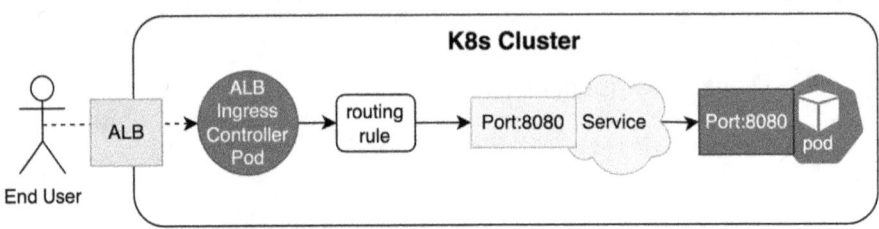

Figure 14-14. Application load balancer ingress controller

ALB requires more configuration steps than the CLB and NLB for the very reasons discussed above. You must install the custom ALB ingress controller from the helm repository. The helm repository is where you can upload helm charts.[10] Like Docker Hub, helm charts may be stored in the helm repository and made accessible to a K8s cluster.

Helm uses a packaging format called charts. A chart is a collection of files that describe a related set of K8s resources. A single chart might be used to deploy a full web application stack with web servers, frontend, and backend services.[11]

---

[9] https://kubernetes-sigs.github.io/aws-load-balancer-controller/v2.2/deploy/configurations/
[10] https://circleci.com/blog/what-is-helm/#:~:text=The%20Helm%20application%20library%20uses,commands%20to%20control%20the%20cluster
[11] https://helm.sh/docs/topics/charts/

CHAPTER 14   THE SERVICE OBJECT

The helm tool automates the creation, packaging, configuration, and deployment of Kubernetes applications by combining configuration files into a single reusable package just like a Docker image.

Requisites for ALB

- You should visit the AWS site to find the latest ALB ingress controller version and instructions.[12]
- You must configure the AWS Identity and Access Management (IAM) OpenID Connect (OIDC) provider for your cluster. You should find the OIDC provider's code in the **oidc.tf** file under the control plane as follows:

```
data "tls_certificate" "oidc" {
  url = aws_eks_cluster.public_endpoint_cluster.
  identity[0].oidc[0].issuer
}

resource "aws_iam_openid_connect_provider" "oidc_openid_connect" {
  client_id_list  = ["sts.amazonaws.com"]
  thumbprint_list = [data.tls_certificate.oidc.
                     certificates[0].sha1_fingerprint]
  url             = data.tls_certificate.oidc.url
}
data "aws_caller_identity" "current" {}
data "aws_iam_policy_document" "oidc_assume_role_policy" {
  statement {
```

---

[12] https://docs.aws.amazon.com/eks/latest/userguide/lbc-helm.html

```
            actions = ["sts:AssumeRoleWithWebIdentity"]
            effect  = "Allow"
            condition {
            test     = "StringEquals"
            variable = "${replace(aws_iam_openid_connect_
                        provider.oidc_openid_connect.url,
                        "https://", "")}:sub"
            values   = ["system:serviceaccount:kube-
                        system:aws-load-balancer-
                        controller-sa"]
            }
            principals {
            identifiers = [aws_iam_openid_connect_provider.
                           oidc_openid_connect.arn]
            type        = "Federated"
            }
        }
    }
    resource "aws_iam_role" "oidc_role" {
      assume_role_policy = data.aws_iam_policy_document.
                           oidc_assume_role_policy.json
      name               = "MyAmazonEKSLoadBalancer
                            ControllerRole"
    }
```

We will defer the OIDC discussion to Chapter 15.

- You should install the Amazon VPC CNI plugin for Kubernetes, kube-proxy, and CoreDNS add-ons. You should find the addons in the **addons.tf** file.

```
resource "aws_eks_addon" "vpc_cni_addon" {
  cluster_name = var.cluster_name
  addon_name   = "vpc-cni"
```

CHAPTER 14   THE SERVICE OBJECT

```
    addon_version = "v1.18.5-eksbuild.1"
     configuration_values = jsonencode({
        env = {
        ENABLE_PREFIX_DELEGATION = "true"
        WARM_PREFIX_TARGET = "1"
        }
    })
}
resource "aws_eks_addon" "kube_proxy_addon" {
  cluster_name = var.cluster_name
   addon_name    = "kube-proxy"
   addon_version =   "v1.31.0-eksbuild.5"
   resolve_conflicts_on_create = "OVERWRITE"
   resolve_conflicts_on_update = "OVERWRITE"
}
resource "aws_eks_addon" "coredns_addon" {
  cluster_name = var.cluster_name
   addon_name    = "coredns"
   addon_version =   "v1.11.3-eksbuild.1"
   resolve_conflicts_on_create = "OVERWRITE"
   resolve_conflicts_on_update = "OVERWRITE"
}
```

Be warned, addons take forever to create, so the cluster creation will be longer than expected if you choose to include the addons in your deployment.

- You must tag your public subnets as follows:

```
tags = {
    "kubernetes.io/role/elb"                         = 1
    "kubernetes.io/cluster/${var.cluster_name}"
    = "shared"
```

CHAPTER 14   THE SERVICE OBJECT

```
    "kubernetes.io/cluster/${var.cluster_name}"
    = "owned"
    Name = "public-subnet-${count.index+1}"
}
```

You should find the public subnet tagging in the subnets.tf file.

- You must attach load balancer controller policy to the cluster nodes:

```
resource "aws_iam_role_policy_attachment" "load-balancer_balancer_controller_policy" {
  policy_arn =  aws_iam_policy.load_balancer_
                 controller_policy.arn
  role       = aws_iam_role.worker_nodes_role.name
}"
```

You should find the policy in the policy.tf file and the creation in the iam.tf file under the node module. The policy is required to grant the load balancer controller permission to the AWS ALB service.

Instance Metadata

The hop limit of the instance metadata service (IMDSv2) can prevent refreshing of cached credentials and could generate the following error message:

ingress Failed build model due to operation error Elastic Load Balancing v2: DescribeLoadBalancers, get identity: get credentials: failed to refresh cached credentials, no EC2 IMDS role found, operation error ec2imds: GetMetadata, canceled, context deadline exceeded

CHAPTER 14 THE SERVICE OBJECT

You avoid this by changing the hop limit of the IMDSv2 from default value of 1 to 2 in the launch template. IMDSv2 uses session-oriented requests to create session tokens that define the session duration, which can be a minimum of one second and a maximum of six hours. During the specified duration, you can use the same session token for subsequent requests. After the specified duration expires, you must create a new session token to use for future requests.[13]

You can use the launch template below to set the hop limit above the default value of 1 to avoid the error. AWS recommends a hop limit of 2 in container environments. The hop limit is the number of network hops that the PUT response is allowed to make. You can set the hop limit to a minimum of 1 and a maximum of 64.

```
resource "aws_launch_template" "launch_template_node_group" {
  name = "launch-template-node-group"
  block_device_mappings {
      device_name = "/dev/sdf"
      ebs {
      volume_size = 50
      }
  }
  ebs_optimized = true
  metadata_options {
      http_tokens         = "optional"
      http_put_response_hop_limit = 2
  }
  network_interfaces {
    associate_public_ip_address = false
  }
}
```

---

[13] https://docs.aws.amazon.com/AWSEC2/latest/UserGuide/configuring-instance-metadata-service.html

CHAPTER 14   THE SERVICE OBJECT

ALB Controller Installation

You should find the command for installing the ALB ingress controller in the script.sh file of the chapter14-alb folder. You can run the script or execute the command line by line.

1. Install the helm on your local machine.
2. Deploy the cluster in the chapter14-alb folder.
3. Make the script.sh file executable.

   chmod +x script.sh

4. Use the script to deploy the AWS load balancer controller.

   ./script.sh

The script.sh

1. The script.sh file starts with setting environment variables for the cluster, AWS region, AWS account ID, and VPC ID.

   ```
   ###initialization #########
   CLUSTER_NAME="public-endpoint-cluster"
   export AWS_REGION=$(aws ec2 describe-availability-zones --output text --query 'AvailabilityZones[0].[RegionName]')
   export ACCOUNT_ID=$(aws sts get-caller-identity --query "Account" --output text)
   export VPC_ID=$(aws ec2 describe-vpcs --filter "Name=tag:Name,Values=public-endpoint-cluster-vpc" --query 'Vpcs[].{id:VpcId}' --output text)
   ```

CHAPTER 14   THE SERVICE OBJECT

2. Switch user context.

    ```
    echo "Switch user context"
    echo "-------------------------------"
    aws eks update-kubeconfig \
        --name ${CLUSTER_NAME} \
        --region ${AWS_REGION}
    ```

3. Create a service account in the kube-system namespace for the load balancer controller.

    ```
    echo "creating lb service account"
    cat >lb-controller-service-account.yml <<EOF
    apiVersion: v1
    kind: ServiceAccount
    metadata:
        name: aws-load-balancer-controller-sa
        namespace: kube-system
    EOF
    kubectl apply -f lb-controller-service-account.yml
    ```

    The service account is retired to grant the ingress controller the right permissions to access AWS services. We will discuss service accounts in detail in the next chapter.

4. Add the helm repository so that you can deploy the ALB with a helm chart.

    ```
    echo "add helm repo"
    echo "-----------------------------------------"
    helm repo add eks https://aws.github.io/eks-charts
    ```

5. Update your local repository.

    ```
    helm repo update eks
    ```

383

6. Install the load balancer controller with a helm chart.

   ```
   helm upgrade aws-load-balancer-controller eks/aws-load-balancer-controller \
     -n kube-system \
     --set clusterName=${CLUSTER_NAME} \
     --set serviceAccount.create=false \
     --set vpcId="vpc-0615e0efcfaae76d6" \
     --set serviceAccount.name=aws-load-balancer-controller-sa
   ```

7. Update the helm chart.

   ```
   kubectl apply -k "github.com/aws/eks-charts/stable/aws-load-balancer-controller/crds?ref=master"
   ```

8. Verify load balancer controller installation.

   ```
   kubectl get deployment -n kube-system aws-load-balancer-controller
   ```

9. You should see:

   ```
   NAME                           READY   UP-TO-DATE   AVAILABLE   AGE
   aws-load-balancer-controller   2/2     2            2           68s
   ```

10. Repeat the command if the output is different.

    ```
    kubectl get deployment -n kube-system aws-load-balancer-controller
    ```

CHAPTER 14   THE SERVICE OBJECT

Troubleshooting Tips

You can employ one of the following to fix errors if the load balancer or the load balancer controller fails to deploy:

kubectl -n <namespace> get all
e.g., kubectl -n kube-system get all
Note the name of the controller and use it to run the next command.
kubectl logs -n <namespace> <controller name>
e.g., kubectl logs -n kube-system deployment.apps/aws-load-balancer-controller

Use the describe command if logs does not work
kubectl describe deployment -n <namespace> <controller name>
e.g. kubectl -n kube-system describe deployment.apps/aws-load-balancer-controller

Verify the ingress controller
kubectl get <LB-type>
e.g., kubectl get ingress
kubectl describe ingress

Verify if services are working
kubectl get service
kubectl describe service <service-name>

Verify if pods are working
kubectl get get
kubectl describe pod <pod-name>

385

CHAPTER 14   THE SERVICE OBJECT

Create the ALB

Run the command to create the ALB:

kubectl apply -f pods/alb.yml

The file content is shown below:

```
---
kind: Pod
apiVersion: v1
metadata:
  name: blueapp-pod
  labels:
    app: blueapp
spec:
  containers:
    - name: blueapp
      image: cloudmanly/eks:blueapp
      imagePullPolicy: Always
      ports:
        - containerPort: 8080
---
apiVersion: v1
kind: Service
metadata:
  name: blueapp-svc
spec:
  selector:
    app: blueapp
  ports:
  - protocol: "TCP"
    port: 80
    targetPort: 8080
```

CHAPTER 14   THE SERVICE OBJECT

```
---
apiVersion: networking.k8s.io/v1
kind: Ingress
metadata:
  name: ingress-alb
  annotations:
    alb.ingress.kubernetes.io/scheme: internet-facing
    alb.ingress.kubernetes.io/target-type: ip
spec:
  ingressClassName: alb
  rules:
    - http:
        paths:
        - path: /
          pathType: Prefix
          backend:
            service:
              name: blueapp-svc
              port:
                number: 80
```

Test the Load Balancer

1. Retrieve the ALB endpoint.

    ```
    kubectl get ingress
    ```

2. Connect to the application with ALB.

    ```
    curl -v  k8s-default-ingressa-efefb7-635.us-east-1.elb.amazonaws.com
    ```

Alternative

1. Go to the AWS console EC2 | Load Balancers.
2. Find the ALB and copy the DNS name created for the blueapp.
3. Paste the URL in your browser.

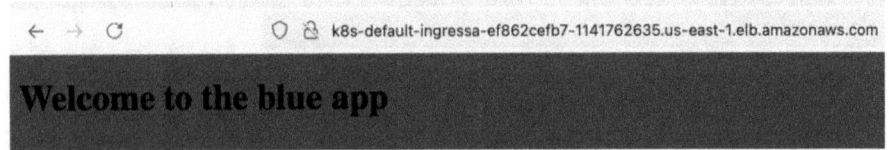

Figure 14-15. Application display with application load balancer endpoint

Summary

By now you should understand how to serve your application to the outside world through proxies and services. As you observed throughout the chapter, you can only access your application through internal connectivity, proxies, or port forwarding which are not useful for production-grade applications. For private node deployment, you would normally interface a public load balancer with NodePort. We set out to show the standard way of exposing pods to the outside world. Network and classic load balancers were easy to deploy because they come with bootstrap controllers installed in K8s clusters. The lack of native controllers made the AWS application load balancer (ALB) quite difficult to deploy. To succeed, you must not forget the following requisites:

- Use the latest controller version.
- Configure the AWS Identity and Access Management (IAM) OpenID Connect (OIDC) provider for the cluster.

CHAPTER 14   THE SERVICE OBJECT

- You should install the Amazon VPC CNI plugin for Kubernetes, kube-proxy, and CoreDNS add-ons.

- Tag subnets appropriately.

- Set the hop limit to at least 2 depending on the method used to deploy the load balancer controller.

We used a service account during the ALB deployment without detailed explanations because we plan to introduce service accounts in the next chapter and deploy more custom controllers.

CHAPTER 15

Pod Service Accounts

Sometimes you would want your applications to interact with AWS or third-party services rather than only K8s objects. For obvious security reasons, third parties and AWS do not enable external access by default. AWS tightly controls any interaction between K8s objects and services in its ecosystem with a strong access control method. Only K8s objects with the right permissions can make API calls to services outside the K8s ecosystem.

This chapter introduces three diverse ways of granting K8s objects access to external services, the role-based access control (RBAC), IAM roles for service accounts (IRSA), and the pod identity methods.

The RBAC Method

Prior to K8s version 1.30, K8s permitted pods to automatically inherit the access rights of their host worker nodes. Any pod running on a node inherits the same privileges as the host whether they need them or not, violating the principle of least privilege. Poor access management may open the door for attackers to piggyback on compromised pods to breach AWS and other cluster resources.

This section will experiment with K8s 1.29 to illustrate the RBAC use case. You will find the Terraform code for this section in the folder chapter15. Most parts of the code remain the same as other chapters except the version changes in the **variables.tf** file under the control plane module.

CHAPTER 15 POD SERVICE ACCOUNTS

```
variable "cluster_name" {
   default = "public-endpoint-cluster"
}
variable "cluster_version" {
  default = "1.29"
}
variable "private_subnet_ids" {}
```

We changed the cluster version deliberately to 1.29 to simulate how pods inherit the privileges of their hosts in K8s 1.29 and lower. You will come across other changes in the code such as the two new IAM policies for the nodes in the **aim.tf** file. The policies authorize pods running on a cluster node to access S3 buckets and secret in the AWS secret manager. The changes in the **iam.tf** file are as follows:

```
#necessary roles for worker nodes
resource "aws_iam_role" "worker_nodes_role" {
  name = "${var.cluster_name}-nodes"
  assume_role_policy = jsonencode({
    Statement = [{
      Action = "sts:AssumeRole"
      Effect = "Allow"
      Principal = {
        Service = "ec2.amazonaws.com"
      }
    }]
    Version = "2012-10-17"
  })
}
...
```

```
resource "aws_iam_role_policy_attachment" "amazon_s3_managed_
policy" {
  policy_arn = "arn:aws:iam::aws:policy/AmazonS3FullAccess"
  role       = aws_iam_role.worker_nodes_role.name
}
resource "aws_iam_role_policy_attachment" "aws_secret_
manager" {
  policy_arn = "arn:aws:iam::aws:policy/
  SecretsManagerReadWrite"
  role       = aws_iam_role.worker_nodes_role.name
}
```

Testing Pod Access After Deployment

We will perform three different tests after the cluster deployment:

- Secret access test
- S3 bucket access test
- ECR repository test

We need a secret in the secret manager before the test. We will create a secret in the secret manager to test our application with the following recipe:

1. Create a secret in the AWS secret manager.

    ```
    aws secretsmanager create-secret \
    --name app-secret-1 \
    --description "test app secret" \
    --secret-string '{"SECRET":"SuperSecret"}' \
    --region us-east-1
    ```

CHAPTER 15   POD SERVICE ACCOUNTS

The value of the secret in the secret manager will be SuperSecret, and the secret ID or name is the app-secret-1.

2. Verify if the secret was created.

    ```
    aws secretsmanager describe-secret --secret-id app-secret-1
    ```

3. Make sure the version of the K8s cluster in the **variables.tf** file of the control plane module is set to **1.29**.

4. Initialize the terraform in the folder Chapter15.

    ```
    terraform init
    ```

5. Deploy the cluster.

    ```
    terraform apply -auto-approve
    ```

6. Update user context.

    ```
    aws eks update-kubeconfig --name public-endpoint-cluster
    ```

7. Create an application YAML for the smapp application. Specify the secret ID you created in step 1 (app-secret-1) and your AWS region as environment variables in the manifest as follows:

    ```
    ---
    kind: Pod
    apiVersion: v1
    metadata:
      name: smapp
      labels:
        app: smapp
    ```

```
   spec:
     containers:
       - name: smapp
         image: cloudmanly/eks:smapp
         imagePullPolicy: Always
         ports:
           - containerPort: 8080
         env:
         - name: REGION
           value: us-east-1
         - name: SECRET_NAME
           value: app-secret-1
```

The smapp accepts the secret ID and displays the secret.

8. Execute the application on the cluster.

   ```
   kubectl apply -f pods/smapp.yml
   ```

Secret Manager Test

1. Verify if your pod is running.

   ```
   kubectl get pods
   ```

2. Start port forwarding.

   ```
   kubectl port-forward smapp 8080
   ```

3. Open your browser and type **http://localhost:8080/**.

CHAPTER 15 POD SERVICE ACCOUNTS

Welcome to Secret Management Test App

Show Secret

Figure 15-1. The secret management application

4. Click the **Show Secret** link of the application to display the secret from the AWS secret manager.

S3 and ECR Access Test

1. Create an S3 bucket in your account.

   ```
   aws s3api create-bucket \
   --bucket my-test-bucket-9000 \
   --region us-east-1
   ```

2. Create an AWS ECR registry.

   ```
   aws ecr create-repository \
       --repository-name docker-images \
       --region us-east-1 \
       --tags '[{"Key":"env","Value":"test"},
         {"Key":"team","Value":"DevOps"}]'
   ```

3. Log in to the running pod.

   ```
   kubectl exec -it smapp -- /bin/bash
   ```

CHAPTER 15 POD SERVICE ACCOUNTS

4. Install the AWS CLI in the pod.

   ```
   apt update && \
   apt install curl wget unzip -y && \
   curl "https://awscli.amazonaws.com/awscli-exe-linux-x86_64.zip" -o "awscliv2.zip" && \
   unzip awscliv2.zip && \
   ./aws/install && \
   aws --version
   ```

5. List S3 buckets in your account from the container.

   ```
   aws s3 ls
   ```

   The command should display all the S3 buckets in the given region of your account.

6. Execute the **list-images** command from the container to list the ECR repository.

   ```
   aws ecr list-images --repository-name docker-images | cat
   ```

7. Delete the cluster after the tests.

   ```
   Terraform destroy -auto-approve
   ```

The **smapp pod** was able to access all the three resources because it inherited the permissions of the host worker nodes. This means that the pod has the same level of access as the node, allowing it to interact with resources both within the cluster and external AWS services.

However, this mode of access poses significant security risk to the cluster. An attacker could exploit application vulnerabilities to potentially gain unauthorized access to both the cluster and other resources outside the cluster. Since the pod inherits the worker node's permissions, a compromise within the pod could lead to a broader attack surface and expose sensitive resources.

CHAPTER 15 POD SERVICE ACCOUNTS

To mitigate this risk, it is essential to implement stricter **security policies**, such as using **Pod Security Policies** (PSPs), hop limit of the instance metadata service version 2 (IMDSv2), IP tables, network policies, and the new K8s versions.[1]

The K8s version 1.30+ removed the ability for pods to inherit permissions of their worker nodes segregating pods' access privileges from that of worker nodes.[2, 3]

IAM Roles for Service Accounts (IRSA)

AWS will not permit K8s objects to access its services or resources without permission. For example, in the preceding example, we created an IAM policy that granted S3 bucket permissions to nodes and demonstrated how pods may inherit the same permission to call S3 bucket's APIs in AWS.

What is more, in Chapter 14 we created a service account that granted the AWS application load balancer (ALB) controller permissions to manage an AWS ALB service with the following script:

```
cat >lb-controller-service-account.yml <<EOF
apiVersion: v1
kind: ServiceAccount
metadata:
    name: aws-load-balancer-controller-sa
    namespace: kube-system
EOF
kubectl apply -f lb-controller-service-account.yml
```

---

[1] https://aws.github.io/aws-eks-best-practices/security/docs/iam/#restrict-access-to-the-instance-profile-assigned-to-the-worker-node
[2] https://kubernetes.io/docs/tutorials/security/apparmor/
[3] https://www.nops.io/blog/kubernetes-1-30-release-updates-for-security-autoscaling-cost-efficiency/

CHAPTER 15 POD SERVICE ACCOUNTS

A service account is one of the ways you can grant permission to a service for service-to-service or machine-to-machine access. This disassociates nodes' permissions from pods' reducing the attack surface.

K8s creates a default service account in each namespace for pods to inherit. It mounts a JSON Web Token (JWT) for the service account in the **/var/run/secrets/kubernetes.io/serviceaccount** folder of each pod. An administrator can use the **kubectl exec** command to display the service account token as follows:

```
kubectl exec <pod-name> -- cat /var/run/secrets/kubernetes.io/serviceaccount/token
```

The default service account (SA) permits only read access to certain internal K8s resources. Hence, it is less powerful and less useful for external access. Luckily, EKS supports custom SA, the IAM roles for service accounts (IRSA) access method. You can assign permissions to pods or applications beyond what the default service account provides with IRSA. Any pod that annotates the custom SA in its manifest can assume the SA role.

IRSA provides credential isolation and accountability through CloudTrail access and event logs. It decouples node permissions from that of pods enhancing least privilege.

IRSA can provide more granular access control support for applications to access external services within and outside AWS. This is possible because AWS IAM now supports the OpenID Connect (OIDC) identity provider (IdP) service. OIDC enables external IdP to establish trust with an AWS account and to grant access to the resources within the account.

OIDC is an authentication protocol. It offloads API authentication from the AWS IAM to a local or an external identity provider (IdP).[4] The caller (the client) making the API call to an AWS account authenticates with the local

---

[4] https://docs.aws.amazon.com/eks/latest/userguide/iam-roles-for-service-accounts.html

or the external IdP other than the AWS IAM. The caller receives a valid OIDC JWT token from the IdP if the authentication succeeds. It then exchanges the token for a temporary AWS Security Service Token (STS) authorization token. The caller presents the STS token to an AWS resource or makes an API call to the AWS resource and receives a response if the token is valid.

The IdP involved in the protocol must be trusted by the service provider (SP), AWS in this case. Trust between AWS (SP) and the IdP is established with a certificate signed by a trusted certificate authority (CA). The IdP shares its certificate with AWS for verification. The parties then establish trust if the certificate is valid.

AWS stores the thumbprint of the third-party CA to eliminate the need to update trusts whenever the IdP renews its certificate.[5]

Thumbprint is a unique value that identifies a certificate. It is the hash value of a certificate computed over all certificate data and its signature. By using the CA's certificate thumbprint, AWS will trust any certificate issued by that CA with the same DNS name as the one already registered.

In K8s's context, the EKS cluster is an internal IdP, and AWS is the external SP. The two must establish trust before IRSA can function.

The IdP (EKS) must create a key pair for token validation. The key pair consists of public and private keys. The private key is for signing the token, while the public key is for signature verification.

EKS (internal IdP) rotates the private signing key every seven days and keeps the public keys until they expire. It also hosts an OIDC endpoint which is used to distribute the public key to any third parties (AWS STS) that want to verify the tokens issued by EKS to client pods.

As an IdP, EKS is responsible for authentication and issuing of tokens to pods (clients). The token is always signed with the EKS private signing key and verified by the public key exposed by the OIDC endpoint. The OIDC endpoint is also called the JSON Web Key Set (JWKS).

---

[5] https://docs.aws.amazon.com/IAM/latest/UserGuide/id_roles_providers_create_oidc_verify-thumbprint.html

CHAPTER 15   POD SERVICE ACCOUNTS

IRSA Flow

The parties involved in the IRSA are clients (pods), an EKS (internal IdP), an authorization server (AWS IAM or STS Assume Role with Web Identity), and AWS, the service provider (SP) as depicted in Figure 15-2.

The linear flow is a simplified representation of the authentication and authorization process. The flow is as follows:

1. A pod makes a service request to EKS (internal IdP).

2. The EKS (internal IdP) validates the request and generates a signed JWT token for the AWS STS token service.

3. The AWS STS token service validates the authentication token and issues an authorization token to the pod if the verification succeeds.

4. The pod uses the authorization token to access the service (S3 bucket).

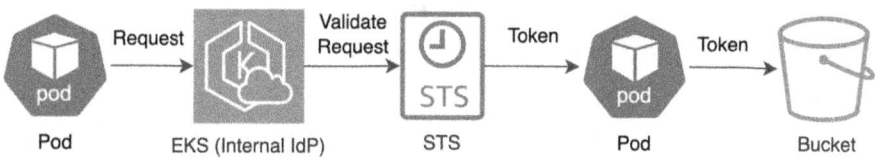

Figure 15-2. Simplified IRSA flow

The service provider (SP) is the entity offering the service such AWS and Google, and the services in this case are S3 bucket, EBS storage, DynamoDB, KMS, etc. The IdP is the entity responsible for authentication of the client applications (pods), EKS in this case. The AWS STS is responsible for authorization.

Figure 15-2 depicts the entire IRSA flow. The breakdown of the main steps is as follows:

- Step 0: Trust establishment between the IdP (EKS) and SP (AWS)
- Steps 1–4: Client authentication
- Steps 5–6: Client authorization
- Step 7: Service access

Trust Establishment

AWS secures communication with OIDC IdPs using a library of trusted certificate authorities (CAs). In step 0 of Figure 15-2, EKS shares its certificate with the AWS STS service. The certificate is signed by AWS which is the CA for both services. The STS service verifies the EKS's CA with the public certificate of the CA and establishes the trust if the verification is successful. The STS service stores the CA's thumbprint for future verification whenever EKS (IdP) updates its certificate. This optimizes the certificate verification process.

You can bring your own thumbprint if your IdP uses a different CA than the AWS-managed CA. If your IdP relies on a certificate that is not signed by one of the AWS trusted CAs, then AWS secures communication with the unmanaged thumbprints you specify.

The EKS certificate is only used to establish trust between the two services (EKS and STS services). It is not involved in the authentication and authorization process.

Once trust is established, the STS service becomes the client of the IdP. Alternatively, the IdP becomes an entity in the STS. The IdP stores the client ID. The client ID is a unique identifier that identifies the application registered with the OIDC provider. AWS uses the client ID to map a claim from the IdP to an RBAC role. The STS also stores the identity of the IdP for future identification.

IRSA Authentication and Authorization Flow

1. K8s issues a service account token and stores it in the **/var/run/secrets/kubernetes.io/serviceaccount** folder like the default token during pod deployment. The token issuing involves JWT token generation and signing with the EKS private key generated at the initial stage. Let me stress that the key here has nothing to do with the certificate used to establish trust.

2. K8s retrieves the service account (SA) token when a pod requests access to an AWS service.

3. K8s fetches the public signing key for the token from EKS's OIDC provider endpoint and verifies the token.

4. K8s requests the AWS STS Assume Role with Web Identity to authorize the token if the token is valid.

5. AWS STS service fetches the public signing key from EKS's OIDC endpoint to verify the token.

6. AWS STS issues an STS temporary token for the pod if the token is valid.

7. The pod makes API calls to the AWS resource with the STS token.

CHAPTER 15   POD SERVICE ACCOUNTS

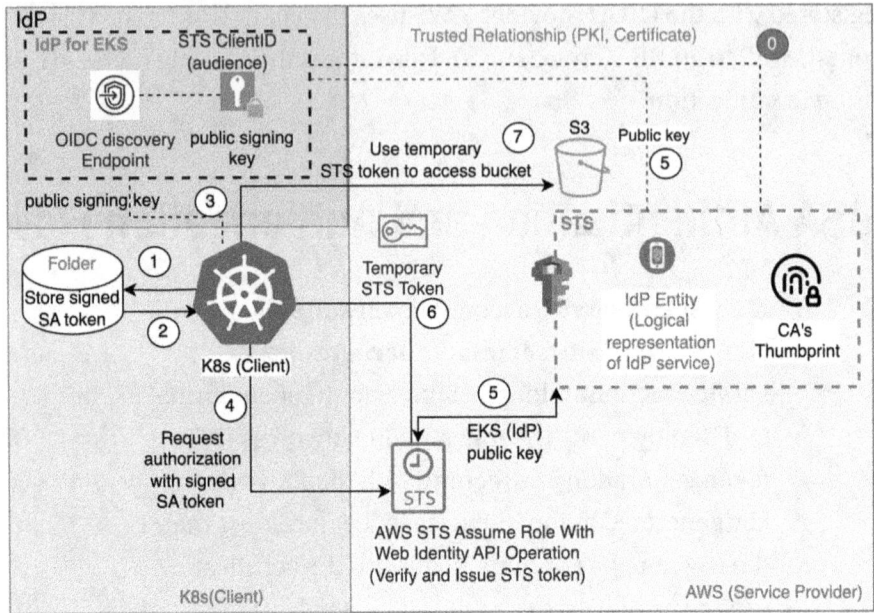

Figure 15-3. IRSA flow

IRSA Manual Trust Establishment

IRSA is complicated to explain. As a result, I will set up the trust between EKS and AWS manually using the flow in Figure 15-3 (step 0 in Figure 15-2) before Terraform automation later in the chapter. This should help you understand the trust establishment process before you move on to the authentication and authorization steps.

1. Destroy the cluster in Chapter15.

   ```
   terraform destroy
   ```

2. Navigate to the **variables.tf** file of the control plane and change the cluster version to the current version.

CHAPTER 15   POD SERVICE ACCOUNTS

```
variable "cluster_version" {
  default = "1.31"
}
```

3. Redeploy the cluster.

   ```
   terraform init
   terraform apply
   ```

4. Copy the OpenID Connect Provider URL of the EKS.

   Navigate to EKS console, click the cluster | Overview, then copy the OpenID Connect Provider URL to the clipboard.

5. Establish the trust between EKS (IdP) and STS.

   Navigate to IAM, click on Identity provider | Add provider, select OpenID Connect, paste the URL of the OpenID Provider you copied in step 4, type sts.amazonaws.com in the Audience, then click Add provider to create the EKS identity provider (IdP).

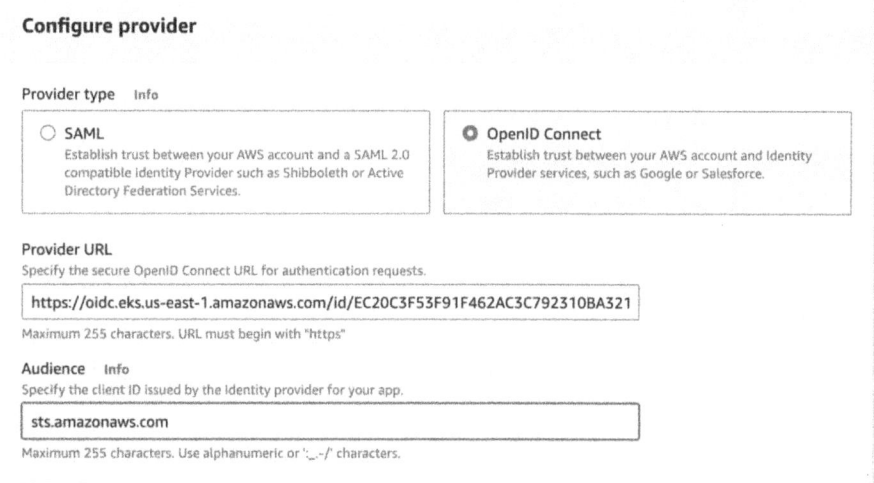

Figure 15-4. Provider configuration-step 1

405

CHAPTER 15   POD SERVICE ACCOUNTS

6. Click the link below the IdP providers (1) to see the summary.

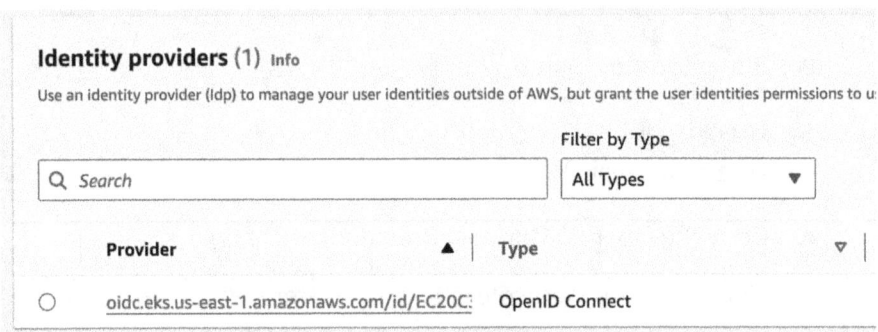

Figure 15-5. *Provider configuration-step 2*

7. You should find **sts.amazonaws.com** under the audiences.

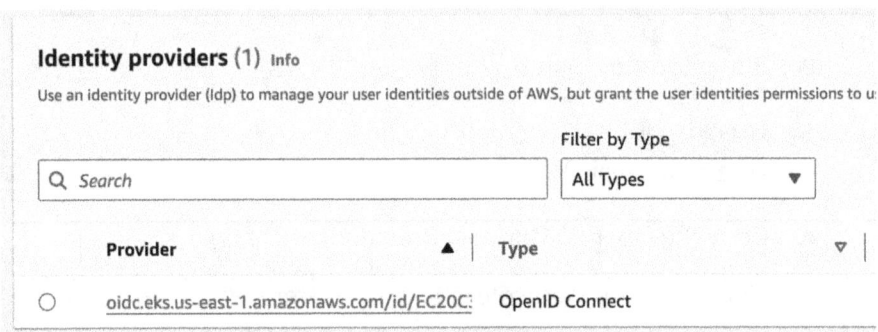

Figure 15-6. *OIDC Audiences*

The audience represents the client ID. Client ID is a unique identifier that identifies the application registered with the OIDC provider. In this case, sts.amazonaws.com is the audience. AWS will use the audience to map a claim from the IdP to a role in STS. The **sts.amazonaws.com** is an initial claim ID; we will replace it with the actual claim ID later.

8. You should also find the thumbprint when you click the Endpoint verification tab. This is what AWS uses to establish trust between the IdP and STS service as explained earlier.

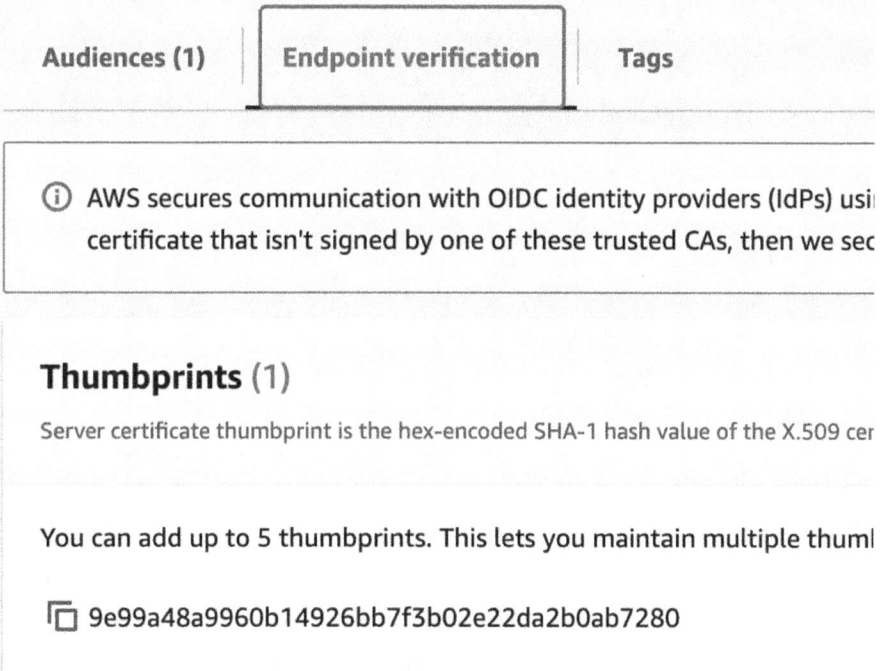

Figure 15-7. OIDC Thumbprints

CHAPTER 15 POD SERVICE ACCOUNTS

9. Attach a role (secret manager and S3 bucket role) to the AWS STS Assume Role with Web Identity.

   Click the Assign role button of the IdP, then select Create a new role.

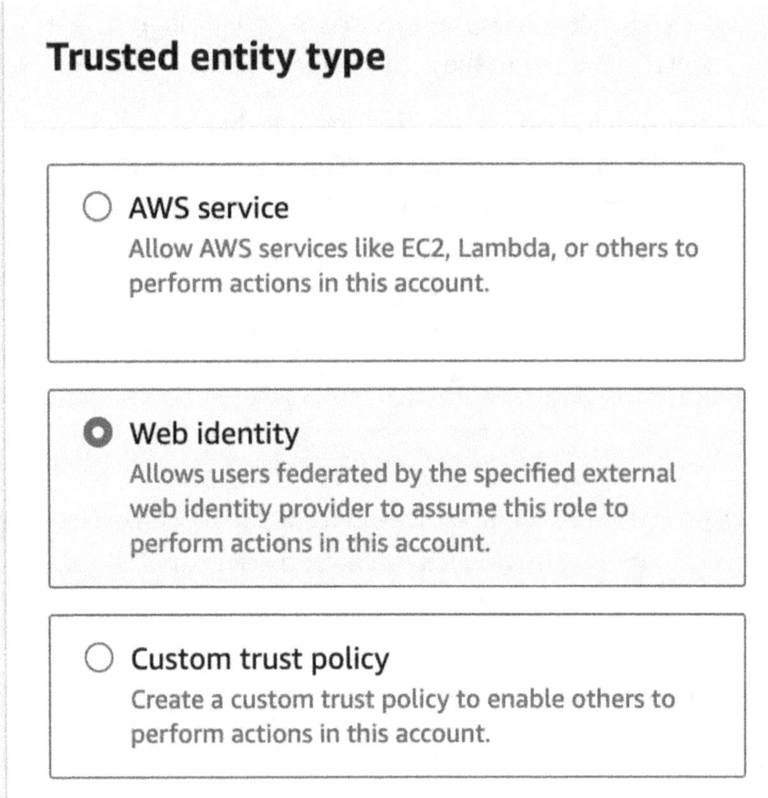

   Trusted entity type

   ○ **AWS service**
   Allow AWS services like EC2, Lambda, or others to perform actions in this account.

   ● **Web identity**
   Allows users federated by the specified external web identity provider to assume this role to perform actions in this account.

   ○ **Custom trust policy**
   Create a custom trust policy to enable others to perform actions in this account.

Figure 15-8. *OIDC configuration-Role assignment*

10. Add permissions.

    Scroll down, select the sts.amazonaws.com under Audience, click Next, type secret in the search bar, then select **SecretsManagerReadWrite permission**.

CHAPTER 15 POD SERVICE ACCOUNTS

Repeat the search for **S3 bucket full access**, select the S3 permission, click Next, type a name for the role **(MyIRSARole)**, then click Create role.

11. Find the role you just created from IAM I Roles (e.g., MyIRSARole).

12. Click the Trust relationship to edit the audiences or the client ID from the initial **sts.awsamazonaws.com** to **system:serviceaccount:default:irsa-service-account** which will map claims from EKS IdP to the **MyIRSARole** in AWS STS. All tokens issued by K8s should include the claim ID.

13. Edit the trust policy and replace the current content with the claim ID as follows:

```
system:serviceaccount:namespace:role-name
{
    "Version": "2012-10-17",
    "Statement": [
        {
            "Effect": "Allow",
            "Principal": {
                "Federated": "arn:aws:iam::
                AccountID:oidc-provider/oidc.
                eks.us-east-1.amazonaws.com/id/
                FE652E.."
            },
            "Action": "sts:AssumeRoleWithWebIdentity",
            "Condition": {
```

```
                    "StringEquals": {
                        "oidc.eks.us-east-1.amazonaws.
                        com/id/FE652E2:sub": "system:
                        serviceaccount:default: irsa-
                        service-account"
                    }
                }
            }
        ]
}
```

The sub is the AWS STS conditional context key. It controls access to a role and specifies which IdP claim can assume a role. If the K8s issues an SA authorization token for a default namespace containing the **irsa-service-account**, then the caller can access or assume the mapping role in STS.

You can choose **aud** or **sub** depending on the type of IdP. Choose **aud** for well-known IdPs like Facebook and Amazon Cognito and **sub** for others.

14. Update the changes to complete the trust establishment between the IdP and the STS service.

Changes to Terraform Code

It is important to understand how the IAM policy for the nodes is set up this time round. Comment out the S3 bucket policy in the **iam.tf** file of the node module because it is no longer needed as we have attached it to the service account.

CHAPTER 15 POD SERVICE ACCOUNTS

However, you need the secret manager permission in both places, the node, and the pod to enable access. Leave the secret manager permission intact.

```
/*
resource "aws_iam_role_policy_attachment" "amazon_s3_managed_policy" {
  policy_arn = "arn:aws:iam::aws:policy/AmazonS3FullAccess"
  role       = aws_iam_role.worker_nodes_role.name
}
*/
resource "aws_iam_role_policy_attachment" "aws_secret_manager" {
  policy_arn = "arn:aws:iam::aws:policy/SecretsManagerReadWrite"
  role       = aws_iam_role.worker_nodes_role.name
}
```

You should add a launch template to the node module to change the IMDSv2 hop limit from one to two to ensure that pods can always access AWS services if they have the right permissions. For example, if you want a browser to access a resource from an application:

```
resource "aws_launch_template" "launch_template_node_group" {
 name = "launch-template-node-group"
 block_device_mappings {
     device_name = "/dev/sdf"
     ebs {
     volume_size = 50
     }
  }
```

```
    ebs_optimized = true
    metadata_options {
       http_tokens       = "optional"
       http_put_response_hop_limit = 2
    }
    network_interfaces {
     associate_public_ip_address = false
    }
}
```

Client Configuration

You must configure the client ID so that the STS service can map the role or the permission on the AWS side after the cluster deployment. The following manifest references the claim ID and the IRSA role name you created in the previous step:

```
---
apiVersion: v1
kind: ServiceAccount
metadata:
  name: irsa-service-account
  namespace: default
  annotations:
    eks.amazonaws.com/role-arn: arn:aws:iam::${ACCOUNT_ID}:role/MyIRSARole
```

The application should specify the service account name K8s will use to create and mount the service account (SA) token:

```
---
kind: Pod
apiVersion: v1
```

```
metadata:
  name: smapp
  labels:
    app: smapp
spec:
  serviceAccountName: irsa-service-account
  containers:
    - name: smapp
      image: cloudmanly/eks:smapp
      imagePullPolicy: Always
      ports:
        - containerPort: 8080
      env:
      - name: REGION
        value: us-east-1
      - name: SECRET_NAME
        value: app-secret-1
```

Testing the s3 Bucket

You can now run the application on the cluster and test the outcome.

1. Update context.

   ```
   aws eks update-kubeconfig --name public-endpoint-cluster
   ```

2. Run the application to verify the service account role.

   ```
   kubectl apply -f pods/smapp.yml
   ```

CHAPTER 15 POD SERVICE ACCOUNTS

3. Verify if the pod is running.

   kubectl get pods

4. Start port forwarding.

   kubectl port-forward pod/smapp 8080

5. Use a web browser to access the URL of the pod.

   localhost:8080

6. You should see the following if you use a browser to open the application.

Figure 15-9. Web page for secret manager access

7. Click the Show secret link to see the secret.

   This is super-duper secret: {"SECRET":"SuperSecret"}

   Home

Figure 15-10. Web page for secret manager access and display

Testing with the Exec Command

1. Log in to the running pod.

   kubectl exec -it smapp -- /bin/bash

2. Install the AWS CLI in the pod.

   ```
   apt update && \
   apt install curl wget unzip -y && \
   curl "https://awscli.amazonaws.com/awscli-exe-linux-x86_64.zip" -o "awscliv2.zip" && \
   unzip awscliv2.zip && \
   ./aws/install && \
   aws --version
   ```

3. List S3 buckets in your account.

   ```
   aws s3 ls
   ```

4. List the secret.

   ```
   aws secretsmanager get-secret-value --secret-id app-secret-1 --no-cli-pager
   ```

   This will output the same secret as before.

Testing with the kotaicode Debug Container

You can choose to test the application with the kotaicode debug container if you do not want to install your own AWS CLI tools. The kotaicode container has built-in CLI for all the major cloud providers.

1. Set the service account and the AWS account ID environment variables for the container.

   ```
   SA=irsa-service-account
   ACCOUNT_ID=<ACCOUNT_ID>
   ```

2. Run the debug app with the service account and wait for the command prompt (it can take longer than expected).

   ```
   kubectl run tmp-shell-0 --rm -i --tty --image kotaicode/ubuntu-devops:24 --overrides '{"spec": {"serviceAccountName":"'$SA'"}}' -- /bin/bash
   ```

3. Verify the caller.

   ```
   aws sts get-caller-identity --no-cli-pager
   ```

4. Test s3 access in the container.

   ```
   aws s3 ls
   ```

5. Test secret manager access in the container.

   ```
   aws secretsmanager get-secret-value --secret-id app-secret-1 --no-cli-pager
   ```

6. List secrets.

   ```
   aws secretsmanager list-secrets --no-cli-pager
   ```

OIDC Terraform Automation

The manual steps were meant for you to understand how to establish trust between EKS and STS and continue from there to activate IRSA. You can automate the same process with the Terraform script. The Terraform code is found in Chapter15-irsa. You should find the OpenID Connect URL in the **oidc.tf** file of the control plane. We explain the code as follows:

CHAPTER 15 POD SERVICE ACCOUNTS

1. Retrieve the TLS certificate for the EKS (IdP).

    ```
    data "tls_certificate" "oidc" {
      url = aws_eks_cluster.public_endpoint_cluster.
      identity[0].oidc[0]. issuer
    }
    ```

2. Register the IdP in the STS.

    ```
    resource "aws_iam_openid_connect_provider" "oidc_openid_connect" {
      client_id_list  = ["sts.amazonaws.com"]
      thumbprint_list = [data.tls_certificate.oidc.
      certificates[0].sha1_fingerprint]
      url = data.tls_certificate.oidc.url
    }
    ```

3. Create an assumed role policy and replace the audience (client ID) with a custom audience.

    ```
    data "aws_iam_policy_document" "oidc_assume_role_policy" {
      statement {
        actions = ["sts:AssumeRoleWithWebIdentity"]
        effect  = "Allow"
        condition {
          test     = "StringEquals"
          variable = "${replace(aws_iam_openid_connect_provider.oidc_openid_connect.url, "https://", "")}:sub"
          values   = ["system:serviceaccount:default:irsa-service-account", "system:serviceaccount:system:my-service-account"]
        }
    ```

```
      principals {
        identifiers = [aws_iam_openid_connect_provider.
        oidc_openid_connect.arn]
        type          = "Federated"
      }
    }
  }
```

4. Create a new IRSA role.

```
resource "aws_iam_role" "oidc_role" {
  assume_role_policy = data.aws_iam_policy_document.
  oidc_assume_role_policy.json
  name               = "IRSARole"
}
```

5. Attach the Amazon S3 policy to the role.

```
resource "aws_iam_role_policy_attachment" "attach_s3_
policy" {
    policy_arn = "arn:aws:iam::aws:policy/
    AmazonS3FullAccess"
  role       = aws_iam_role.oidc_role.name
}
```

6. Attach the secret manager policy to the role.

```
resource "aws_iam_role_policy_attachment" "attach_
secret_access_policy" {
  policy_arn = "arn:aws:iam::aws:policy/
  SecretsManagerReadWrite"
  role       = aws_iam_role.oidc_role.name
}
```

CHAPTER 15   POD SERVICE ACCOUNTS

This part of the code establishes the trust between the IdP and AWS. It automates the manual steps discussed in the previous section.

Cluster Deployment

1. Deploy the cluster in Chapter15-irsa.

    ```
    terraform init
    terraform apply
    ```

2. Update context.

    ```
    aws eks update-kubeconfig --name public-endpoint-cluster
    ```

3. Run the application.

    ```
    kubectl apply -f pods/smapp.yml
    ```

The manifest will create as service account and an application to use the service account as follows:

```
---
apiVersion: v1
kind: ServiceAccount
metadata:
  name: irsa-service-account
  namespace: default
  annotations:
    eks.amazonaws.com/role-arn: arn:aws:iam::
    {ACCOUNT_ID}:role/IRSARole
---
kind: Pod
apiVersion: v1
```

```
metadata:
  name: smapp
  labels:
    app: smapp
spec:
  serviceAccountName: irsa-service-account
  containers:
    - name: smapp
      image: cloudmanly/eks:smapp
      imagePullPolicy: Always
      ports:
      - containerPort: 8080
      env:
      - name: REGION
        value: us-east-1
      - name: SECRET_NAME
        value: app-secret-1
```

Testing Secret Manager with Port Forwarding

1. Start port forwarding.

   `kubectl port-forward pod/smapp 8080`

2. Use a web browser to access the URL of the pod.

   `localhost:8080`

3. You should see the same results as before.

CHAPTER 15 POD SERVICE ACCOUNTS

Testing with the Exec Command

1. Log in to the running pod.

   ```
   kubectl exec -it smapp -- /bin/bash
   ```

2. Install the AWS CLI in the pod.

   ```
   apt update && \
   apt install curl wget unzip -y && \
   curl "https://awscli.amazonaws.com/awscli-exe-linux-x86_64.zip" -o "awscliv2.zip" && \
   unzip awscliv2.zip && \
   ./aws/install && \
   aws --version
   ```

3. List S3 buckets in your account.

   ```
   aws s3 ls
   ```

4. List the secret.

   ```
   aws secretsmanager get-secret-value --secret-id app-secret-1 --no-cli-pager
   ```

This will output the same secret as before.

Testing with the kotaicode Debug Container

You can try the same test with the debug container as before.

1. Set the service account and the AWS account ID environment variables.

   ```
   SA=irsa-service-account
   ACCOUNT_ID=<ACCOUNT_ID>
   ```

421

2. Replace the ${ACCOUNT_ID} with your AWS account.

3. Run the debug application (this may take longer than expected; delete the pod and rerun the command again if it fails).

   ```
   kubectl run tmp-shell-0 --rm -i --tty --image kotaicode/ubuntu-devops:24 --overrides '{"spec": {"serviceAccountName":"'$SA'"}}' -- /bin/bash
   ```

4. Verify the caller.

   ```
   aws sts get-caller-identity --no-cli-pager
   ```

5. Test s3 access.

   ```
   aws s3 ls
   ```

6. Test secret manager access.

   ```
   aws secretsmanager get-secret-value --secret-id app-secret-1 --no-cli-pager
   ```

7. List secrets.

   ```
   aws secretsmanager list-secrets --no-cli-pager
   ```

8. Type exit to exit the debug container.

9. Delete the pods and the service account.

   ```
   kubectl delete -f pod/smapp.yml
   ```

Pod Identity

The Amazon EKS Pod Identity is a simplified version of the IRSA method. It works in the same way as the IRSA method. EKS Pod Identity makes access control more granular at the pod level.[6] As before, only pods configured with a service account can assume the permissions attached to the service account role.[7] This means you can tailor permissions to specific needs of your applications.

Pod identity enables access and event logging through AWS CloudTrail to help facilitate retrospective auditing. No role name is required when creating a service account object with pod identity.

Our third example in this chapter will show how to run the same smapp application with pod identity. As a prerequisite, you must install the EKS Pod Identity addon to activate the EKS Pod Identity solution.

Terraform Code

We will deploy the pod identity code in the folder chapter15-pod-id. Aside the removal of the secret manager role, the other key changes are as follows:

1. Deployment of the pod identity addon. You should find this in the **addons.tf** file.

   ```
   resource "aws_eks_addon" "eks_pod-idenity_addon" {
       cluster_name = var.cluster_name
       addon_name   = "eks-pod-identity-agent"
   }
   ```

---

[6] https://docs.aws.amazon.com/eks/latest/userguide/pod-id-how-it-works.html
[7] https://docs.aws.amazon.com/eks/latest/userguide/pod-identities.html

2. Creation of the assumed role policy for pod identity.

```
data "aws_iam_policy_document" "pod_id_policy" {
  statement {
    effect = "Allow"
    principals {
      type        = "Service"
      identifiers = ["pods.eks.amazonaws.com"]
    }
    actions = [
      "sts:AssumeRole",
      "sts:TagSession"
    ]
  }
}
```

3. Creation of a role for pod identity.

```
resource "aws_iam_role" "pod_identity_role" {
  name               = "pod-identity-role"
  assume_role_policy = data.aws_iam_policy_document.assume_role.json
}
```

4. Attachment of secret manager policy to the role.

```
resource "aws_iam_role_policy_attachment" "secret_manager_policy" {
  policy_arn = "arn:aws:iam::aws:policy/SecretsManagerReadWrite"
  role       = aws_iam_role.pod_identity_role.name
}
```

CHAPTER 15   POD SERVICE ACCOUNTS

5. Attachment of the s3 bucket policy to the role.

   ```
   resource "aws_iam_role_policy_attachment" "s3_bucket_
   policy" {
     policy_arn = "arn:aws:iam::aws:policy/
     AmazonS3FullAccess"
     role       = aws_iam_role.pod_identity_irsa_role.name
   }
   ```

6. Creation of the client ID or audience.

   ```
   resource "aws_eks_pod_identity_association" "pod_
   identity_cliam_id" {
     cluster_name    = var.cluster_name
     namespace       = "default"
     service_account = "pod-service-account"
     role_arn        = aws_iam_role.pod_identity_role.arn
   }
   ```

Cluster Deployment

1. Initialize the terraform code in the chapter15-pod-id folder.

   ```
   terraform init
   ```

2. Deploy the cluster.

   ```
   terraform apply -auto-approve
   ```

3. Update user context.

   ```
   aws eks update-kubeconfig --name public-endpoint-cluster
   ```

CHAPTER 15   POD SERVICE ACCOUNTS

4. Execute the application YAML file in the folder.

   ```
   kubectl apply -f pods/pod-id-smapp.yml
   ```

   The first section of the YAM file creates a service account for the pod in the default namespace. You do not need to specify a role arn.

   ```
   ---
   apiVersion: v1
   kind: ServiceAccount
   metadata:
     name: pod-service-account
     namespace: default
   ```

   The second stanza of the manifest specifies the service account the pod should use. No role arn is needed here.

   ```
   ---
   kind: Pod
   apiVersion: v1
   metadata:
     name: smapp
     labels:
       app: smapp
   spec:
     serviceAccountName: pod-service-account
     containers:
       - name: smapp
         image: cloudmanly/eks:smapp
         imagePullPolicy: Always
         ports:
           - containerPort: 8080
   ```

```
    env:
    - name: REGION
      value: us-east-1
    - name: SECRET_NAME
      value: app-secret-1
```

5. Check if the pod is running.

   ```
   kubectl get pods
   ```

6. Start port forwarding.

   ```
   kubectl port-forward pod/smapp 8080
   ```

7. Use a web browser to access the URL of the pod.

   ```
   localhost:8080
   ```

8. You should see this if you use the Web.

Figure 15-11. Web page for secret access

9. Click the Show secret link to see the secret.

Figure 15-12. Web page for secret display

Testing with CLI

1. Log in to the running pod.

   ```
   kubectl exec -it smapp -- /bin/bash
   ```

2. Install the AWS CLI in the pod.

   ```
   apt update && \
   apt install curl wget unzip -y && \
   curl "https://awscli.amazonaws.com/awscli-exe-linux-x86_64.zip" -o "awscliv2.zip" && \
   unzip awscliv2.zip && \
   ./aws/install && \
   aws --version
   ```

3. List S3 buckets in your account.

   ```
   aws s3 ls
   ```

4. List the secret.

   ```
   aws secretsmanager get-secret-value --secret-id app-secret-1 --no-cli-pager
   ```

Summary

The two means of granting least privileged access to pods to access external resources are the IAM roles for service accounts (IRSA) and pod identity. Pod identity is the simplified and more powerful version of IRSA. It reduces the complexities in setting up service accounts for pods in EKS. There is no need to worry about IMDSv2 hop limit or node policy attachments to grant pod access to external services such as AWS S3 buckets. IRSA is based on the OpenID Connect authentication protocol. It offloads API authentication from the AWS IAM to a local or external identity provider (IdP). The client making the API call to an AWS account authenticates with the IdP and receives a token. It then exchanges the token for a temporary AWS Security Service Token (STS) authorization token used to access an AWS service. In EKS, the IdP is the EKS service itself, and the service provider is AWS. The next chapter will see more applications of service accounts.

CHAPTER 16

Pod Persistence

In the previous chapter, we saw how Kubernetes (K8s) mounts the service account (SA) tokens in a folder within a container running inside a pod. Files or on-disk folders such as the SA folder are ephemeral because they "die" with their pods. In other words, they have the lifetime of their pods. Data stored in the folder is deleted and lost when pods that host them cease to exist. K8s provides ways to persist data to stay permanent even if pods are destroyed. This chapter will discuss options available for creating persistent storages so that data is retained even when pods are destroyed. We will briefly touch on ephemeral volume types before we delve into persistent volumes.

Kubernetes Volumes

Volumes are directories mounted for containers inside pods to store or access data.[1] They present the basic storage object in K8s.

K8s implements two types of volumes, in-tree and out-of-tree volumes. In-tree volumes have storage drivers integrated with K8s binary. They are bootstrap with K8s; hence, no driver or plugin support is required to use them.

In contrast, out-of-tree volumes are supported by third-party storage drivers installed from extrinsic plugins. No bootstrap support exists for such volumes; as a result, cluster operators must deploy the requisite plugins to make them work.

---

[1] https://kubernetes.io/docs/concepts/storage/volumes/

CHAPTER 16   POD PERSISTENCE

You can create two kinds of volumes, ephemeral or persistent volume types whether you are deploying in-tree or out-of-tree volume types. An ephemeral volume has a lifetime of a pod but persists when a container is restarted, whereas a persistent volume exists beyond a pod's lifetime. Figure 16-1 illustrates the two types of volumes.

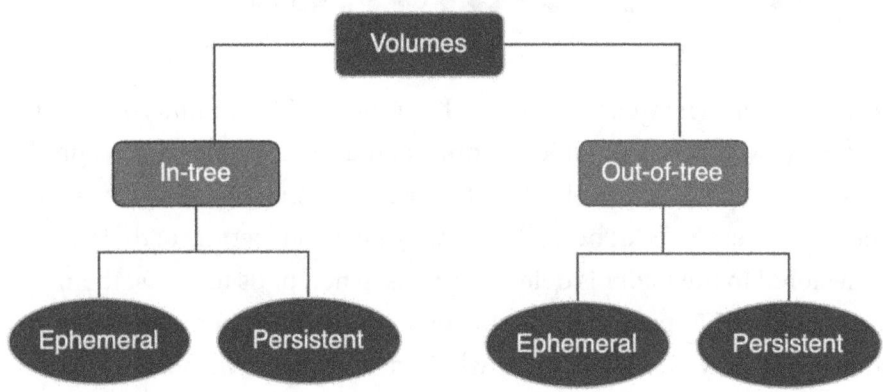

Figure 16-1. *Volume types*

Ephemeral volumes are useful for stateless applications such as cache services, long in-memory computations, and large dataset processing with short-term storage needs.

They are also important for secret storage and configuration management. You may need ephemeral volumes to persist storage across container restart to maintain data consistency in an application.

On the other hand, persistent volumes are useful for stateful applications, applications that require long-term persistent storage.[2]

---

[2] https://kubernetes.io/docs/concepts/storage/volumes/#emptydir

Kinds of Ephemeral Volumes

The lifetime of a K8s ephemeral volume depends on the pod that hosts them. Containers that run inside pods are consigned to the same volume even if you restart them. The new containers that are created after restart will utilize the same volume as the old. Thus, no data is lost across container restarts. However, the volume ceases to exist, and data is lost once a pod terminates.

K8s supports several kinds of ephemeral volumes for different purposes:

- *emptyDir*: K8s creates an empty directory when a pod is assigned to a node and grants containers of the pod read/write access to the directory. K8s deletes the directory once the pod is terminated.

- *ConfigMap, downwardAPI, secret*: You can manage pod secret and environment variables with the downward API and secret object. The downward API is a special volume for environment variables, while the secret object is for secret management. K8s uses these volumes to inject secrets or environment data into pods. The ConfigMap volume on the other hand can store publicly variable configuration for pods to use.

- *CSI ephemeral volumes*: Generic ephemeral volumes for third-party integration. It requires third-party Container Storage Interface (CSI) storage driver support.[3]

---

[3] https://kubernetes.io/docs/concepts/storage/ephemeral-volumes/

CHAPTER 16   POD PERSISTENCE

Ephemeral Volume Implementation

Creating ephemeral storage involves two simple steps. Create the volume and mount the volume in a container. The example below creates a volume named **empty-volume** and mounts it in the blueapp container using the mountPath key. The mount point or path is where the actual data is stored. For example, the /**data** directory in the manifest below is the mount path:

```
---
kind: Pod
apiVersion: v1
metadata:
  name: app-emp
spec:
volumes:
  - name: empty-volume
    emptyDir: {}
  containers:
  - name: blueapp
    image: cloudmanly/eks:blueapp
    ports:
      - containerPort: 8080
    command: ["/bin/sh"]
    args: ["-c", "while true; do echo $(date -u) >> /data/out.txt; sleep 5; done"]
    volumeMounts:
    - name: empty-volume
      mountPath: /data
```

CHAPTER 16   POD PERSISTENCE

The curly brace ({}) indicates that K8s will create an emptyDir with default configuration. The default medium is disk or SSD depending on the environment. You can change the default medium and the volume size to RAM by replacing the {} with the following specification:

```
emptyDir:
  medium: Memory
  sizeLimit: 500MB
```

An emptyDir volume exists with the host pod as shown in Figure 16-2. It is created when a pod is assigned to a node and exists as long as that pod is running on that node. An emptyDir volume is initially empty and accessible to all containers in the same pod; thus, all containers in a pod can read and write to the same emptyDir volume. emptyDir is ephemeral because the data in the emptyDir is lost forever when a pod is removed from a node, dies, or deleted.

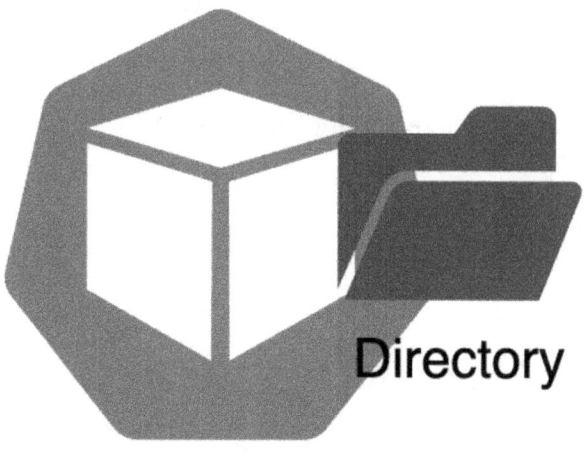

Figure 16-2. EmptyDir volume

CHAPTER 16   POD PERSISTENCE

Testing the Ephemeral Volume

1. Initialize the terraform in Chapter16-in-tree.

   `terraform init`

2. Deploy the cluster.

   `terraform apply -auto-approve`

3. Update user context.

   `aws eks update-kubeconfig --name public-endpoint-cluster`

4. Execute the application YAML file in the pod folder.

   `kubectl apply -f pods/empheral.yml`

5. Log in to the pod.

   `kubectl exec -it blueapp -- /bin/bash`

6. Display the content of the out.txt file.

   `cat /data/out.txt`

You should find the data in the /data/out.txt file.

The Secret Volume

The secret volume is one of the ephemeral volumes. It can store secrets for applications. You implement secret volumes by creating and mounting a secret object in a pod.

CHAPTER 16   POD PERSISTENCE

You can create the secret object as follows:[4]

```
apiVersion: v1
kind: Secret
metadata:
  name: top-secret
data:
  username: Ym9i
  password: c3VwZXItc2VjcmV0
```

The name of the secret is top-secret. It references the username and password in the data section. The secret object accepts base64 encoding for the username and password. The encoding is done with the following commands:

```
echo -n 'bob' | base64
Ym9i
echo -n 'super-secret' | base64
c3VwZXItc2VjcmV0
```

You can now mount the volume in the blue app pod as follows:

```
---
kind: Pod
apiVersion: v1
metadata:
  name: blueapp
spec:
  volumes:
    - name: secret-vol
      secret:
        secretName: top-secret
```

---

[4] https://kubernetes.io/docs/tasks/inject-data-application/distribute-credentials-secure/#provide-prod-test-creds

437

```
containers:
- name: blueapp
  image: cloudmanly/eks:blueapp
  ports:
  - containerPort: 8080
  volumeMounts:
  - name: secret-vol
    readOnly: true
    mountPath: /opt/tomcat/secret-vol
```

Testing the Secret Volume

1. Execute the application YAML file in the folder.

   ```
   kubectl apply -f pods/secret.yml
   ```

2. Log in to the pod.

   ```
   kubectl exec -it blueapp -- /bin/bash
   ```

3. Display the password.

   ```
   cat /secret-vol/password
   ```

4. Display the username.

   ```
   cat /secret-vol/username
   ```

Persistent Volume

Let us move on to persistent volumes. We begin with the host path volume and proceed to more advanced persistent volume implementations.

CHAPTER 16   POD PERSISTENCE

The Host Path Volume

The host path volume provides an easy and quick way of configuring persistent volumes.[5] It mounts a file or a directory from a worker node into a pod as depicted in Figure 16-3.

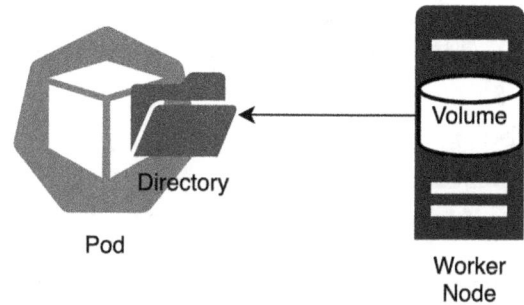

Figure 16-3. Host path volume

The worker node's file (host file) or directory should exist or should be created dynamically with host path field types. The host path volume may be created as follows:

```
---
kind: Pod
apiVersion: v1
metadata:
  name: blueapp
spec:
volumes:
  - name: persistent-vol
    hostPath:
        path: /persistent-data
        type: DirectoryOrCreate
```

---

[5] The Kubernetes Workshop: Learn how to build and run highly scalable workloads on Kubernetes, Zachary Arnold, Sahil Dua, Wei Huang, Faisal Masood, Melony Qin, and Mohammed Abu Taleb

CHAPTER 16   POD PERSISTENCE

```
containers:
- name: blueapp
  image: cloudmanly/eks:blueapp
  ports:
    - containerPort: 8080
  command: ["/bin/sh"]
  args: ["-c", "while true; do echo $(date -u) >> /data/out.txt; sleep 5; done"]
  volumeMounts:
  - name: persistent-vol
    mountPath: /data
```

The manifest file creates a pod and mounts a host path volume in the pod. The hostPath field specifies the host directory (/persistent-data) that should be mounted in the container. The optional **type** field specifies the type of volume.

The type field supports the following values:

- "" (an empty string): This is the default value. Perform no checks before mounting the hostPath volume. The disadvantage of this is that if the path specified does not exist on the node, the pod will still be created without verifying the existence of the path. Hence, the pod will keep crashing indefinitely because of this error.

- DirectoryOrCreate: Creates an empty directory if the specified host path directory does not exist on the host node.

- Directory: The host path directory must exist on the host node. It generates a FailedMount error if the directory does not exist.

- FileOrCreate: Creates the host path file if it doesn't exist on the host.

- File: The file specified must exist on the host node.

- Socket: The socket specified must exist on the host.

- CharDevice: The character device specified must exist.

- BlockDevice: The block device specified must exist on the host.

The pod accesses the data in the host path volume from the /data directory mounted in the pod or the blue app container. The value of the args field under the container specification is a loop that prints date to the out.txt file.

Testing the Host Path Volume

1. Execute the application YAML file in the folder.

    ```
    kubectl apply -f pods/hostpath.yml
    ```

2. Log in to the pod.

    ```
    kubectl exec -it blueapp -- /bin/bash
    ```

3. Display the content of the out.txt file.

    ```
    cat /data/out.txt
    ```

Testing for Persistence of the Host Path Volume

1. Delete the blue app pod.

    ```
    kubectl delete pod blueapp
    ```

CHAPTER 16   POD PERSISTENCE

2. Navigate to EC2, select an instance, then click Connect | Session Manager.

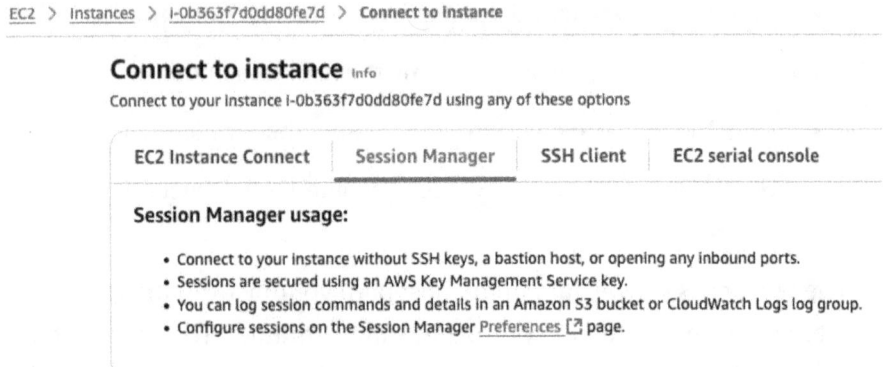

Figure 16-4. Log in to an instance

3. Verify if the data exists after pod deletion.

   sh-5.2$ cat /persistent-data/out.txt

4. You should see the following output:

   Wed Jan 8 04:57:38 UTC ...
   Wed Jan 8 04:57:43 UTC ...
   Wed Jan 8 04:57:48 UTC ...
   Wed Jan 8 04:57:53 UTC ...
   Wed Jan 8 04:57:58 UTC ...

The host path data persists after the pod deletion. The pod will reload the data in the persistent-data location when you redeploy it.

The host path volume is for quick tests or fixes. Even though host path volume persists data, there is no guarantee of data integrity if a pod is rescheduled on a different node.

It also a huge security risk to the cluster security. Avoid the host path volume if you can because it opens access to a host file system which can expose privileged system credentials (e.g., kubelet secrets) or privileged APIs (such as the container runtime socket). Attackers can take advantage of this vulnerability to escape your container or attack other parts of your cluster.

The Persistent Volume Subsystem

The configuration of persistent volumes with the persistent volume subsystem APIs is more demanding than the host path volume type because it involves multiple K8s objects, a persistent volume (PV) object which represents the block storage, a storage class object (SC) which determines the volume type, and a persistent volume claim (PVC) object which requests a portion of the PV for a pod to mount in a container.

SCs optimize storage management in K8s. It helps PVs to adapt to the varying storage needs of applications. It specifies storage types, their characteristics, and the provisioners responsible for creating PVs on the fly.

Once the PV is set up with your preferred SC, you can bind the PV to an application. Binding allows you to claim part of the PV for use in a pod. You do that by creating a persistent volume claim that requests a portion of the storage from PV. The request should at least specify the SC and the access mode. SC determines the PV that should be provisioned to satisfy the request.

SCs control volume types and their characteristics. You can specify any kind of SC in a PVC request depending on the application preferences. SC types are default SC, static, dynamic, standard, or custom SC.

K8s creates default SC for every cluster and uses it to create PV when a PVC request does not specify any SC. It ensures that K8s provide storage resources even when a PVC request does not contain a specific SC. K8s provisions a storage resource from a preexisting volume when a PVC request specifies static SC. The preexisting must have been created manually in the cluster by an administrator.

CHAPTER 16   POD PERSISTENCE

K8s provisions new storage resources according to the needs of an application on the fly with dynamic SC. Standard SC instructs K8s to provision an AWS EBS volume with the gp2 type and ext4 file system. A PVC request can include a custom SC for more specific use cases and requirements.

Figure 16-5 describes the basic steps in creating and using a PV. The storage class describes the characteristics of the type of volume to create. K8s creates the volume. PVC requests how much of the pie is needed in an application and mounts the portion in the application. The request will specify the SC which determines which kind of PV K8s should deploy.

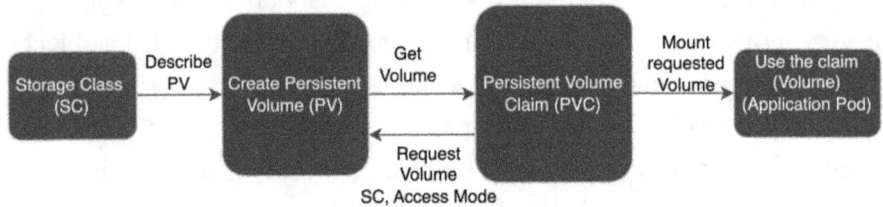

Figure 16-5. Persistent volume creation

Persistent Volume Creation and Testing

You can follow the steps below to create and test a network file share (NFS) persistent volume:

1. Create a persistent volume with the AWS gp2 storage class.

   ```
   apiVersion: v1
   apiVersion: v1
   kind: PersistentVolume
   metadata:
     name: persistent-volume
   spec:
     storageClassName: gp2
   ```

444

```
capacity:
    storage: 5Gi
volumeMode: Filesystem
accessModes:
    - ReadWriteMany
persistentVolumeReclaimPolicy: Retain
nfs:
    server: <IPAdress_of_the_nfs_server>
    path: /mnt/nfs_share/
```

K8s will dynamically provision an AWS EBS volume with the gp2 type, ext4 file system and default gp2 storage class (SC).

The capacity specifies the storage capacity, 5GB in this case; volume mode is file system for the volume. K8s supports two volume modes, the default file system mode and the block volume mode. Block mode is presented to a pod as a block device, without any file system on it. This speeds up access because there is no intermediate file system layer between the pod and the volume.

The access mode determines the mode of access. The **read write many** access mode means K8s will mount the volume on many nodes and allow pods to read or write to the volume. Other modes are **read write once, read only many**, etc.[6]

The reclaim policy determines what K8s should do with the volume after PVC has released the portion of the volume it claimed and how to manage the

---

[6] https://kubernetes.io/docs/concepts/storage/persistent-volumes/

volume when it is not in use. The retain reclaim policy means K8s cannot release the volume for another PVC claimant even though the previous PVC claimant has released it. The previous claimant's data remains on the volume until an administrator deletes it manually.

The delete reclaim policy will delete the storage resources and everything associated with it after a claim is released.

The nfs section specifies the type of volume to deploy. K8s implements volume types as plugins. Kubernetes currently supports the following plugins:

- csi: Container Storage Interface (CSI)
- fc: Fibre Channel (FC) storage
- hostPath: HostPath volume
- iscsi: iSCSI (SCSI over IP) storage
- local: Local storage devices mounted on nodes
- nfs: Network File System (NFS) storage

2. Create a persistent volume claim.

```
---
apiVersion: v1
kind: PersistentVolumeClaim
metadata:
  name: nfs-pvc
spec:
  storageClassName: gp2
  resources:
```

CHAPTER 16 POD PERSISTENCE

```
      requests:
        storage: 200Mi
    volumeMode: Filesystem
    accessModes:
      - ReadWriteMany
    selector:
      matchLabels:
        environment: "dev"
```

The claim specifies the SC (gp2) to correspond to that of the standard PV specified in step 1. It requests a portion of storage (200MB) instead of the entire 5GB of storage. The volume type is file system, and the access mode is read/write/many.

3. Mount the volume in a pod. This where you call the PV and the PVC.

```
---
kind: Pod
apiVersion: v1
metadata:
  name: blueapp
spec:
  containers:
  - name: blueapp
    image: cloudmanly/eks:blueapp
    ports:
      - containerPort: 8080
    command: ["/bin/sh"]
    args: ["-c", "while true; do echo $(date -u)
    >> /data/out.txt; sleep 5; done"]
    volumeMounts:
```

447

```
        - name: persistent-storage
          mountPath: /data
      volumes:
        - name: persistent-storage
          persistentVolumeClaim:
            claimName: nfs-pvc
```

We mount the volume in the blueapp pod by referencing the PV and PVC.

Testing the Persistent Volume

1. Using the cluster in Chapter16-in-tree.

2. Execute the application YAML file in the pod folder.

   ```
   kubectl apply -f pod/persistent-gp2.yml
   ```

3. Verify if PV is running.

   ```
   kubectl get PV
   ```

4. Verify if PVC is running.

   ```
   kubectl get pvc
   ```

   PVC will be pending.

5. Verify why PVC is pending.

   ```
   kubectl describe nfs-pvc
   ```

   You should find a message like this:

   ```
   Normal  WaitForFirstConsumer  22s  persistentvolume-
   controller  waiting for first consumer to be created
   before binding
   Normal  ExternalProvisioning  9s (x2 over 22s)
   persistentvolume-controller  Waiting for a volume to
   ```

be created either by the external provisioner 'ebs. csi.aws.com' or manually by the system administrator. If volume creation is delayed, please verify that the provisioner is running and correctly registered.

6. Verify if the external provisioner is running.

   ```
   kubectl -n kube-system get pod -o wide
   NAME
   aws-node-xzvkj
   coredns-789f8477df-7mwj8
   coredns-789f8477df-vxww5
   kube-proxy-jhc7w
   ```

   You should find no ebs.csi.aws.com provisioner here.

7. Verify provisioner with logs.

   ```
   kubectl logs ebs.csi.aws.com -n kube-system
   ```

   You should find an error message.

The describe command should explain why the persistent volume claim is pending. Notice that the default ebs.csi.aws.com provisioner could not create the persistent volume claim (PVC) because first it is not the correct plugin or driver for the NFS volume. Secondly, we could not find it in the kube system namespace, suggesting the provisioner may not run or register correctly. We will return to the AWS EBS provisioner later in the chapter.

Lastly, the PVC description message suggests that an administrator should create the volume because it could not automate the PVC process. No one wants to create a volume manually if it can be automated with a provisioner. A provisioner is a plugin or a driver that can automate the creation of PV and PVC. The next section shows how to automate an NFS PV and PVC with an NFS driver.

CHAPTER 16   POD PERSISTENCE

Out-of-Tree NFS Provisioner

We deployed a new manifest in the persistent-provisioner.yml file. The code has no PV but just a storage class which does all the heavy lifting creating a PV and PVC. It specifies the NFS provisioner and volume type attributes. The provisioner creates the PV and the PVC for the pods to mount:

```
apiVersion: storage.k8s.io/v1
kind: StorageClass
metadata:
  name: nfs-csi
provisioner: nfs.csi.k8s.io
parameters:
  server: ip_address_of_nfs_server
  share: /mnt/nfs_share/
reclaimPolicy: Delete
volumeBindingMode: Immediate
```

The SC specifies the IP address of the NFS server and the share where persistent data is stored and shared. This means you must create an NFS server, replace ip_address_of_nfs_server with the IP address of the NFS server before you can create the PV and the PVC.

You will find the Terraform code for the NFS server in the nfs module as below:

```
resource "aws_instance" "instances" {
  ami             = data.aws_ami.ubuntu.id
  instance_type   = var.instance-type
  key_name        = var.sshkey
  metadata_options {
    http_endpoint = "enabled"
    http_tokens   = "required"
  }
```

CHAPTER 16 POD PERSISTENCE

```
    subnet_id                  = var.subnet_id
    vpc_security_group_ids     = [aws_security_group.sg.id]
    associate_public_ip_address = true

    user_data = <<-EOL
       #!/bin/bash -xe
       sudo apt update
       sudo apt -y install nfs-kernel-server
       sudo systemctl enable nfs-kernel-server.service
       sudo systemctl start nfs-kernel-server.service
       sudo apt -y install nfs-common
       sudo mkdir -p /mnt/nfs_share
       sudo chown -R nobody:nogroup /mnt/nfs_share/
       sudo chmod 777 /mnt/nfs_share/
       sudo echo '/mnt/nfs_share 10.0.0.0/16(rw,sync,no_subtree_
       check)' >> /etc/exports
       sudo exportfs -rav
       sudo systemctl restart nfs-kernel-server.service
    EOL

    tags = {
      "Name" : var.instance-tags
    }
}
```

The module creates an EC2 instance for the NFS server and installs the NFS package on it. It creates the share directory and grants the required permissions. The user data script creates an entry in the /etc/exports file. The parameter for the entry is explained as follows:

- rw: Nodes will have both read and write access to the volumes.

- sync: Write changes to disk before replying.

- no_subtree_check: Disables the subtree checking as recommended.

Finally, the script updates the export file and restarts the NFS server.

Testing the NFS Provisioner Deployment

1. Delete the failed gp2 deployment.

   ```
   kubectl delete -f pod/persistent-gp2.yml
   ```

2. Replace the IP address in the **persistent-provisioner.yml** with the IP address of the NFS server deployed with the cluster.

   ```
   apiVersion: storage.k8s.io/v1
   kind: StorageClass
   metadata:
     name: nfs-csi
   provisioner: nfs.csi.k8s.io
   parameters:
     server: 10.0.5.194 #replace it with yours
     share: /mnt/nfs_share/
   reclaimPolicy: Delete
   volumeBindingMode: Immediate
   ```

3. Install the CSI NFS provisioner on the cluster because it is an out-of-tree plugin.

   ```
   curl -skSL https://raw.githubusercontent.com/kubernetes-csi/csi-driver-nfs/v4.5.0/deploy/install-driver.sh | bash -s v4.5.0 --
   ```

4. Verify if the provisioner is running.

   ```
   kubectl -n kube-system get pod -o wide -l app=csi-nfs-controller
   kubectl -n kube-system get pod -o wide -l app=csi-nfs-node
   ```

5. Execute the NFS provisioner deployment file in the pod folder.

   ```
   kubectl apply -f pods/persistent-provisioner.yml
   ```

6. Verify if the blue app is running.

   ```
   kubectl get pods
   ```

7. Log in to the pod.

   ```
   kubectl exec -it blueapp -- /bin/bash
   ```

8. Display the content of the out.txt file.

   ```
   cat /data/out.txt
   ```

   You should find the data in the /data/out.txt file.

9. Verify if out.txt is created on the NFS server.

   ```
   cd /mnt/nfs_share/
   ls
   cd pvc-xxxx && ls
   ```

You should find the out.txt file in the shared directory.

Persistent Volume with AWS

Cluster administrators would prefer cloud-native storage such as the Amazon Elastic Block Store (EBS) volume for persistent volume to NFS persistent volume.

This may call for out-of-tree AWS plugins or provisioners to manage the volume. Cluster administrators must install AWS add-ons and additionally permit them to make the API calls necessary for volume management. This is where the IAM roles for service accounts (IRSA) become necessary.

As you have already read from the previous section, volume creation involves three stages. The first is the description of the volume you want to mount using K8s's StorageClass (SC) object. The second is the creation of the actual volume by K8s using the PersistentVolume (PV) object. The final stage is a request for storage by a pod using the PersistentVolumeClaim (PVC) object. The claim is fulfilled by a PV based on an SC.

PVC exists to handle the different storage demands of pods, for example, to fulfill the shared storage or dedicated storage demands for pods.

The next section will demonstrate the setup for the AWS Elastic Block Store (EBS) followed by a discussion on the merit of EBS and why we may need the elastic file storage (EFS).

EBS Volume

EBS is a block-based storage that can be mounted as a volume in a pod. Typically, it is attached to a single Elastic Compute Cloud (EC2) instance in a single availability zone (AZ).[7]

It is categorized by performance characteristics from general purpose (gp2 and gp3) and high performance (io1 and io2) as well as SSD and HDD (magnetic) types.

SSD-backed volumes are optimized for transactional workloads involving frequent read/write operations with small I/O size, where the dominant performance attribute is IOPS. SSD-backed volume types include General Purpose (GP) SSD and Provisioned IOPS SSD. Table 16-1 summarizes the characteristics of the SSD-backed volumes.

---

[7] https://docs.aws.amazon.com/ebs/latest/userguide/ebs-volume-types.html

Table 16-1. Characteristics of EBS volume

Volume Type	GP3	GP2	io2	io1
Durability	99.8%–99.9% (0.1%–0.2% annual failure rate)		99.999% durability (0.001% annual failure rate)	99.8%–99.9% durability (0.1%–0.2% annual failure rate)

EBS Implementation

You need a service account to mount an EBS volume in a pod. So, you start by creating a service account for the EBS add-on and the EBS controllers with Terraform. You will find the code in the **oidc.tf** and **addons.tf** files under the control plane folder. Refer to Chapter 15 for a detailed discussion on service accounts for K8s.

The oidc.tf file creates the OIDC provider and the service account that will grant permissions to the EFS and the EBS controllers to manage the volume. It creates two service accounts in the kube-system name. The ebs-csi-controller-sa is the service account for the EBS volume, and the efs-controller-sa is the service account for the EFS volume.

```
data "tls_certificate" "oidc" {
  url = aws_eks_cluster.public_endpoint_cluster.identity[0].
  oidc[0].issuer
}
resource "aws_iam_openid_connect_provider" "oidc_openid_
connect" {
  client_id_list  = ["sts.amazonaws.com"]
  thumbprint_list = [data.tls_certificate.oidc.certificates[0].
  sha1_fingerprint]
  url             = data.tls_certificate.oidc.url
}
```

CHAPTER 16 POD PERSISTENCE

```
data "aws_iam_policy_document" "assume_role_policy" {
  statement {
    actions = ["sts:AssumeRoleWithWebIdentity"]
    effect  = "Allow"
    condition {
      test     = "StringEquals"
      variable = "${replace(aws_iam_openid_connect_provider.
      oidc_openid_connect.url, "https://", "")}:sub"
      values   = ["system:serviceaccount:kube-system:ebs-csi-
      controller-sa",
      "system:serviceaccount:kube-system:efs-csi-
      controller-sa"]
    }

    principals {
      identifiers = [aws_iam_openid_connect_provider.oidc_
      openid_connect.arn]
      type        = "Federated"
    }
  }
  depends_on = [aws_iam_openid_connect_provider.oidc_openid_
  connect]
}
```

The addon.tf file specifies the drivers or the addons for the EBS and the EFS volume as follows:

```
resource "aws_iam_role" "ebs" {
  assume_role_policy = data.aws_iam_policy_document.assume_
  role_policy.json
  name               = "ebs-role"
}
```

CHAPTER 16   POD PERSISTENCE

```
resource "aws_iam_role_policy_attachment" "ebs" {
  policy_arn = "arn:aws:iam::aws:policy/service-role/
  AmazonEBSCSIDriverPolicy"
  role       = aws_iam_role.ebs.name
}
resource "aws_iam_role" "efs" {
  assume_role_policy = data.aws_iam_policy_document.assume_
  role_policy.json
  name               = "efs-role"
}
resource "aws_iam_role_policy_attachment" "efs" {
  policy_arn = "arn:aws:iam::aws:policy/service-role/
  AmazonEFSCSIDriverPolicy"
  role       = aws_iam_role.efs.name
}
resource "aws_eks_addon" "ebs-csi" {
  cluster_name             = aws_eks_cluster.public_endpoint_
                             cluster.name
  addon_name               = "aws-ebs-csi-driver"
  addon_version            = "v1.31.0-eksbuild.1"
  service_account_role_arn = aws_iam_role.ebs.arn
  tags = {
    "eks_addon" = "ebs-csi"
    "terraform" = "true"
  }
    resolve_conflicts_on_create = "OVERWRITE"
    resolve_conflicts_on_update = "OVERWRITE"
    depends_on = [aws_iam_openid_connect_provider.oidc_openid_
    connect]
}
```

CHAPTER 16 POD PERSISTENCE

```
resource "aws_eks_addon" "efs-csi" {
  cluster_name              = aws_eks_cluster.public_endpoint_
                              cluster.name
  addon_name                = "aws-efs-csi-driver"
  addon_version             = "v2.0.2-eksbuild.1"
  service_account_role_arn = aws_iam_role.efs.arn
  tags = {
    "eks_addon" = "efs-csi"
    "terraform" = "true"
  }
    resolve_conflicts_on_create = "OVERWRITE"
    resolve_conflicts_on_update = "OVERWRITE"
    depends_on = [ aws_iam_openid_connect_provider.oidc_
    openid_connect ]
}
```

Now deploy the cluster to mount the volumes in the pods. We will start with the EBS volume and continue with the EFS volume.

Testing the EBS Volume

We use the following manifest to set up the volume in the blue app pod. The manifest has three stanzas, each depicting the two of the three stages involved in creating a volume. The first stanza creates the Storage Class which describes the type of volume you want to mount with the StorageClass object. No PV is specified because the EBS provisioner takes care of it.

The second stanza is a request for storage by a pod using the PersistentVolumeClaim (PVC) object which is fulfilled by a PV based on an SC. The third stanza is where the pod mounts the volume at an internal mount path and references the persistent volume claim.

```
---
kind: StorageClass
apiVersion: storage.k8s.io/v1
metadata:
  name: storage-name
provisioner: ebs.csi.aws.com
parameters:
  type: standard
  encrypted: 'true'
volumeBindingMode: WaitForFirstConsumer
reclaimPolicy: Delete
---
apiVersion: v1
kind: PersistentVolumeClaim
metadata:
 name: ebs-claim
spec:
  accessModes:
    - ReadWriteOnce
  storageClassName: storage-name
  resources:
    requests:
      storage: 4Gi
---
apiVersion: v1
kind: Pod
metadata:
  name: ebs-app
spec:
  containers:
  - name: blueapp
    image: cloudmanly/eks:blueapp
```

```
    ports:
      - containerPort: 8080
    command: ["/bin/sh"]
    args: ["-c", "while true; do echo $(date -u) 
    >> /data/out.txt; sleep 5; done"]
    volumeMounts:
    - name: persistent-storage
      mountPath: /data
  volumes:
  - name: persistent-storage
    persistentVolumeClaim:
      claimName: ebs-claim
```

1. Initialize the terraform in Chapter11-out-of-tree.

   `terraform init`

2. Deploy the cluster.

   `terraform apply -auto-approve`

3. Update user context.

   `aws eks update-kubeconfig --name public-endpoint-cluster`

4. Execute the application YAML file in the folder.

   `kubectl apply -f pods/ebs-app.yml`

5. Log in to the pod.

   `kubectl exec -it ebs-app -- /bin/bash`

6. Display the content of the out.txt file.

   `cat /data/out.txt`

You will find the physical volume on one of the nodes in the cluster if you log in to the nodes. The data in the volume will persist even if you delete the pod.

EFS File Storage

EFS is a shared storage platform unlike EBS. The way you access the storage and how the storage is created are quite different. EFS is a shared storage solution that can be used across multiple availability zones (AZs), while EBS is normally used to provide persistent volumes within a single AZ with high throughput.

It is not possible to mount EBS on multiple nodes because EBS does not support read write many operations.[8] You can use node affinity and label to have multiple pods run on the same node, but that will not take advantage of load distribution across nodes. Lack of load distribution means some nodes may not have enough resources to run new pods, complicating pod scaling.

It is impossible to do full CI/CD applications update without human action. You may need to regularly delete deployment to force K8s to update the pod image.

AWS removed node labels during the node upgrade; hence, each update of nodes would involve relabeling of nodes. Hence, lifecycle and backup management is easier for EFS than EBS.

---

[8] https://hervekhg.medium.com/stop-using-ebs-as-persistant-volume-for-eks-pod-use-efs-instead-fev-2023-d9ee4a9b9eeb

CHAPTER 16   POD PERSISTENCE

EFS Experiment

You need additional steps to deploy the EFS file storage in AWS. So, we updated the Terraform code to set up the EFS file storage before we deploy our application. The changes are as follows:

```
resource "aws_efs_file_system" "efs-storage" {
   creation_token = "efs-storage"
   performance_mode = "generalPurpose"
   throughput_mode = "bursting"
   encrypted = "true"
  tags = {
     Name = "EfsStorage"
   }
}
#mount point
 resource "aws_efs_mount_target" "efs-mt-storage" {
   file_system_id  = aws_efs_file_system.efs-storage.id
   security_groups = [var.security_group_id]
   subnet_id = var.subnets_id[0]
 }
```

The code creates a general-purpose EFS storage for the application pods to mount volumes. It creates a mount point on nodes and a security group to allow network access.

Once the cluster is deployed, you will need the file system ID to mount the volume in your pod. You find the file system ID from the terraform state file (terraform.tfstate). You can use the ID to list mount points on the cluster nodes.

```
aws efs describe-mount-targets \
 --file-system-id fs-0af3dedd \
```

```
  --query "MountTargets[*]. {id:MountTargetId,az:AvailabilityZon
    eName, subnet:SubnetId,EFSIP:IpAddress}" \
  --output table
```

You can create more mount targets in subnets with the following commands:

```
#create the mount target
aws efs create-mount-target \
 --file-system-id fs-0af3ded \
 --security-groups sg-0c28acf68  \
 --subnet-id subnet-0876b8c2
```

You can describe the mount target to see how many exist.

```
aws efs describe-mount-targets \
 --file-system-id fs-0af3ded \
 --query "MountTargets[*]. {id:MountTargetId,az:Availability
    ZoneName, subnet:SubnetId,EFSIP:IpAddress}" \
 --output table
```

Testing the EFS Volume

Use the manifest pods/efs-app.yml to create the EFS volume in the blue app. Make sure you change the file system ID to your file system ID before you deploy the pod.

```
---
kind: StorageClass
apiVersion: storage.k8s.io/v1
metadata:
 name: efs-sc
provisioner: efs.csi.aws.com
parameters:
```

```
  provisioningMode: efs-ap
  fileSystemId: fs-0af3d
  directoryPerms: "700"
---
apiVersion: v1
kind: PersistentVolumeClaim
metadata:
  name: efs-claim
spec:
  accessModes:
    - ReadWriteMany
  storageClassName: efs-sc
  resources:
   requests:
      storage: 5Gi
---
apiVersion: v1
kind: Pod
metadata:
  name: efs-app
spec:
  containers:
  - name: blueapp
    image: cloudmanly/eks:blueapp
    ports:
      - containerPort: 8080
    command: ["/bin/sh"]
    args: ["-c", "while true; do echo $(date -u) >> /data/out.txt; sleep 5; done"]
    volumeMounts:
    - name: persistent-storage
      mountPath: /data
```

```
volumes:
- name: persistent-storage
  persistentVolumeClaim:
    claimName: efs-claim
```

1. Execute the application YAML file in the folder.

   ```
   kubectl apply -f efs-app.yml
   ```

2. Display the PV: kubectl get pv

3. Display the PVC: kubectl get pvc

4. Display logs: kubectl logs efs-csi-controller -n

5. Log in to the pod.

   ```
   kubectl exec -it efs-app -- /bin/bash
   ```

6. Display the content of the out.txt file.

   ```
   cat /data/out.txt
   ```

Summary

This chapter set out to discuss and experiment with ephemeral and persistent storage. We reviewed the in-tree and out-of-tree volumes and went through configurations of each kind. While ephemeral storage was quite straightforward to set up, persistent storage was a lot more demanding because of many objects' involvements. We noticed that the storage class object controls and enhances the management of persistent storage. The type of storage K8s provisions depends on the storage class of the object. You can configure K8s to service multiple persistent volumes with different storage class types to meet application demands. Again, we saw applications of addons in persistent storage implementation. The next chapter will focus on how to scale pods in K8s.

CHAPTER 17

Pod Scaling

Up until now, we have not taken advantage of scale in our cluster deployment. We only deploy a pod on a node or two and destroy the cluster after experimentations. We now want to shift our attention from running a single pod on a node to deploying replicas of pods on multiple worker nodes.

Typically, you would want to run reliable and resilient applications. One of the ways to ensure that in K8s is application replication. The ability to run replicas and even multiple versions of the same application improves reliability and resilience. Running an application as a single pod in production is a recipe for disaster. The entire application could become inaccessible if a node becomes unhealthy, a zone becomes unavailable, or the application pod fails.

Apart from failures and fault intolerance, deploying an application as multiple pod replicas ensures better load balancing across the replicas such that no single pod is overwhelmed with unbearable requests, allowing the application to handle high traffic volumes without major service degradation.

If one replica fails, the other replicas will be available to serve end users. Load balancing application traffic with application replicas makes an application resilient. You can always create more replicas to scale applications and increase their capacity to handle more traffic.

This chapter will introduce you to pod scaling in K8s. We will experiment with two common replication controllers to demonstrate pod scaling in K8s clusters.

CHAPTER 17 POD SCALING

Kubernetes Controllers

K8s pod scaling creates replicas of the same pod to make applications resilient. K8s relies on controllers to scale applications and nodes. It supports both built-in and third-party controllers. We rely on the built-in controllers such as ReplicaSets, Deployments, DaemonSets, StatefulSets, and Jobs to manage pods in the cluster. They ensure that the desired number of pods is always running on the cluster.

Similarly, third-party controllers such as AWS autoscaler and karpenter are deployed to manage worker nodes, ensuring that the desired number of nodes is always deployed. You can run third-party controllers as a set of pods on control planes, worker nodes, or even outside a cluster.

Replica Sets

A replica set is simply a set of identical pods controlled by K8s's ReplicaSet controller as shown in Figure 17-1. Like a thermostat, a ReplicaSet controller maintains the desired number of pods running in a cluster at any given time. As such, it is often used to guarantee the availability of a specified number of identical pods.[1] Even if someone accidentally deletes a running pod, the replica set will ensure that a new pod is created to replace it.

---

[1] https://kubernetes.io/docs/concepts/workloads/controllers/replicaset/

CHAPTER 17   POD SCALING

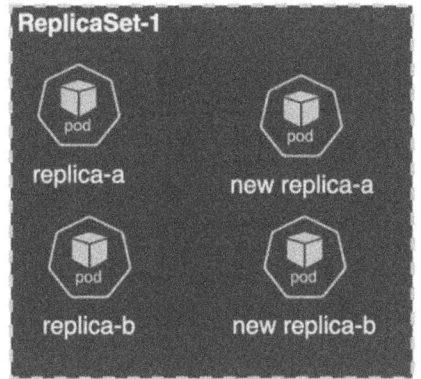
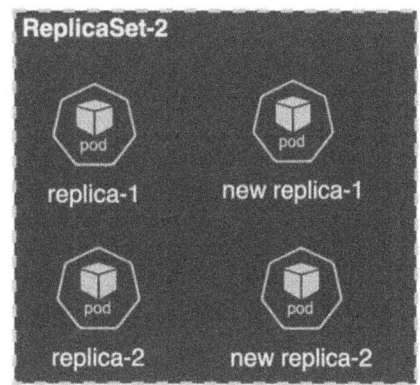

Figure 17-1. Replica sets

Replica set controllers monitor pods across different nodes in a cluster and terminate or start new pods to match the specification of the replica set's template.

Replica Set Manifest

Let us use the following manifest to illustrate how replica sets scale and maintain the state of pods:

```
---
apiVersion: apps/v1
kind: ReplicaSet
metadata:
  name: blueapp
  labels:
    app: blueapp
spec:
  replicas: 3
  selector:
    matchLabels:
```

```
    environment: dev
template:
  metadata:
    labels:
      environment: dev
  spec:
    containers:
      - name: blueapp
        image: cloudmanly/eks:blueapp
        imagePullPolicy: Always
```

The breakdown of the manifest is as follows:

1. The first section of the manifest specifies the kind of the resources, resource name, and a label.

   ```
   apiVersion: apps/v1
   kind: ReplicaSet
   metadata:
     name: blueapp-replicaset
     labels:
       app: blueapp
   ```

2. The second section of the manifest creates three replicas of the blueapp pod as shown below:

   ```
   spec:
   ```
   replicas: 3
   selector:
   ```
       matchLabels:
         environment: dev
   ```
   template:
   ```
       metadata:
         labels:
   ```

```
        environment: dev
    spec:
      containers:
        - name: blueapp
          image: cloudmanly/eks:blueapp
          imagePullPolicy: Always
```

The replica field sets the number of replicas. K8s will set the number of replicas to one if nothing is specified in the replica field. This number represents the desired state or desired number of pods for the deployment. The replica set will create or delete pods to match the number of replicas.

The selector field specifies the label selectors the replica set controller can use to identify which pods to manage, where the template section is reserved for pod specification. The replica set uses the template section to create new pods whenever there is a need for more.

As the main function, the replica set creates pods, checks status of the rollouts to see if they succeeded, and acts to maintain states of pods according to configuration requirements.

Replica Set Experiment

You should deploy the Terraform code in folder chapter17 and run the following commands to experiment with the replica set:

1. Update user context.

   ```
   aws eks update-kubeconfig --name public-endpoint-cluster
   ```

2. Deploy the replica set.

   ```
   kubectl apply -f pods/replica.yml
   ```

3. Display the number of replica pods.

   ```
   kubectl get pods
   ```

CHAPTER 17 POD SCALING

4. Find the replica set controller.

    ```
    kubectl describe rs blueapp
    ```

    You can observe that the pod is controlled by a replica set with the name ReplicaSet/blueapp.

5. Simulate pod failure with pod deletion.

    ```
    Kubectl get pod
    kubectl delete pod <pod_name>
    ```

6. Verify if the replica set restored the state.

    ```
    kubectl get pods
    ```

7. Scale the number of replicas from three to four.

    ```
    kubectl scale --replicas=4 rs blueapp
    ```

8. Verify the number of replicas.

    ```
    kubectl get pods
    ```

9. Scale down the number of replicas.

    ```
    kubectl scale --replicas=1 rs blueapp
    ```

10. Verify the number of replicas.

    ```
    kubectl get pods
    ```

The replica set creates a new pod to maintain the desired state of the pods it manages in the cluster whenever you delete one. It does so with the pod configuration in the template section of the replica set manifest. Even if you delete all the pods under the control of a replica set, the replica set will recreate them repeatedly.

Deployment

Deployments rely on the deployment controller controllers to upscale or downscale pods in a cluster. Beneath the deployments are replica sets which do the actual scaling work for the deployment controller as shown in Figure 17-2.

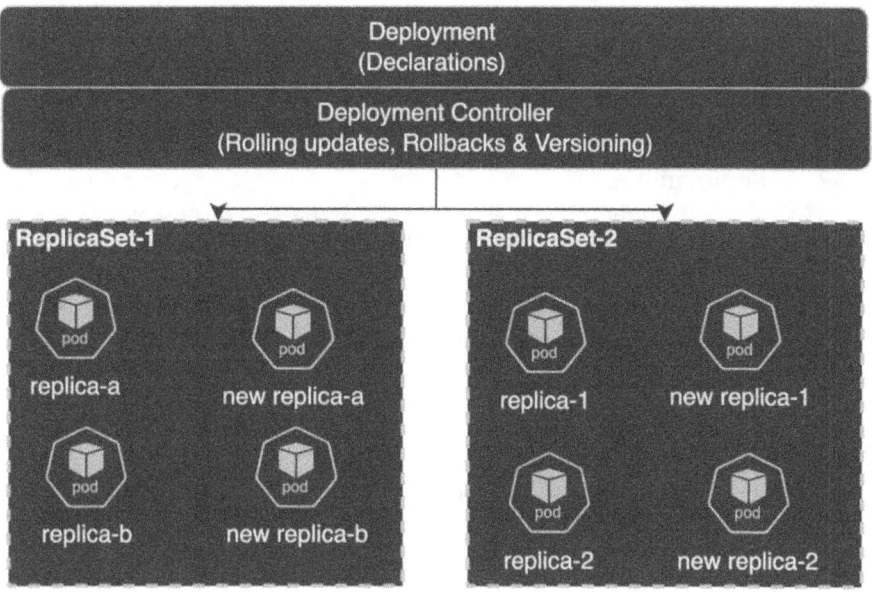

Figure 17-2. Deployment controller

A deployment controller is responsible for managing a set of pods in the form of replica sets and hash-based labels. It can roll out new versions of an application or roll back to old versions of an application through replica sets.

Deployments add to the basic scaling and self-healing features of replica sets, rolling updates, rollbacks, and application versioning. The versioning feature makes it possible to run multiple versions of the same application in a cluster. This makes it easy to roll back applications to their previous version if needed. The rolling updates enable seamless updates of applications with reduced downtime.

The functions of deployments are listed as follows:[2]

1. Create replica sets to handle pod creation.
2. Verify the status of the rollouts to see if they succeed.
3. Use the rollback functionality to roll back the earlier deployment revision if the current deployment is not stable. Each rollback updates the revision of the deployment.
4. Scale up the deployment to increase workload.
5. Pause the rollout to apply multiple fixes to its PodTemplateSpec and then resume it to start a new rollout.
6. Monitor rollout status.
7. Clean up older replica sets.
8. Declare the new state of the pods by updating the PodTemplateSpec in the deployment manifest to create a new replica set that moves the pods from the old replica set to the new one at a controlled rate. Each new replica set then updates the revision of the deployment.

---

[2] https://kubernetes.io/docs/concepts/workloads/controllers/deployment/

Deployment Manifest

You implement deployment by describing a desired state in a deployment manifest for the deployment controller to change the actual state to the desired state at a controlled rate. Additionally, you can define deployments to create new replica sets or to remove existing deployments and adopt all their resources with new deployments.

```
---
apiVersion: apps/v1
kind: Deployment
metadata:
  name: blueapp-deployment
  labels:
    app: blueapp
spec:
  replicas: 3
  strategy:
    type: RollingUpdate
    rollingUpdate:
      maxUnavailable: 1
      maxSurge: 1
  selector:
    matchLabels:
      app: blueapp
      environment: dev
  template:
    metadata:
      labels:
        app: blueapp
        environment: dev
    spec:
```

```
    containers:
      - name: blueapp
        image: cloudmanly/eks:blueapp
        imagePullPolicy: Always
```

As before, the first section of the manifest specifies the kind of the resources, a name, and a label as shown below:

```
apiVersion: apps/v1
kind: Deployment
metadata:
  name: blueapp-deployment
  labels:
    app: blueapp
```

The second section of the manifest creates three replicas of the blueapp pod using the rolling update strategy as shown below:

```
spec:
  replicas: 3
  strategy:
    type: RollingUpdate
    rollingUpdate:
      maxUnavailable: 1
      maxSurge: 1
  selector:
    matchLabels:
      app: blueapp
      environment: dev
  template:
    metadata:
      labels:
        app: blueapp
```

```
      environment: dev
  spec:
    containers:
      - name: blueapp
        image: cloudmanly/eks:blueapp
        imagePullPolicy: Always
```

A strategy is used to update a deployment without having any downtime. K8s deployment comes with the rolling updates and the recreate strategies which can be configured in multiple ways to implement continuous deployment in DevOps methodologies such as

- Blue-green deployment
- Canary deployment
- Recreate deployment
- A/B testing deployment

Rolling Update Strategy

A rolling update is K8s's default deployment strategy. The strategy replaces the existing version of pods by updating them one by one with new ones.[3] It uses the readiness probe checks to determine the readiness of a recent version of a pod. It then deletes the previous version of a pod once the new one is ready without any application downtime.

Rolling update strategy is helpful when you want to update the pod template specification without incurring any application downtime. However, two application versions would exist at the same time during the update, one representing the old pods and the other for the new

---

[3] https://spot.io/resources/kubernetes-autoscaling/5-kubernetes-deployment-strategies-roll-out-like-the-pros/

application. End users who are served by the old application will still see the previous version of the application, while others will see the latest version at least during the updating period.

You can stop the update and roll back without stopping the entire cluster if you encounter any issue. You can specify two optional parameters, maxSurge and maxUnavailable, in the deployment manifest to refine your deployment strategy.

MaxSurge specifies the maximum number of pods the deployment can create at one time. You can specify this as a whole number (e.g., 5) or as a percentage of the total required number of pods (e.g., 20%, always rounded up to the next whole number). If you do not set MaxSurge, the implicit, default value is 25%.

MaxUnavailable specifies the maximum number of pods that can be unavailable during the rollout. Like MaxSurge, you can define it as an absolute number or a percentage.

At least one of these parameters must be larger than zero. By changing the values of these parameters, you can define other deployment strategies, as shown below:

```
strategy:
  type: RollingUpdate
  rollingUpdate:
    maxUnavailable: 1
    maxSurge: 1
```

Deployment Experiment

You should deploy the Terraform code in folder chapter17 and run the following commands to experiment with the deployment. You can find more scenarios here.[4]

---

[4] https://kubernetes.io/docs/concepts/workloads/controllers/deployment/

CHAPTER 17   POD SCALING

1. Update user context.

   ```
   aws eks update-kubeconfig --name public-endpoint-cluster
   ```

2. Create a deployment.

   ```
   kubectl apply -f pods/deployment.yml
   ```

3. Display the number of pods.

   ```
   kubectl get pods
   ```

4. Verify if deployment was created.

   ```
   kubectl get deployments
   ```

5. Find the deployment controller.

   ```
   kubectl describe blueapp-deployment
   ```

   Observe that the pod is controlled by a deployment with the name Deployment/blueapp-deployment.

6. Simulate pod failure with pod deletion.

   ```
   Kubectl get pod
   kubectl delete pod <pod_name>
   ```

7. Verify if the replica set restored the state.

   ```
   kubectl get pods
   ```

8. Scale the number of replicas from three to five.

   ```
   kubectl scale deployment/blueapp-deployment --replicas=5
   ```

9. Verify the number of pods.

    kubectl get pods

10. Scale down the number of pods.

    kubectl scale deployment/blueapp-deployment --replicas=3

11. Verify the number of pods.

    kubectl get pods

12. See the Deployment rollout status.

    kubectl rollout status deployment/blueapp-deployment

13. Find the replica set of the deployment.

    kubectl get rs

    The figure after the name of the deployment is the hash value of the replica set's pod template.

14. Delete the replica set.

    Kubectl delete rs blueapp-deployment-546488b678

15. Verify if the pods are recreated.

    kubectl get pods

You should see pods recreated.

Summary

We set out to experiment with pod scaling and how it works in K8s, focusing on replica sets and deployments. We reviewed how these controllers work to upscale and downscale applications. Deployment controllers rely on replica sets to function. However, they do more than just upscale and downscale applications. They add to the scaling functionalities rolling updates and ability to manage multiple versions of applications for better application maintenance strategy. Deployments can potentially reduce application downtime during an application the entire lifecycle. They provide better support for application rollout strategies such as blue-green, canary, recreate deployments, and even A/B testing. We will spend the next chapter on pod monitoring, focusing on how administrators can gain visibility into pods.

CHAPTER 18

Pod Monitoring

Kubernetes (K8s) provides a lot of information for operators to gain insight into the cluster itself and the underlying infrastructure. There are many tools that can support cluster monitoring with kubectl being one of them. You can use kubectl to log and debug cluster issues such as when a controller failed, or if pods are running. However, kubectl is not easy to use for logging, tracing, troubleshooting, and collection of metrics. Developers or cluster administrators often turn to alternative tools, which provide more advanced features than the kubectl for cluster monitoring. Some of these tools are K8s dashboard; Lens; CloudWatch; Prometheus; Elasticsearch, Logstash, and Kibana (ELK); Rancher; and more. This chapter introduces cluster monitoring and how to implement some of the cluster visualization tools to monitor K8s clusters and their objects. We will focus on three tools in this chapter, K8s dashboard, Lens, and K9s. We will implement other tools such as CloudWatch in Chapter 20.

Kubefwd

We will employ the kubefwd proxy tool to make the K8s dashboard available on our local machine. We experimented with the kube-proxy command in the previous chapters to access cluster resources. The kubefwd makes it easy to perform the same task as the kube-proxy. It is a bulk port forwarder for K8s. It allows access to any K8s service from a local workstation just as you would do with kube-proxy but in a slightly better way.

CHAPTER 18 POD MONITORING

This is how you would installation and execution the kubefwd on MacOS for cluster monitoring.

1. Install kubefwd on your Mac.

   `brew install txn2/tap/kubefwd`

2. To upgrade kubefwd

   `brew upgrade kubefwd`

K8s Dashboard Manifest

The next step is to deploy the K8s dashboard after the cluster deployment. The dashboardwill be made accessible through the kubefwd. The two ways to install the K8s dashboard are to use a manifest or helm chart.

You can install the K8s dashboard with a helm chart as follows:

```
Add kubernetes-dashboard repository
helm repo add kubernetes-dashboard https://kubernetes.github.io/dashboard/
# Deploy a Helm Release named "kubernetes-dashboard" using the kubernetes-dashboard chart
helm upgrade --install kubernetes-dashboard kubernetes-dashboard/kubernetes-dashboard --create-namespace --namespace kubernetes-dashboard
```

You would need the K8s dashboard manifest to deploy the dashboard on the cluster. You should find the manifest in the **k8s-dashboard.yml** file that comes with the code for this chapter. The breakdown of the manifest is as follows.

Namespace

The first section of the manifest creates the namespace for the dashboard as follows:

```
apiVersion: v1
kind: Namespace
metadata:
  name: kubernetes-dashboard
```

A namespace isolates the kubernetes dashboard from other resources. You can use namespace to control who can access the dashboard.

Service Account

The second stanza in the file is the service account creation. The K8s dashboard needs permission to access and visualize the cluster objects and their metrics.

```
apiVersion: v1
kind: ServiceAccount
metadata:
  labels:
    k8s-app: kubernetes-dashboard
  name: kubernetes-dashboard
  namespace: kubernetes-dashboard
```

The name of the service account is kubernetes-dashboard, and it is in the same namespace as the dashboard.

Service

The third stanza in the K8s dashboard manifest is the service part. As we discussed earlier, pods are private objects unreachable from the outside world. You expose pods through service objects.

```
kind: Service
apiVersion: v1
metadata:
  labels:
    k8s-app: kubernetes-dashboard
  name: kubernetes-dashboard
  namespace: kubernetes-dashboard
spec:
  ports:
    - port: 443
      targetPort: 8443
  selector:
    k8s-app: kubernetes-dashboard
```

The third section of the manifest uses a service to expose the K8s dashboard pod on port 443.

The next three stanzas create secret objects for the dashboard to store secrets.

Secret

The service part of the dashboard is encrypted on port 443 to secure the cluster information and metrics. K8s needs encryption certificates and keys to secure the dashboard. The following sections handle the secret generation part of the dashboard. The three security tokens are the certs, secret key, and a secret for cross-site request forgery (csrf).

```
---
apiVersion: v1
kind: Secret
metadata:
  labels:
    k8s-app: kubernetes-dashboard
  name: kubernetes-dashboard-certs
  namespace: kubernetes-dashboard
type: Opaque
---
apiVersion: v1
kind: Secret
metadata:
  labels:
    k8s-app: kubernetes-dashboard
  name: kubernetes-dashboard-csrf
  namespace: kubernetes-dashboard
type: Opaque
data:
  csrf: ""
---
apiVersion: v1
kind: Secret
metadata:
  labels:
    k8s-app: kubernetes-dashboard
  name: kubernetes-dashboard-key-holder
  namespace: kubernetes-dashboard
type: Opaque
```

CHAPTER 18   POD MONITORING

Access Control

What can the dashboard do once deployed? This section lists all the permissions that will be granted to the dashboard's service account. It includes secret access, service access, metrics access, and more.

```
---
kind: ConfigMap
apiVersion: v1
metadata:
  labels:
    k8s-app: kubernetes-dashboard
  name: kubernetes-dashboard-settings
  namespace: kubernetes-dashboard
---
kind: Role
apiVersion: rbac.authorization.k8s.io/v1
metadata:
  labels:
    k8s-app: kubernetes-dashboard
  name: kubernetes-dashboard
  namespace: kubernetes-dashboard
rules:
  # Allow Dashboard to get, update and delete Dashboard
  exclusive secrets.
  - apiGroups: [""]
    resources: ["secrets"]
    resourceNames: ["kubernetes-dashboard-key-holder",
    "kubernetes-dashboard-certs", "kubernetes-dashboard-csrf"]
    verbs: ["get", "update", "delete"]
    # Allow Dashboard to get and update 'kubernetes-dashboard-
    settings' config map.
```

```yaml
    - apiGroups: [""]
      resources: ["configmaps"]
      resourceNames: ["kubernetes-dashboard-settings"]
      verbs: ["get", "update"]
      # Allow Dashboard to get metrics.
    - apiGroups: [""]
      resources: ["services"]
      resourceNames: ["heapster", "dashboard-metrics-scraper"]
      verbs: ["proxy"]
    - apiGroups: [""]
      resources: ["services/proxy"]
      resourceNames: ["heapster", "http:heapster:",
      "https:heapster:", "dashboard-metrics-scraper",
      "http:dashboard-metrics-scraper"]
      verbs: ["get"]
---
kind: ClusterRole
apiVersion: rbac.authorization.k8s.io/v1
metadata:
  labels:
    k8s-app: kubernetes-dashboard
  name: kubernetes-dashboard
rules:
  # Allow Metrics Scraper to get metrics from the
  Metrics server
  - apiGroups: ["metrics.k8s.io"]
    resources: ["pods", "nodes"]
    verbs: ["get", "list", "watch"]
```

CHAPTER 18 POD MONITORING

```yaml
---
apiVersion: rbac.authorization.k8s.io/v1
kind: RoleBinding
metadata:
  labels:
    k8s-app: kubernetes-dashboard
  name: kubernetes-dashboard
  namespace: kubernetes-dashboard
roleRef:
  apiGroup: rbac.authorization.k8s.io
  kind: Role
  name: kubernetes-dashboard
subjects:
  - kind: ServiceAccount
    name: kubernetes-dashboard
    namespace: kubernetes-dashboard
---
apiVersion: rbac.authorization.k8s.io/v1
kind: ClusterRoleBinding
metadata:
  name: kubernetes-dashboard
roleRef:
  apiGroup: rbac.authorization.k8s.io
  kind: ClusterRole
  name: kubernetes-dashboard
subjects:
  - kind: ServiceAccount
    name: kubernetes-dashboard
    namespace: kubernetes-dashboard
```

Deployment

The actual dashboard application and internal service objects are specified in the deployment section of the manifest. You should find two deployments, one for the application and the other for the metric scraper.

```
---
kind: Deployment
apiVersion: apps/v1
metadata:
  labels:
    k8s-app: kubernetes-dashboard
  name: kubernetes-dashboard
  namespace: kubernetes-dashboard
spec:
  replicas: 1
  revisionHistoryLimit: 10
  selector:
    matchLabels:
      k8s-app: kubernetes-dashboard
  template:
    metadata:
      labels:
        k8s-app: kubernetes-dashboard
    spec:
      securityContext:
        seccompProfile:
          type: RuntimeDefault
      containers:
        - name: kubernetes-dashboard
          image: kubernetesui/dashboard:v2.7.0
          imagePullPolicy: Always
```

```
        ports:
          - containerPort: 8443
            protocol: TCP
        args:
          - --auto-generate-certificates
          - --namespace=kubernetes-dashboard
          # Uncomment the following line to manually specify
          Kubernetes API server Host
          # If not specified, Dashboard will attempt to auto
          discover the API server and connect
          # to it. Uncomment only if the default does
          not work.
          # - --apiserver-host=http://my-address:port
        volumeMounts:
          - name: kubernetes-dashboard-certs
            mountPath: /certs
            # Create on-disk volume to store exec logs
          - mountPath: /tmp
            name: tmp-volume
        livenessProbe:
          httpGet:
            scheme: HTTPS
            path: /
            port: 8443
          initialDelaySeconds: 30
          timeoutSeconds: 30
        securityContext:
          allowPrivilegeEscalation: false
          readOnlyRootFilesystem: true
          runAsUser: 1001
          runAsGroup: 2001
```

```
      volumes:
        - name: kubernetes-dashboard-certs
          secret:
            secretName: kubernetes-dashboard-certs
        - name: tmp-volume
          emptyDir: {}
      serviceAccountName: kubernetes-dashboard
      nodeSelector:
        "kubernetes.io/os": linux
      # Comment the following tolerations if Dashboard must not
      be deployed on master
      tolerations:
        - key: node-role.kubernetes.io/master
          effect: NoSchedule
---
kind: Service
apiVersion: v1
metadata:
  labels:
    k8s-app: dashboard-metrics-scraper
  name: dashboard-metrics-scraper
  namespace: kubernetes-dashboard
spec:
  ports:
    - port: 8000
      targetPort: 8000
  selector:
    k8s-app: dashboard-metrics-scraper
```

CHAPTER 18 POD MONITORING

```yaml
---
kind: Deployment
apiVersion: apps/v1
metadata:
  labels:
    k8s-app: dashboard-metrics-scraper
  name: dashboard-metrics-scraper
  namespace: kubernetes-dashboard
spec:
  replicas: 1
  revisionHistoryLimit: 10
  selector:
    matchLabels:
      k8s-app: dashboard-metrics-scraper
  template:
    metadata:
      labels:
        k8s-app: dashboard-metrics-scraper
    spec:
      securityContext:
        seccompProfile:
          type: RuntimeDefault
      containers:
        - name: dashboard-metrics-scraper
          image: kubernetesui/metrics-scraper:v1.0.8
          ports:
            - containerPort: 8000
              protocol: TCP
          livenessProbe:
            httpGet:
              scheme: HTTP
```

```
      path: /
      port: 8000
    initialDelaySeconds: 30
    timeoutSeconds: 30
  volumeMounts:
    - mountPath: /tmp
      name: tmp-volume
  securityContext:
    allowPrivilegeEscalation: false
    readOnlyRootFilesystem: true
    runAsUser: 1001
    runAsGroup: 2001
serviceAccountName: kubernetes-dashboard
nodeSelector:
  "kubernetes.io/os": linux
# Comment the following tolerations if Dashboard must not be deployed on master
tolerations:
  - key: node-role.kubernetes.io/master
    effect: NoSchedule
volumes:
  - name: tmp-volume
    emptyDir: {}
```

Admin User Service Account

The last two sections create the admin user service account and bind the cluster admin role. This will allow the admin user to have full access to the dashboard.

CHAPTER 18   POD MONITORING

```
---
apiVersion: v1
kind: ServiceAccount
metadata:
  name: admin-user
  namespace: kubernetes-dashboard
---
apiVersion: rbac.authorization.k8s.io/v1
kind: ClusterRoleBinding
metadata:
  name: admin-user
roleRef:
  apiGroup: rbac.authorization.k8s.io
  kind: ClusterRole
  name: cluster-admin
subjects:
  - kind: ServiceAccount
    name: admin-user
    namespace: kubernetes-dashboard
```

The manifest deploys the K8s dashboard user interface (UI) for developers to troubleshoot applications and manage the cluster resources. Developers can scale a deployment, initiate a rolling update, restart a pod, or deploy new applications with the support of the dashboard. They can also see information about the state of cluster resources and any errors that may have occurred.

Dashboard Deployment with kubefwd

You can use the kubefwd application to enable local access to the dashboard through port forwarding. The steps are as follows:

CHAPTER 18 POD MONITORING

1. Deploy in the folder chapter18.

2. Update cluster context.

   ```
   aws eks update-kubeconfig --name public-
   endpoint-cluster
   ```

3. Deploy the K8s dashboard application and the two other applications in the pod folder.

   ```
   kubectl apply -f /pods
   ```

4. Start the kubefwd dashboard.

   ```
   sudo kubectl port-forward -n kubernetes-dashboard svc/kubernetes-dashboard 443
   ```

5. Go to the browser and type https://localhost/.

6. Click advanced and accept the risk.

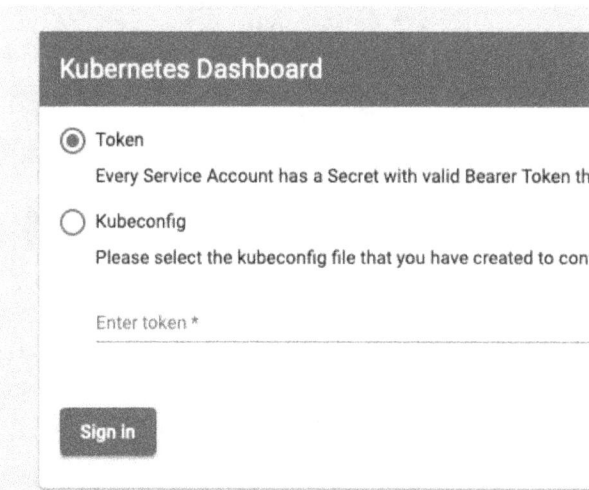

Figure 18-1. Kubernetes dashboard setup

CHAPTER 18 POD MONITORING

7. Generate a password.

   ```
   kubectl -n kubernetes-dashboard create token admin-user
   ```

8. Copy and paste the token in the browser.

   ```
   eyJhbGciOiJSUzI1NiIsImtpZCI6IjI3NDM1MmI3OWMxZDBjZmIONz
   U5NzQzNzIzNjgOMGY2NTEyZTQ2...9JIQ4E3MiD9_1JvffdB_615ufD4y
   kTvpI2fVn9Qz4xnNO4TCM3uNQ
   ```

9. You may browse the objects in the dashboard and make changes as needed.

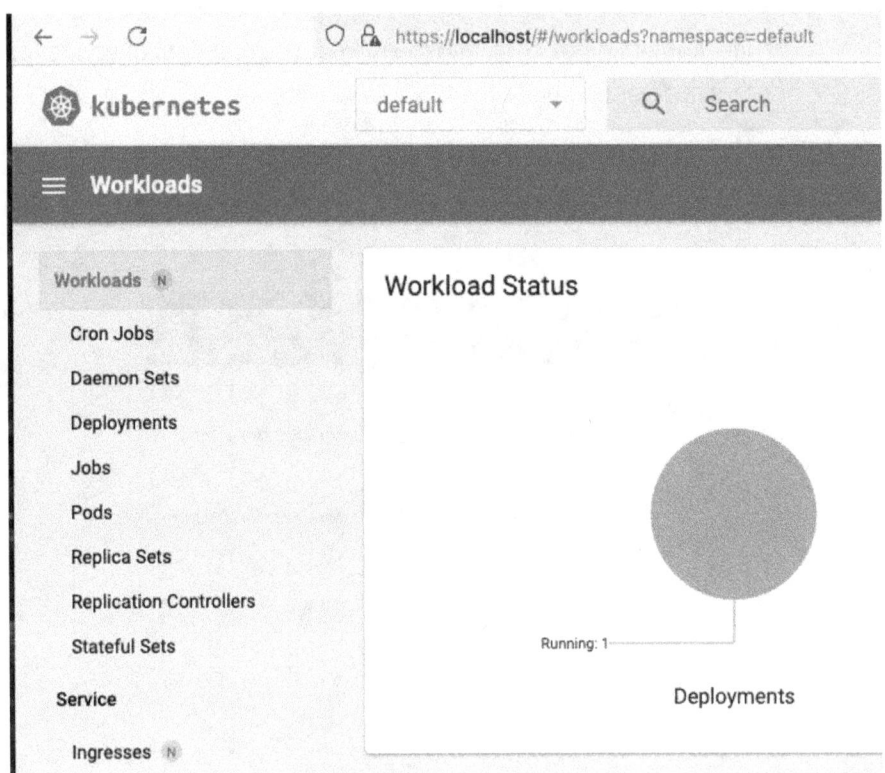

Figure 18-2. Kubernetes dashboard

CHAPTER 18   POD MONITORING

Lens

Lens is another visualization tool like the K8s dashboard. However, Lens is not free as the K8s dashboard. Lens supports seamless interaction with Kubernetes clusters. It provides an environment for secure and effective work within teams and organizations. You may set up Lens with the following steps:

1. Update cluster context.

   ```
   aws eks update-kubeconfig --name public-endpoint-cluster
   ```

2. Configure the .kube/config file to recognize Lens when it starts.

   ```
   kind: Config
   preferences: {}
   users:
   - name: arn:aws:eks:us-east-1:ACCOUNT_ID:cluster/cluster-name
       env:
         - name: AWS_PROFILE
           value: default
   ```

   Update the configuration under the users section. Reference your AWS profile under the env section. You may find your AWS profile in .aws/credentials. The profile name in the .aws/credentials file should be the same as the value you supply in the .kube/config file above. My profile name is default in this example, and as such the env value is also default.

3. Download and install Lens from the website of Lens. https://k8slens.dev/

499

CHAPTER 18 POD MONITORING

4. Open Lens.

5. Register Lens.

6. Open the Lens application again to load the cluster objects.

7. Select the current cluster.

8. Review the objects.

Figure 18-3. Lens dashboard

You can also launch Lens from the command line with the **open -a lens** command.

K9s

K9s is another tool that eases cluster monitoring. You can download it from the K9s website.[1]

---

[1] https://k9scli.io/topics/install/

CHAPTER 18   POD MONITORING

1. Install K9s.

   ```
   brew install derailed/k9s/k9s
   ```

2. Verify the version.

   ```
   k9s version
   ```

3. Use help.

   ```
   k9s help
   ```

4. Open K9s.

   ```
   k9s + enter or k9s -c dp
   ```

The K9s dashboard shows the shortcuts and commands you can use to access the cluster objects. For example, <0> means all objects and y means YAML file. You should find the type of object (pod, deployment, service, etc.) at the bottom taskbar.

You may see the interface when you start K9s with the k9s + enter command.

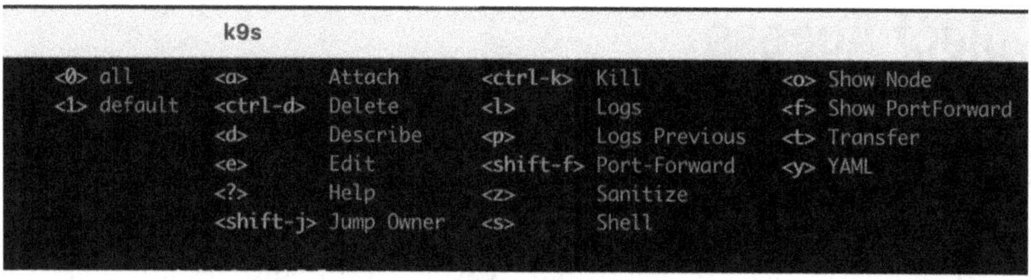

```
            k9s
<0> all        <a>        Attach      <ctrl-k>  Kill           <o> Show Node
<1> default    <ctrl-d>   Delete      <l>       Logs           <f> Show PortForward
               <d>        Describe    <p>       Logs Previous  <t> Transfer
               <e>        Edit        <shift-f> Port-Forward   <y> YAML
               <?>        Help        <z>       Sanitize
               <shift-j>  Jump Owner  <s>       Shell
```

Figure 18-4. K9s interface

Pressing 0 will show all namespaces of what you are viewing (pod deployments, etc.).

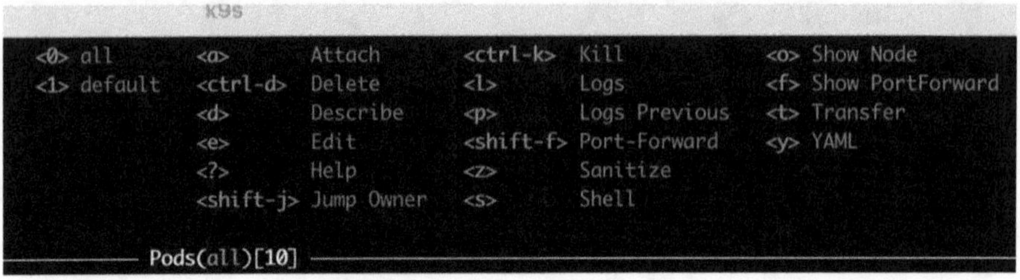

Figure 18-5. K9s interface options

Press 1 to show only the default namespace, all pods in the default namespace.

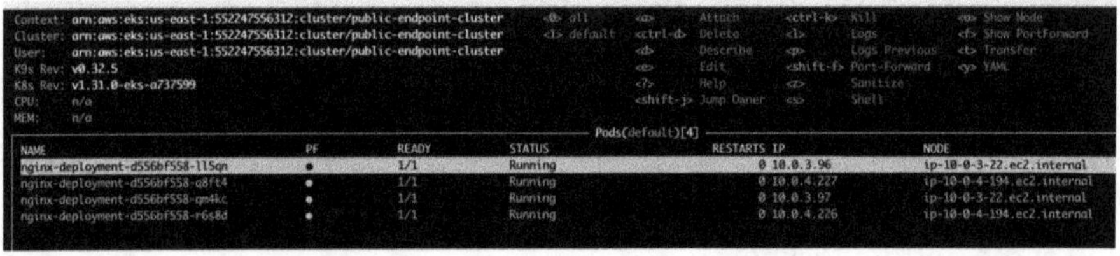

Figure 18-6. K9s interface - output for namespaces

Object Access

Use the colon (:) to bring up the command-line interface in K9s. Follow it up with the name of an object, for example, pod, deployment, service, etc. You can also combine the two commands as pod **or: deployment**.

You jump out of an object with the escape command (esc). You use the forward slash (/) or the equal to (=) sign for searching. For example, the **wk /nginx, wk app=nginx, /image etc. wk** command means workload.

CHAPTER 18   POD MONITORING

Other Common Commands

- : deployment
- : ns
- : Workload /
- : Wk /
- : Workloads
- Searches
- / pod
- / ns
- Step into Yaml file with y
- Step into metadata with /meta
- Use shell to exec into a container and exit to come out
- Use esc to escape an object

Summary

There are many tools you can rely on to monitor your cluster if you decide against kubectl commands such as kubectl describe, kubectl logs, and kubectl get events. K9s will be a go-to tool for basic monitoring and troubleshooting. K9s is like kubectl but a little more interactive. You can use the built-in K8s dashboard with a proxy to monitor your cluster. You can also go for commercial and more advanced tools such as Lens, Rancher, and ELK. You can rely on AWS to monitor your cluster with X-Ray, CloudWatch, and Elasticsearch. We close this part of the book with a brief and basic introduction to cluster monitoring using three simple monitoring tools. The last part of this book will focus on more advanced K8s concepts, including advanced monitoring tools in AWS.

PART 3

CHAPTER 19

Cluster Autoscaling

In the final part of this book, we will focus on advanced Amazon EKS concepts, beginning with cluster autoscaling, and then move on to service mesh in the following chapter. In Chapter 17, we discussed pod scaling using replica sets and deployments. These mechanisms are designed to scale the number of pods based on workload demand. However, they do not have the ability to scale the cluster infrastructure itself, such as the nodes that run the pods.

This chapter will focus on scaling the cluster infrastructure by using Cluster Autoscaler (CA) and Karpenter. These tools automatically adjust the number of nodes in your EKS cluster based on the resource needs. They make sure that your cluster can scale dynamically in response to changing demand while optimizing cost efficiency. We'll explore how these tools work, their setup, and how you can leverage them to enhance the flexibility and efficiency of your EKS infrastructure.

The Cluster Autoscaler

ReplicaSets create pods for the K8s scheduler to deploy them on a selected node. The pods remain in the pending state when the scheduler cannot find nodes with enough memory, CPU, or network resources (e.g., IP address) to deploy them unless node capacity is manually or automatically increased by adjusting the number or the size of the node.

CHAPTER 19 CLUSTER AUTOSCALING

If the scheduler cannot find nodes with sufficient resources such as memory, CPU, or network resources (e.g., IP addresses), the pods are made to stay in the pending state.

This issue arises because the cluster's current capacity cannot accommodate the new pods. The cluster operator must adjust the cluster's node capacity either manually, by adding more nodes or resizing the existing ones. Alternatively, they can automate the adjustment with services like Cluster Autoscaler (CA) or Karpenter.

CA and Karpenter can dynamically increase the node capacity based on the demands of the pods, preventing pending pods and making the cluster efficient in handling workloads.

Amazon EKS provides three techniques for automating node scaling to accommodate more pods based on demand:

1. *Cluster Autoscaler (CA)*: This service automatically adjusts the number of nodes in your cluster. It scales up the cluster by adding more nodes when there are insufficient resources (e.g., CPU, memory) to schedule pods, and it scales down the cluster by removing underutilized nodes when resource demand decreases.

2. *Vertical Pod Autoscaler (VPA)*: VPA automatically adjusts the CPU and memory resource requests for running pods. It helps optimize resource allocation for each pod based on observed usage, ensuring that each pod gets the appropriate resources for efficient performance.

3. *Horizontal Pod Autoscaler (HPA)*: HPA automatically scales the number of pod replicas based on observed metrics such as CPU or memory usage.

CHAPTER 19 CLUSTER AUTOSCALING

It ensures that the number of pods increases or decreases depending on the demand, maintaining the desired application performance.[1]

In this section, we will focus on CA. Cluster Autoscaler adds nodes when there are pending pods and removes nodes when they are empty. In EKS, CA depends on the AWS autoscaling group (ASG) to adjust nodes depending on resource demands.[2]

As illustrated in Figure 19-1

1. The scheduler detects lack of resources when a pod is in a pending state.

2. CA (controller) detects a new pod request in a pending state.

3. CA calls the AWS ASG service (APIs) to launch a new node.

4. The ASG launches a new node to increase the node capacity.

5. The K8s scheduler detects a newly registered node and deploys the pending pods.

K8s registers the newly provisioned node with the control plane to make it available to the scheduler to schedule the pending pod. One of the bottlenecks of the CA is the dependency on the ASG orchestrator to adjust node capacity. Such reliance reduces the overall efficiency of the entire autoscaling process.

---

[1] https://kubernetes.io/docs/concepts/configuration/manage-resources-containers/
[2] https://kubernetes.io/docs/concepts/cluster-administration/cluster-autoscaling/

CHAPTER 19   CLUSTER AUTOSCALING

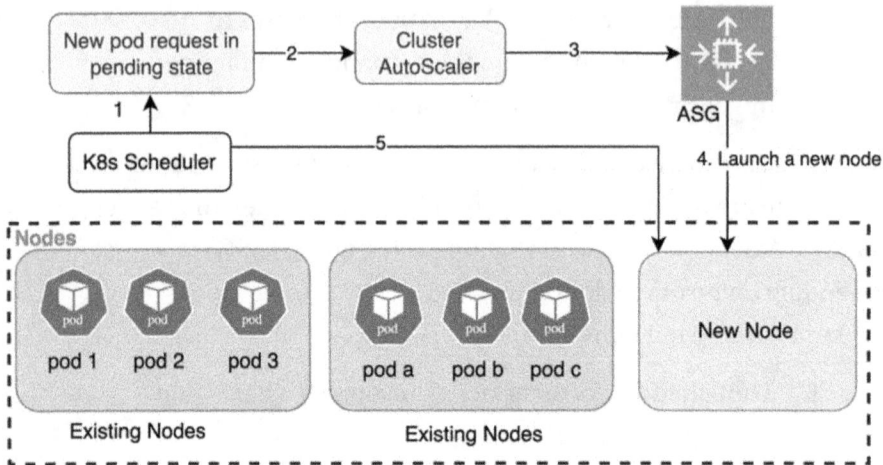

Figure 19-1. AWS Autoscaler

Autoscaling Demonstration

You will find the example code in the chapter19-autoscaler folder. We highlight the key modification as follows:

1. Tags

    You must configure the nodes with special tags for CA to discover them: **k8s.io/cluster-autoscaler/enabled**. You should find the code in the workers.tf file.

    ```
    tags = {
    "k8s.io/cluster-autoscaler/enabled" = "true"
    "k8s.io/cluster-autoscaler/${var.cluster_name}"
    = "owned"
      }
    ```

2. Service account

The CA controller needs a service account with permission to call the AWS APIs. You should find the code in the oidc.tf file under the control plane folder as follows:

```
data "tls_certificate" "oidc" {
  url = aws_eks_cluster.autoscaler_cluster.identity[0].
  oidc[0].issuer
}
resource "aws_iam_openid_connect_provider" "oidc_
provider" {
  client_id_list  = ["sts.amazonaws.com"]
  thumbprint_list = [data.tls_certificate.oidc.
  certificates[0].sha1_fingerprint]
  url             = data.tls_certificate.oidc.url
}

data "aws_iam_policy_document" "assume_role_policy" {
  statement {
     actions = ["sts:AssumeRoleWithWebIdentity"]
     effect  = "Allow"
     condition {
     test     = "StringEquals"
     variable = "${replace(aws_iam_openid_connect_
     provider.oidc_provider.url, "https://", "")}:sub"
     values   = ["system:serviceaccount:kube-
     system:cluster-autoscaler"]
     }
```

```
          principals {
            identifiers = [aws_iam_openid_connect_provider.
            oidc_provider.arn]
            type        = "Federated"
          }
       }
    }
}
```

We created the service account in the kube-system namespace where the controller will be deployed.

3. The second part of the OIDC code creates policies and attaches them to the service account role. You should find the code in the **oidc.tf** file.

You must create a policy to grant the CA the needed permission to call the AWS APIs as follows:

```
# Creating IAM Policy for auto-scaler
resource "aws_iam_policy" "autoscaler" {
  name = "eks-autoscaler-policy"
  policy = jsonencode({
  "Version": "2012-10-17",
  "Statement": [
    {
      "Effect": "Allow",
      "Action": [
        "autoscaling:DescribeAutoScalingGroups",
        "autoscaling:DescribeAutoScalingInstances",
        "autoscaling:DescribeLaunchConfigurations",
        "autoscaling:DescribeScalingActivities",
        "autoscaling:DescribeTags",
        "ec2:DescribeImages",
```

CHAPTER 19 CLUSTER AUTOSCALING

```
        "ec2:DescribeInstanceTypes",
        "ec2:DescribeLaunchTemplateVersions",
        "ec2:GetInstanceTypesFromInstanceRequirements",
        "eks:DescribeNodegroup"
      ],
      "Resource": ["*"]
    },
    {
      "Effect": "Allow",
      "Action": [
        "autoscaling:SetDesiredCapacity",
        "autoscaling:TerminateInstanceInAutoScalingGroup"
      ],
      "Resource": ["*"]
    }
  ]
  })
}
```

The policy has all the permissions EKS needs to make the autoscaler work.

4. Create a CA role

Create a role that will be used by the service account to make the API calls and attach the CA's policy.

```
resource "aws_iam_role_policy_attachment" "cluster_auto_scaler" {
  policy_arn = aws_iam_policy.autoscaler.arn
  role       = aws_iam_role.cluster_autoscaler_controller_role.name
}
```

```
#attach policy to the role
resource "aws_iam_role_policy_attachment" "cluster_
auto_scaler" {
  policy_arn = aws_iam_policy.autoscaler.arn
  role       = aws_iam_role.cluster_autoscaler_
controller_role.name
}
```

5. Autoscaler cluster security group

    The new nodes by CA should operate with the same security group as the bootstrap nodes to be able to join the cluster. You attach the security group to the CA nodes with the following code:

```
resource "aws_ec2_tag" "cluster_primary_security_
group" {
  resource_id = aws_eks_cluster.autoscaler_cluster.
vpc_config[0].cluster_security_group_id
  key         = "autoscaler.sh/discovery"
  value       = var.cluster_name
}
```

Testing the CA

Create the cluster in folder chapter19-autoscaler:

```
terraform init
terraform apply
```

Review the script.sh file that comes with the code:

```
#!/bin/bash
echo "Setting environment for autoscaler
\n******************************"
aws eks update-kubeconfig --name autoscaler-cluster
ACCOUNT=$(aws sts get-caller-identity --query "Account" --output text)
```

Run the **script.sh** script to update the kube config context and set the environment variable for your AWS ACCOUNT ID:

```
chmod +x script.sh
./script.sh
```

Deploy Autoscaler Controller

Deploy the cluster autoscaler controller by executing the autoscalercontroller.yml file. Before then, find the version of the autoscaler that matches your K8s version (e.g., K8s 1.31 corresponds to autoscaler v1.26.2).

We have already downloaded and configured the autoscalercontroller.yml in the chapter19 folder. You can skip steps 1–5 below if you want to use the file that comes with the book:

1. Download the latest version of the autoscaler controller yaml file with the following command:

    ```
    curl -o cluster-autoscaler-autodiscover.yaml https://raw.githubusercontent.com/kubernetes/autoscaler/master/cluster-autoscaler/cloudprovider/aws/examples/cluster-autoscaler-autodiscover.yaml
    ```

2. Modify the service account object as follows:

```
---
apiVersion: v1
kind: ServiceAccount
metadata:
  labels:
    k8s-addon: cluster-autoscaler.addons.k8s.io
    k8s-app: cluster-autoscaler
  annotations:
    eks.amazonaws.com/role-arn: arn:aws:iam::${ACCOUNT_ID}:role/ClusterAutoScalerRole-autoscaler-cluster
  name: cluster-autoscaler
  namespace: kube-system
---
```

3. Replace the service account name with yours and check if the version number corresponds to your K8s version.

```
serviceAccountName: cluster-autoscaler
      containers:
        - image: registry.k8s.io/autoscaling/cluster-autoscaler:v1.26.2
          name: cluster-autoscaler
          resources:
            limits:
              cpu: 100m
              memory: 600Mi
            requests:
              cpu: 100m
              memory: 600Mi
```

CHAPTER 19 CLUSTER AUTOSCALING

4. Replace the cluster name with your cluster name.

   node-group-auto-discovery=asg:tag=k8s.io/cluster-autoscaler/enabled,k8s.io/cluster-autoscaler/<YOUR CLUSTER NAME>

5. Add command switches under the autodiscover tagline (line 165) to allow the autoscaler to balance more effectively across availability zones and scale autoscaling node groups to zero:

   - --balance-similar-node-groups
   - --skip-nodes-with-system-pods=false

   Make sure the role is the same as the OIDC service account role.

6. Deploy the autoscaler controller.

   kubectl create -f autoscalercontroller.yml

7. Check if the controller is running.

   kubectl get po -n kube-system

8. Monitor controller logs.

   kubectl -n kube-system logs -f deployment.apps/cluster-autoscaler

9. Run the inflated app that comes with the code.

   kubectl apply -f inflate-app.yml

10. Check if the pod is running.

    kubectl get po -n kube-system

CHAPTER 19   CLUSTER AUTOSCALING

11. Validate the account ID environment variable or the role name if you encounter an error. Copy the controller's name and run **kubectl logs -f cluster-autoscaler-5d576889b-dj44j -n kube-system** command on it if you get errors.

12. Show the number of nodes.

    ```
    kubectl get nodes
    ```

13. Scale the app and wait for the autoscaler to add more nodes.

    ```
    kubectl scale deployment inflate --replicas 3
    ```

14. Check if pods are running or pending.

    ```
    kubectl get po
    ```

15. Wait for a while and check again; pods should be in the running state.

    ```
    kubectl get po
    ```

16. Show the number of nodes; nodes should increase from one to three.

    ```
    kubectl get nodes
    ```

17. You can scale down and up to observe the behavior.

AWS Karpenter

Karpenter is a more intelligent autoscaler designed to overcome the limitations of the Cluster Autoscaler (CA). CA relies on simple metrics such as pending pods, CPU, and memory limits to launch a new node.

It does not consider unused computing resources and the instance type that will best serve the needs of the cluster, resulting in waste and low utilization efficiency.

Unlike Karpenter, CA is slow in provisioning because it relies on a third-party orchestrator such as AWS ASG to launch new nodes to keep up with demands. For example, it takes about 30–60 seconds for CA to issue a scale-up request to an autoscaler orchestrator of a cloud provider. It takes several minutes for the autoscaler orchestrator of the cloud provider to create a node, resulting in delays and possible performance degradation of applications.[3]

Karpenter does not rely on any third-party orchestrator. It manages each instance directly, enabling retries in milliseconds instead of minutes. It leverages several metrics to make decisions, thus making it flexible, efficient, and high performance.[4]

Karpenter improves application availability and cluster efficiency by rapidly launching right-sized compute resources in response to changing application load. It provides just-in-time compute resources to meet application needs.

Karpenter automatically optimizes a cluster's compute resource to reduce costs and improve performance.

It functions by observing the aggregated resource requests of unscheduled pods and makes decisions to launch new nodes and terminate the old ones to reduce scheduling latencies and infrastructure costs as shown in Figure 19-2. In Figure 19-2, the Karpenter controller detects the pending pod and immediately goes to work to provision or deprovision the right node to handle the event.

---

[3] https://aws.amazon.com/blogs/aws/introducing-karpenter-an-open-source-high-performance-kubernetes-cluster-autoscaler/

[4] https://aws.amazon.com/blogs/aws/introducing-karpenter-an-open-source-high-performance-kubernetes-cluster-autoscaler/

CHAPTER 19   CLUSTER AUTOSCALING

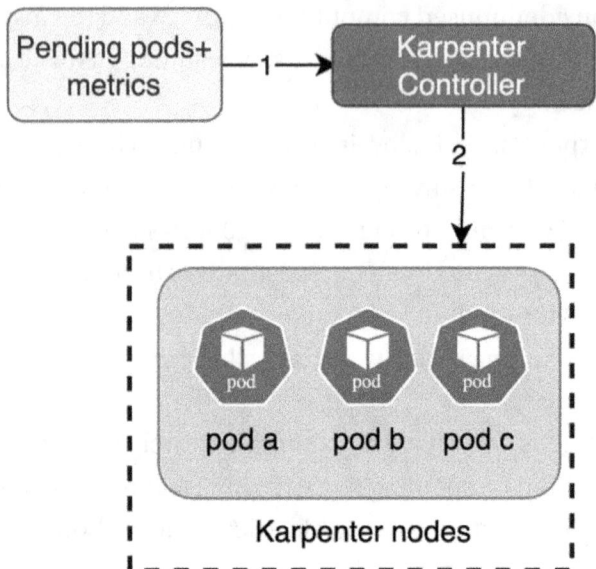

Figure 19-2. Karpenter CA

Karpenter Implementation

The sample code is found in the chapter19-karpenter folder. You should create a service account to grant the Karpenter controller permission to call AWS APIs. The service policy is found in the **policy.tf** file. We downloaded the controller policy from the karpenter.sh site but argumented it with the following IAM permissions:

```
"iam:GetInstanceProfile",
"iam:CreateInstanceProfile",
"iam:TagInstanceProfile",
"iam:AddRoleToInstanceProfile",
"iam:AddRoleToInstanceProfile"
```

CHAPTER 19 CLUSTER AUTOSCALING

Karpenter requires the coredns addon and at least two nodes. You may schedule these nodes exclusively for Karpenter pods using toleration as follows:

```
resource "aws_eks_addon" "coredns" {
  # Allow CoreDNS to run on the same nodes as the Karpenter
  controller
  # use during cluster creation when Karpenter nodes do not
  yet exist
  cluster_name              = var.cluster_name
  addon_name                = "coredns"
  addon_version             = "v1.11.4-eksbuild.2"
  configuration_values = jsonencode({
      tolerations = [
        {
          key     = "karpenter.sh/controller"
          value   = "true"
          effect  = "NoSchedule"
        }
      ]
  })
  resolve_conflicts_on_create = "OVERWRITE"
  resolve_conflicts_on_update = "OVERWRITE"
  depends_on = [aws_iam_openid_connect_provider.oidc_provider]
}
```

The toleration section ensures that EKS reserves the nodes for only Karpenter pods or pods with **karpenter.sh/controller** keys isolating the Karpenter controller nodes from the worker nodes. Karpenter will deploy all application pods on new nodes except they have the same key as the controller.

CHAPTER 19   CLUSTER AUTOSCALING

Toleration is the opposite of taint.[5] Setting a taint on a node tells the scheduler not to run a pod on it unless the pod is explicitly labeled to tolerate that taint.

You should identify the Karpenter nodes with special labels and tags for Karpenter to distinguish between worker and non-worker nodes:

```
labels = {
    "karpenter.sh/controller" = "true"
  }
tags = {
    "karpenter.sh/discovery"  = var.cluster_name
  }
```

Similarly, you should add the karpenter.sh/discovery tag to all subnets where Karpenter should deploy new nodes:

```
tags = {
   Name = "private-subnet-${count.index+1}"
   "kubernetes.io/role/internal-elb"            = 1
   "karpenter.sh/discovery"  = var.cluster_name
  }
```

Karpenter requires VPC CNI, kube-proxy, and coredns addons. You could deploy the three addons as follows:

```
resource "aws_eks_addon" "vpc_cni_addon" {
  cluster_name = var.cluster_name
  addon_name   = "vpc-cni"
   configuration_values = jsonencode({
     env = {
     ENABLE_PREFIX_DELEGATION = "true"
```

---

[5] https://karpenter.sh/docs/concepts/scheduling/

```
      WARM_PREFIX_TARGET = "1"
      }
  })
      resolve_conflicts_on_create = "OVERWRITE"
      resolve_conflicts_on_update = "OVERWRITE"
}
resource "aws_eks_addon" "eks_kube_proxy_addon" {
  cluster_name = var.cluster_name
  addon_name   = "kube-proxy"
  resolve_conflicts_on_create = "OVERWRITE"
  resolve_conflicts_on_update = "OVERWRITE"
}
resource "aws_eks_addon" "coredns" {
  cluster_name              = var.cluster_name
  addon_name                = "coredns"
      configuration_values = jsonencode({
      tolerations = [
          {
          key    = "karpenter.sh/controller"
          value  = "true"
          effect = "NoSchedule"
          }
      ]
      })
      resolve_conflicts_on_create = "OVERWRITE"
      resolve_conflicts_on_update = "OVERWRITE"
}
```

CHAPTER 19   CLUSTER AUTOSCALING

You will need a service account for the Karpenter controller. We opted for pod identity which requires pod identity addon and configuration file. You should find the addon in the **addons.tf** file and the configuration code in the **pod-id.tf** file.

Karpenter Deployment

Deploy the cluster and run the bash script that comes with the code to install the Karpenter controller. The script simply installs the controller with a helm chat and deploys Karpenter pods in the karpenter namespace. The version argument specifies the version of the Karpenter we want to deploy.

```bash
#!/bin/bash
CLUSTER_NAME=karpenter-cluster
KARPENTER_VERSION=1.1.1
ACCOUNT_ID=$(aws sts get-caller-identity --query "Account" --output text)
CLUSTER_ENDPOINT=$(aws eks describe-cluster --name karpenter-cluster --query "cluster.endpoint" --output text)
SERVICE_ACCOUNT=KarpenterControllerRole-karpenter-cluster

#switch context and create karpenter namespace
aws eks update-kubeconfig --name karpenter-cluster && kubectl create ns karpenter
echo "add helm repo"
echo "-----------------------------------------"
helm repo add eks https://aws.github.io/eks-charts
echo "installing karpenter\n*******************************"
docker logout public.ecr.aws
```

```
#install karpeneter
helm upgrade --install karpenter oci://public.ecr.aws/
karpenter/karpenter --version ${KARPENTER_VERSION} \
  --namespace karpenter \
  --set "settings.clusterName=${CLUSTER_NAME}" \
  --set clusterEndpoint=${CLUSTER_ENDPOINT} \
  --set serviceAccount.annotations."eks\.amazonaws\.com/role-
    arn"="arn:aws:iam::${ACCOUNT_ID}:role/${SERVICE_ACCOUNT}" \
  --set controller.resources.requests.cpu=1 \
  --set controller.resources.requests.memory=1Gi \
  --set controller.resources.limits.cpu=1 \
  --set controller.resources.limits.memory=1Gi \
  --set logLevel=debug \
  --wait
```

Install Karpenter Controller

You may follow the recipe below to install the Karpenter controller:

1. Deploy the cluster in the chapter19-karpenter folder.

2. Install the Karpenter controller onto the cluster with the **script.sh** file.

   ```
   chmod +x script.sh
   ./script.sh
   ```

3. Verify if Karpenter is working.

   ```
   kubectl get pods -n karpenter
   ```

   You should expect running Karpenter pods with the following output:

   ```
   karpenter-77b5f57d4c-mpb6z    1/1    Running    0    33s
   karpenter-77b5f57d4c-zldb2    1/1    Running    0    33s
   ```

4. Open another terminal and run the following command to monitor Karpenter logs if you want to monitor the controller:

   ```
   kubectl logs -f -n karpenter -l app.kubernetes.io/
   name=karpenter
   ```

Deploy Node Pool

Once Karpenter is installed successfully, the next step is to deploy a NodePool.[6] A NodePool specifies how you want to configure the new worker nodes the Karpenter controller is about to create. NodePool allow you to specify the constraints for the nodes and the pods that can run on them. The NodePool manifest can perform tasks such as

- Defining taints to limit the pods that can run on a new Karpenter created node
- Limiting node creation to certain zones, instance types, and computer architectures
- Setting default values for node expiration

Deploy the NodePool manifest in the nodepool.yml file with the following command:

```
kubectl apply -f deployment/nodepool.yml
```

The node pool file contains the following configurations:

```
---
apiVersion: karpenter.k8s.aws/v1
kind: EC2NodeClass
```

---

[6] https://karpenter.sh/docs/concepts/nodepools/

```yaml
metadata:
  name: default
spec:
  amiSelectorTerms:
    - alias: bottlerocket@latest
  role: KarpenterNodeRole-karpenter-cluster
  subnetSelectorTerms:
    - tags:
      karpenter.sh/discovery: karpenter-cluster
  securityGroupSelectorTerms:
    - tags:
      karpenter.sh/discovery: karpenter-cluster
  tags:
      karpenter.sh/discovery: karpenter-cluster
---
apiVersion: karpenter.sh/v1
kind: NodePool
metadata:
  name: default
spec:
  template:
    spec:
    nodeClassRef:
    group: karpenter.k8s.aws
    kind: EC2NodeClass
    name: default
    requirements:
    - key: "karpenter.k8s.aws/instance-category"
        operator: In
        values: ["c", "m", "r"]
```

```
          - key: "karpenter.k8s.aws/instance-cpu"
            operator: In
            values: ["4", "8", "16", "32"]
          - key: "karpenter.k8s.aws/instance-hypervisor"
            operator: In
            values: ["nitro"]
          - key: "karpenter.k8s.aws/instance-generation"
            operator: Gt
            values: ["2"]
  limits:
    cpu: 1000
  disruption:
    consolidationPolicy: WhenEmpty
    consolidateAfter: 30s
```

First it specifies the object kind as EC2NodeClass. It set the Amazon Machine Image to a bottle rocket image and the role for the new worker nodes as KarpenterNodeRole-karpenter-cluster. This role was created in the aim.tf file under the node module. Furthermore, it specifies the network selector and security groups each identified by a tag.

The second stanza is the creation of the NodePool which references the EC2NodeClass and sets the requirements for the nodes.

Application Deployment

1. Deploy the inflate application.

   ```
   kubectl apply -f deployment/inflate-app.yml
   ```

2. Check the number of nodes.

   ```
   kubectl get nodes
   ```

CHAPTER 19 CLUSTER AUTOSCALING

You may use the AWS console to observe the changes. You will see changes fast on the console.

3. Scale the inflate app and observe how fast Karpenter will spin up new nodes and deploy the pod.

   ```
   kubectl scale deployment inflate --replicas 4
   ```

4. Check the nodes that were created by Karpenter.

   ```
   kubectl get nodes
   ```

5. Scale down the inflated app to see how Karpenter reacts.

   ```
   kubectl scale deployment inflate --replicas 1
   ```

Karpenter vs. Cluster Autoscaler[7]

Feature	Cluster Autoscaler	Karpenter
Resource management	Based on the resource utilization of existing nodes, Cluster Autoscaler takes a reactive approach to scale nodes.	Based on the current resource requirements of unscheduled pods, Karpenter takes a proactive approach to provision nodes.
Node management	Cluster Autoscaler manages nodes based on the resource demands of the present workload, using predefined autoscaling groups.	Karpenter scales, provisions, and manages nodes based on the configuration of custom provisioners.

(continued)

---

[7] https://www.nops.io/blog/karpenter-vs-cluster-autoscaler-vs-nks/

CHAPTER 19 CLUSTER AUTOSCALING

Feature	Cluster Autoscaler	Karpenter
Scaling	Cluster Autoscaler focuses on node-level scaling, which means it can effectively add more nodes to meet any increase in demand. But this also means it may be less effective in downscaling resources.	Karpenter offers more effective and granular scaling functionalities based on specific workload requirements. In other words, it scales according to the actual usage. It also allows users to specify scaling policies or rules to match their requirements.
Scheduling	With Cluster Autoscaler, scheduling is simpler as it is designed to scale up or down based on the present requirements of the workload.	Karpenter can effectively schedule workloads based on distinct factors like availability zones and resource requirements. It can try to optimize for the cheapest pricing via spot but is unaware of any commitments like RI's or Savings Plans.

Summary

This chapter introduced cluster autoscaler and Karpenter to scale the cluster nodes. Karpenter is a more intelligent autoscaler design to overcome the limitations of the K8s Cluster Autoscaler (CA). To recap, CA only uses simple metrics such as pending pods, CPU, and memory limits to launch a new node. It does not consider unused computing resources and the instance type that will best serve the needs of the cluster, resulting in waste and low utilization efficiency. CA is slow in provisioning because it relies on a third-party orchestrator such as AWS ASG to launch new nodes to keep up with demands. You can use Karpenter to save money as it can find the right instance for your workload. The next chapter will introduce service mesh and how to manage them.

CHAPTER 20

Service Mesh and VPC Lattice

We will introduce the service mesh concepts and show how you can implement them in EKS. Service mesh is a technique for networking independent applications or services using configurations rather than code. The application network becomes an avenue for application metrics collection, an infrastructure for application security and resilience. It relieves developers from manually coding applications or service-to-service communication and saves them time for more productive tasks. The AWS version of service mesh is known as App Mesh. App Mesh allows you to create a distributed application or service network infrastructure in EKS for application observability, security, and resilience. You should understand the mesh architecture and be able to configure it by the time you finish this chapter.

Service Orchestration

If you deployed the cluster in Chapter 14 and ran the corresponding **blueapp.yml** manifest, you should notice an internal service exposing the blue app pod to the outside world through a load balancer as depicted in Figure 20-1.

CHAPTER 20   SERVICE MESH AND VPC LATTICE

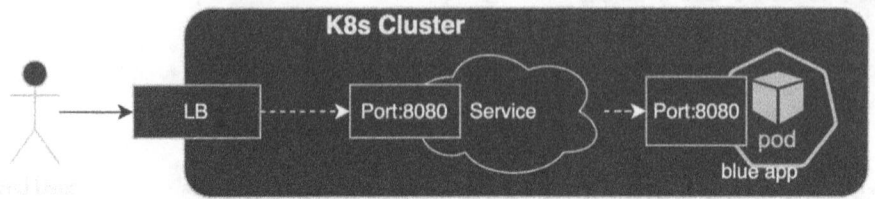

Figure 20-1. *Load balancer to service communication*

The blue app pod is a simple application with a single user interface (UI). Imagine the blue app were to be a complex application with multiple modules such as authentication, order, payment, inventory, messaging, etc. The architecture style would correspond to a single humongous pod placed behind a load balancer as depicted in Figure 20-2.

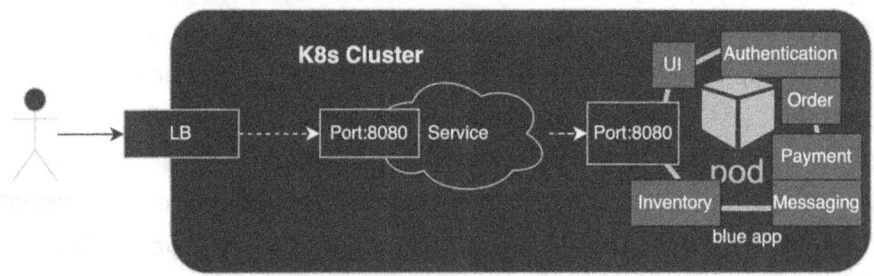

Figure 20-2. *Monolithic application*

The challenge with this kind of monolithic architecture is that it makes development more complex and slower.[1] It is tightly coupled and impossible to scale the individual components or modules. An error in one part of the module could affect the entire application. Monolithic applications constrain technology and are bad for an agile way of work.

An independent pod per module would be a better architecture and a better way of dealing with the shortcomings of monolithic architecture. Figure 20-3 shows how you may move from monolithic architecture to microservice architecture.

---

[1] Microservices patterns with exmaples in Java, Manning, Chris Richard

CHAPTER 20 SERVICE MESH AND VPC LATTICE

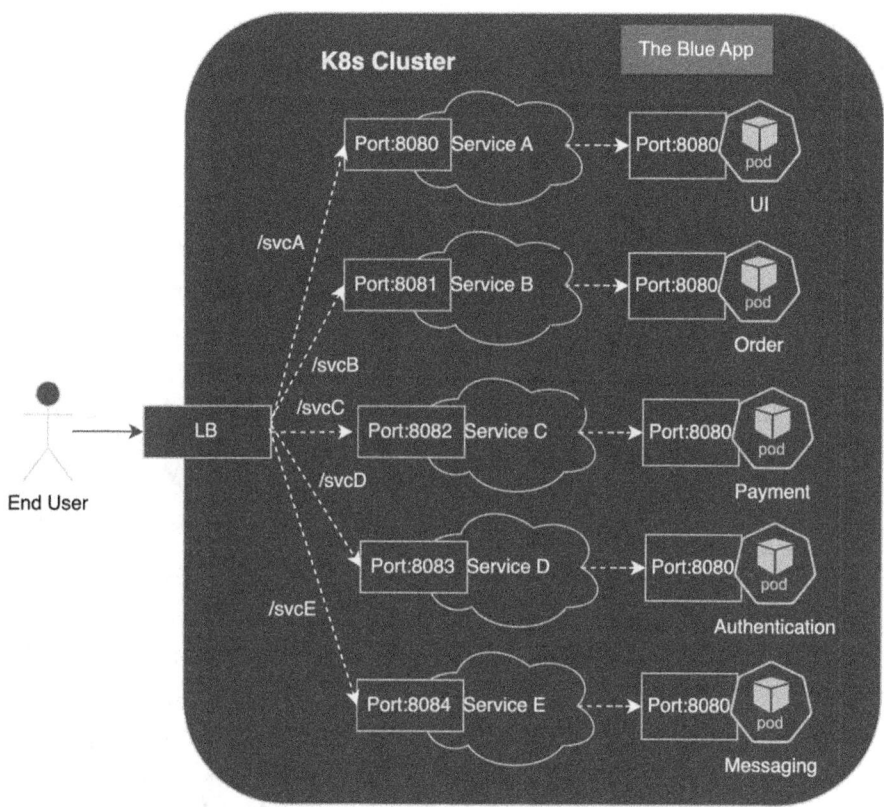

Figure 20-3. *Pod per module*

In this architecture, each module runs in its own pod with its own service. You can develop and scale the pod independently. This decouples the architecture and promotes an agile way of working. Teams can work independently on their assigned modules and deploy frequently without affecting other services enabling flexible release cycles. They can experiment with new features and roll back if the feature fails. Teams can develop in the technology of their choice and still be able to work with other modules or teams enhancing resilient and technological flexibility.

CHAPTER 20 SERVICE MESH AND VPC LATTICE

The microservices architecture is not complete if the services cannot talk to each other. For example, a simple order may involve the UI module or service, the order, payment, and the messaging modules. This would require the services to communicate with each other for an end user to place an order as depicted in Figure 20-4.

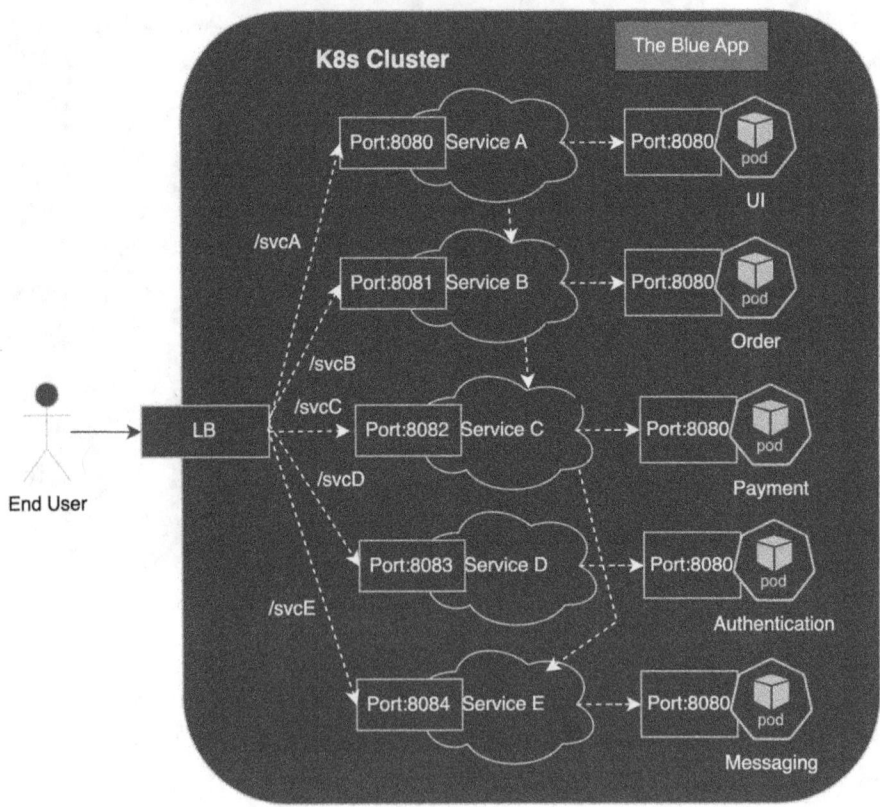

Figure 20-4. Service mesh

Connecting independent services increases the complexities to microservice architectures. It can make logging, monitoring, and troubleshooting more complex since the services may run on different machines. Further, it decreases operational excellence as it becomes difficult to collect the necessary metrics.

Service mesh was introduced to address some of these shortcomings in microservice architectures. Service mesh answers operational excellence as well as security questions. For example, how do you ensure that services are working properly? How do you know if all the services are operating at the same level? How do you know if they are responding to requests quickly as they should? The following sections introduce AWS service mesh and experiments with examples to show how you can address some of the challenges of microservices.

AWS App Mesh

AWS App Mesh is the AWS version of the service mesh orchestrator. A service mesh is an application infrastructure layer dedicated to handling service-to-service communication. It is a managed service that relies on arrays of lightweight envoy proxies deployed alongside applications to observe and control service-to-service communication within a cluster. It standardizes service-to-service communication, traffic management, security, and observability without changing application code.[2] App Mesh ensures consistent and end-to-end visibility and makes applications highly available.

Service-to-service communication occurs through envoy proxies. An envoy is a sidecar container that handles traffic directly before it reaches an application or container. The services no longer communicate with each other directly but over envoy proxies or the sidecar container as shown in Figure 20-5.

---

[2] https://docs.aws.amazon.com/app-mesh/latest/userguide/what-is-app-mesh.html

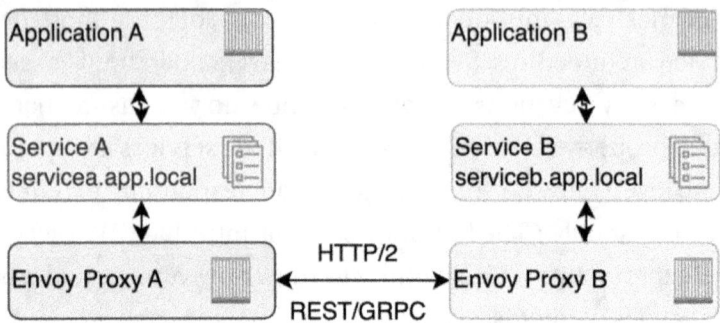

Figure 20-5. *Service mesh*

In Figure 20-5, when application A wants to send a message to application B, it sends the message to service A; service A forwards the message to the envoy proxy A for it to deliver the message to the envoy proxy B. The envoy proxy B then sends the message to application B through the service B.

Service A communicates with service B indirectly through the envoy proxies deployed alongside application pods A and B. The envoy proxy is a container image implemented as the sidecar container. A sidecar is the container instance of an envoy proxy image. It reads the App Mesh configuration and directs traffic appropriately. An envoy proxy is a self-contained, high-performance application server with a small memory footprint.

An envoy proxy has the following capabilities:[3, 4]

- *Service discovery*: A mechanism for finding the periodically updated list of healthy endpoints of services.

---

[3] https://www.envoyproxy.io/docs/envoy/latest/intro/what_is_envoy
[4] Istio in Action, Christian E. Posta and Rinor Maloku

- *Health checking*: A subsystem that can optionally perform active health checking of upstream service clusters and use the result with the service discovery information to determine healthy targets.

- *Advanced load balancing*: Since envoy is a self-contained proxy instead of a library, it can implement advanced load balancing techniques such as automatic retries, circuit breaking, global rate limiting via an external rate limiting service, request shadowing, and outlier detection in a single place.

- *Client-side load balancing*: Envoy proxies provide clients with the list of endpoints and let them decide which ones to call.

- *Circuit breaking*: Sheds load to services that are misbehaving for a while to make the application more resilient.

- *Bulkheading*: Limits client resource usage with explicit thresholds (connections, threads, sessions, and so on) when making calls to a service.

- *Timeouts*: Enforce time limitations on requests, sockets, liveness, and so on when making calls to a service.

- *Retry budgets*: Apply constraints to retries, that is, limit the number of retries in each period (e.g., only retry 50% of the calls in a 10-second window).

- *Deadlines*: Give requests context about how long a response may still be useful; if outside the deadline, disregard processing the request.

- *Front/edge proxy support*: Envoy has a feature set that makes it well suited as an edge proxy for most modern web application use cases, including TLS termination, HTTP/1.1, HTTP/2, and HTTP/3 support, as well as HTTP L7 routing. This provides added benefit in using the same software at the edge for observability, management, identical service discovery, load balancing, etc.

- *Observability*: Envoy includes robust statistics support for all subsystems; statsd is the currently supported statistics sink, though plugging in a different one would not be difficult. Statistics are also viewable via the administration port. Envoy also supports distributed tracing via third-party providers.

App Mesh Data Plane

AWS App Mesh creates a "cluster" on top of a cluster. It has its own data and control planes. The data plane is formed by the sidecar containers together with microservices of the application pods. Microservices refer to the actual K8s services represented by the cluster IP service. It exposes application pods such that they can communicate with other services.

CHAPTER 20 SERVICE MESH AND VPC LATTICE

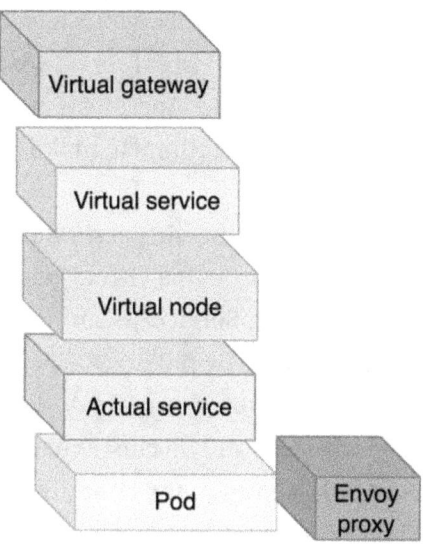

Figure 20-6. *App Mesh components*

As in Figure 20-6, App Mesh functions with virtual services which are the abstractions of the actual K8s services (microservices) that wish to communicate with each other. The main components of App Mesh data plane are the microservices, (also known as actual services), virtual nodes, virtual services, and virtual gateways. The rest are virtual routers and routes. The virtual gateway, virtual routers, and routes are optional components. They are required for traffic management. They determine the weight or the percentage of traffic an App Mesh can route to different versions of an application. They can manage canary, blue/green, and other deployment strategies.

You can easily implement the blue/green application deployment strategy with App Mesh where you test two versions of the same application, the old and the latest version, before deciding whether to replace the outdated version of the application with the new one. No code changes are required.

Virtual services are for exposing applications to services within the App Mesh. Like the actual services, a virtual service exposes a virtual node or virtual router to other services in the App Mesh. It exposes the service endpoints of virtual nodes or virtual routers to make them discoverable by other services.

From a communication viewpoint, virtual services are the entry point to the mesh. Every request goes through a virtual service to reach the actual or microservices beneath it. Service-to-service communication goes from an envoy proxy to another envoy proxy.

You identify a virtual service with a domain name defined with the **awsName** field in a service manifest. The cluster uses the native CoreDNS service to resolve the domain names to the IP address of the microservice in question for the sidecar container. The envoy proxy or the sidecar container piggybacks on this to find the actual service (microservice) that must receive the traffic within the cluster.

External clusters may require external DNS to resolve the microservice IP for the envoy proxy to find the target service. You can create a dummy service alongside a virtual service in a configuration manifest to instruct the CoreDNS to resolve the virtual service DNS name into a microservice IP.

A virtual node is a pointer to an actual microservice. It is a virtual endpoint to an actual microservice. For that matter, you must configure the same name for both virtual node and an actual service. You use a service to make a set of pods available on the network so that other services can interact with it.[5]

A virtual gateway exposes virtual services to resources outside the mesh so that an external request can reach a microservice. It makes services inside the mesh accessible to services outside the mesh. For example, you can connect an external load balancer to an App Mesh

---

[5] https://kubernetes.io/docs/concepts/services-networking/service/

cluster through a virtual gateway. Virtual gateways depend on a stand-alone or an independent envoy proxy responsible for managing the external communication to the App Mesh. A stand-alone envoy proxy is different from a sidecar proxy in the sense that it is not attached to any application. Sidecars are injected into containers like we attach a sidecar to a car.

App Mesh Control Plane

The second part of App Mesh is the control plane managed by AWS. The control plane is a collection of controls for App Mesh microservice management.

It is the policy enforcer and configuration manager. It ensures that the App Mesh envoy operates according to policies set by the cluster administrator or the desired state set in the deployment manifest. Figure 20-7 is a component of the App Mesh control plane in relation to the data plane. The observability component controls the generation of rich metrics, logs, and traces to troubleshoot and monitor the microservices.

The network management component provides fine-grained control over traffic between microservices. It ensures that routing rules of the virtual routers are implemented as desired. It supervises traffic splitting by gradually moving traffic between service versions, enabling techniques like canary deployment, A/B testing, and blue-green deployments.

Instead of manually coding service-to-service communication, you can specify it at the high level for App Mesh to do the mapping. App Mesh integrates with the AWS Cloud Map for service discovery. Cloud Map allows you to maintain a centralized registry of microservice names, service IPs and ports. The service discovery component controls the service discovery part of the App Mesh cluster.

CHAPTER 20   SERVICE MESH AND VPC LATTICE

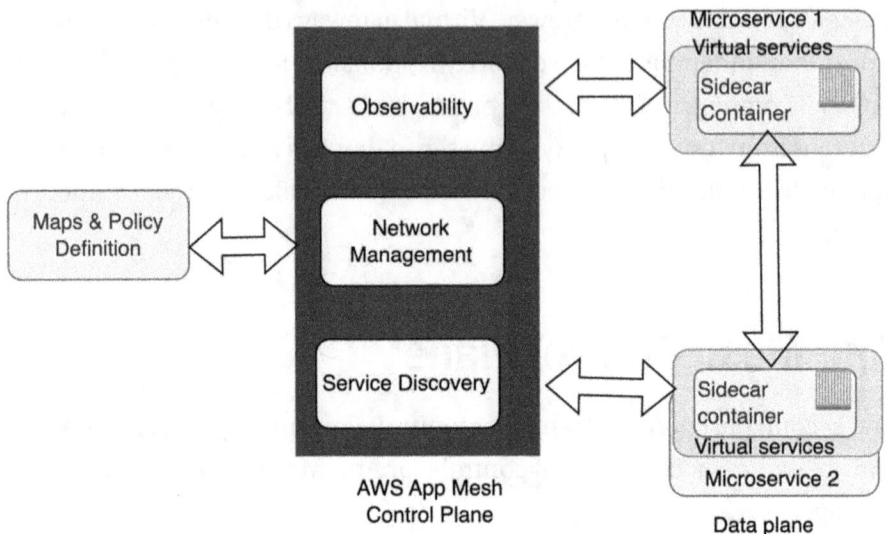

Figure 20-7. App Mesh control plane and data plane

App Mesh Implementation

It is now time to demonstrate a few App Mesh implementation scenarios. We will begin with cluster deployment and the changes we have made to the cluster code to implement the App Mesh. We will continue with a couple of App Mesh deployment scenarios, from a service mesh with only two services to a service mesh with three services. We develop further to connect the service mesh to an external load balancer and finally try blue/green application deployment. We will end with monitoring and traceability in App Mesh.

Since AWS is deprecating App Mesh service soon, you may jump to the "VPC Lattice" section after you are done with the first two examples.

CHAPTER 20   SERVICE MESH AND VPC LATTICE

The App Mesh Cluster

The chapter20 folder contains the cluster code for an App Mesh deployment. The three key changes are the introduction of the launch template, new security group rules, and the policy codes in the data plane module. You should find the changes in the launch-tp.tf, sg.tf, and the policy.tf files.

The launch template configures the AWS instance metadata service version 2 (IMDSv2) to enable pods in the App Mesh call services outside their containers. The hop limit is the key change here. It is the number of network hops that the PUT response is allowed to make.[6] The hop limit is between 1 and 64. The recommended hop limit for container applications is 2. We use the launch template to set the hop limit for App Mesh containers as shown in the code snippet below:

```
resource "aws_launch_template" "launch_template_node_group" {
  name = "launch-template-node-group"
  block_device_mappings {
      device_name = "/dev/sdf"
      ebs {
        volume_size = 50
      }
  }
  ebs_optimized = true
  metadata_options {
      http_tokens     = "optional"
      http_put_response_hop_limit = 2
  }
  network_interfaces {
     associate_public_ip_address = false
  }
}
```

---

[6] https://docs.aws.amazon.com/AWSEC2/latest/UserGuide/instancedata-data-retrieval.html#imds-considerations

CHAPTER 20 SERVICE MESH AND VPC LATTICE

The hop limit of 2 means pods in App Mesh can communicate with the outside world.

You should find two policies in the policy.tf file. The first policy authorizes the envoy proxy for all virtual nodes, even if they don't use TLS. Proxy authorization requires that the **appmesh:StreamAggregated Resources** permission is specified in an IAM policy. You must attach the policy to an IAM role, and that IAM role must be attached to the compute resource that hosts the envoy proxy.[7]

```
resource "aws_iam_policy" "appmesh" {
  name = "AWSAppMeshControllerIAMPolicy"
  path        = "/"
  description = "my aws envoy policy"
  policy = <<POLICY
{
    "Version": "2012-10-17",
    "Statement": [
        {
            "Effect": "Allow",
            "Action": "appmesh:StreamAggregatedResources",
            "Resource": "*"
        }
    ]
}
  POLICY
}
```

---

[7] https://docs.aws.amazon.com/app-mesh/latest/userguide/proxy-authorization.html

CHAPTER 20   SERVICE MESH AND VPC LATTICE

The second policy is a load balancer controller policy. It is an optional policy but needed for connecting the App Mesh to an external load balancer. You can create the policy from your Terraform code or with a script outside the Terraform code.

The third change is the security group rules. Most important of them is the local administration interface port for the envoy proxy (9901). The envoy port is used to query and modify various aspects of the envoy proxy server. You can retrieve health check information, change log level, and so on. You must open port 9901 to enable communication.

The rest of the rules are for applications. For example, port 80 will allow the load balancer to send requests on port 80 to an App Mesh service.

```
resource "aws_security_group_rule" "allow_pod_port_9901-egress" {
  type              = "egress"
  from_port         = 9901
  to_port           = 9901
  protocol          = "tcp"
  cidr_blocks       = ["10.0.0.0/16"]
  security_group_id = var.cluster_security_group_id
}

resource "aws_security_group_rule" "allow_pod_port_9901-ingress" {
  type              = "ingress"
  from_port         = 9901
  to_port           = 9901
  protocol          = "tcp"
  cidr_blocks       = ["10.0.0.0/16"]
  security_group_id = var.cluster_security_group_id
}
```

```
resource "aws_security_group_rule" "allow_pod_port_443-
egress" {
  type               = "egress"
  from_port          = 443
  to_port            = 443
  protocol           = "tcp"
  cidr_blocks        = ["10.0.0.0/16"]
  security_group_id  = var.cluster_security_group_id
}
resource "aws_security_group_rule" "allow_pod_port_443-
ingress" {
  type               = "ingress"
  from_port          = 443
  to_port            = 443
  protocol           = "tcp"
  cidr_blocks        = ["10.0.0.0/16"]
  security_group_id  = var.cluster_security_group_id
}
```

App Mesh Cluster Deployment

1. Initialize the terraform in the chapter20 folder.

   ```
   terraform init
   ```

2. Deploy the cluster.

   ```
   terraform apply -auto-approve
   ```

CHAPTER 20 SERVICE MESH AND VPC LATTICE

App Mesh Deployment Scenario 1

We will start with a simple App Mesh with two services, service A and service B. We will label them as green and blue services as shown in Figure 20-8. The green service listens on port 8081, while the blue service listens on port 8080. We want the two services to communicate with each other using App Mesh.

Figure 20-8. *Blue and green service communication*

We begin with a partial App Mesh implementation with only actual services for applications A and B, virtual nodes, and virtual services. No virtual gateway or virtual routers as shown in Figure 20-9.

We will inject the envoy proxy's sidecar container during the application deployment. On top of the application are the microservice and a virtual node. The virtual node creates the endpoint for the actual service. The virtual service exposes the node or the virtual endpoint within the cluster.

CHAPTER 20   SERVICE MESH AND VPC LATTICE

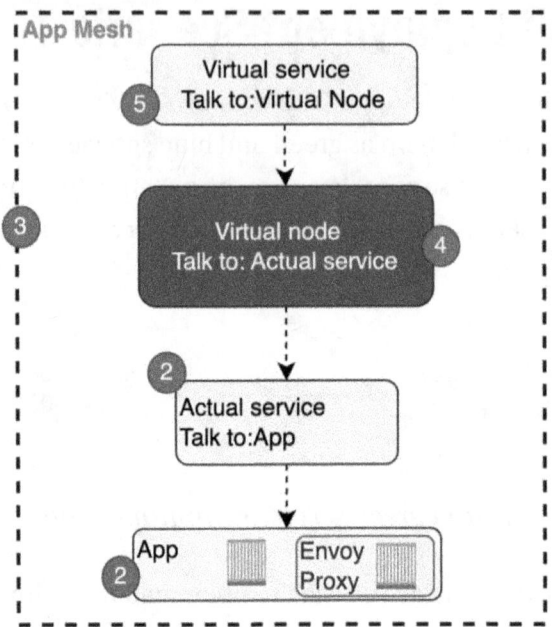

Figure 20-9. Simple App Mesh setup

Install App Mesh Controller

Before we configure the service-to-service communication, we must install the App Mesh controller on the cluster. The App Mesh controller controls the sidecar container. The controller will automatically inject a sidecar container to any pod in the App Mesh namespace[8] except the pods for the gateway envoy proxy.

You should find the App Mesh controller script in the chapter20/appmeshBG/1-script folder. The script creates an OIDC provider, a namespace, and a service account and installs the App Mesh controller in the appmesh-system namespace.

---

[8] https://docs.aws.amazon.com/app-mesh/latest/userguide/getting-started-kubernetes.html

You should first run the **appmesh.sh** script followed by the **kubectl -n appmesh-system get all** command. The command will show if the controller is active. You should run the command a couple of times to make sure the controller is active. You cannot deploy App Mesh if the controller is not active. You can rerun the appmesh.sh again if the controller is not active after trying the kubectl command a couple of times.

You may use the following commands to troubleshoot errors if the controller is not running:

- `kubectl -n appmesh-system get all`

  Note the name of the controller and use it to run the next command.

- `kubectl logs -n <namespace> <controller name>`

  For example, kubectl logs -n appmesh-system appmesh-5tsggs

- `kubectl get pods -A`

  Note the name of the envoy proxy and use it to run the next command.

- `kubectl describe deployment -n <namespace> <controller name>`

  Describes the App Mesh controller deployment.

- `kubectl logs -n <namespace> <pod name> envoy`

The App Mesh controller script (appmesh.sh) is as follows:

```bash
#! /bin/bash
CLUSTER_NAME="appmesh-cluster"
#########################initialization #########################
export AWS_REGION=$(aws ec2 describe-availability-zones --output text --query 'AvailabilityZones[0].[RegionName]')
```

```
echo "Update context"
echo "-------------------------------"
aws eks update-kubeconfig \
   --name ${CLUSTER_NAME} \
   --region ${AWS_REGION}
echo "create oidc provider"
echo "-------------------------------"
eksctl utils associate-iam-oidc-provider \
      --region=${AWS_REGION} \
      --cluster=${CLUSTER_NAME} --approve
####################clean up ################################
kubectl delete ns appmesh-system
echo "delete sa "
echo "-------------------------------------"
eksctl delete iamserviceaccount --cluster ${CLUSTER_NAME} \
 --name appmesh-controller-sa \
 --namespace appmesh-system

echo "Create the app mesh namespace"
echo "-------------------------------"
kubectl create ns appmesh-system

#stack
aws cloudformation delete-stack \
    --stack-name eksctl-appmesh-cluster-addon-
    iamserviceaccount-appmesh-system-appmesh-controller-sa

################service account ############################
echo "create appmesh controller sa with managed policy"
echo "-------------------------------"
eksctl create iamserviceaccount --cluster ${CLUSTER_NAME} \
 --name appmesh-controller-sa \
 --attach-policy-arn arn:aws:iam::aws:policy/
```

CHAPTER 20 SERVICE MESH AND VPC LATTICE

```
AWSAppMeshFullAccess \
 --override-existing-serviceaccounts \
 --namespace appmesh-system \
 --approve

#########################helm chat ###########################
echo "add helm repo"
echo "---------------------------------------"
helm repo add eks https://aws.github.io/eks-charts

 helm install appmesh-controller eks/appmesh-controller \
 --namespace appmesh-system \
 --set region=${AWS_REGION} \
 --set serviceAccount.create=false \
 --set serviceAccount.name=appmesh-controller-sa

echo "--------------output----------------"
kubectl -n appmesh-system get all
```

Rerun the script in case the App Mesh controller installation fails. You should see the following when the controller is active:

```
NAME                                           DESIRED  CURRENT  READY  AGE
replicaset.apps/appmesh-controller-9f9857547   1        1        1      24s
```

Run the App Mesh

You should find the code for the App Mesh configuration in the appmeshBG/2-mesh folder.

1. Create a namespace.

    ```
    kind: Namespace
    apiVersion: v1
    metadata:
    ```

551

```
      name: bgns
      labels:
        name: bgns
```

You create a namespace to isolate your App Mesh deployment. This step is optional but is a good practice to organize your deployment with namespaces.

2. Deploy the blue and green applications and services (micro- or actual services) with the following manifest:

```
---
apiVersion: apps/v1
kind: Deployment
metadata:
  namespace: bgns
  name: blue
spec:
  selector:
    matchLabels:
      app: blue
  replicas: 1
  template:
    metadata:
      labels:
        app: blue
    spec:
      containers:
      - image: cloudmanly/eks:blue
        imagePullPolicy: Always
        name: blue
```

```
      ports:
      - containerPort: 8080
---
apiVersion: v1
kind: Service
metadata:
  namespace: bgns
  name: blue
  labels:
    app: blue
spec:
  ports:
    - port: 8080
      protocol: TCP
  selector:
    app: blue

---
apiVersion: apps/v1
kind: Deployment
metadata:
  namespace: bgns
  name: green
spec:
  selector:
    matchLabels:
      app: green
  replicas: 1
  template:
    metadata:
      labels:
        app: green
```

```
    spec:
      containers:
      - image: cloudmanly/eks:green
        imagePullPolicy: Always
        name: green
        ports:
        - containerPort: 8081

---
apiVersion: v1
kind: Service
metadata:
  namespace: bgns
  name: green
  labels:
    app: green
spec:
  ports:
    - port: 8081
      protocol: TCP
  selector:
    app: green
```

The selectors and the service ports are very important for service-to-service communications. The manifest deploys the blue and green applications and their services.

3. Create the App Mesh object.

   ```
   apiVersion: appmesh.k8s.aws/v1beta2
   kind: Mesh
   metadata:
     name: bgmesh
   ```

```
spec:
  namespaceSelector:
    matchLabels:
      mesh: bgmesh
---
apiVersion: v1
kind: Namespace
metadata:
  name: bgns
  labels:
    mesh: bgmesh
    gateway: ingress-gateway
    appmesh.k8s.aws/sidecarInjectorWebhook: enabled
```

The manifest creates the App Mesh object (bgmesh) and enables the App Mesh's sidecar container web hook (appmesh.k8s.aws/sidecarInjectorWebhook: **enabled**) in the bgns namespace for all pods that will be deployed in the namespace except the gateway pod. This means apart from the gateway envoy proxy pod, the App Mesh controller will automatically inject a sidecar pod to any pod deployed in the bgns namespace.[9]

The gateway envoy proxy is an exception because it must run as a stand-alone pod. We implement the exception with the **gateway:ingress-gateway** label in the namespace object of the manifest above. In

---

[9] https://aws.github.io/aws-app-mesh-controller-for-k8s/reference/injector/

CHAPTER 20 SERVICE MESH AND VPC LATTICE

addition, the virtual gateway pod must carry the same label (**ingress-gateway**) to enable the exception.[10]

4. Create virtual nodes.

```
---
apiVersion: appmesh.k8s.aws/v1beta2
kind: VirtualNode
metadata:
  name: green
  namespace: bgns
spec:
  podSelector:
    matchLabels:
      app: green
  listeners:
    - portMapping:
        port: 8081
        protocol: http
      healthCheck:
        protocol: http
        path: '/'
        healthyThreshold: 2
        unhealthyThreshold: 2
        timeoutMillis: 2000
        intervalMillis: 5000
  backends:
    - virtualService:
        virtualServiceRef:
```

---

[10] https://aws.github.io/aws-app-mesh-controller-for-k8s/reference/injector/

            namespace: bgns
            name: blue
      serviceDiscovery:
        dns:
          hostname: green.appns.svc.cluster.local
---
apiVersion: appmesh.k8s.aws/v1beta2
kind: VirtualNode
metadata:
  name: **blue**
  namespace: bgns
spec:
  podSelector:
    matchLabels:
        app: blue
  listeners:
    - portMapping:
        port: 8080
        protocol: http
      healthCheck:
        protocol: http
        path: '/'
        healthyThreshold: 2
        unhealthyThreshold: 2
        timeoutMillis: 2000
        intervalMillis: 5000
  backends:
    - **virtualService:**
        virtualServiceRef:
            namespace: bgns

```
          name: green
serviceDiscovery:
  dns:
    hostname: blue.appns.svc.cluster.local
```

The virtual node is a pointer to the actual service. The main requirement here is that the virtual nodes and the actual services must have the same name to point to each other. **The configuration will fail if you miss this point.** Nothing will work if the name of the actual service is different from the virtual node. The two names must be the same.

The backends field specifies which service the node can talk to. In this example, the blue node will talk to the green node and vice versa.

5. Create a virtual service to expose the nodes.

```
---
apiVersion: appmesh.k8s.aws/v1beta2
kind: VirtualService
metadata:
  name: blue
  namespace: bgns
  labels:
    app: blue
spec:
  awsName: blue.bgns.svc.cluster.local
  provider:
    virtualNode:
      virtualNodeRef:
        name: blue
        namespace: bgns
```

CHAPTER 20 SERVICE MESH AND VPC LATTICE

```
---
#dummy core dns service
apiVersion: v1
kind: Service
metadata:
  name: blue
  namespace: bgns
  labels:
    app: blue
spec:
  ports:
  - port: 8080
    name: http
  selector:
    app: blue
---
apiVersion: appmesh.k8s.aws/v1beta2
kind: VirtualService
metadata:
  name: green
  namespace: appns
  labels:
    app: green
spec:
  awsName: green.bgns.svc.cluster.local
  provider:
    virtualNode:
      virtualNodeRef:
        name: green
        namespace: bgns
```

CHAPTER 20   SERVICE MESH AND VPC LATTICE

```
---
#dummy core dns service
apiVersion: v1
kind: Service
metadata:
  name: green
  namespace: bgns
  labels:
     app: green
spec:
  ports:
  - port: 8081
    name: http
  selector:
     app: green
```

The virtual service makes the nodes visible or accessible within the App Mesh. Each virtual service should include a dummy service to enable the native CoreDNS to resolve the virtual service's domain name, **blue.bgns.svc.cluster.local**, to the IP address of the microservice for the envoy sidecar. The virtual service can use any name, but we maintain the same names (blue, green) for the sake of simplicity.

6. Execute the code in the folder.

    ```
    kubectl apply -f appmeshBG/2-mesh
    ```

7. Verify if actual services are running.

    ```
    kubectl get svc -n bgns
    ```

CHAPTER 20 SERVICE MESH AND VPC LATTICE

You should find

```
blue    ClusterIP    172.20.25.188    <none>    8080/TCP    19s
green   ClusterIP    172.20.203.13    <none>    8081/TCP    18s
```

8. Verify if pods are running.

   `kubectl get pod -n bgns`

   You should find the following:

   ```
   blue-f94845bbb-rsdrx      1/1    Running    0    35s
   green-88dcd8df4-h2hdt     1/1    Running    0    34s
   ```

   Note that each application has only one pod because the sidecar is hidden. You should refresh the deployment for the controller to inject the sidecar.

9. Inject the envoy proxy for the blue app.

   `kubectl rollout restart deployment blue -n bgns`

10. Inject the envoy proxy for the green app.

    `kubectl rollout restart deployment green -n bgns`

11. Verify the envoy proxy injection.

    `kubectl get pod -n bgns`

    You should find two running pods instead of one.

    ```
    NAME                         READY   STATUS     RESTARTS   AGE
    blue-6f4d59c79d-bxgnp        2/2     Running    0          30s
    green-78b894859f-x4j8l       2/2     Running    0          24s
    ```

12. Deploy the nodes and the virtual services.

    `Kubectl apply -f appmeshGB/4-virtualize`

CHAPTER 20   SERVICE MESH AND VPC LATTICE

Testing the AB Services

1. Get pods.

    kubectl get pod -n bgns

2. Log in to the blue application.

    kubectl exec -it blue-6f4d59c79d-bxgnp -n bgns -- /bin/bash

    You should see the following:

    Defaulted container "blue" out of: blue, envoy, proxyinit (init)
    root@blue-6f4d59c79d-bxgnp:/code#

3. Call the application service from blue.

    curl -v http://green.bgns.svc.cluster.local:8081

    You should see {"Hello":"green"}.

4. Repeat the same for the green application.

    curl -v http://blue.bgns.svc.cluster.local:8080

5. You should see {"Hello":"blue"}.

We demonstrated that we could use App Mesh to make blue and green services communicate with each other through envoy proxies as explained before. The blue microservice can be called the green microservice and vice versa.

CHAPTER 20 SERVICE MESH AND VPC LATTICE

The Three-Application Scenario

You can experiment with three services. You can find the code in the appmeshGBR folder. Follow the same steps as above to deploy the App Mesh and access the services as before. Service G can call services B and R, service B can call services G and R, and service R can call services B and G.

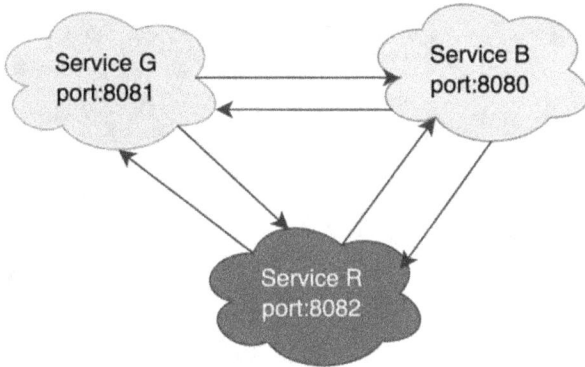

Figure 20-10. *Three-application scenario*

App Mesh with Load Balancer Implementation

We want to deploy a load balancer in front of the App Mesh so that the end user can access the microservices through a browser. The architecture for this implementation is shown in Figure 20-11.

563

Chapter 20 Service Mesh and VPC Lattice

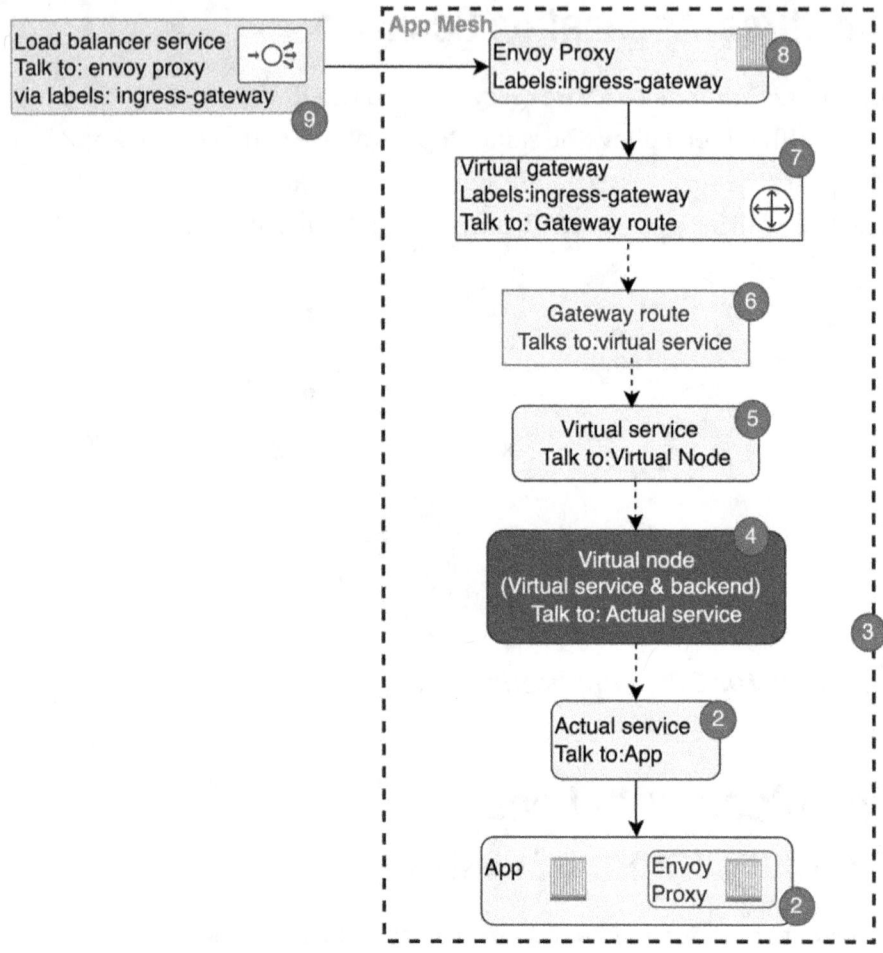

Figure 20-11. *Adding load balancer to App Mesh*

In Figure 20-11, we introduce an ingress gateway and a stand-alone envoy proxy on top of the virtual gateway. We then connected the external load balancer to the envoy proxy of the gateway.

The App Mesh implementation is counterintuitive to the App Mesh communication shown in Figure 20-9. You often start from the bottom up with the mesh and end with the load balancer. You should find the manifest in chapter20/appmeshLB folder.

CHAPTER 20 SERVICE MESH AND VPC LATTICE

1. Run the script in the folder to create the load balancer controller.

2. We create a new namespace for the load balancer App Mesh:

   ```
   kind: Namespace
   apiVersion: v1
   metadata:
    name: lbns
    labels:
       name: lbns
   ```

3. We deploy the blue application and the actual service with the following deployment:

   ```
   ---
   apiVersion: apps/v1
   kind: Deployment
   metadata:
     namespace: lbns
     name: blue
   spec:
     selector:
       matchLabels:
         app: blue
     replicas: 1
     template:
       metadata:
         labels:
           app: blue
       spec:
         containers:
         - image: cloudmanly/eks:blueapp
   ```

```
            imagePullPolicy: Always
            name: blue
            ports:
            - containerPort: 8080
---
apiVersion: v1
kind: Service
metadata:
  namespace: lbns
  name: blue
  labels:
    app: blue
spec:
  ports:
    - port: 8080
      protocol: TCP
  selector:
    app: blue
```

4. We create the mesh (lbmesh) with the following manifest:

```
apiVersion: appmesh.k8s.aws/v1beta2
kind: Mesh
metadata:
  name: lbmesh
spec:
  namespaceSelector:
    matchLabels:
      mesh: lbmesh
---
apiVersion: v1
```

```
      kind: Namespace
      metadata:
        name: lbns
        labels:
          mesh: lbmesh
          gateway: ingress-gateway
          appmesh.k8s.aws/sidecarInjectorWebhook: enabled
```

5. Create a virtual node for the actual service. The backend for the virtual node is the blue virtual service. The virtual node has the same name as the actual service.

```
      ---
      apiVersion: appmesh.k8s.aws/v1beta2
      kind: VirtualNode
      metadata:
        name: blue
        namespace: lbns
      spec:
        podSelector:
          matchLabels:
              app: blue
        listeners:
          - portMapping:
              port: 8080
              protocol: http
            healthCheck:
              protocol: http
              path: '/'
              healthyThreshold: 2
              unhealthyThreshold: 2
```

```
              timeoutMillis: 2000
              intervalMillis: 5000
        backends:
          - virtualService:
              virtualServiceRef:
                  namespace: lbns
                  name: blue
        serviceDiscovery:
          dns:
            hostname: blue.lbns.svc.cluster.local
```

6. Create a virtual service to reference the virtual nodes.

```
---
apiVersion: appmesh.k8s.aws/v1beta2
kind: VirtualService
metadata:
  name: blue
  namespace: lbns
  labels:
      app: blue
spec:
  awsName: blue.lbns.svc.cluster.local
  provider:
    virtualNode:
      virtualNodeRef:
        name: blue
        namespace: lbns
#dummy service
---
apiVersion: v1
```

```yaml
kind: Service
metadata:
  name: blue
  namespace: lbns
  labels:
    app: blue
spec:
  ports:
  - port: 8080
    name: http
  selector:
    app: blue
```

7. Create a gateway route to route the traffic to the virtual service.

```yaml
---
apiVersion: appmesh.k8s.aws/v1beta2
kind: GatewayRoute
metadata:
  name: app-route
  namespace: lbns
spec:
  httpRoute:
    match:
      prefix: "/"
    action:
      target:
        port: 8080
        virtualService:
          virtualServiceRef:
            name: blue
            namespace: lbns
```

CHAPTER 20   SERVICE MESH AND VPC LATTICE

8. Create a virtual gateway to connect the envoy proxy to the App Mesh.

   ```
   ---
   apiVersion: appmesh.k8s.aws/v1beta2
   kind: VirtualGateway
   metadata:
     name: ingress-gateway
     namespace: lbns
   spec:
     namespaceSelector:
       matchLabels:
         gateway: ingress-gateway
     podSelector:
       matchLabels:
         app: ingress-gateway
     listeners:
       - portMapping:
           port: 8088
           protocol: http
   ```

9. Create an envoy proxy to forward traffic from the load balancer to the virtual gateway. The envoy proxy must carry the **virtual-gateway** label. Otherwise, you may get this error message "admission webhook "mpod.appmesh.k8s.aws" denied the request: sidecarInject enabled but no **matching VirtualNode or VirtualGateway found**." You should run **kubectl get virtualgateway -n lbns** to find the arn of the virtual gateway and use it to configure the stand-alone envoy proxy. This is already done for you in the code below, but you should replace the account ID with yours:

CHAPTER 20 SERVICE MESH AND VPC LATTICE

```
#run this command to export ACCOUNT_ID=$(aws sts get-caller-identity --query "Account" --output text)
---
apiVersion: apps/v1
kind: Deployment
metadata:
  name: standalone-envoy-proxy
  namespace: lbns
  labels:
    app: ingress-gateway
spec:
    replicas: 2
    selector:
     matchLabels:
        app: ingress-gateway
    template:
     metadata:
      labels:
        app: ingress-gateway
     spec:
      containers:
        - name: envoy #name must be envoy
          image: 840364872350.dkr.ecr.us-east-1.amazonaws.com/aws-appmesh-envoy:v1.27.2.0-prod
          env:
            - name: APPMESH_RESOURCE_ARN
              value: arn:aws:appmesh:us-east-1:$ACCOUNT_ID:mesh/pod-service-mesh/virtualGateway/ingress-gateway_lbns
```

```
          - name: ENVOY_LOG_LEVEL
            value: "debug"
        ports:
          - containerPort: 8088
```

10. Create the load balancer to connect to the stand-alone envoy proxy.

    ```
    ---
    apiVersion: v1
    kind: Service
    metadata:
      name: external-nlb-svc
      namespace: lbns
      annotations:
        service.beta.kubernetes.io/aws-load-balancer-type:
        external
        service.beta.kubernetes.io/aws-load-balancer-nlb-
        target-type: ip
        service.beta.kubernetes.io/aws-load-balancer-
        scheme: internet-facing
    spec:
      ports:
        - port: 80
          targetPort: 8088
          protocol: TCP
      type: LoadBalancer
      loadBalancerClass: service.k8s.aws/nlb
      selector:

        app: ingress-gateway
    ```

App Mesh with Load Balancer Deployment

Find the code in the chapter20/appmeshLB folder.

1. You may delete the old App Mesh deployment.
2. Install the load balancer controller.

   ./appmeshLB/1-script/appmesh.sh

3. Create the mesh and the applications.

   kubectl apply -f appmeshLB/2-mesh

4. Roll out the deployment to inject the sidecar.

   ./appmeshLB/3-script/rollout.sh

5. Create nodes and virtual services.

   kubectl apply -f appmeshLB/4-virtualizer

6. Create a gateway and load balancer.

   kubectl apply -f appmeshLB/5-load-balancer

Testing the AB Services

1. Get services.

   kubectl get svc -n lbns

   You should find the URL of the load balancer.

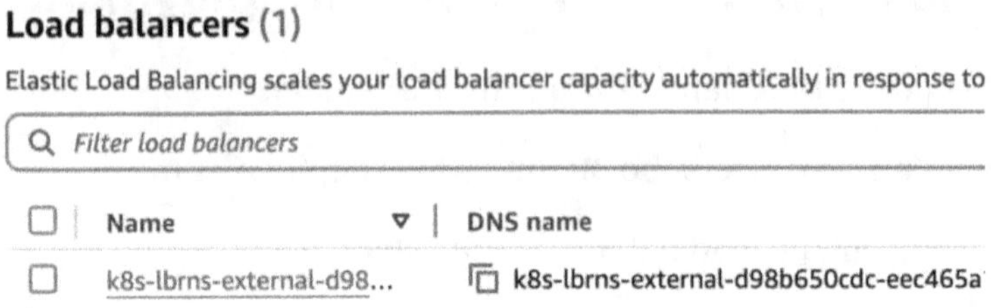

Load balancers (1)

Elastic Load Balancing scales your load balancer capacity automatically in response to

	Name	▽	DNS name
☐	k8s-lbrns-external-d98...		k8s-lbrns-external-d98b650cdc-eec465a

Figure 20-12. Load balancer console

2. Go to the EC2 console and to the load balancer. Refresh it and wait for it to be active.

3. Connect to the blue application with curl or with your browser.

```
curl -v URL of the load balancer
```

App Mesh Traffic Management Implementation

We introduce additional steps to demonstrate App Mesh traffic management – specifically, blue/green deployment strategy. This requires a router that will distribute traffic to different versions of an application, the old and the new. We represent the outdated version of the application by the blue app and the new application version by the green app.

The traffic will come from the load balancer to the virtual service of the virtual router via the virtual gateway as shown in Figure 20-13. The router determines the weight or the percentage of traffic that should be forwarded to the different versions of the application. For example, you can send 20% of the traffic to the latest version of the application and 80% to the outdated version of the application until you are comfortable switching all traffic to the latest version of the application.

CHAPTER 20 SERVICE MESH AND VPC LATTICE

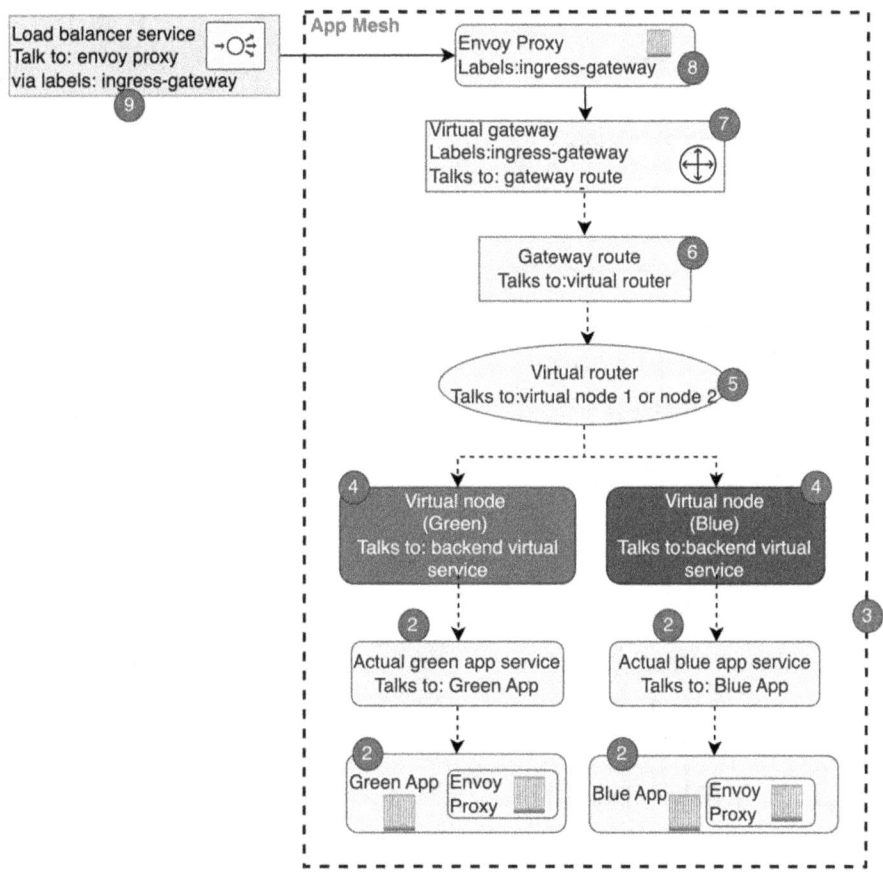

Figure 20-13. *Adding virtual router to App Mesh*

The actual service forwards the traffic to the application as routed by the router. Again, we start from the bottom of the stack to the top of the stack.

1. Create the namespace for the App Mesh.

    ```
    kind: Namespace
    apiVersion: v1
    ```

```
    metadata:
      name: lbrns
      labels:
        name: lbrns
```

2. Deploy the blue and green apps and their services.

```
---
apiVersion: apps/v1
kind: Deployment
metadata:
  namespace: lbrns
  name: blue
spec:
  selector:
    matchLabels:
      app: blue
  replicas: 1
  template:
    metadata:
      labels:
        app: blue
    spec:
      containers:
      - image: cloudmanly/eks:blue
        imagePullPolicy: Always
        name: blue
        ports:
        - containerPort: 8080
---
apiVersion: v1
kind: Service
```

```yaml
metadata:
  namespace: lbrns
  name: blue
  labels:
    app: blue
spec:
  ports:
    - port: 8080
      protocol: TCP
  selector:
    app: blue

---
apiVersion: apps/v1
kind: Deployment
metadata:
  namespace: lbrns
  name: green
spec:
  selector:
    matchLabels:
      app: green
  replicas: 1
  template:
    metadata:
      labels:
        app: green
    spec:
      containers:
        - image: cloudmanly/eks:green
          imagePullPolicy: Always
          name: green
```

```
        ports:
        - containerPort: 8081
---
apiVersion: v1
kind: Service
metadata:
  namespace: lbrns
  name: green
  labels:
    app: green
spec:
  ports:
    - port: 8081
      protocol: TCP
  selector:
    app: green
```

3. Create a mesh and inject the sidecar container in the lbrns namespace.

```
apiVersion: appmesh.k8s.aws/v1beta2
kind: Mesh
metadata:
  name: lbrmesh
spec:
  namespaceSelector:
    matchLabels:
      mesh: lbrmesh
---
apiVersion: v1
kind: Namespace
```

CHAPTER 20 SERVICE MESH AND VPC LATTICE

```
metadata:
  name: lbrns
  labels:
    mesh: lbrmesh
    gateway: ingress-gateway

    appmesh.k8s.aws/sidecarInjectorWebhook: enabled
```

4. Create nodes for the blue and the green apps.

```
---
apiVersion: appmesh.k8s.aws/v1beta2
kind: VirtualNode
metadata:
  name: blue
  namespace: lbrns
spec:
  podSelector:
    matchLabels:
        app: blue
  listeners:
    - portMapping:
        port: 8080
        protocol: http
      healthCheck:
        protocol: http
        path: '/'
        healthyThreshold: 2
        unhealthyThreshold: 2
        timeoutMillis: 2000
        intervalMillis: 5000
```

```yaml
    serviceDiscovery:
      dns:
        hostname: blue.lbrns.svc.cluster.local
---
apiVersion: appmesh.k8s.aws/v1beta2
kind: VirtualNode
metadata:
  name: green
  namespace: lbrns
spec:
  podSelector:
    matchLabels:
      app: green
  listeners:
    - portMapping:
        port: 8081
        protocol: http
      healthCheck:
        protocol: http
        path: '/'
        healthyThreshold: 2
        unhealthyThreshold: 2
        timeoutMillis: 2000
        intervalMillis: 5000
  serviceDiscovery:
    dns:
      hostname: green.lbrns.svc.cluster.local
```

Create virtual services for the blue and the green apps.

```
---
apiVersion: appmesh.k8s.aws/v1beta2
kind: VirtualService
metadata:
  name: blue
  namespace: lbrns
  labels:
    app: blue
spec:
  awsName: blue.lbrns.svc.cluster.local
  provider:
    virtualNode:
      virtualNodeRef:
        name: blue
        namespace: lbrns

#dummy CoreDNS service
---
apiVersion: v1
kind: Service
metadata:
  name: blue
  namespace: lbrns
  labels:
    app: blue
spec:
  ports:
  - port: 8080
    name: http
  selector:
    app: blue
```

```yaml
---
apiVersion: appmesh.k8s.aws/v1beta2
kind: VirtualService
metadata:
  name: green
  namespace: lbrns
  labels:
      app: green
spec:
  awsName: green.lbrns.svc.cluster.local
  provider:
    virtualNode:
      virtualNodeRef:
        name: green
        namespace: lbrns

#dummy CoreDNS service
---
apiVersion: v1
kind: Service
metadata:
  name: green
  namespace: lbrns
  labels:
    app: green
spec:
  ports:
  - port: 8081
    name: http
  selector:
    app: green
```

CHAPTER 20 SERVICE MESH AND VPC LATTICE

5. Create a virtual router.

   ```
   ---
   apiVersion: appmesh.k8s.aws/v1beta2
   kind: VirtualRouter
   metadata:
     namespace: lbrns
     name: app-router
   spec:
     listeners:
       - portMapping:
           port: 8085
           protocol: http
     routes:
       - name: app-route
         httpRoute:
           match:
             prefix: '/'
           action:
             weightedTargets:
               - virtualNodeRef:
                   name: green
                 weight: 50
                 port: 8081
               - virtualNodeRef:
                   name: blue
                 weight: 50
                 port: 8080
   ```

   The virtual router will route 50% of the traffic to the green app and the other 50% to the blue app. You can change the percentage according to your requirements.

Create a virtual service for the router.

```
---
apiVersion: appmesh.k8s.aws/v1beta2
kind: VirtualService
metadata:
  namespace: lbrns
  name: router-v-svc
spec:
  awsName: router-v-svc.lbrns.svc.cluster.local
  provider:
    virtualRouter:
      virtualRouterRef:
        name: app-router

#dummy coredns service
---
apiVersion: v1
kind: Service
metadata:
  name:  router-v-svc
  namespace: lbrns
  labels:
    app: router-v-svc
spec:
  ports:
    - port: 8085
      name: http
  selector:
    app: router-v-svc
```

CHAPTER 20 SERVICE MESH AND VPC LATTICE

6. Create a gateway route.

    ```
    ---
    apiVersion: appmesh.k8s.aws/v1beta2
    kind: GatewayRoute
    metadata:
      name: app-route
      namespace: lbrns
    spec:
      httpRoute:
        match:
          prefix: "/"
        action:
          target:
            port: 8085
            virtualService:
              virtualServiceRef:
                name: router-v-svc
                namespace: lbrns
    ```

7. Create a virtual gateway.

    ```
    ---
    apiVersion: appmesh.k8s.aws/v1beta2
    kind: VirtualGateway
    metadata:
      name: ingress-gateway
      namespace: lbrns
    spec:
      namespaceSelector:
        matchLabels:
          gateway: ingress-gateway
      podSelector:
    ```

```
    matchLabels:
       app: ingress-gateway
 listeners:
 - portMapping:
      port: 8088
      protocol: http
```

8. Create the envoy proxy.

```
---
apiVersion: apps/v1
kind: Deployment
metadata:
  name: standalone-envoy-proxy
  namespace: lbrns
  labels:
    app: ingress-gateway
spec:
   replicas: 1
   selector:
    matchLabels:
       app: ingress-gateway
   template:
    metadata:
     labels:
       app: ingress-gateway
    spec:
     containers:
       - name: envoy #name must be envoy
         image: 840364872350.dkr.ecr.us-
         east-1.amazonaws.com/aws-appmesh-
         envoy:v1.27.2.0-prod
```

```
            env:
            - name: APPMESH_RESOURCE_ARN
              value: arn:aws:appmesh:us-
              east-1:552247556312:mesh/pod-service-mesh/
              virtualGateway/ingress-gateway_lbrns
            - name: ENVOY_LOG_LEVEL
              value: "debug"
            ports:
              - containerPort: 8088
```

9. Create a load balancer.

```
    ---
    apiVersion: v1
    kind: Service
    metadata:
      name: external-nlb-svc
      namespace: lbrns
      annotations:
        service.beta.kubernetes.io/aws-load-balancer-type:
        external
        service.beta.kubernetes.io/aws-load-balancer-nlb-
        target-type: ip
        service.beta.kubernetes.io/aws-load-balancer-
        scheme: internet-facing
    spec:
      ports:
        - port: 80
          targetPort: 8088
          protocol: TCP
```

CHAPTER 20   SERVICE MESH AND VPC LATTICE

```
type: LoadBalancer
loadBalancerClass: service.k8s.aws/nlb
selector:
  app: ingress-gateway
```

10. Deploy controllers (do not run this command if you have run it before).

    `./appmeshLBR/appmesh.sh`

11. Verify if the controller is running.

    ```
    kubectl -n appmesh-system get all
    kubectl get deployment -n kube-system aws-load-balancer-controller
    ```

12. Deploy the mesh.

    `kubectl apply -f appmeshLBR/1-virtualizer`

13. Roll out applications.

    `./appmeshLBR/rollout.sh`

14. Verify the envoy proxy injection.

    `kubectl get pod -n lbrns`

    You should find two running pods instead of one.

NAME	READY	STATUS	RESTARTS	AGE
blue-6f4d59c79d-bxgnp	2/2	Running	0	30s
green-78b894859f-x4j8l	2/2	Running	0	24s

15. Deploy the router and gateway.

    `kubectl apply -f appmeshLBR/4-routing`

16. Verify if actual services are running.

    ```
    kubectl get svc -n lbrns
    ```

17. Verify if pods are running.

    ```
    kubectl get pod -n lbrns
    ```

18. Deploy the backend application. The backend is a stand-alone application for responding to traffic to the virtual service. It is an optional application. We will remove the backend application in the next example.

    ```
    kubectl apply -f appmeshLBR/5-backend
    ```

19. Roll out the backend application.

    ```
    kubectl rollout restart deployment backend -n lbrns
    ```

Testing the Traffic Management App Mesh

1. Get services.

    ```
    kubectl get svc -n lbrns
    ```

2. Wait for the load balancer to deploy and run multiple curl commands against the load balancer.

    ```
    curl -v  k8s-lbrns-external-6c0935a8dc-f14b9dab3cbc8aba.elb.us-east-1.amazonaws.com
    ```

You should see 50% of the traffic to the green application and another 50% to the blue application.

CHAPTER 20   SERVICE MESH AND VPC LATTICE

Logging with App Mesh

Logging is one of the pillars of observability. A log is a record of events occurring within a computer network or a system. It is usually composed of timestamped entries with each entry containing information related to a specific event that has occurred within the system or the network.[11]

Logs are useful for debugging, troubleshooting, security investigations, performance monitoring, and optimization. They are also useful for security incident investigation and postmortem analysis.

Logs are also important for establishing baselines, identifying operational trends, and supporting internal investigations, including audit and forensic analysis. Logs come from several sources, including software, applications, systems, networks, and devices.

Software Log Sources

Software logs may come from device drivers, databases, web browsers, and office suites. Others may come from security software such as antimalware, intrusion detection, and prevention systems.

Additionally, security-related software logs may come from remote access software such as Virtual Private Networks (VPNs), web proxies, firewalls, vulnerability management, and identity and access management software.

Operating System Log Sources

Operating systems (OSs) are another source of logs. They record system events and user actions that include system shutdown, system restart, service starting, and service started. Typically, operating systems record

---

[11] NIST, Guide to computer security logs, SP 800-92

failed and successful events alongside custom events specified by an administrator. They may also log information from security software and other software running on the platform.

Audit Logs

Audit logs on the other hand record security events related to end users. Audit logs capture events such as successful and failed authentication attempts, access to files, and security policy changes. Other events include account changes which may cover account creation, deletion, privilege assignment, and usages.

Application Log Sources

Applications assist users to execute specific tasks on a device or a system. It is therefore common to find audit logs which record successful and failed authentication attempts, account changes, and privilege access.

In addition, applications may record client requests and server responses, user interactions, and business transactions. Specifically, an application can capture each user request, email address, sender, recipients, subject name, and URLs.

Applications also log usage information and operational actions covering application startup and shutdown, application failures, errors, and major application configuration changes.

Network Log Sources

The last log source is networks. Networks can generate flow logs and network traffic for content inspection, threat monitoring, and troubleshooting.

Fluent Bit is an open source and multi-platform log processor and forwarder. It can collect data logs from diverse sources and unify and send them to different destinations such as CloudWatch Logs.[12]

It is fully compatible with Docker and Kubernetes environments. It uses a daemon set to send container logs from an EKS cluster to CloudWatch Logs for log storage and analytics.

Fluent Bit default log sources include application, host, and data plane and performance. You can find them in the following locations on the EKS nodes:

- /aws/containerinsights/Cluster_Name/application
- /aws/containerinsights/Cluster_Name/host
- /aws/containerinsights/Cluster_Name/dataplane
- /aws/containerinsights/Cluster_Name/performance

The application log group or source stores the stdout logs of containers. Containers write their logs to the stdout, and they are stored in the application log group.

You can also find additional logs in the following log sources:

- /var/log/containers
- /var/log/dmesg
- /var/log/secure
- /var/log/messages
- /var/log/journal

The /var/log/journal log source contains logs for kubelet.service, kubeproxy.service, and docker.service.

---

[12] https://aws.amazon.com/blogs/containers/fluent-bit-integration-in-cloudwatch-container-insights-for-eks/

Changes to Terraform Configuration

We want to use CloudWatch to store and process logs from the App Mesh. The App Mesh will need permission to access the CloudWatch service. You add the CloudWatchAgentServerPolicy policy to the worker nodes to grant the permission. This is already included in the chapter20-logging code.

```
#AWS cloud watch - terraform
resource "aws_iam_role_policy_attachment" "aws_cloudwatch-agent" {
  policy_arn = "arn:aws:iam::aws:policy/
  CloudWatchAgentServerPolicy"
  role       = aws_iam_role.worker_nodes_role.name
}
```

The next change is the CloudWatch addon. The addon can collect and analyze container logs for the cluster. We enable container insight with the following addon:

```
resource "aws_eks_addon" "cloudwatch-addon" {
  addon_name   = "amazon-cloudwatch-observability"
  cluster_name = var.cluster_name
}
```

CloudWatch container insight collects, aggregates, and summarizes metrics and logs from your containerized applications and microservices.[13]

Logging Configuration

We will collect containers with Fluent Bit and send them to CloudWatch for analysis. Fluent Bit is an open source and multi-platform log processor and forwarder that allows you to collect data and logs from various

---

[13] https://docs.aws.amazon.com/AmazonECS/latest/developerguide/cloudwatch-container-insights.html

CHAPTER 20 SERVICE MESH AND VPC LATTICE

sources, including docker containers, and unify and send them to different destinations, including CloudWatch Logs. With Fluent Bit, you can send container logs from your EKS clusters to CloudWatch Logs for log storage and analytics.[14] You can configure Fluent Bit to collect logs as follows:

1. Set an environment variable for Fluent Bit.

    ```
    CLUSTER_NAME="appmesh-cluster"
    export AWS_REGION=$(aws ec2 describe-availability-
    zones --output text --query 'AvailabilityZones[0].
    [RegionName]')
    export ACCOUNT_ID=$(aws sts get-caller-identity --query
    "Account" --output text)
    FluentBitHttpPort='2020'
    FluentBitReadFromHead='Off'
    [[ ${FluentBitReadFromHead} = 'On' ]] &&
    FluentBitReadFromTail='Off'|| FluentBitReadFromTail='On'
    [[ -z ${FluentBitHttpPort} ]]
    && FluentBitHttpServer='Off' ||
    FluentBitHttpServer='On'Create
    ```

2. Create a Config map for Fluent Bit.

    ```
    Kubectl create configmap fluent-bit-cluster-info \
    --from-literal=cluster.name=${CLUSTER_NAME \
    --from-literal=http.server=${FluentBitHttpServer} \
    --from-literal=http.port=${FluentBitHttpPort} \
    --from-literal=read.head=${FluentBitReadFromHead} \
    --from-literal=read.tail=${FluentBitReadFromTail} \
    --from-literal=logs.region=${AWS_REGION} -n amazon-
    cloudwatch-n amazon-cloudwatch
    ```

---

[14] https://aws.amazon.com/blogs/containers/fluent-bit-integration-in-cloudwatch-container-insights-for-eks/

CHAPTER 20   SERVICE MESH AND VPC LATTICE

3. Install Fluent Bit daemonset.

    ```
    kubectl apply -f https://raw.githubusercontent.com/aws-
    samples/amazon-cloudwatch-container-insights/latest/
    k8s-deployment-manifest-templates/deployment-mode/
    daemonset/container-insights-monitoring/fluent-bit/
    fluent-bit.yaml
    ```

4. Validate the installation.

    ```
    kubectl get pods -n amazon-cloudwatch
    NAME                READY   STATUS    RESTARTS   AGE
    fluent-bit-d2gbp    1/1     Running   0          12s
    fluent-bit-x79mp    1/1     Running   0          12s
    ```

5. Add log sections to the App Mesh YAML files. For example, the virtual gateway manifest will include logging as follows:

    ```
    ---
    apiVersion: appmesh.k8s.aws/v1beta2
    kind: VirtualGateway
    metadata:
      name: ingress-gateway
      namespace: lbrns
    spec:
      namespaceSelector:
        matchLabels:
          gateway: ingress-gateway
      podSelector:
        matchLabels:
          app: ingress-gateway
      listeners:
        - portMapping:
    ```

595

```
        port: 8088
        protocol: http
logging:
    accessLog:
        file: path: "/dev/stdout"
```

6. The envoy proxy will become as follows:

```
---
apiVersion: apps/v1
kind: Deployment
metadata:
  name: standalone-envoy-proxy
  namespace: lbrns
  labels:
    app: ingress-gateway
spec:
    replicas: 1
    selector:
     matchLabels:
        app: ingress-gateway
    template:
     metadata:
      labels:
        app: ingress-gateway
     spec:
      containers:
        - name: envoy #name must be envoy
          image: 840364872350.dkr.ecr.us-
          east-1.amazonaws.com/aws-appmesh-
          envoy:v1.27.2.0-prod
          env:
```

CHAPTER 20 SERVICE MESH AND VPC LATTICE

```
- name: APPMESH_RESOURCE_ARN
  value: arn:aws:appmesh:us-
    east-1:552247556312:mesh/pod-service-mesh/
    virtualGateway/ingress-gateway_lbrns
- name: ENVOY_LOG_LEVEL
  value: "debug"
ports:
  - containerPort: 8088
```

You can configure debugging and other logs for the envoy to write to the stdout. These logs are useful for gaining insights into both envoy's communication with App Mesh and service-to-service traffic.

The envoy access log configuration will contain both container and access logs of the envoy proxy. You can switch off the envoy container log if you are interested in exporting only the envoy access logs. You do this by turning off the log as follows:

```
- name: ENVOY_LOG_LEVEL
  value: "off"
```

The above configurations only forward logs to the standard out; you need a cluster log forwarder such as Fluent Bit to send the logs to a storage or a log processing service such as CloudWatch Logs.

App Mesh Deployment

1. Deploy controllers.

   ./appmeshLogging/1-script/appmesh.sh

2. Verify if the App Mesh controller is running.

   kubectl -n appmesh-system get all

You should see the following:

```
NAME                                READY  UP-TO-DATE  AVAILABLE  AGE
deployment.apps/appmesh-controller  1/1    1           1          3m28s

NAME                                          DESIRED  CURRENT  READY  AGE
replicaset.apps/appmesh-controller-5c798f4f6f 1        1        1      3m28s
```

3. Verify if the load balancer controller is running.

   ```
   kubectl get deployment -n kube-system aws-load-balancer-controller
   ```

   The command should output the following:

   ```
   NAME                          READY  UP-TO-DATE  AVAILABLE  AGE
   aws-load-balancer-controller  2/2    2           2          12m
   ```

   Rerun the script in step 1 if any of the controllers fails to deploy.

4. Deploy the mesh.

   ```
   kubectl apply -f appmeshLogging/2-virtualizer
   ```

5. Roll out applications.

   ```
   ./appmeshLogging/3-rollout/rollout.sh
   ```

6. Verify the envoy proxy injection.

   ```
   kubectl get pod -n lbrns
   ```

   You should find two running pods instead of one.

   ```
   NAME                      READY  STATUS   RESTARTS  AGE
   blue-6f4d59c79d-bxgnp     2/2    Running  0         30s
   green-78b894859f-x4j8l    2/2    Running  0         24s
   ...
   ```

7. Deploy the router and gateway.

   `kubectl apply -f appmeshLogging/4-routing`

8. Verify if pods are running.

   `kubectl get pod -n lbrns`

9. Get services.

   `kubectl get svc -n lbrns`

10. Wait for the load balancer to deploy and run multiple curl commands against the load balancer.

    `curl -v k8s-lbrns-external-6c0935a8dc-f14b9dab3cbc8aba.elb.us-east-1.amazonaws.com`

    You should see 50% of the traffic to the green application and another 50% to the blue application.

11. Deploy the Fluent Bit.

    `kubectl apply -f appmeshLogging/5-fluentbit/fleuntbit.sh`

12. Verify if the Fluent Bit is running.

    `kubectl get pods -n amazon-cloudwatch`

Log Review

You see the following log group created in CloudWatch. It takes a few minutes to see all the log groups.

CHAPTER 20 SERVICE MESH AND VPC LATTICE

Log group	Log class	Anomaly d...	Data..
/aws/containerinsights/appmesh-cluster/application	Standard	Configure	-
/aws/containerinsights/appmesh-cluster/dataplane	Standard	Configure	-
/aws/containerinsights/appmesh-cluster/performance	Standard	Configure	-

Figure 20-14. *Log review*

The default retention period is never expired, which means your logs will be retained forever. You can manually delete the logs, or you can set the retention period from the action menu. Select a log group, go to Actions, and select Edit retention and set the date.

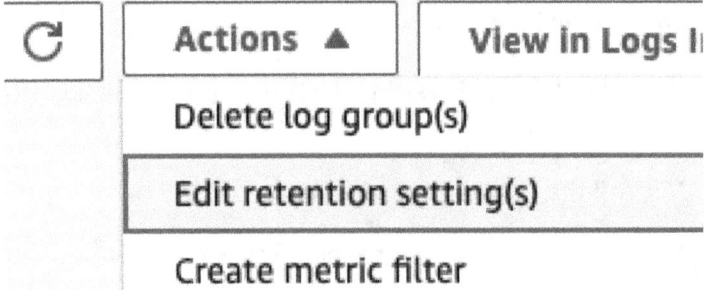

Figure 20-15. *Log review–editing retention settings*

You can use the CloudWatch Trace Map to review nodes and trace errors.

600

CHAPTER 20 SERVICE MESH AND VPC LATTICE

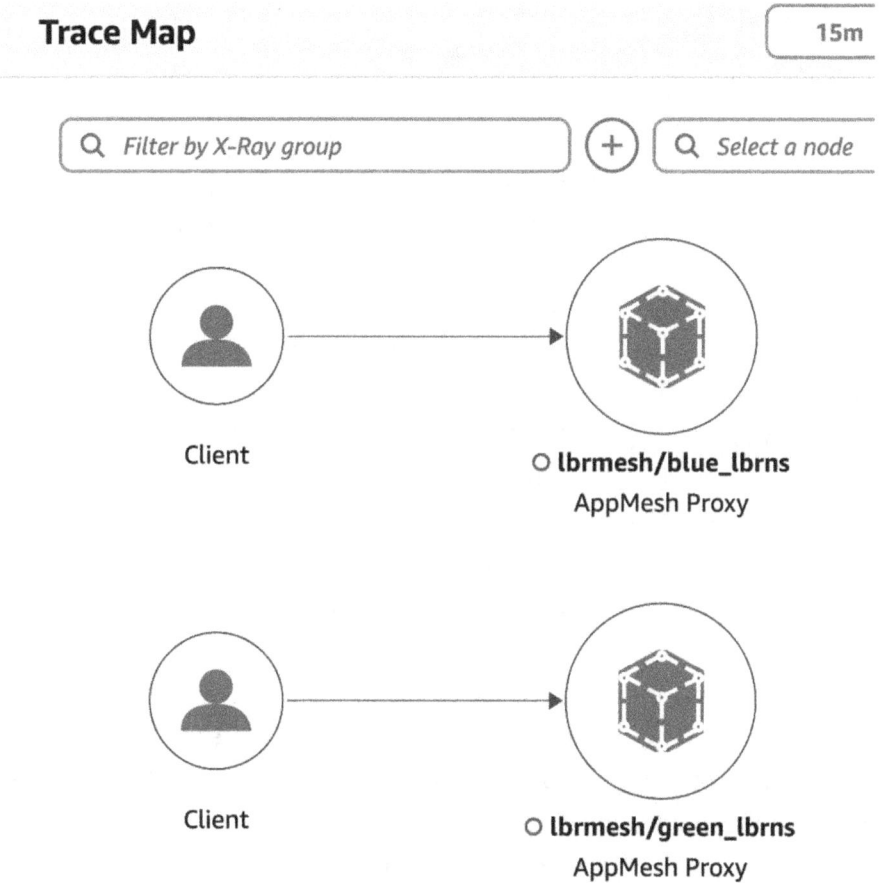

Figure 20-16. *Trace Map*

We want to shorten the discussion here and more on to the next generation App Mesh in the next section. There are a lot we can discuss here, but since App Mesh is soon deprecated, it gives less value to deep dive into observability and security discussions.

CHAPTER 20 SERVICE MESH AND VPC LATTICE

VPC Lattice

Fortunately, or unfortunately, AWS has decided to deprecate App Mesh from 2026 and replace it with Amazon VPC Lattice. The case for VPC Lattice is simplicity and elimination of sidecar or envoy proxy.

AWS is moving away from a mesh network to a lattice network with no envoy proxies running as sidecar containers for traffic routing, resilience, metrics collection, and security. VPC Lattice provides a managed control plane and data plane, eliminating the need for additional components within your pods.[15]

For observability, App Mesh requires you to install the Amazon CloudWatch Agent with Prometheus Metrics Collection, which forwards the metrics to Amazon CloudWatch. No such installations are needed in VPC Lattice. VPC Lattice provides a built-in metrics collector for CloudWatch. This is important since it reduces and simplifies configurations.

Lattice incorporates Load Balancer and AWS Resource Access Manager (RAM) natively, allowing Kubernetes Services to be accessed from the outside world or other AWS resources running in different AWS Accounts. As depicted in Figure 20-17, the load balancer, virtual gateway, and envoy proxy are no longer components for service-to-service communication in AWS VPC Lattice architecture.

---

[15] https://aws.amazon.com/blogs/containers/migrating-from-aws-app-mesh-to-amazon-vpc-lattice/#:~:text=Architecturally%2C%20App%20Mesh%20relies%20on,additional%20components%20within%20your%20Pods

CHAPTER 20 SERVICE MESH AND VPC LATTICE

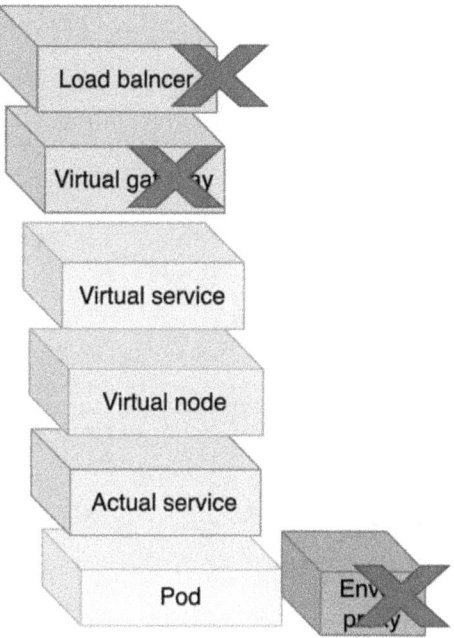

Figure 20-17. *App Mesh and VPC*

Additionally, VPC Lattice supports AWS Identity and Access Management (IAM) authentication through Auth Policies, enabling coarse-grained authorization for your microservices.

CHAPTER 20   SERVICE MESH AND VPC LATTICE

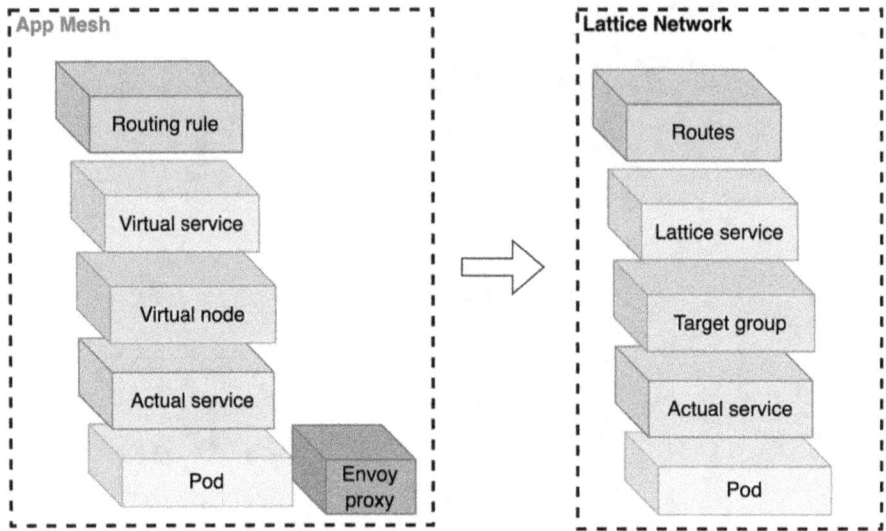

Figure 20-18. App Mesh vs. VPC Lattice

In Figure 20-18, App Mesh and VPC Lattice both provide traffic management and application-aware networking, but they differ in their underlying concepts and architectures. The pod and actual services remain the same for both App Mesh and VPC Lattice. Virtual nodes become the target group, virtual service becomes lattice service, and routing rules become routes.

The service network is a shareable, managed logical grouping that contains services and policy. Service represents an Application Unit with a DNS name and can extend across all computers, instances, containers, and serverless. It is made up of listener, target groups, and target.

The Benefits of VPC Lattice

As an application layer networking service, VPC Lattice gives you a consistent way to connect, secure, and monitor service-to-service communication without any prior networking expertise.[16]

---

[16] https://www.eksworkshop.com/docs/networking/vpc-lattice/

CHAPTER 20   SERVICE MESH AND VPC LATTICE

You can configure network access, traffic management, and network monitoring to enable service-to-service communication consistently across VPCs and accounts, regardless of the underlying compute type, including Kubernetes clusters. VPC Lattice takes care of common networking tasks such as discovering components, routing traffic between individual workloads, and authorizing access, eliminating the need for developers to do this themselves through additional software or code.

Developers can configure policies to define how their applications should communicate without any prior networking expertise.

The primary benefits of using Lattice are

- *Increased productivity*: Lattice handles networking, security, and observability challenges in a uniform way across all compute platforms for developers, letting them focus on building features that matter to their business.

- *Improved security posture*: Lattice enables developers to easily authenticate and secure communication across applications, without the operational overhead of current mechanisms (e.g., certificate management). With Lattice access policies, developers and cloud admins can enforce granular access control. Lattice can also enforce encryption for traffic in-transit, further increasing security posture.

- *Improved application scalability and resilience*: Lattice makes it easy to create a network of deployed applications with rich routing, authentication, authorization, monitoring, and more. Lattice provides all these benefits with no resource overhead on workloads and can support large-scale deployments and many requests per second without adding significant latency.

- *Deployment flexibility with heterogeneous infrastructure*: Lattice provides consistent features across all compute services – EC2, ECS, EKS, Lambda – and can include services living on-premises, allowing organizations the flexibility to choose the optimal compute infrastructure for their use case.

AWS Gateway API Controller

The Gateway API controller must be deployed before you can run VPC Lattice. It is an open source project managed by the K8s networking community. It is a collection of resources that model application networking in K8s.

The components of the gateway control the various VPC Lattice services. The Gateway API supports resources such as GatewayClass which is managed by AWS. AWS integrates Amazon VPC Lattice with the AWS Gateway API controller. When installed in your cluster, the controller watches for the creation of Gateway API resources, such as gateways and routes, and provisions the corresponding Amazon VPC Lattice objects according to the mapping in Figure 20-18.

The Gateway is configured by the cluster operator. It maps to the VPC Lattice service network. The HttpRoute maps to the VPC Lattice service, and services correspond to the VPC Lattice target groups as in Figure 20-18.

CHAPTER 20 SERVICE MESH AND VPC LATTICE

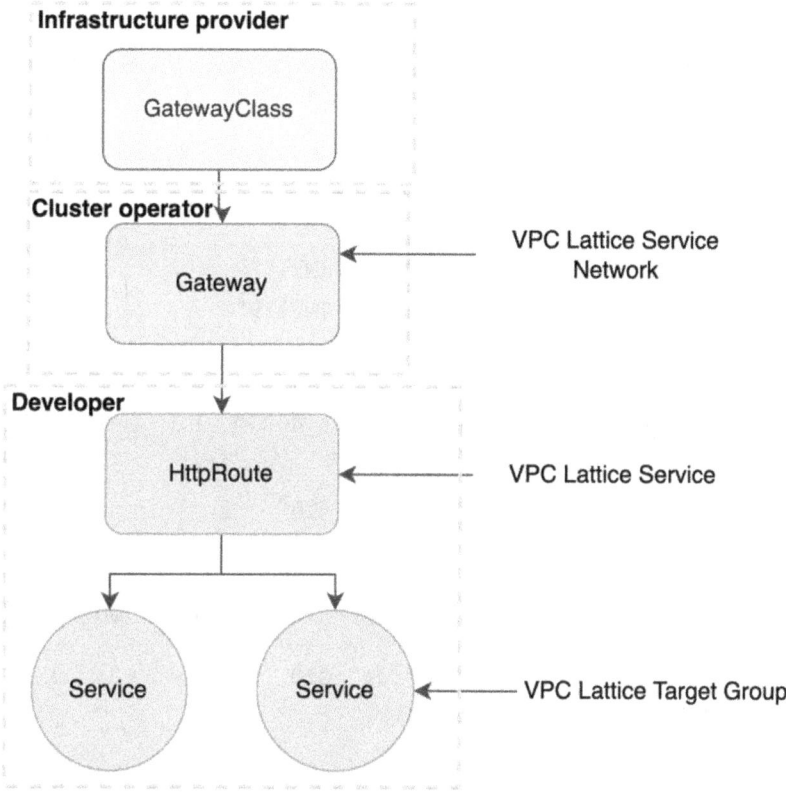

Figure 20-19. Gateway API controller and VPC Lattice

Implementation Changes to Terraform Code

You will find the Terraform code for the VPC Lattice in the chapter20-lattice folder. We added CNI and pod identity addons to the code. We will use the pod identity to create a service account for the gateway controller of the VPC Lattice. The CNI addon performs the usual network functions:

```
resource "aws_eks_addon" "vpc_cni_addon" {
  cluster_name  = var.cluster_name
  addon_name    = "vpc-cni"
  addon_version = "v1.18.5-eksbuild.1"
```

607

CHAPTER 20 SERVICE MESH AND VPC LATTICE

```
  configuration_values = jsonencode({
    env = {
    ENABLE_PREFIX_DELEGATION = "true"
    WARM_PREFIX_TARGET = "1"
    }
  })
  resolve_conflicts_on_create = "OVERWRITE"
  resolve_conflicts_on_update = "OVERWRITE"
}

resource "aws_eks_addon" "pod_idenity_addon" {
  cluster_name = var.cluster_name
  addon_name   = "eks-pod-identity-agent"
}
```

We created a policy for the VPC Lattice controller in the policy.tf file:

```
resource "aws_iam_policy" "vpc_lattice" {
 name = "VPCLatticeControllerIAMPolicy"
 path        = "/"
 description = "VPC Lattice Controller IAM Policy "
 policy = <<POLICY
{
    "Version": "2012-10-17",
    "Statement": [
        {
            "Effect": "Allow",
            "Action": [
                "vpc-lattice:*",
                "ec2:DescribeVpcs",
                "ec2:DescribeSubnets",
                "ec2:DescribeTags",
                "ec2:DescribeSecurityGroups",
```

CHAPTER 20 SERVICE MESH AND VPC LATTICE

```
                "logs:CreateLogDelivery",
                "logs:GetLogDelivery",
                "logs:DescribeLogGroups",
                "logs:PutResourcePolicy",
                "logs:DescribeResourcePolicies",
                "logs:UpdateLogDelivery",
                "logs:DeleteLogDelivery",
                "logs:ListLogDeliveries",
                "tag:GetResources",
                "firehose:TagDeliveryStream",
                "s3:GetBucketPolicy",
                "s3:PutBucketPolicy"
            ],
            "Resource": "*"
        },
        {
            "Effect" : "Allow",
            "Action" : "iam:CreateServiceLinkedRole",
            "Resource" : "arn:aws:iam::*:role/aws-
            service-role/vpc-lattice.amazonaws.com/
            AWSServiceRoleForVpcLattice",
            "Condition" : {
                "StringLike" : {
                    "iam:AWSServiceName" : "vpc-lattice.
                    amazonaws.com"
                }
            }
        },
        {
            "Effect" : "Allow",
            "Action" : "iam:CreateServiceLinkedRole",
```

```
                "Resource" : "arn:aws:iam::*:role/aws-
                service-role/delivery.logs.amazonaws.com/
                AWSServiceRoleForLogDelivery",
                "Condition" : {
                    "StringLike" : {
                        "iam:AWSServiceName" : "delivery.logs.
                        amazonaws.com"
                    }
                }
            }
        ]
    }
 POLICY
 }
```

Attach the policy to the pod identity role and create the gateway controller service account:

```
data "aws_iam_policy_document" "assume_role" {
  statement {
    effect = "Allow"
    principals {
      type        = "Service"
      identifiers = ["pods.eks.amazonaws.com"]
    }
    actions = [
      "sts:AssumeRole",
      "sts:TagSession"
    ]
  }
}
```

```
resource "aws_iam_role" "pod_identity_role" {
  name                = "pod-identity-vpc-lattice-role"
  assume_role_policy = data.aws_iam_policy_document.assume_
  role.json
}

resource "aws_iam_role_policy_attachment" "vpc_lattice_gateway_
controller_policy" {
  policy_arn = aws_iam_policy.vpc_lattice.arn
  role       = aws_iam_role.pod_identity_role.name
}

resource "aws_eks_pod_identity_association" "gateway_
controller_sa" {
  cluster_name    = var.cluster_name
  namespace       = "aws-application-networking-system"
  service_account = "gateway-api-controller"
  role_arn        = aws_iam_role.pod_identity_role.arn
}
```

VPC Lattice Configuration for Blue-Green Deployment

The configuration file is in the chapter20-lattice/scripts folder.

1. Install the gateway controller.

    ./1-scripts/1-install-controller.sh

2. Create a VPC Lattice network.

    ./1-scripts/2-create-vpc-lattice.sh

CHAPTER 20   SERVICE MESH AND VPC LATTICE

3. Create VPC Lattice services.

./1-scripts/3-create-service.sh

The service script creates the gateway class:

```
# Create a new Gateway Class for AWS VPC lattice provider
apiVersion: gateway.networking.k8s.io/v1beta1
kind: GatewayClass
metadata:
  name: amazon-vpc-lattice
spec:
  controllerName: application-networking.k8s.aws/gateway-api-controller
```

The service gateway listens on port 80:

```
apiVersion: gateway.networking.k8s.io/v1beta1
kind: Gateway
metadata:
  name: color-app
spec:
  gatewayClassName: amazon-vpc-lattice
  listeners:
  - name: http
    protocol: HTTP
    port: 80
```

The routes:

```
apiVersion: gateway.networking.k8s.io/v1beta1
kind: HTTPRoute
metadata:
  name: color
```

```
spec:
  parentRefs:
  - name: color-app
    sectionName: http
  rules:
  - backendRefs:
    - name: blue
      kind: Service
      port: 80
      weight: 50
    - name: green
      kind: Service
      port: 80
      weight: 50
```

The applications and microservices:

```
---
apiVersion: apps/v1
kind: Deployment
metadata:
  name: blue
spec:
  selector:
    matchLabels:
      app: blue
  replicas: 1
  template:
    metadata:
      labels:
        app: blue
      spec:
```

```
      containers:
      - image: cloudmanly/eks:blue
        imagePullPolicy: Always
        name: blue
        ports:
        - containerPort: 8080
        env:
        - name: PodName
          value: "Blue pod"
---
apiVersion: v1
kind: Service
metadata:
  name: blue
  labels:
    app: blue
spec:
  ports:
    - port: 80
      protocol: TCP
      targetPort: 8080
  selector:
    app: blue
---
apiVersion: apps/v1
kind: Deployment
metadata:
  name: green
spec:
  selector:
    matchLabels:
      app: green
```

```
    replicas: 1
    template:
       metadata:
       labels:
       app: green
       spec:
       containers:
       - image: cloudmanly/eks:green
         imagePullPolicy: Always
         name: green
         ports:
         - containerPort: 8080
         env:
         - name: PodName
             value: "green pod"
---

apiVersion: v1
kind: Service
metadata:
   name: green
   labels:
      app: green
spec:
   ports:
      - port: 80
        protocol: TCP
        targetPort: 8081
      selector:
        app: green
```

Testing

Retrieve the service DNS from the VPC Lattice console and use it to test the deployment.

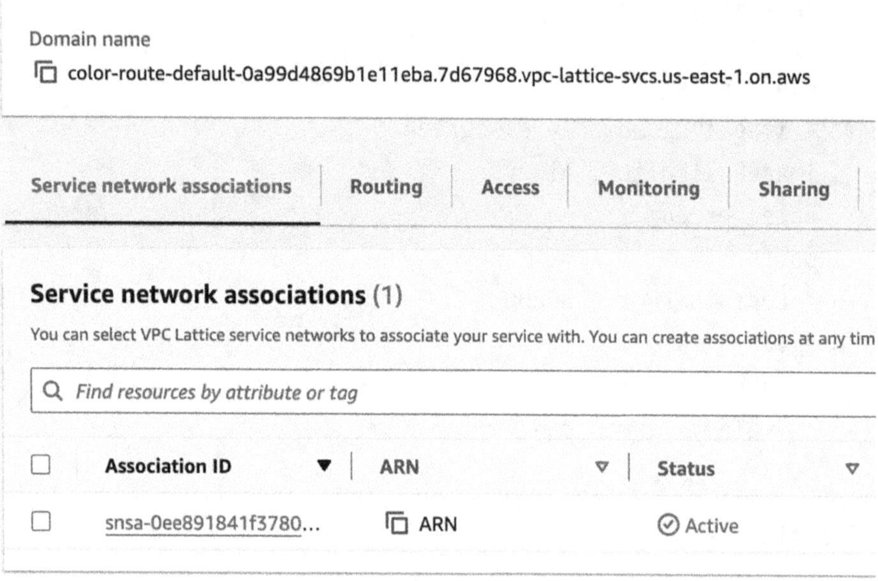

Figure 20-20. Service network association

Alternatively, retrieve the VPC Lattice service DNS with the following command:

```
export COLORAPP_DNS="http://$(kubectl get httproute color-route -o json | jq -r '.metadata.annotations["application-networking.k8s.aws/lattice-assigned-domain-name"]')"
echo "Print out Color app Lattice DNS is $COLORAPP_DNS"
```

Test the blue and green deployment:

```
kubectl exec deploy/green -- curl -s $COLORAPP_DNS
```

Run the command multiple times. You should see 50% output for each application or service.

Istio Service Mesh

Istio is an open source service mesh; unlike the proprietary AWS App Mesh, Istio is cloud agnostic. It has less complex architecture and is easy to implement. Since AWS will soon deprecate App Mesh, customers who want to stick to the good old service mesh may fall on Istio as a natural alternative.

Figure 20-21 shows the basic Istio service mesh components. The components have no virtual gateway and virtual nodes.

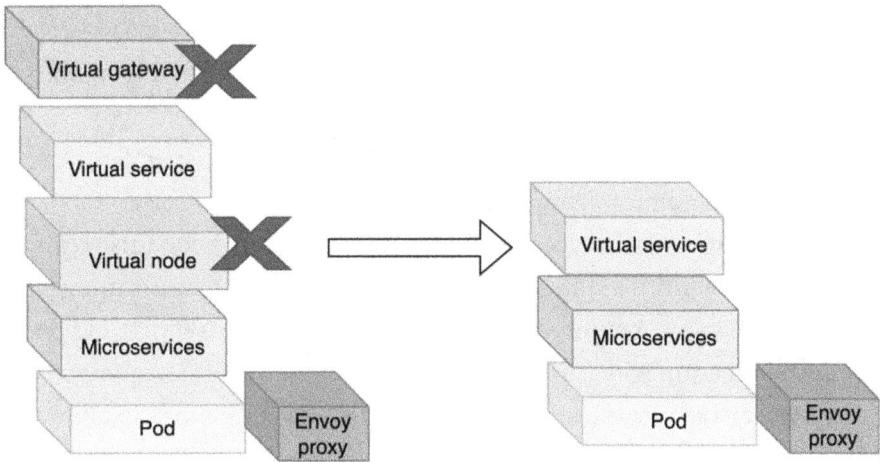

Figure 20-21. Basic Istio service mesh components

Figure 20-21 depicts the architecture of two microservices (A and B) and how they can communicate over an Istio service mesh. The traffic flow is like the App Mesh service mesh except that Istio's version is more simplified.

CHAPTER 20   SERVICE MESH AND VPC LATTICE

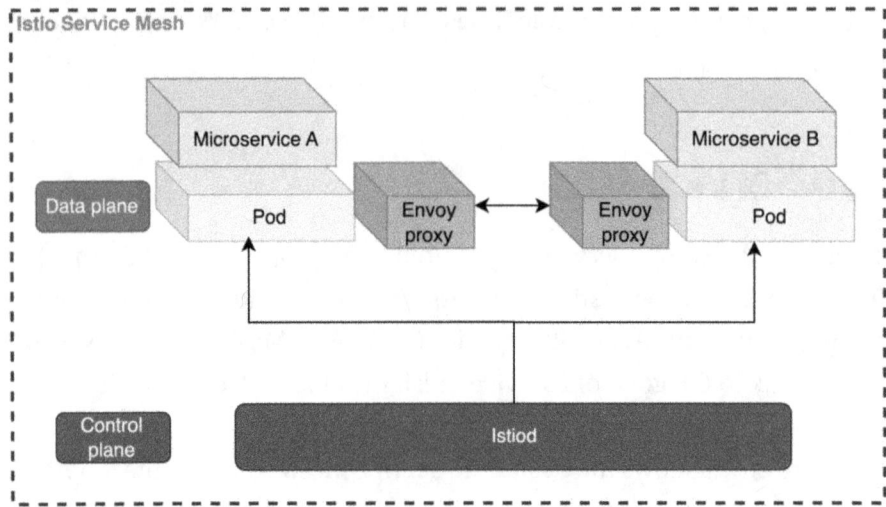

Figure 20-22. *Istio service mesh architecture*

According to the Istio documentation,[17] the functions of the Istiod are service discovery and certificate management. It converts high-level routing rules that control traffic behavior into envoy-specific configurations and propagates them to the sidecars at runtime.

Istiod abstracts platform-specific service discovery mechanisms and synthesizes them into a standard format that any sidecar conforming with the envoy API can consume. It enables strong service-to-service and end-user authentication with built-in identity and credential management. It acts as a certificate authority (CA) and generates certificates to allow secure mTLS communication in the data plane.

You can use Istiod to configure Istio envoy proxies to handle routing, security, and telemetry data and make service mesh architecture resilient.

---

[17] https://istio.io/latest/docs/ops/deployment/architecture/

CHAPTER 20   SERVICE MESH AND VPC LATTICE

Istio Implementation

You should find the Istio cluster in the chapter20-istio folder. You may follow these steps to install and deploy Istio service mesh:

1. Deploy the Istio cluster in the folder chapter20-istio.

   ```
   terraform init
   terraform apply
   ```

2. Use the installation guide from Istio to install the istioctl[18] tool.

3. Run the istio.sh script to install the Istio controller on your EKS cluster.

   ```
   #!/bin/bash
   CLUSTER_NAME="istio-cluster"
   export AWS_REGION=$(aws ec2 describe-availability-zones --output text --query 'AvailabilityZones[0].[RegionName]')
   echo "Update context"
   echo "-------------------------------"
   aws eks update-kubeconfig \
       --name ${CLUSTER_NAME} \
       --region ${AWS_REGION}
   kubectl create ns istio-system
   istioctl install --set profile=demo -y
   kubectl get pod -n istio-system
   kubectl -n appmesh-system get all
   ```

---

[18] https://istio.io/latest/docs/setup/install/istioctl/

CHAPTER 20 SERVICE MESH AND VPC LATTICE

You should see the following output:

```
NAME                                      READY   STATUS    RESTARTS   AGE
istio-egressgateway-7c78d99db7-xdd8r      1/1     Running   0          9s
istio-ingressgateway-78c97cd8c9-fm6ks     1/1     Running   0          8s
istiod-6487b86f99-b5r6n                   1/1     Running   0          16s
```

The script updates the user context, creates istio-system namespace, installs Istio, and displays the Istio system pods.

4. Create a namespace for the Istio service mesh and enable sidecar container injection in the namespace with the following manifest:

```
kind: Namespace
apiVersion: v1
metadata:
 name: istions
 labels:
    name: istions
---
kind: Namespace
apiVersion: v1
metadata:
  name: istions
  labels:
    istio-injection: enabled
```

620

CHAPTER 20 SERVICE MESH AND VPC LATTICE

The first stanza of the manifest creates the istions namespace, while the second part enables the sidecar injection, meaning any pod in the namespace should inherit a sidecar.

5. Roll out the blue and the green applications and their microservices.

    ```
    kubectl apply -f istio/2-apps.yml
    ```

    The manifest for the applications is displayed below. The keynote here is the service port. You configured port 80 for both microservices because we want to reach them by the same port.

    ```
    ---
    apiVersion: apps/v1
    kind: Deployment
    metadata:
      name: blue
      namespace: istions
    spec:
      selector:
        matchLabels:
          app: blue
      replicas: 1
      template:
        metadata:
        labels:
        app: blue
        spec:
        containers:
        - image: cloudmanly/eks:blue
          imagePullPolicy: Always
    ```

```yaml
      name: blue
      ports:
      - containerPort: 8080
---
apiVersion: apps/v1
kind: Deployment
metadata:
  name: green
  namespace: istions
spec:
  selector:
    matchLabels:
      app: green
  replicas: 1
  template:
    metadata:
    labels:
    app: green
    spec:
    containers:
    - image: cloudmanly/eks:green
      imagePullPolicy: Always
      name: green
      ports:
      - containerPort: 8081
---
apiVersion: v1
kind: Service
metadata:
  name: green
```

```
    namespace: istions
    labels:
       app: green
spec:
  ports:
  - name: http
    port: 80
    protocol: TCP
    targetPort: 8081
  selector:
     app: green

---
apiVersion: v1
kind: Service
metadata:
  name: blue
  namespace: istions
  labels:
     app: blue
spec:
  ports:
  - name: http
    port: 80
    protocol: TCP
    targetPort: 8080
  selector:
     app: blue
```

CHAPTER 20   SERVICE MESH AND VPC LATTICE

6. Verify the application pods in the istions namespace.

   ```
   kubectl get pod -n istions
   ```

   You should observe the following output:

   ```
   blue-f94845bbb-nsh9f      2/2    Running   0    3m31s
   green-88dcd8df4-2gtdw     2/2    Running   0    3m31s
   ```

Testing the Service Mesh

1. Access one of the pods.

   ```
   kkubectl exec -it blue-f94845bbb-nsh9f -n istions -- /bin/bash
   ```

2. Verify access to the services from the blue app container.

   ```
   curl http://blue
   curl http://green
   ```

You should see the **{"Hello":"blue"}** and **{"Hello":"green"}** as the outputs.

The result shows that we can call one microservice from another through the sidecar containers. Our Istio service mesh is active and working.

Istio Ingress Gateway

We want to introduce you to the Istio ingress gateway and a quick way of distributing traffic in Istio service mesh in this section. The gateway will enable external access to the microservices without using the **kubectl exec** command.

CHAPTER 20 SERVICE MESH AND VPC LATTICE

You should find the manifest for the gateway in the 3-ingress.yml file.

1. Access one of the pods.

    ```
    apiVersion: networking.istio.io/v1alpha3
    kind: Gateway
    metadata:
      name: istio-gateway
      namespace: istions
    spec:
      selector:
        istio: ingressgateway  # use istio default
        controller
      servers:
      - port:
          number: 80
          name: http
          protocol: HTTP
        hosts:
        - "*"
    ---
    apiVersion: networking.istio.io/v1alpha3
    kind: VirtualService
    metadata:
      name: blue-green
      namespace: istions
    spec:
      hosts:
      - "*"
      gateways:
      - istio-gateway
      http:
      - match:
    ```

625

```
        - uri:
          prefix: "/"
      route:
        - destination:
            host: green
            weight: 50
        - destination:
            host: blue
            weight: 50
```

The first part of the manifest deploys the Istio default gateway for servers running on port 80. The second section specifies the traffic distribution implemented by the Istio virtual service. The service runs in the istions namespace and refers to the Istio gateway.

2. Deploy the gateway.

   `kubectl apply -f istio/3-ingress.yml`

3. Go to the AWS console ➤ EC2 ➤ Load balancer, then copy the load balancer URL and open it in your browser. You should see the same output as before in your browser.

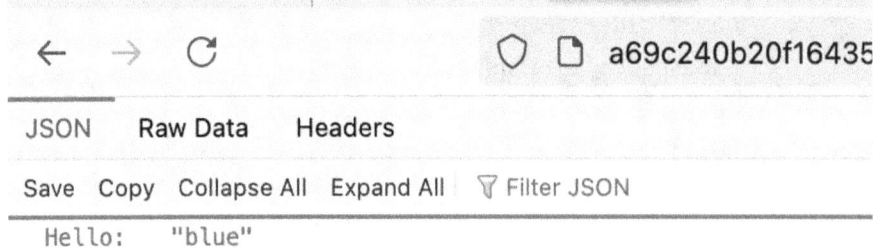

Figure 20-23. The blue app interface

CHAPTER 20 SERVICE MESH AND VPC LATTICE

We have just scratched the surface of Istio in this section for you to dig deeper. You should use this as a springboard to further explore the world of Istio.

Summary

This has been the longest chapter in the entire book. The chapter introduced App Mesh concepts and implementation examples. As you notice, App Mesh is complex and even more complicated with hundreds of microservices. AWS is moving away from App Mesh in EKS to VPC Lattice with the goal of reducing the complexities and managing more application network services for developers and cluster administrators. This chapter only introduced you to VPC Lattices in EKS for you to continue exploring the big world of VPC Lattice for services beyond EKS. The first part of the chapter was important to understand the case for VPC Lattice and even rethinking the future application network architecture design. For those who want to continue with the old application network pattern, you can explore Istio on EKS. Istio is like App Mesh and less complicated. It uses the envoy proxy pattern just like the AWS App Mesh.

Index

A

AB services, 562, 573, 574
A/B testing deployment, 477
Access control, 79, 239, 240, 488–490
Access mode, 445
Access policies, 268
ACK, *see* AWS controller for Kubernetes (ACK)
Actual services, 539, 575
Addons, 60, 230, 233, 234, 302, 379, 522
    ACK controller deployment, 236, 238
    code review, 227, 228
    and controllers (*see* Controllers)
    deployment and validation, 228, 230, 232
    documentation, 219
    implementation, 225, 226
    operational capabilities, 215
    self-managed, 224
    updates, 231
    version upgrade, 232–234
    VPC CNI, 233, 234
Advanced load balancing, 537

ALB, *see* Application load balancer (ALB)
AmazonEC2Container RegistryReadOnly, 55
AmazonEKSCluster AdminPolicy, 272
AmazonEKSClusterPolicy, 44
AmazonEKS_CNI_Policy, 55
AmazonEKSWorkerNode Policy, 55
Amazon Machine Images (AMIs), 10, 90, 103, 157, 161, 162, 176, 177, 184
AmazonSMMManaged InstanceCore, 55
Amazon Web Services (AWS)
    console, 10
    K8s cluster, 9
    security group console, 144, 145
    self-managed nodes, 10
    worker nodes, 10
AMIs, *see* Amazon Machine Images (AMIs)
Annotations, 346
API, *see* Application programming interface (API)

INDEX

Application load balancer (ALB), 368, 370, 398
  application display, 388
  configuration, 376
  controller installation, 382
  creation, 386, 387
  external/internal HTTP(S) access, 376
  ingress controller, 376
  instance metadata, 380, 381
  requisites, 377–380
  script.sh file, 382–384

Application programming interface (API), 14, 17, 298

App Mesh, 531
  capabilities, 536–538
  cluster, 543–546
  cluster deployment, 546
  components, 539
  control plane, 541, 542
  data plane, 538–542
  defined, 535
  deployment, 597–599
  deployment scenario
    green and blue services, 547
    install controller, 548–551
    running, 551–561
    setup, 548
    testing AB services, 562
    three application scenario, 563
  envoy proxies, 535, 536
  implementation, 542
  load balancer implementation (*see* Load balancer)
  logging, 590–592
  terraform configuration, 593
  traffic management implementation
    actual service, 575
    adding virtual router, 575
    backend application, 589
    blue and green apps, 576–578
    blue/green deployment strategy, 574
    controllers, 588
    envoy proxy, 586
    gateway route, 585
    lbrns namespace, 578
    load balancer, 587
    namespace, 575
    nodes, 579
    roll out applications, 588
    router and gateway, 588
    testing, 589
    virtual gateway, 585
    virtual router, 583
    virtual services, 580, 582, 584
  and VPC, 603
  vs. VPC Lattice, 604

ASG, *see* Autoscaling group (ASG)
Audit logs, 591
Auth whoami command, 244
Autoscaler cluster security group, 514
Autoscaler controller, 515–518

Autoscaling demonstration, 510–514
Autoscaling group (ASG), 509
    configuration, 166
    service, 160
Autoscaling strategy, 134
Availability zone (AZ), 47, 454, 461
AWS, *see* Amazon Web Services (AWS)
Aws-auth ConfigMap access control method, 239, 241, 247, 248
    authentication, 242–245
    with code editor, 261–263
    making Alice cluster administrator, 251–253
    making Alice default namespace admin, 253, 254
    manual editing, 255, 256
AWS console, code visualization
    addons, 60
    CLI, 62
    cluster endpoint, 59
    cluster ENIs, 60, 61
    cluster network tab, 59
    cluster overview tab, 59
    node security groups, 61
    testing cluster, 63, 64
AWS controller for Kubernetes (ACK), 221, 222
Aws eks command, 9
Aws eks update-kubeconfig command, 150

AWS Nitro System, 208, 209
AZ, *see* Availability zone (AZ)

B

Bastion hosts
    access control mechanisms, 90
    additional-sg.tf and cluster-sg.tf files, 88
    authentication, 93
    connecting cluster, 114–117
    connecting instance, 115
    entry points, 129
    private/internal resources, 88
    public subnet, 91
    security group, 91–93, 129
    selecting instance, 115
    VPC ID, 91
Bastion module, 87
Bastion security group, 129
    validation, 110, 111
Behind-the-scenes mapping, 267–269
Block mode, 445
Blue app interface, 626
Blue app pod, 532
Blue/green deployment strategy, 539, 574
Borg
    cluster, 4
    container, 5
    job quota, 5
    power *vs.* casual users, 6
    resource allocations, 5

INDEX

Borg (*cont.*)
   resource-intensive
      applications, 5
   scalability, 5
Bulkheading, 537

C

CA, *see* Certificate authority (CA);
      Cluster autoscaler (CA)
Canary deployment, 477
Certificate authority (CA), 242, 400,
      405, 618
Charts, 376
CIDR, *see* Classless inter-domain
      address (CIDR)
Circuit breaking, 537
Classic load balancers (CLBs),
      368, 370–372
Classless inter-domain address
      (CIDR), 46, 47
CLBs, *see* Classic load
      balancers (CLBs)
CLI, *see* Command line
      interface (CLI)
Client-side load balancing, 537
Cloud Map, 541
CloudWatch, 593, 594
CloudWatchAgentServer
      Policy, 593
Cluster administrators, 272
Cluster autoscaler (CA), 507–510
   limitations, 518
   testing, 514

   See also Karpenter
Cluster deletion, 76
Cluster endpoint, 58, 59
   access console, 146
   configuration, 66, 67
Cluster ENIs, 60, 61
Cluster events, 299
Cluster inbound rule, 72
Cluster network access control,
      22, 23, 31
Cluster nodes, 51, 52
Cluster/object controllers, 17
Cluster outbound rule, 72, 73
Cluster policy
   attach EKS, 85
   create EKS, 84, 85
Cluster public endpoint, 59
Cluster review
   additional security group
      review, 145, 146
   additional security group
      validation, 113, 114
   bastion security group
      validation, 110, 111
   cluster security group, 110,
      143, 145
   validation, 111, 113
   network and security menu, 112
   removing rules, 113
Cluster security
   IAM, 64
   network security, 69, 71
   public access endpoint
      restrictions, 65–68

INDEX

Cluster security group, 20–22, 61, 62, 71–73, 110, 112, 114
    additional-sg.tf file, 105
    clean up, 143, 145
    cluster ENIs, 101
    code review, 104, 105, 135, 136
    default, 106
    EKS, 103
    inbound rule, 102, 105
    recommendation, 102
    terraform code
        deployment, 107–109
    validation, 111, 113
Cluster stability, 74–76
Cluster testing, 63, 64
Cluster VPC configuration, 69, 70
Command line interface (CLI), 62
Computing resources, 191
Container image, 313
    building, 319, 320
    custom, 317–319
Containerized applications, 314
Container packaging, 311–314
Container registry, 317
Controllers
    cluster, 217, 221
    and deployment, 235, 236
    extrinsic, 218–224
    instability, 215
    intrinsic, 217, 218
    K8s object, 216
    manager component, 17, 18, 301
    monitor events, 18
    synchronization, 216

Control plane
    API server component, 17
    App Mesh, 541
    AWS components, 16
    cluster events, 16, 298
    controller manager
        component, 17, 18
    deployment
        arguments, 40
        aws_eks_cluster, 39
        resource block, 39, 40
        role assignment, 42, 44
        security groups, 44
        terraform code, 38
        vpc_config block, 40
    ETCD component, 17
    K8s components, 16
    module, 133, 134
    route 55, 19
    scheduler component, 18
CRDs, *see* Custom resource
    definitions (CRDs)
Cross-site request forgery
    (csrf), 486
csrf, *see* Cross-site request
    forgery (csrf)
Customer network, 37
Customer VPC, 20, 21, 45
Custom launch template
    AMI images, 169
    AWS CLI command, 168
    configurations, 171
    EKS node group console, 172, 173

INDEX

Custom launch template (*cont.*)
  instantiation, 173, 174
  launch-template.tf file, 169
  operational overheads, 168
  properties, 168
  terraform code
    execution, 171–173
  user data file, 174, 175
Custom objects, 224
Custom resource, 223
Custom resource definitions
  (CRDs), 222

D

Data plane
  App Mesh, 538–541
  architecture, 47
  cluster security group and
    ENIs, 20–22
  customer VPC, 20
  kubelet and container
    runtime, 315
  VPC, 45–47
Deadlines, 537
Decision-making algorithm, 300
Decision-making process, 18
Default security groups, 106
DevOps methodologies, 477
Distributed systems, 17
Docker desktop installation,
  315, 316
Docker Hub, 317
Docker Hub public registry

creating container, 328
home page, 327
IdP login page, 326
registration, 326, 327
running images on
  EKS, 329–331

E

EBS, *see* Elastic Block Store (EBS)
EC2, *see* Elastic Compute
  Cloud (EC2)
ECR, *see* Elastic container
  registry (ECR)
EFS, *see* Elastic file storage (EFS)
EKS, *see* Elastic Kubernetes
  Service (EKS)
EKS addon controllers, 219, 221
EKS implementation
  cluster deletion, 76
  cluster nodes, 51, 52
  cluster security, 64–73
  cluster stability, 74–76
  code visualization with AWS
    console, 58–64
  control plane
    deployment, 38–40
  data plane VPC, 45–47
  endpoint public access
    cluster, 35–38
  IAM, 42
  main.tf file, 56
  network infrastructure, 49–51
  node security, 53–55

INDEX

subnets, 47, 48
terraform code
    deployment, 56, 58
Elastic Block Store (EBS), 453
    implementation, 455, 456, 458
    setup, 454
    testing, 458–461
    volume, 454, 455
Elastic Compute Cloud (EC2), 454
Elastic container registry (ECR),
    317, 325, 332
Elastic file storage (EFS), 454
    experiment, 462, 463
    file storage, 461
    testing, 463–465
Elastic Kubernetes Service
    (EKS), 295
    add-ons, 9, 213 (*see*
        also Addons)
    architecture, 14, 15
    AWS services, 9, 10
    challenges, 9
    cluster nodes, 100
    console, 144
    control plane (*see* Control plane)
    description, 8
    IAM, 240–242
    implementation (*see* EKS
        implementation)
    K8s, 295
    K8s clusters, 8
    lifecycle management
        processes, 9
    planes, 9
    running custom containers, 325
    worker nodes, 10
Elastic Load Balancers
    (ELBs), 367–370
Elastic Network Interfaces (ENIs),
    20–22, 54, 98, 192
ELBs, *see* Elastic Load
    Balancers (ELBs)
EmptyDir volume, 435
Empty-volume, 434
Endpoint hybrid access cluster,
    25–28, 131
    attach EKS describe policy, 125
    bastion host, 129, 130
    cluster review, 143–146
    code structure, 127, 128
    configuring AWS credential file,
        126, 127
    connecting cluster
        hybrid endpoint, 146, 147
        private cluster access
            test, 147–150
        public cluster access test, 147
    create user to assume role,
        123, 124
    creating EKS describe policy,
        124, 125
    external and internal service, 121
    network setup, 130–134
    role creation, 122, 123
    test public endpoint access
        restrictions, 151, 153
    troubleshooting, 140–143
    worker nodes, 134–140

INDEX

Endpoint private access cluster, 23–25, 95
   access key ID and secret access key, 79
   attach EKS described policy, 85
   bastion host code, 90–93
   cluster review, 109–114
   cluster security group, 101–109
   code structure, 87–89
   configuring AWS credential file, 85, 86
   connecting bastion host, 114–117
   create EKS described policy, 84, 85
   create user to assume role, 81–83
   creating bridge, 87
   MFA and external ID restrictions, 80
   network setup, 94–99
   role creation, 80, 81
   security controls, 118
   worker nodes, 99, 101
Endpoint public access cluster, 28–30, 41
   cluster_name variable, 37
   cluster_version, 37
   control-plane module, 36
   data-plane module, 36
   folder structure, 36
   kube config file, 38
   pod/deployment folders, 38
   script.sh file, 37, 38
   terraform, 35
   variables.tf file, 37
Endpoint public access restrictions, *see* Public access endpoint restrictions
End-user communication, 31
ENIs, *see* Elastic Network Interfaces (ENIs)
Ephemeral volumes
   defined, 432
   emptyDir, 435
   implementation, 434, 435
   purposes, 433
   secret volume, 436–438
   specification, 435
   stateless applications, 432
   testing, 436
ETCD component, 17, 299
Events, 349, 350
Exec command, 414, 415, 421
External clusters, 540
Extrinsic controllers
   ACK, 221, 222
   defined, 218
   EKS addon controllers, 219, 221
   operator, 223
   third-party addons, 223

F

Fargate nodes, 10, 16, 103, 161, 162
Fluent Bit, 592–594
FQDNs, *see* Fully qualified domain names (FQDNs)
FROM command, 318

INDEX

Front/edge proxy support, 538
Fully qualified domain names (FQDNs), 19

G

Gateway API controller, 606, 607
General-purpose remote procedure calls (gRPC), 368
Graceful update strategy, 186–190
gRPC, *see* General-purpose remote procedure calls (gRPC)

H

Health checking, 537
Hop limit, 543, 544
Horizontal pod autoscaler (HPA), 508
Host path volume, 439
    creation, 439
    defined, 439
    login to instance, 442
    testing, 441
    testing persistence, 441–443
    values, field type, 440, 441
HPA, *see* Horizontal pod autoscaler (HPA)
Hybrid endpoint, 146, 147

I

IaC, *see* Infrastructure-as-code (IaC)
IAM, *see* Identity and access management (IAM)
IAM roles for service accounts (IRSA), 454
    ALB, 398
    credential isolation and accountability, 399
    flow, 404
        authentication and authorization process, 401, 403
        simplification, 401
        steps, 402
        trust establishment, 402, 403
    granular access control support, 399
    IdP, 400
    K8s, 399
    manual trust establishment, 404–410
    OIDC configuration, 399, 406–408
    provider configuration, 405, 406
    S3 bucket permissions, 398
    thumbprint, 400
    token validation, 400
Identity and access management (IAM), 28, 42, 53–55, 64, 80, 81, 122, 123, 377, 603
    adding cluster editor role, 256, 258, 263, 264
    aws-auth ConfigMap access control method, 239, 242–245, 247, 248
    cluster creators, 239
    EKS, 240–242

INDEX

Identity and access management
        (IAM) (*cont.*)
    K8s RBAC roles, 248, 249
    kube config file, 245, 247
    manual editing, 255,
        256, 261–263
    role assignment
        demonstration role
        configure aws-auth
            ConfigMap, 251–254
        creating test user, Alice,
            250, 251
    using custom groups, 258–260
Identity-based policies, 83
Identity provider (IdP), 399
IdP, *see* Identity provider (IdP)
Image optimization, 324, 325
IMDSv2, *see* Instance metadata
        service version 2 (IMDSv2)
Infrastructure-as-code (IaC), 35
Instance metadata service version
        2 (IMDSv2), 398, 543
Internet gateways, 20, 27, 181, 182
Internet protocol (IP) address, 47
    cluster deployment and
        review, 194–199
    exhaustion, 191
    nodes, 192–194
    pod density (*see* Pod density)
    prefix assignment mode
        demonstration, 208–213
    primary and secondary,
        201, 203
    VPC CNI, 199, 200

In-tree volumes, 431
Intrinsic controllers, 217, 218
IP address management daemon
        (IPAMD), 200
IPAMD, *see* IP address
        management
        daemon (IPAMD)
IRSA, *see* IAM roles for service
        accounts (IRSA)
Istio service mesh
    architecture, 617, 618
    components, 617
    documentation, 618
    implementation, 619–624
    ingress gateway, 624, 626, 627
    platform-specific service
        discovery mechanisms, 618
    testing, 624

J

Jenkins code pipeline, 25
JSON Web Key Set (JWKS), 400
JSON Web Token (JWT), 399
JWKS, *see* JSON Web Key
        Set (JWKS)
JWT, *see* JSON Web Token (JWT)

K

K8s dashboard
    access control, 488–490
    admin user service account,
        495, 496

INDEX

deployment, 491–493, 495
installation, 484
namespace, 485
secret, 486, 487
service, 486
service account, 485
K8s RBAC roles, 248, 249
K9s, 500–502
Karpenter, 508
   application deployment, 528
   controller, 519
   controller/addon, 161
   defined, 519
   deployment
      install controller, 525
      version argument, 524
   implementation, 520–524
   just-in-time compute
      resources, 519
   NodePool, 526, 528
   vs. CA, 520, 529, 530
KarpenterNodeRole-karpenter-
      cluster, 528
Kotaicode debug container, 415,
      416, 421, 422
Kube config file, 245, 247, 248
Kubectl cluster-info dump
      command, 307
Kubectl command, 240
Kubectl exec command, 24, 352,
      399, 624
Kubectl exec deployment/
      catalog, 22
Kubectl logs, 22

Kubectl proxy, 353
Kubefwd proxy tool, 483, 484
Kubelet component, 301
Kube-node-lease namespace, 343
Kube-proxy component, 302
Kubernetes (K8s)
   addons, 302
   application development, 7
   architecture
      API server component, 298
      cluster, 300
      components, 297
      controller manager
         component, 301
      etcd component, 299
      global decisions, 298
      kubelet component, 301
      kube-proxy component, 302
      scheduler component, 300
      visual representation, 297
   benefits, 296, 297
   clusters, 9
   component illumination,
      303–305, 307–309
   containerized applications, 7, 8
   controllers, 468
   dashboard, 497, 498
   JWT, 399
   objects, 9
   orchestrator, 295
   pods, 303
   private endpoint access, 22
   registers, 509
   running apps

INDEX

Kubernetes (K8s) (*cont.*)
    building container image, 319, 320
    containerized applications, 314
    container packaging, 311–314
    custom container image, 317–319
    Docker desktop installation, 315, 316
    Docker Hub public registry, 326–331
    finding layers, 320–323
    image optimization, 324, 325
    private repository, 332–335
    running containers on cluster, 316, 317
    running custom containers on EKS, 325
  types, 74
  volumes, 431, 432
Kube-system namespace, 141

L

Labels, 345, 346
Launch template, 159–161, 163, 167, 176–180, 543
Lens, 499, 500
L-IPAM, *see* Local IP address management (L-IPAM)
Litmus test, 198

Load balancer, 32, 366, 367, 387, 531, 532, 587
  adding, 564
  architecture, 563
  blue application and actual service, 565
  communication, 564
  console, 574
  controller, 598
  controller policy, 545
  create gateway route, 569
  deployment, 573
  envoy proxy, 570, 572
  ingress gateway, 564
  mesh manifest, 566
  namespace, 565
  testing AB services, 573, 574
  virtual gateway, 570
  virtual node, 567
  virtual service, 568
Load distribution, 461
Local IP address management (L-IPAM), 200
Local registries, 325
Logging
  applications, 591
  audit, 591
  configuration, 593–599
  defined, 590
  networks, 591, 592
  Oss, 590
  review, 599–601
  software log sources, 590

M

main.tf file, 56
Managed nodes, 103, 157–159
Manual editing, 255, 256, 261–263
MaxSurge, 478
MaxUnavailable, 478
MFA, *see* Multifactor authentication (MFA)
Microservices architecture, 534
Monolithic architecture, 532
MountPath key, 434
Multifactor authentication (MFA), 64
Multithreading, 5

N

Namespace
   administrator, 249, 272, 282
   cluster administrators, 342
   commands, 342
   defined, 341
   demonstration, 343, 344
   initial, 343
   production environment, 342
   resources, 342
Network address translation (NAT) gateways, 20
Network file share (NFS), 444
Network infrastructure, 49–51
Network interface, 195, 196
   attachment, 197
   card, 193
   EC2 instances, 194
   IDs, 204
   secondary, 197, 198
   VPC container, 199, 200
Network load balancer (NLB), 27, 368, 369, 373–375
Network log sources, 591, 592
Network management, 541
Network security, 69, 71
Network setup, 94–99
   administrators and services, 130
   control plane module, 133, 134
   subnets, 131, 132
New cluster access management
   access entries and policy association, 268, 269
   access policies, 268
   assigning IAM permissions, 286–289
   authentication modes, 273, 274
   behind-the-scenes mapping, 267
   built-in access entry policy, 270–272
   cluster creators, 268
   create cluster admin, 280, 282
   creating access entry with EKS console, 289, 290
   disable cluster creator, 290, 291
   granting creator to Alice, 275–277, 279
   granting custom permissions with K8s RBAC, 284–286
   implementation, 274, 275
   managed policies, 272

INDEX

New cluster access
      management (*cont.*)
  namespace access, 282, 283
  process, 269
NFS, *see* Network file share (NFS)
NLB, *see* Network load
      balancer (NLB)
Node controller, 301
Node groups, 156, 157
NodePool, 526, 528
Node Port service
  example, 359, 360
  and public network, 361–364
Nodes, 345, 579
  cluster upgrade tips, 189, 190
  creating image with
      packer, 181–185
  custom launch
      templates, 167–175
  definition, 155
  graceful node group
      update, 186–190
  IP addressing, 192–194
  managed node code review,
      162, 163
  managed node deployment,
      164, 165
  managed node deployment
      review, 165–167
  and pods, 155, 156
  self-managed node
      deployment, 175–181
  types
    Fargate, 161, 162
    launch template, 159–161
    managed nodes, 157–159
    self-managed, 161
Node security
  group rules, 53
  groups, 61
  IAM, 53–55
Node selectors, 347
Nonprogrammatic outbound
      communication, 24

O

Object access, 502
Observability, 538, 541, 590, 602
OIDC, *see* OpenID Connect (OIDC)
OIDC terraform automation, 416,
      418, 419
On-demand nodes, 158
Open container initiative (OCI) file
      system, 312
OpenID Connect (OIDC), 377, 399
Operating systems (OSs), 590
Operator controllers, 223
OSs, *see* Operating systems (OSs)
Out-of-tree NFS provisioners
  creation, 450
  parameter entry, 451
  terraform code, 450
  testing deployment, 452, 453
Out-of-tree volumes, 431
Overlay file system, 312

P

Packer, 181–185
Parallel processing, 5
Path-based routing, 368
Performance metrics, 308
Persistent volume
   with AWS, 454
   creation, 444–448
   defined, 432
   host path, 439–443
   subsystem, 443, 444
   testing, 444–449
Persistent volume claim (PVC), 449, 454, 458
Planning access control, 248
Plugins, *see* Addons
Pod density, 200–202
   demonstration, 202–207
   with prefix, 207, 208
Pod identity, 423
Pod monitoring
   commands, 503
   dashboard deployment with kubefwd, 496, 498
   K8s dashboard manifest, 484–496
   K9s, 500–502
   kubefwd, 483, 484
   lens, 499, 500
   object access, 502
Pods, 303
   deployment, 351, 352
   monitoring (*see* Pod monitoring)
   parameter experiment
      annotations, 346
      events, 349, 350
      labels, 345, 346
      name/ID, 341
      namespace, 341–344
      nodes, 345
      node selector, 347
      priority, 344
      QoS, 347
      service account, 345
      status, 346, 347
      steps, 338–341
      toleration, 348, 349
   scale (*see* Pod scaling)
   specification, 337, 338
   testing after deployment, 393–395
Pod scaling
   deployment
      controllers, 473
      experiment, 478–480
      functions, 474
      manifest, 475, 477
   failures and fault intolerance, 467
   K8s controllers, 468
   reliability and resilience, 467
   replica (*see* Replica sets)
   rolling update, 477, 478
Pod security policies (PSPs), 398
Pod service accounts
   client configuration, 412, 413
   cluster deployment, 419, 420, 425, 427, 428

INDEX

Pod service accounts (*cont.*)
   identity, 423
   IRSA (*see* IAM roles for service accounts (IRSA))
   OIDC terraform automation, 416, 418, 419
   RBAC method, 391–398
   terraform code, 410, 412, 423–425
   testing exec command, 414, 415, 421
   testing kotaicode debug container, 415, 416, 421, 422
   testing s3 bucket, 413, 414
   testing secret manager with forwarding, 420
Port forwarding, 354, 355
Prefix assignment mode demonstration, 208–213
Primary ENI deletion, 198
Private cluster access test, 147–150
Private repository
   demonstration, 332
   Docker Hub, 333
   grant exclusive access, 332
   running ECR image, 334, 335
Private_subnet_ids, 37
Programmatic outbound communication, 24
Prometheus Metrics Collection, 602
Proxy, 355

PSPs, *see* Pod security policies (PSPs)
Public_access_cidrs argument, 134
Public access endpoint restrictions
   with CLI command, 68
   with code, 68
   with web console, 65–67
Public cluster access test, 147
Public endpoint access restrictions, 151, 153
Public_endpoint_cluster, 37, 39
Public Internet, 29
Public registries, 325
Public subnets, 24
PVC, *see* Persistent volume claim (PVC)

Q

Quality of service (QoS), 347

R

RAM, *see* Resource Access Manager (RAM)
RBAC, *see* Role-based access control (RBAC)
Reclaim policy, 445
Recreate deployment, 477
ReplicaSet controller, 301
Replica sets, 469
   controllers, 468
   defined, 468

experiment, 471, 472
manifest, 469–471
Resource Access Manager (RAM), 602
Resource-based policies, 83
Retry budgets, 537
Role assignment, 42, 44
Role-based access control (RBAC), 28, 247, 267
    host worker nodes, 391
    S3 and ECR access test, 396–398
    secret manager test, 395, 396
    stimulation, 392
    testing pod access after deployment, 393–395
Rolling update strategy, 477, 478
Route 55, 19, 44
Route table, 182, 183

S

S3 bucket, 396–398, 413, 414
SC, *see* Storage class object (SC)
Scheduler, 300
Scheduler component, 18
Secret management, 395, 396
Secret volume, 436–438
Security controls, 118
Security group rules, 545
Security groups, 20, 44, 71–73
    See also Cluster security group
Security policies, 398
Security service token (STS), 400

Self-managed addons, 224
Self-managed nodes, 102, 103, 161
    deployment, 175–181
Service account, 345, 511
Service discovery, 536
Service mesh, 531, 534–536
Service network association, 616
Service object, 358, 359
    ALB, 375–384
    application API display, 356
    application display, 355
    CLBs, 370–372
    ELBs, 367–370
    expose pods, 351
    implementation, 358
    and ingress controllers, 357
    internal access to application, 352, 353
    load balancer IP, 364
    load balancers, 366, 367
    NLB, 373–375
    Node Port, 359–364
    pod deployment, 351, 352
    port forwarding, 354, 355
    testing cluster IP service, 364–366
    troubleshooting tips
        alternative, 388
        creating ALB, 386, 387
        fix errors, 385
        testing load balancer, 387
    types, 357–359
    using proxy, 355

INDEX

Service orchestration
    independent services, 534
    load balancer, 531
    microservices architecture, 534
    monolithic application, 532
    pod per module, 532, 533
Service provider (SP), 400, 401
Service-to-service communication, 531, 535, 540, 541, 602, 605
Shared responsibility model, 224
Smapp pod, 397
SNAT, see Source NAT (SNAT)
Software logs, 590
Source NAT (SNAT), 24
SP, see Service provider (SP)
Spot instances/nodes, 158
SSD-backed volumes, 454
Statement element, 83
Status, 346, 347
Storage class object (SC), 443
Subnets, 47, 48
System masters, 255

T

Taints mark nodes, 349
Task isolation, 6
Terraform, 35, 40, 44, 303
Terraform apply command, 232
Terraform code deployment, 56, 58, 137–140
Third-party addons/controllers, 223
Third-party controllers, 468

Thumbprint, 400
Timeouts, 537
Toleration, 348, 349, 521, 522
Trace Map, 601

U

UFS, see Union file system (UFS)
UI, see User interface (UI)
Underlay network, 199
Union file system (UFS), 312
User access, 32
User interface (UI), 496, 532

V

Version element, 82
Vertical pod autoscaler (VPA), 508
Virtual gateway, 539, 540, 570, 585
Virtual nodes, 539, 540, 556, 558, 567
Virtual private cloud (VPC), 14
Virtual router, 575, 583
Virtual services, 539, 540, 558, 560, 568, 580, 582, 584
Volumes
    EBS (see Elastic Block Store (EBS))
    ephemeral (see Ephemeral volumes)
    in-tree, 431
    out-of-tree, 431, 450–453
    persistent (see Persistent volume)
    types, 432

VPA, *see* Vertical pod
    autoscaler (VPA)
VPC, *see* Virtual private cloud (VPC)
VPC Container Network Interface
    (VPC CNI), 199, 200
VPC Lattice
    benefits, 604–606
    blue-green deployment, 611–615
    gateway API controller, 606, 607
    IAM, 603
    mesh network, 602
    observability, 602
    service network, 604
    terraform code, 607
    testing, 616, 617
VPC resources, 65

W, X, Y, Z

Warm pools, 200
Web socket protocols, 368
Worker nodes, 37, 44, 52,
    70, 99, 101
    additional security group
        code, 136–140
    batch processing
        workloads, 134
    cluster security group code,
        135, 136
    mission-critical
        workloads, 134
    spot instances, 134
Workload demand, 507